ODYSSEYS OF RECOGNITION

NEW STUDIES IN THE AGE OF GOETHE

New Studies in the Age of Goethe, sponsored by the Goethe Society of North America, aims to publish innovative research that contextualizes the "Age of Goethe," whether within the fields of literature, history (including art history and history of science), philosophy, art, music, or politics. Though the series editors welcome all approaches and perspectives, they are especially interested in interdisciplinary projects, creative approaches to archival or original source materials, theoretically informed scholarship, work that introduces previously undiscovered materials, and projects that reexamine traditional epochal boundaries or open new channels of interpretations.

TITLES IN THE SERIES

Ellwood Wiggins, *Odysseys of Recognition: Performing Intersubjectivity in Homer, Aristotle, Shakespeare, Goethe, and Kleist*

Seán Williams, *Pretexts for Writing: German Romantic Prefaces, Literature, and Philosophy*

Vance Byrd, *A Pedagogy of Observation: Nineteenth-Century Panoramas, German Literature, and Reading Culture*

Christine Lehleiter, *Romanticism, Origins, and the History of Heredity*

Benjamin Bennett, *Aesthetics as Secular Millenialism: Its Trail from Baumgarten and Kant to Walt Disney and Hitler*

Mary Helen Dupree, *The Mask and the Quill: Actress-Writers in Germany from Enlightenment to Romanticism*

Peter J. Schwartz, *After Jena: Goethe's Elective Affinities and the End of the Old Regime*

Brian Tucker, *Reading Riddles: Rhetorics of Obscurity from Romanticism to Freud*

ODYSSEYS OF RECOGNITION

Performing Intersubjectivity in Homer, Aristotle, Shakespeare, Goethe, and Kleist

Ellwood Wiggins

Bucknell University | University Press
Lewisburg, Pennsylvania

Library of Congress Cataloging-in-Publication Data

Names: Wiggins, Ellwood H., Jr., author.
Title: Odysseys of recognition : performing intersubjectivity in Homer, Aristotle, Shakespeare, Goethe, and Kleist / by Ellwood Wiggins.
Description: Lewisburg : Bucknell University Press, 2019. | Series: New studies in the age of Goethe | Includes bibliographical references and index.
Identifiers: LCCN 2018029485 | ISBN 9781684480388 (cloth) | ISBN 9781684480371 (pbk.)
Subjects: LCSH: Recognition in literature. | Intersubjectivity in literature. | Homer—Criticism and interpretation. | Aristotle—Criticism and interpretation. | Shakespeare, William, 1564–1616—Criticism and interpretation. | Goethe, Johann Wolfgang von, 1749–1832—Criticism and interpretation. | Kleist, Heinrich von, 1777–1811—Criticism and interpretation.
Classification: LCC PN56.R33 W54 2019 | DDC 809/.93353—dc23
LC record available at https://lccn.loc.gov/2018029485

A British Cataloging-in-Publication record for this book is available from the British Library.

∞ The paper used in this publication meets the requirements of the American National Standard for Information Sciences—Permanence of Paper for Printed Library Materials, ANSI Z39.48-1992.

www.bucknell.edu/UniversityPress

Distributed worldwide by Rutgers University Press

Manufactured in the United States of America

FOR SARA

Alle Hypothesen hinder den ἀναγνωρισμός, das Wiederbeschauen, das Betrachten der Gegenstände, der fraglichen Erscheinungen von allen Seiten.

—Goethe, *Maxime und Reflexionen* (HA, 12, 447)

CONTENTS

OVERVIEW OF CONTENTS

ABBREVIATIONS

Al	Plato, *Alcibiades*, trans. D. S. Hutchinson, in *Complete Works*, ed. John M. Cooper (Indianapolis: Hackett, 1997), 557–595. Cited by Stephanus page number. Unless noted otherwise, references to other Platonic dialogues are from this edition and will also be cited by Stephanus number.
HA	Johann Wolfgang von Goethe, *Werke*, Hamburger Ausgabe, ed. Erich Trunz, 14 vols. (Munich: Deutscher Taschenbuch Verlag, 1986). Cited by volume and page or line numbers.
Il	Homer, *The Iliad*, trans. Richmond Lattimore (1951; repr., Chicago: University of Chicago Press, 1961). Greek from *Iliad*, trans. and ed. A. T. Murray and William F. Wyatt, Loeb Classical Library 170–171, vols. 1–2 (Cambridge, Mass.: Harvard University Press, 1999). Cited by book and line numbers.
Iph	Euripides, *Iphigenia among the Taurians*, in Euripides, *Trojan Women, Iphigenia among the Taurians, and Ion*, ed. and trans. David Kovacs, Loeb Classical Library 10, vol. 4 (Cambridge, Mass.: Harvard University Press, 1999). Cited by line number.
LS	H. G. Liddell and Robert Scott, *An Intermediate Greek-English Lexicon* (Oxford: Oxford University Press, 1945).
LSJ	H. G. Liddell, Robert Scott, and Henry Jones, *A Greek-English Lexicon* (Oxford: Oxford University Press, 1996).
NE	Aristotle, *Nicomachean Ethics*. Greek from *The Nicomachean Ethics*, trans. and ed. H. Rackham, Loeb Classical Library 73 (Cambridge, Mass.: Harvard University Press, 1934). Cited by Bekker page number.

Od Homer, *The Odyssey*, trans. Richmond Lattimore (1965; repr., New York: Harper Perennial, 1991); Greek from *Odyssey*, trans. and ed. A. T. Murray and George E. Dimock, Loeb Classical Library 104–105, vols. 1–2 (Cambridge, Mass.: Harvard University Press, 1998). Cited by book and line numbers.

P Aristotle, *Poetics*. Greek from *Poetics*, ed. Stephen Halliwell et al., Loeb Classical Library 199 (Cambridge, Mass.: Harvard University Press, 1995). Cited by chapter, Bekker page, and line numbers.

Penth Heinrich von Kleist, *Sämtliche Werke und Briefe* (Munich: Carl Hanser Verlag, 1993). Cited by scene and line number. English is from *Penthesilea*, trans. Joel Agee (New York: Harper Perennial, 1998). Cited by page number.

Ph Aristotle, *Physics*. Greek from *Physica*, ed. W. D. Ross (1950; repr., Oxford: Oxford University Press, 1988). Cited by Bekker page number.

TC Shakespeare, *Troilus and Cressida*, ed. David Bevington (London: Arden Shakespeare; Thomson Learning, 1998), first published 1609. Cited by act, scene, and line numbers.

A NOTE ON TRANSLATIONS AND ORTHOGRAPHY

Unless otherwise noted, translations are mine.

A note on orthography: Double quotation marks are used for exact quotations and as scare quotes. Italics are used throughout to draw attention to terms as terms as well as for foreign terms and for special emphasis. In block quotes, Greek lettering is preserved; when quoting in the text, Greek words and phrases are transliterated into Roman script.

ODYSSEYS OF RECOGNITION

Introduction

Performing Recognition

THE MOST ICONIC recognition scene in contemporary American culture took place a long time ago in a galaxy far, far away. *The Empire Strikes Back* (1980) climaxes when Luke Skywalker comes face-to-mask with his evil nemesis, Darth Vader. After winning a virtuoso lightsaber duel, Vader beckons to him and declares, "I am your father."[1] The tableau of Vader extending his arm to a cowering Luke is a ubiquitous symbol for surprise revelations on T-shirts, posters, and internet memes. Yet it avoids all the traditional tropes of recognition scenes. Vader offers no proof of his parentage: he does not tell Luke about a unique birthmark on his son's thigh or open his own body armor to reveal an identifying scar or amulet. He does not try to move Luke with tender stories of his mother. Instead, the only evidence Vader offers is the single sentence, "Search your feelings; you know it to be true."[2] This one line encapsulates a radical but hidden shift in the modern conception of recognition. Today's audiences assume that recognition is an internal operation of the mind: search *within* and you will find knowledge about others.

In the *Odyssey*, in contrast, Penelope's long testing and her eventual acknowledgment of Odysseus are processes of external performance rather than internal cognition or feeling. This understanding of interpersonal recognition has become strange and counterintuitive. Aristotle long ago identified recognition (*anagnōrisis*: a change in knowledge leading to friendship or enmity) as a constitutive element of powerful drama, "the greatest means by which tragedy moves the soul."[3] Hollywood blockbusters routinely climax with a scene of discovery and revelation, and so this may seem to be an unchanging universal in human storytelling. Today's common sense says that recognition is a cognitive operation that must occur in the brain. This assumption is so deeply rooted in the modern world that it is difficult not to impose its consequences when reading drama and fiction from other eras or cultures. We have all succumbed to the dark force of Vader's rhetoric of self-sufficient interiority. A principal argument of this book, however, is that recognition is *not* simply an internal function of the brain but rather a process that takes place between people in the world. Recognition, in short, is performance.

Understanding recognition as intersubjective performance is important not merely for interpreting Aristotle and ancient drama but also as a contribution to contemporary discourses in philosophy and politics. For one thing, a performative conception of recognition complements and challenges the work of scholars in identity politics and social justice. This strand of political theory, which emphasizes the importance of institutional recognition for minority groups within a society, may seem to be a far cry from the dramas of separation and reunion from which Aristotle distilled the technical term *anagnorisis*. Yet it is dangerous to be blind to the narrative structures underlying the political concept. Many recognition theorists, such as Charles Taylor, Axel Honneth, and Patchen Markell, take their inspiration from Hegel's "Struggle for Recognition" (*Kampf um Anerkennung*), as narrated in the *Phenomenology of Spirit* (1807). In this emblematic myth, two subjects vie for mutual recognition in order to validate their own independent subjectivity, with the logical consequence being a battle for mastery ultimately leading to death. The drama of this conflict unfolds along lines that are implicit in Aristotle's definition of anagnorisis. Recognition and acknowledgment, I argue, are not as easily separable as commonly held.

Though Hegelian *Anerkennung* and Aristotelian anagnorisis are both usually rendered in English as *recognition*, many would correctly argue that this connection is misleading. In German, for instance, there is no danger of conflating anagnorisis (*Wiedererkennung*: knowing again) with acknowledgment (*Anerkennung*). In English, *recognition* commonly refers to the internal cognitive operation of knowledge and *acknowledgment* to the public avowal of that cognition. In the prevalent way of speaking, the difference seems relatively clear: recognition indicates private knowledge; acknowledgment signifies public announcement. One might question, for instance, when it is that Penelope *recognizes* Odysseus. Does she know her husband during their first interview in book 19, as some readers since antiquity have claimed, or not until he finally passes the bed test, as Telemachus and most scholars assume? It is clear, however, that she does not *acknowledge* him until book 23. In this book, I call into question this simplistic contrast between recognition and acknowledgment by challenging the notion that the internal and external processes of coming to know are so distinct. It is not the case in the *Odyssey* that interior representational knowledge is necessarily antecedent to external semiotic communication. Knowledge is something that happens through and consists in the mutual performances between people. This central claim is will be explored, quizzed, and tested through all the readings in the book.

These connections to the philosophy of consciousness and politics underline two common but problematic assumptions about recognition. The first is evident in the *Star Wars* vignette: recognition is an interior operation of the mind. The second is implicit in the tendency to separate recognition from acknowledgment: recognition is a momentary flash of realization. Instead, close attention to anagnorisis scenes reveals that people come to know one another as friends or enemies through involved processes that take place in intersubjective performance. Before expanding on this positive claim, it is prudent to clarify the two paradoxes in modern conceptions of the time and space of recognition. Two popular TV shows and one ancient tragedy will help illustrate the consequences of imagining recognition to be internal and instantaneous.

INTERIORITY ILLUSION

The smart and savvy Canadian science-fiction thriller *Orphan Black* (2013–2018) would seem to be proof against sentimental claptrap. It is premised on the radically constructivist assumption that human clones—people born with the exact same genetic makeup and identical appearance—grow into profoundly different characters. Despite having the same DNA, Sarah Manning's clones take on remarkably diverse identities and personalities. Even things as seemingly ineluctable as sexual orientation and gender identity prove to be constructs of a combination of choice and social pressure rather than essentially inborn in the world of the show. The development of the plot and the characters appear almost designed as a thought experiment to prove Judith Butler's claims about the performativity of identity.[4] Yet by the fourth episode of the first season, even this sophisticated understanding of selfhood cannot withstand the desire for nonmediated recognition. In that episode, one of Sarah's identical clones (both played by virtuoso Tatiana Maslany) impersonates her perfectly enough to fool even Sarah's foster mother. Yet Sarah's young daughter, who has been estranged from her mother for nearly a year, sees right through the disguise and immediately knows that the identical clone who flawlessly imitates her mother's accent and mannerisms is an imposter. An internal core of selfhood is inscrutably independent of outward appearance and behavior and can only be accessed by mysterious ties of kinship and "true love."

This plot twist echoes the conceit of a popular children's book *I'd Know You Anywhere, My Love*, published in the same year as the first season of *Orphan Black*. In this book, a mother assures her child that even if he were to turn into a rhinoceros, camel, or pig, she would know and love him just the same. Every page features an Ovidian (or, imagined without the cute accompanying illustrations, quite Kafkaesque) metamorphosis into an alarming creature and the mother's immediate recognition of her son "by the gleam of [his] eye" or his "*magical* smile."[5] A mother's love sees right through external appearance to the "true self" within.

The phantasm of modern recognition comprises two incompatible delusions:

1. Your true identity is something unique and immutable that is independent of outward appearance or behavior.
2. This "inner core" is immediately knowable to others who truly love you (parents, lovers, siblings).

This children's book merely articulates a fantasy of recognition that is perpetuated by countless films and TV shows like *Orphan Black*. Inner knowledge becomes a fetishized focus of desire and a test of "authentic" love, parentage, and friendship. Imagine how easily the *Oedipus* tragedy, which was Aristotle's example of the most beautiful kind of recognition, could have been avoided if only these basic modern conditions of parenthood had been in place. The grown Oedipus returning to Thebes was no rhinoceros: how silly of Jocasta not to know her son by the gleam of his eyes rather than allowing them to be extinguished by the terror of recognition.

INSTANTANEOUSNESS ILLUSION

On May 23, 2010, the ancient dramatic device of recognition enjoyed a shining moment of power on television sets around the world. The last episode of the final season of the popular show *Lost* (2004–2010) aired on ABC. During the course of its six-year run, the series had notoriously drawn watchers in by opening up more and more mysteries in an increasingly intricate plot involving multiple time lines, alternate realities, and evolving mythologies. By the time the final season began airing, internet sites in many different languages were dedicated to speculating on the puzzles presented by the show and sported pages upon pages of "theories" with legions of adherents and opponents. Lists of unanswered questions raised by the plot and its background numbered in the hundreds. Over the course of the sixth season, which many fans expected to settle these enigmas once and for all, the lists expanded rather than shrank. So as the final episode loomed, fans had to pin all their hopes for getting answers to six years of mystery on this last two-and-a-half-hour extravaganza. When the credits began rolling after its close, however, many of these questions—both major and nitpicky—still remained open and even unaddressed.[6] One would have expected a massive outpouring of rage and frustration on the show's many internet message boards and chat rooms, where fans would exchange their reactions while each episode aired and then their theories afterward as the debates and debunking began in earnest. But the opposite occurred. On one popular website, *Lostpedia*, the reactions in the hours after the show were overwhelmingly positive. I counted around nine gushing reviews for every scathing one. The few negative reactions were virulently so—and predictably, they complained about the lack of answers to the questions in which fans had invested so much of their time and energy. There was nothing in between these two extremes. Here is a small sampling from the first hour after the show aired:

- OMFG what an episode.
- I feel very satisfied. There are still questions of course, but overall I have a warm fuzzy feeling. And I'm pretty sure it isn't just the red wine I drank tonight.
- I have to say that it was well worth the wait, the six year wait. For an ending like this, I would've waited 10 years if I had to.
- It was a beautiful end to a beautiful six years. The plot is still open, but that is a good thing . . . we all still have something to debate and discuss. Emotionally and thematically, however, we were given closure.
- That was beautiful. I was moved to tears at every re-union in the episode. Absolutely the ending it deserved.
- I love love loved it!!!![7]

Why was initial viewer reaction to this episode generally so positive despite its failure to satisfy the curiosity about so many plot points the show had insisted on raising? Several critics and fans attempted to answer this question by claiming that *Lost* was really more about the characters than about the plot.[8] But this claim evades rather than addresses the puzzle: *Lost* perhaps more than any other recent show continually drove home the point that character (in both the literary and ethical senses of the word) consists in the choices people make and the actions people take—that is, as Aristotle would say, character is subordinate to plot.

So what *is* the plot of the final episode? How does one construct a story that satisfies most viewers while leaving so many loose ends and unresolved questions? The episode is made up of a series of successively intensified recognition moments—scenes in which characters, who had learned to love and care for each other over the course of their adventures on the island, suddenly come to know each other again in an alternate universe in which their plane had never crashed. The secret to the episode's emotional and narrative success lies in the peculiar nature of dramatic recognition.

Aristotle emphasized the soul-moving potential of anagnorisis. People are, apparently, hard-wired to react with fear and pity to beholding a sudden change in fortune or a change in characters' understanding of who they are. These moments of dramatic turnaround are ideally situated not only to grab spectators' attention and tug at their heartstrings but also to display knowledge in action. He defines anagnorisis as "a change from ignorance to knowledge into either friendship or enmity among people destined for good or bad fortune" (*P*, 11, 1452a, 29–31). This is precisely what happens to characters in the "flash sideways" world of *Lost*. The "reunions" that so many bloggers and critics claimed repeatedly brought tears to their eyes are anagnorisis moments. Characters who never knew one another in their own reality suddenly become aware of relationships they had forged in an alternate universe and immediately embrace their newfound, long-lost friends.

One major reason the end of the show proved satisfying (despite its failure to gratify viewers' curiosity about so many questions) lies in the structure of dramatic recognition. Anagnorisis always has the *form* of knowledge—it is, after all, a coming-to-know. Even though the *content* of this particular knowledge in *Lost* has nothing whatsoever to do with the many mysteries raised by the show's intricate plot, viewers are nonetheless treated to a dramatic dose of cognitive realization—and in the *Lost* finale, this happens over and over again. The reason more fans did not blow up in frustration over the lack of any confirmation (or disproval) of their pet theories is that the plot of *Lost* culminated in these scenes of anagnorisis. Dramatic knowledge served as a proxy and substitute for the satisfaction of factual knowledge.[9]

The recognition scenes in *Lost* not only conform to the interior fallacy diagnosed above (a single touch implants a host of visualized memories in the internal minds of characters) but furthermore happen instantaneously. Most literary critics who invoke anagnorisis in their analyses write about a "moment of recognition," and they conjure the image of a split-second cognitive operation in which realization "flashes." Wikipedia currently defines *anagnorisis* as "a moment in a play or other work when a character makes a critical discovery," and it goes on to call it "a hero's sudden awareness."[10] The recognition scenes in the final season of *Lost* fully corroborate this temporality of sudden recognition. In the alternate reality in which Oceanic Flight 815 did not crash, passengers come to recognize their fellows in sudden flashes of insight triggered by special encounters with strangers who had been near and dear to them in the island reality. Flashback images from the previous seasons suddenly rush into the perceivers' heads; the change in knowledge is instantaneous and complete.

Although these recognition scenes in *Lost* comport precisely with the language of most critics and the assumptions of most people about recognition, I will argue that it never actually happens this way in texts from Homer to the twentieth century. It is important to note that Aristotle describes anagnorisis in the *Poetics* as part of the plot—the mythos or story—of a tragedy. And story, in turn, is the imitation of an action, of praxis. Hence recognition for Aristotle is an action in the world—a process involving mental as well as relational, spatial, and sensory capacities—not a cognitive operation that occurs instantaneously within the confines of our skulls. The investigations of this book were motivated by precisely this discovery: that anagnorisis unfolds through a series of interactions over time.

The recognition scenes in *Lost* reveal two important aspects of anagnorisis. First, by satisfying (many) viewers despite all of their unanswered questions, these scenes demonstrate the enormous power of recognition in dramatic denouements. Second, by staging the recognition moments as instant flashes of sudden and complete knowledge, the scenes and their narrative scaffolding reveal the peculiar temporality of recognition. In order to make the momentary recognition seem believable, the show must first make viewers accept such unlikely things as time travel, alternate universes, psychic connections with the dead, and magical islands that occasionally disappear and rematerialize at entirely new coordinates. Only under these fantastical conditions do the momentary recognitions as presented in the final episode seem at all plausible or likely. In all other cases, it is a process, often long and arduous—in short, an action, as Aristotle implies. The *Lost* finale thus underscores both the ultimate impossibility of the kind of instant anagnorisis it portrays as well as the paradoxical drive to understand recognition as instantaneous.

Think again about Aristotle's favorite example, *Oedipus the King* by Sophocles. Though many people write about the "moment" of reversal and recognition in *Oedipus*,[11] if one tries to pinpoint the instant of realization and turnaround—if one attempts to locate a single lightning-like flash of illumination in the play—one gets into trouble. In fact, the action of Oedipus's coming to know himself is brought about only by a long and involved process, driven forward by Oedipus's own obstinate and inexorable efforts to discover the truth. Every episode adds another piece to the puzzle for Oedipus gradually to assemble, and there is no single moment when they all come together in a perfect picture. Fear and doubt begin to gnaw at him slowly, and it is not possible to point to a singular instant when the balances turn and one can identify a before and after between Oedipus's ignorance and knowledge. On the other hand, it is equally impossible to think of the play in a meaningful way without positing such a moment: the play takes on sense and power when one conceives of its unstoppable, central sweep as a swift and fateful turning point or peripeteia. Aristotle is not wrong to identify such a scenario in the play,[12] even if a careful reading of the text reveals it to be a fabrication: it is a symptom of human nature (which he clearly diagnoses elsewhere)[13] and a consequence of equating sight with knowledge to see conglomerations of parts as organic wholes and to grasp gradual processes in instantaneous cognitions.[14]

If one accepts that recognition is not a momentary, internal flash of insight, one is next obliged to ask *what kind of an action* it is. How does recognition unfold in time and in the world? The answer, which will be explored and elaborated in great detail over the course of the readings in this book, may at first sound deceptively simple and unhelpfully vague: the action of interpersonal recognition consists in performance. In coming to know and acknowledge one another, people bring a host of capacities and practices to bear in sussing out the actions and words of others and in gauging their own deeds and speeches in response. They are simultaneously actors and spectators in this negotiation of interpretive and perlocutionary acts in constant recalibration and adjustment. Recognition happens *between* people in this performative space: they necessarily play roles to one another while judging and responding to the roles played in return.

RECOGNITION AS PERFORMANCE

This claim will be fleshed out—both theoretically (chapter 2) and phenomenologically (passim)—in the chapters to come, but for now, a brief example from a twentieth-century film can serve as a good illustration of what it entails. *The Best Years of Our Lives* was released in 1946, and it immediately met with both popular and critical success, making box office records in the United States and Great Britain and garnering seven Academy Awards, including Best Picture. It follows the careers of three American servicemen as they return home from the Second World War and try to reestablish themselves and their relationships with family, friends, and society at large. In the film's opening scenes, the three soldiers meet in a military plane where they have hitched a ride to get back to their hometown. Their excitement about the impending reunions with loved ones is tinged with tangible apprehension about how they will be received. The eldest of the three is named Al (played by Frederic March), who had been a successful banker before the war. As he wrings his hands in nervous trepidation about the encounters awaiting him with wife and children in his swank apartment, he remarks, "Feels as if I were going in to hit a beach."[15] The impending reunion with his family is here given a military metaphor: his wife and children become enemies behind fortifications that Al must assault. The anticipated trials of *nostos* and recognition are as nerve-racking as the expectation of artillery barrages and carnage on the shores of Normandy. He might as well have been warned, as Agamemnon cautions Odysseus in Hades, to beware the fatal dangers of homecoming. Al's admission reveals the full force behind the clause in Aristotle's definition requiring recognition to lead to friendship or enmity, and the decision between friend and foe will figure largely in this book (especially chapters 4 and 9).

When he finally crosses the threshold of his old home, the reunions with his wife, son, and daughter are joyous but incredibly stiff and awkward. There is no question of Al's identity, as there was with Odysseus, but that does not make a reestablishment of his familial relations any less fraught. The resonance of this scene with the Aristotelian formula of anagnorisis is clear: Al first approaches his wife with the same dread and apprehension reserved for encountering enemies. A spouse does not have to be surrounded by dozens of rapacious suitors to render a reunion after long separation dangerous and frightening: time and distance alone can accomplish this estrangement. He is finally driven by the unbearable discomfort of the entire situation to demand that they all go out for a night on the town, where Al proceeds to drink himself silly. At one bar, he boozily asks his wife, Milly (played by Myrna Loy), for a dance. As he lurches with her around the dance floor, he looks into her face with sudden surprise:

> AL. You're a bewitching little creature. In a way, you remind me of my wife.
> MILLY. But you never told me you're married.
> AL. Oh yeah, a little woman, two kiddies, back there in the States.
> MILLY. But let's not think of them now.
> AL. Oh, you're so right. This night belongs only to us.[16]

For the first time during this exchange, the entire patina of self-conscious awkwardness dissipates, and husband and wife are able to interact with natural affection. Only through this little pageant of explicit role-play can a modicum of normalcy return to their relations. It is here that a *change* in knowledge leading to back to friendship—the precise formula of anagnorisis—is set in motion. The choreography of negotiations between the two actors, where recognition inevitably takes place, is palpable on the screen through the pushes and pulls, the glances and grimaces, of their dance. Of course, all of their negotiated interactions before and after this dance also involve playing roles, testing reactions, and responding to perceived applause or hostility, but it is as if this one episode of unabashed performativity (the first time they stop pretending not to pretend) allows the estranged husband and wife to begin the process of resuming their relations of faithful companionship.

The explicit role-play reinstates the couple's trust even though it is loaded with an implicit confession of unfaithfulness. Milly must take on the role of a coquettish mistress to a philandering soldier in foreign climes: she must herself play a woman with whom her husband is presumably about to have a fling. Al's improvised scene with the "bewitching little creature" is a fiction in the present, but it points in very nonfictional ways to both the past and the future. Playing out this invented scenario of the affair has very real consequences for the future lives of husband and wife, as it constitutes the turning point of their relations from a nervous fear of hostility to a promise of comfortable friendship. It also points to the past as a thinly veiled admission of Al's infidelity. Milly's willing assumption of the role of adulteress could also be read as an absolution of Al's transgressions (not only his possible unfaithfulness but also his abandonment of the family to go to war). In this way, the performance of recognition here provides the precise remedies that Hannah Arendt identifies as the only responses to the two ineluctable perils of human action: promise for the unknowable future and forgiveness for the unchangeable past.[17] As in the interactions between Odysseus and Penelope explored below, it is paradoxically the very ambiguity involved in playacting that creates this space for the reparations of recognition.

Again, a brief glance to Sophocles's *Oedipus* provides a helpful illustration of the performative nature of anagnorisis. Oedipus's self-knowledge is not complete with the shepherd's report that proves he is the son of Laius and Jocasta. Mere information is not enough to bring about the horror of recognition that he declares the gods demand. Nor even is the act of gouging out his eyes sufficient to enact the *nefas*, the unspeakable transgression, of his self-knowledge. Instead, Oedipus must return to the stage and make a show of his blindness; it must be seen and acknowledged by the chorus, by Creon, and by his daughters. Only in interactive performance with the present community of those from whom he implores banishment does Oedipus's self-recognition become actualized.

AIMS AND SCOPE OF READINGS

This book explores the ways in which exemplary scenes of dramatic recognition, such as these in *Oedipus* and *The Best Years of Our Lives*, function as performative modes of enacting knowledge about other people (and ourselves). *Anagnorisis*, a technical term with which Aristotle labeled a very specific movement within a certain class of Attic tragedies, suggestively binds together knowledge, action, and narrative in a figure that strains to transcend the formal bounds of poetics. It describes not only compelling junctures of great dramas but also more fundamental questions of epistemology and the ethical decisions of everyday life. It is perhaps no wonder that Aristotle, as a philosopher attempting to give an account of poetry, hit on formulae so richly suggestive in other fields of human endeavor. For this reason, this study takes Aristotle's formulation of anagnorisis in the *Poetics* as its point of departure. But it is not strictly a study of Aristotle. The readings conducted in the chapters that follow do not aim to illustrate any kind of comprehensive interpretation of this *terminus technicus* in the *Poetics*. Nor do the readings "apply" an Aristotelian understanding of anagnorisis to the texts as a hermeneutic device. Though reflections on the *Poetics* provide helpful impulses to the readings staged in this book, Aristotle accompanies the following chapters as an evocatory spirit, not as a programmatic demon. His ideas wander through the reflections as a kind of theoretical stimulus in the same way that the character of Odysseus provides a recurring touchstone in the subject matter.

A good way to distinguish the aims and limits of this book is in reference to important studies of two terms in its title: *recognition* and *performance*. In bringing these discourses together, the book amends a mutual neglect between performance theorists and recognition scholars. Of many recent studies of recognition, three books in particular deserve mention: one work of literary scholarship, one of philosophy, and one of political science. None attends to the performative aspects of recognition. Unlike Terence Cave's monumental achievement of cataloguing the changing attitudes toward recognition in Western literary theory and practice over the centuries in his *Recognitions*,[18] this book does not aim at constructing an intellectual history of the term. Nor is my ambition to devise an all-encompassing construction of self, other, and world, as Paul Ricoeur endeavors in his elegant *Course of Recognition*.[19] Finally, though similar in scope to Patchen Markell's brilliant critique of political theories of recognition in *Bound by Recognition*,[20] this book does not deconstruct an entire school of normative political theory.

Cave's work is an erudite encyclopedia of impressive breadth, but it avoids pursuing its promising initial insight about the status of recognition as a *skandalon* to its radical theoretical conclusions. Ricoeur's rich and comprehensive philosophical argument, meanwhile, presents a reductive reading of Homer's *Odyssey* that, paradoxically, reveals the excessive optimism of Ricoeur's epistemological account of intersubjective recognition. My reading of the *Odyssey* addresses both of these issues by constructing a definition of recognition as performance with Aristotle's concepts of *energeia* (actualization) and *dynamis* (potency; chapter 2) and by analyzing how recognition thus defined functions in the text (chapters 3–5). The very fact that Ricoeur denies the *Odyssey* the mutual recognition I show to be at work in the poem underscores the central problem of anagnorisis: it consists *fundamentally* in performance and is precisely *not* the external representation of internal states of knowledge. Recognition itself can only be perceived—in fact only exists—as the outward signs of interpretation qua performance. The careful inscrutability of the relation between Penelope and Odysseus is the text's own performance of this interpretive conundrum. The *Odyssey* thus demonstrates the scandal of recognition at an extreme never explored by Cave and in so doing calls into question the positive hopes that Ricoeur harbors for its ethical promise.

Markell's insights about the (often tragic) limits of recognition projects[21] are central to the understanding of recognition presented here, but I depart from Markell in three important ways. First, Markell makes a very convincing case that Aristotelian anagnorisis is useful in understanding one trajectory of political thought that first springs from Hegel's description of the struggle for *Anerkennung* and then flows into the influential school of recognition politics today. There is, however, another thread of political discourse that Markell overlooks even though it is equally pertinent to Aristotle's definition of anagnorisis. The clause requiring anagnorisis to lead to friendship or enmity has direct (though unexplored) resonances with Carl Schmitt's definition of the political, which he locates in the decision between friend and enemy. The debates about friendship and politics informed by this controversial claim, from Jacques Derrida to Giorgio Agamben, all pivot on different answers to the question of recognition, and the anagnorisis scenarios in the works discussed below are a testing ground for claims made on all sides.[22] The very act of "deciding" between friend and enemy turns out to emphasize the impossible distance between recognition and acknowledgment in which anagnorisis has to abide. This book, then, lays open fields of human experience, as represented in a series of literary texts, in which the tropes and conventions of dramatic recognition reveal connections and insights otherwise hidden from view.

Second, despite his astute critique of the double binds that necessarily tie up the well-intentioned advocates of recognition politics, Markell's account is still caught up in the cognitive ideal of representational knowledge. The readings below repeatedly show the dangers and traps of such assumptions of input/output models of consciousness in encounters between people. Third, Markell does not attend to the *performative* nature of the process of recognition. His brilliant reading of *Antigone*, for instance, remains situated at the level of the text and does not take into account either the performative acts between characters or the performance of the actors for the Athenian audience. The studies in this book, in contrast, pay careful attention not only to the words of the text but also to the (re)enactments of which the words are a part.

This brings me to the other word from the book's title: *performance*. This concept helps me get beyond the impasse in which a discursive investigation into the self-signification of the word *recognition* dead-ends: the unavoidable nostalgia for an irretrievable past (chapter 1). It would seem that the ephemeral "ontology of performance"[23] Peggy Phelan diagnoses could never escape the deferral of meaning set in motion by the desire of recognition. Yet Homeric scholarship and ancient physics offer a way beyond this strict deconstruction of authenticity. Reenactment, in the sense that Gregory Nagy elucidates to describe the mimesis of Homeric poetry,[24] together with Aristotle's concepts of *energeia* and *dynamis*, invites a definition of recognition as performance (chapter 2): it is a change that can never find fulfillment *and* an action with beginning, middle, and end; it is the actualization of interpersonal knowledge *as* potential. This derivation provides a philosophical grounding for Richard Schechner's undertheorized notion of "restored behavior."[25] This conception further jibes with Rebecca Schneider's championing of the gestic endurance of performance.[26] Her eloquent study reveals an unexpected kind of authenticity in the missteps of historical reenactment, found sculpture, and experimental theater, and my book makes a similar move in its textual readings of Homer, Shakespeare, and Goethe.

The astute analysis of the performance of self to others by two moral philosophers, J. David Velleman (in *How We Get Along*) and Hilde Lindemann (in *Holding and Letting Go*), meanwhile, underpins the notions of human interaction fleshed out in these readings.[27] I show that recognition inheres in the theatrical space between actors, and the consequences of this claim call into question the possibility of "authentic" self-presentation, on which the philosophers still rely. It is not a matter of strictly denying the possibility of authenticity, à la Adorno, but rather of seeing that it is inextricable from deception. This seeming contradiction is at work in the scene from *The Best Years of Our Lives*, in which only through conscious pretending does a palpable and positive change in the relationship between Al and Milly occur. "Authentic" gestures and the possibility for more honest recognition emerge directly out of necessarily "inauthentic" pretense.

The following readings insist that recognition is a poetic and, more specifically, theatrical device (described in an emblematic and evocative way by Aristotle) that can shed illuminating light on concepts beyond poetics, particularly at the intersection of ethics and epistemology. The *Poetics* itself already hints at some of these ramifications. A large part of the motivation for reading Aristotle closely in these investigations of recognition is his way of seeing anagnorisis as a *perception and judgment in action*, the performance of a mental operation within the circumstances of a plot, gestures, and ongoing acting onstage. This is the fundamental point Aristotle contributes to the thinking about recognition presented in this book: in perceiving, knowing, and judging, the mind is necessarily in action in the world. It is the post-Cartesian radical separation of mind and world—a widely accepted input/output model of cognitive representation—that the readings here challenge by returning to Aristotle. The notions of "action in perception" and an enactive view of consciousness, currently making a revolution among a new generation of cognitive scientists, resonate very well with the claims I make about anagnorisis and performance in this book. Instead of recognition taking place within the brain (as a result of sensory stimuli and consequently leading to particular behaviors), recognition consists of the actions performed between people in the world. By substituting *people* for *world*, Alva Noë's pronouncement about consciousness can apply equally to recognition: it "is not something that happens inside us, it is something we do, actively, in our dynamic interaction with the [people] around us."[28] Of course, this involves the mind—but only as an integrated part of the entire scene of recognition. The ultimate failure of Cartesian models of consciousness is dramatized in my reading of Heinrich von Kleist's *Penthesilea* in the final chapter.

The choice of epochs and cultures presented in this constellation of readings, though disparate, is not random, and the trajectory to Germany via Homer and Shakespeare makes historical as well as thematic sense. Both Homer and Shakespeare served as vital catalysts to the burgeoning sense of German identity in the late eighteenth and early nineteenth centuries in general and for the two writers considered here in particular. Johann Wolfgang von Goethe's admiration for Homer as a poet is surpassed only by his awe of Shakespeare. Goethe imagined himself as Homer's Odysseus while developing his botanical theories in Italy, and Goethe's debt to Shakespeare's Hamlet is echoed by the hero of his own *Wilhelm Meister's Apprenticeship*, whose performance of *Hamlet* constitutes the turning point of the entire novel. The twenty-four scenes of Kleist's *Penthesilea*, meanwhile, only make sense by considering them together with the twenty-four books of Homer's *Iliad*. The self-understandings of Goethe and Kleist as authors were fundamentally fashioned by their reception of Homer and Shakespeare, and the readings below flesh out the acts of recognition discernable in the intertextual performances of their works.

This constellation of texts—Homer, classical Greek philosophy, Shakespeare, then Goethe and Kleist—may seem to perpetuate a Hellenized self-understanding in German culture that developed from Goethe to Adorno and from Hölderlin to Heidegger. Although the succession of authors reenacts this canonical intellectual history, the content of the readings undermines any attempt to narrate a history of cultural progress or classicizing nostalgia. The elements of recognition explored through Homer and Aristotle show up in strangely familiar but deviously altered guises in the newer texts. Instead of tracing the Grecophile or Shakespearean roots of modern German concepts and tropes, the book makes a show of their metamorphoses.

One example of this kind of trajectory in the book is its inversion of the Romantic idea of the subject as a construction of interiority (*Innerlichkeit*), which comes about by leaving the enclosed self in order to return richer and different.[29] The assumptions underlying this conception of consciousness are so embedded in modern ways of thinking that many readers impose ideas of interiority on their apprehensions even of ancient texts to which such ideas would be entirely foreign. This book first makes a show of the *scene* of recognition between people in Homer and Aristotle (chapters 1–5). Then it turns to reveal how knowledge about other people continues to be a matter of intersubjective action rather than interior cognizance even in modernity. Although Harold Bloom discerns the invention of the interior subject in Shakespeare, this book shows a complex constellation of exterior surfaces in *Troilus and Cressida* (chapter 6). Whereas the cult of interiority had come to reign supreme by the late eighteenth century, my readings of Goethe reveal selves that are constituted by their interplay with others (chapters 7–9). Far from celebrating any kind of Romantic subject, Kleist's *Penthesilea* even demonstrates the tragic consequences of taking interiority literally (chapter 10). This book does not merely call for a return to premodern conceptions of consciousness but instead shows how radical intersubjectivy is at work even in the famous poets of interiority. Both movements in the Fichtean construction of individual consciousness, leaving and returning, are hence revealed to be illusory. The self is constituted *in*, *during*, and *by* the enacted recognition of the other.

The book is made up of ten chapters divided into two parts. The five chapters of the first part unpack the elements of Aristotle's definition of *anagnorisis* (self-signification, change, knowledge, friendship and enmity, and fortune) through readings of Homer's *Odyssey.* This allows for a natural progression as I unpack the concept of recognition by establishing its semantic field (chapter 1) before deriving my own definition of it as performance (chapter 2), which is then evaluated in terms of epistemology (chapter 3), the ethics of friendship (chapter 4), and the fate of identity (chapter 5). The corresponding chapters of the second part reveal the metamorphoses of these elements in modern recognition scenarios. Each chapter takes off from an Odysseus-figure who functions as a foil, catalyst, or retardant for the scenes of recognition in the work at hand. Odysseus is at once the master of disguise and discernment, cunning and action, *mētis* and praxis. He is a consummate actor who makes a peerless candidate for showcasing the performative aspects of recognition.

Part I, chapter 1, "Just as the Name Itself Signifies," shows how the structure of the word *recognition* challenges a series of dualities fundamental to Western thought (e.g., Same/Other, natural/conventional), which cohere through a paradoxical logic of nostalgia.[30] This analysis reveals surprising structural links between semiotics and the theory of epic poetry. In chapter 2, "Recognition Is a Change," I give substance to the notion of recognition as performance by probing Aristotle's definition of change and adducing the model of rhapsodic performance. Recognition, I claim, is the actualization of imperfectible knowledge of other people *as* potentiality. Chapter 3, "From Ignorance to Knowledge," takes up this definition in the problem of other minds. A Penelopean reading of the *Odyssey* offers a model for how knowledge of other people consists in intersubjective performance. The illegibility of recognition in books 19–23 of the *Odyssey* forces a reevaluation of the difference between recognition and acknowledgment. In chapter 4, "Into Friendship or Enmity," the relationship between Odysseus and Penelope offers a vista beyond Derrida's claims about the impasse between ancient and modern friendship and opens up the possibility for an ethics of recognition. The fifth chapter, "For Those Bound for Good or Bad Fortune," finally marks the limits of human agency in recognition by tracing the ineluctable aspects of identity construction.

Part II, "Outing Interiority," follows Homer's traces in Shakespeare, Goethe, and Kleist. Its five chapters correspond to the fields of recognition opened up by the chapters of part I: the self (*to auto*), change (*metabolē*), knowledge (*gnosis*), friendship (*philia*), and fortune (*tukhē*). These five basic elements of Aristotelian recognition undergo striking metamorphoses in modernity, surprising both in their differences and similarities with the ancient models. The self-signification interrogated in chapter 1 points toward the fundamental need for self-knowledge (chapter 6). The definition of recognition as a type of change (chapter 2) suggests the metamorphoses analyzed in chapter 7. Change changes in modernity: Aristotle moves to *metabolē* (change) by way of *kinēsis* (motion); Goethe attends primarily to *Übergänge* (transitions) to develop his morphology. The problem of knowledge then expands from the world of Penelope (chapter 3) to that of Goethe (chapter 8), but its basic challenge of requiring action in the face of indeterminacy remains the same. The ethics of friendship (chapter 4) undergirds fundamental political dimensions in Goethe's *Iphigenie* (chapter 9). The fortune of identity (chapter 5), meanwhile, returns to tear down both self and other in a Cartesian understanding of subjectivity (chapter 10).

Chapter 6, "Self-Knowledge between Plato and Shakespeare," reads Ulysses's colloquy with Achilles in *Troilus and Cressida* as a parody of the Platonic *Alcibiades I*. The dialogue's famous staging of the formation of self through the other's gaze is critically revealed to fall apart in Shakespeare's play. In fact, it repeats the performative structure of Plato's aporetic dialogues and questions the very possibility of following the Delphic injunction to know oneself.

The next four chapters examine the performative work of recognition at the height of the cult of interiority. It first delineates the convergence of drama, epistemology, and ethics in the figure of recognition in Goethe's work, and then observes their explosion in a play by his contemporary, Kleist. Chapter 7, "Metamorphoses of Recognition," is a reading of Goethe's short biographical account of his friendship with Schiller, "Fortunate Event," that shows it to unite three different orders of knowledge discernable from the *Poetics* in one dramatic peripeteia: the recognition of people, of things, and of actions.

Chapters 8 and 9 lay out two readings of Goethe's reworking of Euripides's *Iphigenia in Tauris*. First, in "Epistemologies of Recognition," the famous anagnorisis between Iphigenie and Orest provides only one focus of the many concentric spirals of interlocking recognition scenes in Goethe's play, which demonstrates the surprising modes of knowledge involved in recognizing self and other: both processes rely on intertextual performance. This conclusion leads to a reappraisal of Goethe's interpretation of catharsis. The following chapter, "Politics of Recognition," continues to read *Iphigenie* through the lens of the friend-enemy distinction, which pits Schmitt's concept of the political against those of recognition politics. Goethe's play represents a state of exception that brings about a tolerant, more open society that is compromised by its reliance on the rhetoric of kinship. Iphigenie's final speech in the drama reveals the performativity inherent in Hannah Arendt's inflection of *action*[31] and its antidotes of promise and forgiveness.

Chapter 10, "The Fate of Recognition," picks back up on the ancient trope of coming to see oneself in the mirror of another's gaze, introduced in *Alcibiades*, as an anagnorisis scenario. By looking to instances of both reflection and mise en abyme in Kleist's *Penthesilea*, this reading brings together the two strands of mirroring (knowing self) and performing (knowing others) that thread their way through the book. Far from being an Other thoroughly alien to Western ways of thought, as many contend, *Penthesilea* is in fact the embodiment of radical Cartesian epistemology. I argue that the drama stages the failures of recognition necessitated by insisting on the possibility of representing and recognizing internal states of knowledge.

Finally, some concluding reflections show how Kleist's drama, in its implicit critique of the modern subject, points forward to twentieth-century readings of *The Odyssey*. Hans Blumenberg's and Franz Kafka's representations of recognition suggestively echo and magnify the interrogations of the preceding chapters.

Thus through these successive scenes of nostalgia and reflection, change and metamorphosis, epistemology and poetics, friendship and politics, fate and identity, love and war, this book explores the structure of human knowledge in performative action through texts that teach about the limits and potentials of both. As seen above, the recognition scenes in the *Lost* finale demonstrate the emotional power and entertainment value of anagnorisis even in the lack of a satisfactory plot that solves the problems it has opened up. The series stages both the impossibility of recognition transpiring in a momentary flash of knowledge and the intense desire to conceive of it as such. A similar paradox is at work in the final scenes of the episode. The remarkable anagnorisis moments in the flash-sideways universe allow characters eventually to enter an idealized community in which all sources of misunderstanding and contention between people have been transcended, in which everyone understands and respects everyone else. This space displays the positivist, enlightened goal of all struggles for recognition. It becomes increasingly clear as the scenes progress, however, that this idyllic community is the afterlife: all its inhabitants are dead. As will be seen in the *Odyssey*, the only setting in which recognition happens automatically and does not consist in an endless back-and-forth of improvisational playacting, the only place in which recognition is ever complete rather than ongoing—the only time in which recognition can come to a conclusion—is among the shades of the dead in Hades. The end (in the sense of *telos*) of recognition is complete, final knowledge, and it is only possible when its performance comes to an end (in the sense of cessation). As the chorus at the close of *King Oedipus* proclaims, no one can be fully known until "he passes life's last limit" (line 1530).[32] The end of recognition is death.[33]

As long as humans live, they will constantly strive to know one another. The goal of this striving—namely, stable representational knowledge of the true self of other person—is absolutely impossible. Yet the goal must necessarily be posited as a real object of desire in order to motivate the process of recognition in which humans are inescapably enmeshed and through which ethical action transpires in the world. In contrast to *Lost*, no one is trapped on an island, for self and other have their being in the shifty bridges of intersubjective interaction. In the TV show's finale, people reliably know one another only in death; in life, we find ourselves lost in the performance of recognition.

Part I

Marking the Limits of Recognition

Between Aristotle and the *Odyssey*

ἀναγνώρισις δέ, ὥσπερ καὶ τοὔνομα σημαίνει, ἐξ ἀγνοίας εἰς γνῶσιν μεταβολή, ἢ εἰς φιλίαν ἢ εἰς ἔχθραν, τῶν πρὸς εὐτυχίαν ἢ δυστυχίαν ὡρισμένων (*P*, 11, 1452a, 29–31)

(Recognition, just as the name itself signifies, is a change from ignorance to knowledge, into either friendship or enmity, among those bound for good or bad fortune.)

ARISTOTLE'S DEFINITION OF anagnorisis makes a promise it doesn't keep. The first clause claims that the name should signify itself: *anagnorisis* and *recognition* both imply "knowing again." Yet the ensuing definition has nothing to do with the recurrence signaled by the word's construction. A "change from ignorance to knowledge" does not require repetition and in fact suggests that recognition is a matter of learning something new rather than revisiting something old. It is as if the logical formulation of the definition quickly hides away the recursive "again" suggested by the word itself. Though tucked away and ignored, however, the introductory clause intimates and foreshadows the repetitions that will arise again at incongruent moments in Aristotle's analysis.

There is no requirement for any modern theory of recognition—whether in political, theatrical, or philosophical discourses—to look to Aristotle's *Poetics* as a source of authority. But over and over again in contemporary accounts of this hot-button topic in current academia, the same pattern staged in Aristotle's definition repeats itself. Theorists attempt to contain and define the phenomenon of recognition, only to discover that it has gotten away from them and appeared in a different guise in another venue.[1] This stubborn recurrence of recognition is not the only fortuitous kinship between Aristotle's formulation and recent studies of recognition. Aristotle's definition entails three disjunctive pairs that modify the course of recognition along binary nodal points. These dyads correspond precisely to problematic areas in contemporary recognition studies: the move from ignorance to knowledge points to questions of epistemology and cognition, the binary friendship or enmity pertains to the entire ethical dimension of recognition in politics, and the determination of good or bad fortune implicates the ineluctable aspects of identity in society. Chapters 3 through 5 are devoted to each of these dichotomies in succession. It turns out that the unkept promise concerning the name's self-signification also involves a series of opposing binaries, and I trace their emergence and complication in chapter 1. The central element of Aristotle's formula, however, is the single word that makes up the defining predicate: *change*. Chapter 2 shows how change also encompasses a dual structure, though instead of an opposing relation, as in the other binaries, the performative change of recognition works through the complementarity of potency and actuality.

Though these five chapters open up discourses implicit in the key parts of Aristotle's definition of anagnorisis, the primary text for part I is the ultimate poem of recognition, the *Odyssey*. This epic provides a rich font of important recognition scenarios, in its language and narratives as well as in the performative practices through which it evolved as a poetic work. Aristotle himself noticed this feature of the Homeric poem: "The *Odyssey* is recognition through and through" (*P*, 24, 1459b). How seriously should one take this claim, which almost appears as an aside in a late chapter of the *Poetics*? Scholars have long analyzed the second half of the epic (books 13–24), which narrates Odysseus's arrival home in Ithaca, as of a series of formulaic recognition sequences between Odysseus and the various members of his household. The most technical of these studies confidently concludes that "recognition scenes are confined to the second half of the *Odyssey*."[2] Yet the first half also abounds in recognition. In the first part, the so-called Telemachy (books 1–4), Odysseus's son leaves Ithaca with an unrecognized, mentoring goddess to seek out news of his father among other returnees from the Trojan War. Each of his encounters with his father's old friends and their retinues involves episodes where Telemachus is not only identified as the son of Odysseus but then recognized to be like his father in some important way. In the second part (books 5–8), Odysseus lands naked on a foreign shore and must present himself to the natives in such a way that they reward him with lavish gifts and conveyance home. This self-presentation includes the third part (books 9–12), in which Odysseus narrates an account of his journeys since leaving Troy. All the first-contact scenarios with strange creatures and cultures during his travels can figure as recognition scenes, in which characters must assess each other as friends or enemies. The entire narration, meanwhile, is part of his endeavor to be recognized as a hero worthy of honor and booty by his Phaeacian audience.

The recognition scenes in the two halves of the *Odyssey* are different in kind. In the second half, the confrontations between Odysseus and his servants and family members on Ithaca are reunions that reestablish a broken *oikos* (household). In the first half, in contrast, Telemachus and his father were previously unacquainted with the people they encounter. Interestingly, most classical scholars who write about recognition in Greek literature concentrate almost exclusively on the scenes in the second half. They assume that recognition implies reunion between estranged members of a family or household.[3] Philosophers and comparatists, on the other hand, want the term to apply more broadly to a wide range of human interactions.[4] Their definitions of recognition encompass the variety of encounters in the first half of the book as well as those on Ithaca.

The readings below show how neither of these seemingly incompatible scholarly treatments are wrong. Recognition is *both* a ubiquitous experience of human intersubjectivity *and* a phenomenon limited to the restoration of familial bonds. The underlying desire of recognition, which haunts Aristotle's definition in the fleeting nod toward the word's self-signification, injects into all interactions a longing to return home. Anagnorisis is always already a process of elusive *nostos*.

This nostalgia of recognition is the subject of the first chapter. As each chapter takes off from a clause of Aristotle's definition, key episodes of the *Odyssey* offer confirmations, complications, and challenges. First, attention to the composition of the word *anagnorisis* itself reveals the illusory desire that is the motivating engine for recognition stories such as the *Odyssey* and for fundamental oppositions in genre studies, ontology, and semiotics. The hidden recognitions between Menelaus and Helen are emblematic of this self-signifying desire (chapter 1). Second, since recognition is a kind of change for Aristotle, it makes sense to examine how change functions in his system. This analysis allows me, with the help of recent Homeric scholarship, to gloss Aristotle's definition of recognition as performance. Two instances of Odysseus's performative weeping serve as examples of the dynamics of this articulation of recognition (chapter 2). This explanation then enables a profitable exploration of three opposing pairs in Aristotle's formulation. The change "from ignorance to knowledge" demands an inquiry into the epistemology of recognition, which, it turns out, is contingent entirely on a propensity to forget. Penelope's interview with Odysseus in book 19 of the *Odyssey* serves as a perfect exemplum of the indeterminacy of recognition (chapter 3). The exclusive disjunction, "friendship or enmity," then forces the problem of recognition into the fields of ethics and, per Schmitt and Derrida, politics. The famous reunion of Odysseus with his dog provides a limit case to understand the dissimulation at the heart of human friendship (chapter 4). Finally, the nodal horizon for good or bad fortune, which closes off Aristotle's definition, offers a vantage from which to view the frailty of recognition. Odysseus's encounters with three women (Circe, Nausicaa, and Athena) reveal a spectrum of the inescapable checks that identity holds over human agency (chapter 5).

It will become clear that *both* classicists and philosophers are justified in their opposing efforts to limit and expand, respectively, recognition's reach in the *Odyssey*. The universalizing tendencies of the former require the constructivist assumptions of the latter—and vice versa—to make the distinctions either insists on. Recognition is a matter of hermeneutics writ both large and small. Any attempt to grasp the essential action of recognition will find that that it eludes conceptual stability. It constantly escapes onto different stages (*andere Schauplätze*, to borrow Freud's phrase). This means both that recognition will appear with strangely familiar features in unexpected places and that many sightings of it will prove errant. Even when observed closely, this protean activity, so central to human agency, is devilishly difficult to hold still.

CHAPTER ONE

"Just as the Name Itself Signifies"

Under the Sign of Nostalgia

WHAT'S IN A name? If the construction of a word reveals its own meaning, a definition should be superfluous. Aristotle prefaces his own definition of recognition by claiming that the word is self-explanatory: "Anagnorisis, *just as the name itself signifies*."[1] He then goes on to provide an explanation of the term that is by no means obvious from its component parts. Though Aristotle never explicitly addresses the etymological roots or compound structure of the word—presumably its signification is too self-evident to warrant explication—these questions launch this chapter, leading to four important claims about recognition. First, the word itself invites reflection on the iterative nature of recognition, revealing a deep connection between recognition and nostalgia. The specific illustration of this link in the *Odyssey* with the homecomings of Agamemnon and Menelaus then leads to the identification of a distinct Atreidian mode of recognition in anticipatory contrast to that of Odysseus and Penelope. Next, the consequences of nostalgic recognition offer insight into the theory of epic poetry. Tragedy and epic both sport their own paradoxes of recognition that simultaneously contradict and complement the other. What's more, the dual logic of recognition echoes and amplifies a series of fraught dualities: surprisingly, the relationships Same/Other, simple/complex, and natural/conventional all share features of the seemingly generic divide between epic and tragedy. Finally, the temporality of epic forces a return and reevaluation of the very nature of signing and signification itself. Semiotics, it turns out, is predicated on the nostalgic paradox of recognition: the artificial arbitrariness of mediating signs necessary for the functioning of language makes possible the idea of and longing for natural signs and immediate communication.

NOSTALGIA AND RECOGNITION

An obvious place to begin investigating what "the name itself signifies" would be the elements that make up the noun: *ana* (again) + *gnōrisis* (acquaintance, knowledge) = knowing again. The term is most often translated as "recognition." This English word fortuitously indicates its own meaning as well: *re* (again) + *cognition* (mental action, acquisition of knowledge) = knowing again. Of course, this kind of explanation simply passes the buck. Saying that recognition means to know something or someone again gets us no closer to an understanding of knowledge. What does it mean to know something or someone in the first place? What concept of time is implied by the adverb *again*? By directing attention to the elements of the term, Aristotle's parenthetical aside is an answer that begs more questions. It does, however, serve to emphasize two fields of meaning implicit in every instance of recognition: epistemology and time. What is the temporality of knowledge assumed behind dramatic anagnorisis?

Before returning to the assumptions behind these two complex notions, however, some alternative explanations of the word *anagnōrisis* merit mention. Several translations of the *Poetics* render the term as "discovery."[2] This name signifies itself in a way quite appropriate to many instances of tragic recognition cited by Aristotle, but the elements of the word *discovery* are very different from those that make up *recognition* and *anagnorisis*. *Discovery* entails an uncovering or disconcealment. It involves the revelation of a preexistent but hidden truth. In fact, discovery is rather suggestive of Martin Heidegger's creative etymology for the Greek word for truth. He derives *alētheia* from *lanthanein* (to escape notice) via an older form (*lēthein*) that is connected to *lēthē* (forgetting) by adding a negating alpha primitive. Hence one should understand truth as a kind of not-forgetting—or, as Heidegger puts it, *Unverborgenheit* (unconcealedness).[3] Heidegger uses this etymological strategy to reveal his notion of truth as disclosure, which he opposes to the prevalent but distorting correspondence conceptions of truth. The connections between dis*closure* and dis*covery* may ring true to a poetic ear, and thinking through interpersonal recognition in terms of Heideggerian ontology could be a thrilling enterprise.[4] Yet the suggestive self-disclosure of the word *discovery* clearly signifies itself in a lexical field very different from that of *anagnorisis*. For one thing, *recognition* and *unconcealedness* require radically different notions of agency. Heideggerian disclosure is a feature of the world in which humans are situated; Aristotelian recognition is an action that subjects engage in. Certainly the *Odyssey* could yield very enlightening readings that illustrate and challenge Heidegger's phenomenology in terms of recognition as disclosure: for seven years, Odysseus languishes on the island of Calypso, whose very name means hidden. Only by finally rejecting the immortality of concealment in favor of the transience of disclosure does Odysseus open himself up to the vicissitudes of discovery. Such a study, however, is an undertaking for a different book. It may turn out that certain aspects of recognition as analyzed below will reveal functions analogous to disclosure, but they make up parts of a performative process and by no means signify the whole action of anagnorisis.

Another etymology of *anagnorisis*, more whimsical than plausible, shares with Heidegger's *alētheia* a predilection for privatives. One could read the initial *an* as a negating prefix before *agnōrisis*, which in turn would mean ignorance by consisting of another alpha-privative + *gnōrisis* (knowledge).[5] Recognition would thus mean not-not-knowing. The Heideggerian implications of this construction are ready to hand. Unconcealedness as a removal of hiddenness is easily kin to a deprival of ignorance. This double negative is clever but unlikely. No such word as *agnōrisis* is attested.[6] In fact, because the prefix *ana* is often an intensifier, meaning "much," "very," or "well," it is far more likely that the common positive meaning would be understood rather than a double negative. A primary definition for *anagignōskein*, for instance, a verb closely related to *anagnōrizein*, is "to know well, to know fully."

The prefix *ana* has sundry denotations, and like the meanings of prepositions in any language, they can be bafflingly idiosyncratic. In compounds, it can give the sense of "upward"; "increase, strengthening"; "again"; or "back." Clearly, several inventive definitions for anagnorisis could be concocted from this grab bag. One plausible suggestion is that the prefix could be understood as "up," as in "taking something up into awareness," rather than "back" or "again."[7] This understanding of the word comes much closer to the sense of a sudden realization or revelation—in short, an epiphany. One could easily discover motifs of recognition in literary epiphanies, such as the ones James Joyce staged in his stories and novels, or in philosophical epiphanies, such as those that constitute Emmanuel Levinas's grounding of morality in the experience of the face-to-face encounter with the Other.[8]

Yet it is difficult to understand how reading the prefix *ana* as "up" rather than "again" would make the phrase "just as the name signifies" any more transparent—indeed, the clause in that case becomes more mystifying as an explanatory interjection. If the word itself signifies taking knowledge "up," it is an explanation that explains nothing and raises no pressing questions. Had Aristotle meant his dramatic device to be epiphanic, he could easily have used that very term. Epiphany derives from the Greek *epiphaneia* (appearance, coming into view), which "signifies itself" in a very distinctive way. Yet, if anything, the sense of the word *epiphany* has undergone an even greater change since antiquity than *recognition*. In classical Greek, no less than in the early church writings, an *epiphany* was an "appearing upon/unto," often of a god to a human.[9] It was the god who did the shining and the mortal who received the rays of illumination. In modern parlance, especially since Joyce gave the term its intellectual chic, an *epiphany* is a transformative realization that occurs within a single person's consciousness. Far from an intersubjective process with necessary consequences in the world, a modernist epiphany is a momentary bursting of awareness occasioned by a chance event, encounter, or object. It may even remain entirely unnoticed by other people. The change in meaning for *epiphany* is more radical even than the one this book is exploring with *recognition* and deserves its own archeological interrogation. The instances of recognition I explore will often coincide with epiphanies for the characters involved and for the readers or spectators looking on. But for reasons that will soon become clear, my investigation will take its impetus from the recognitive rather than the epiphanic aspects of these encounters.

Despite the indisputable attractions of *discovery* and *epiphany*, *recognition* has one advantage that the other compounds lack. Both *recognition* and *anagnorisis* share a compelling ambiguity. They invite but do not insist on a reference to time and recurrence. *Recognition* implies an "again" with its prefix, but many uses of the noun and verb do not denote any return. When one state recognizes another, what is being repeated? When someone longs for recognition in her job or community, where is the recurrence? *Anagnōrizein* and the related verb *anagignōskein* share in this diverse range of meanings.[10] Yet even in these nonrepetitive denotations, the presence of the *re* carries the whisper of return.

Although he initially calls our attention to the composition of the word itself, Aristotle's explanation in the lines that follow significantly leaves out the self-defining feature of the *ana-*, the "again" to which he is presumably referring in his parenthetical postpositive. "A transition out of ignorance into knowing" (*ex agnoias eis gnōsin metabolē*) is the properly defining formula of the sentence. Recognition is a change. What kind of change? A change from ignorance to knowledge. What kind of coming to know? One that leads to friendship or enmity. Where in this definition is the self-defining feature of the word's composition? Where are the implicit recurrence and return with which Aristotle introduces the notion?

The paragraph as a whole makes no further overt reference to the notion of *again* outside the initial attention Aristotle draws to the construction of the word and its telling prefix. Indeed, it is at first unclear how the example for the best form of recognition cited by Aristotle in the following lines is a case of *re*cognition at all. Oedipus's realization of who he is and what he has done can hardly be described as a reunion with someone or something with which he had been previously familiar. But by pointing to Sophocles's play as the ideal showcase of effective recognition, the text underscores the fact that in the discovery of his own identity, Oedipus is suddenly confronted with the knowledge that he is not the stranger to Thebes he had always held himself to be: in fact, his arrival years before had been a return and his first sight of Jocasta, a *Wiedersehen*.

Though he does not spell it out explicitly, by framing this defining paragraph on anagnorisis first with the parenthetical clause "just as the name signifies" and then with the concluding example of Oedipus—by surrounding the body of his definition with two subtle reminders of "again"—Aristotle invites readers to focus their view on the recurrent nature of recognition. Recognition necessarily implies a return—just as it equally presumes a prior leave-taking. Even if one doesn't buy into the Platonic Socrates's occasional notion of knowledge as recollection (and Aristotle certainly does not), there is the inescapable smack of repetition about recognition; a *wieder* is involved in any instance of *erkennen*.

Recognition involves return. The converse is equally true. As a poem of homecoming, the *Odyssey* is "recognition through and through" (*P* 24, 1459b). Recognition is the means by which Odysseus secures his homecoming. Desire for home is synonymous with a longing to be sure of friends and family. This process is the tension at the heart of all *nostoi*, the stories of the heroes returning from the Trojan (or indeed any) War. The yearning for home and reestablishment of the household in the *Odyssey* is always tinged with pain and loss. Recognition in the epic poem of return, therefore, is an operation of nostalgia.

Nostalgia is not a Greek word. It was first coined in the seventeenth century by Johannes Hofer (1669–1752) as a medical term for the debilitating homesickness of Swiss mercenaries. As Svetlana Boym writes, "*Nostalgia* is only pseudo-Greek, or nostalgically Greek."[11] Appropriately enough for a word meant to describe a phenomenon of traveling, it comprises a portmanteau: *nostos* (homecoming) + *algos* (pain). The two components of the modern word both feature prominently in the preamble to the *Odyssey* and set the tone for all twenty-four songs that follow. The poem is about the pain of homecoming. Norman Austin argues convincingly that nostalgia is the key pathos of the entire epic, just as wrath (*mēnis*) is the principle emotion of the *Iliad*.[12] I would go further by claiming that the central action related to this pathos of nostalgia is recognition.

A form of *nostos* appears three times in the first thirteen lines of the poem, first as an object of struggle (*Od*, 1.5), then deprivation (*Od*, 1.19), and finally yearning (*Od*, 1.13). It is closely tied to recognition:

> Tell me, Muse, of the man of many ways, who was driven
> far journeys, after he had sacked Troy's sacred citadel.
> Many were they whose cities he saw, whose minds he learned of (ἔγνω),
> Many the pains (ἄλγεα) he suffered in his spirit on the wide sea,
> Struggling for his own life and the homecoming (νόστον) of his companions. (*Od*, 1.1–5)

Recognition, *nostos*, and *algos* make up the three most defining features of Odysseus's character: he *knew* the minds of many people (*gignōskein*; *Od*, 1.3), suffered many pains (*algea*; *Od*, 1.4), and struggled for his companions' homecoming (*nostos*; *Od*, 1.5). Recognition is Odysseus's heroic excellence (skill or virtue, even: *aretē*)—knowing people is what he's good at. The formula by which Odysseus knows men's minds ties recognition to *nostos* even more closely: "*noon egnō*" (he knew the mind). The verb for knowledge here, *gignōskein*, is a cognate with the root of anagnorisis. *Nous* (the later Attic form of the Homeric *noos*) is etymologically related to *nostos*. To know another's mind is a kind of coming home. Both derive from the Proto-Indo-European root *nes-*, which means, according to Douglas Frame, "to return to light and life."[13] It is clear how the *Odyssey* is constructed out of many interlocking versions of this basic motif: Odysseus's escape from the dark hiddenness of Calypso's island, for instance, leads to the bright openness of his public acknowledgment by the Phaeacians. He even returns to the world of the living from the literal death of the underworld. Odysseus's characteristic skill at reading other people is deeply embedded in his longing for home. *Nous* requires and enables *nostos*.

Yet are *nous* and *nostos* necessarily bound to *algos* in the *Odyssey*? Certainly characters must endure sufferings in order to achieve homecoming.

But the poem is commonly understood to end happily: Odysseus has been reunited with his son, wife, father, and loyal servants. His household has been restored and the rapacious suitors and miscreant domestics punished. How can such resounding success admit notes of discord?

In fact, the undeniable joys of reunion in the *Odyssey* are suffused with melancholy. Odysseus reestablishes his household and kingship, but his new reign is far from identical with his old stewardship of the island. The twelve ships full of Ithacans he led from Troy (not counting the many who must have died of wounds or disease on Ilion's plains), doubtless his staunchest young male supporters from Ithaca, are all dead. In order to gain control of his household, he has had to shed even more blood. Odysseus graphically executes not only all of the suitors but also twelve maidservants. In book 24, the Ithacans themselves rise up against their erstwhile king in disgust at this carnage. Only the intervention of Athena prevents a violent and likely protracted civil war on the island. The peace that she decrees is predicated on the Ithacans forgetting their just grievances so that they may be friends again. Zeus instructs her to "make them forget (*eklēsis*) the death of their brothers / and sons, and let them be friends with each other, as in the time past" (*Od*, 24.484–485). The only way for Odysseus to regain any legitimacy as the ruler of Ithaca is by making his subjects forget his crimes. Just a few lines before, Agamemnon praises Penelope, who enabled her husband's happy return because of "how well she remembered (*eu memnēt'*) Odysseus" (*Od*, 24.195). Though the cultivated memories of Penelope effected his homecoming, the careful excision of memories from the people is necessary for Odysseus to sustain his return in the long run.

In one sense, the *algos* of *nostos* is transferred from Odysseus and his family to his subjects. In other senses, it will tinge even the relations of the reestablished hierarchies of returnee's household. Introducing her haunting, seminal study of nostalgia, Svetlana Boym suggested that the *Odyssey* was a poem that consistently skirted misrecognition and hence always suggested the tragedy that could easily develop out of any of its episodes.[14] I claim that *algos* taints even the most seemingly successful recognitions and *nostoi* in the poem.

RECOGNITIONS IN MYCENAE AND SPARTA

I will return to examine the tensions in Odysseus's own day of homecoming below (chapters 3–4), but two counter examples of the nostalgia of recognition come much earlier. In many ways, the *Odyssey* displays a paradigmatic spectrum for the sorrows of homecoming and recognition long before the Ithacan reunions in the second half of the poem. At the extremes of the spectrum are the two brothers who dragged Odysseus to war in the first place: Agamemnon and Menelaus. The former arrives home triumphant after finally leading the Greek forces to victory at Troy, only to be killed by his wife and her lover. Agamemnon misreads Clytemnestra's smiles on his return to Mycenae and dooms his entire brood of offspring to a generation of recognition tragedies.[15] This negative poster child for *nostos* gone awry appears as a ghost to Odysseus in the *Odyssey*. The shade of Agamemnon warns him to be careful in coming home and doles out advice about recognition: Odysseus should make his arrival secretly and not be open even with his wife (*Od*, 11.441–443, 454–456). If Agamemnon's trusting homecoming led to the stuff of tragedy with the sudden recognition of hidden enemies, Odysseus's devious return is epic material in the slow discovery of friends.

Seemingly in stark contrast to Agamemnon's bloody return is the peaceful household of Menelaus in Sparta, which we see through the eyes of Telemachus. Like his father in Phaeacia and Ithaca, Telemachus arrives at the court of Menelaus without immediately disclosing his identity. Even the ways that his hosts recognize their young guest's identity have their parallels in the other courts.[16] His sojourn in Sparta is the final stage of Telemachus's educational expedition in which the young man is exposed to the ways of heroic Greek culture and hospitality. The regal pair of Menelaus and Helen gives Telemachus his crowning lesson on becoming a hero worthy of his pedigree. By the end of his stay, he so impresses his hosts with his judicious mastery of cultural norms that they shower him with gifts and praise.

With the possible exception of Alcinous's court, no other household in the *Odyssey* is as replete with riches as that of Menelaus. Menelaus seems to have it all. Among his splendid trophies, he can even count the most beautiful woman in the world as his wife. Telemachus is constantly in awe of the glamorous possessions that deck Sparta's halls. Yet though Telemachus arrives on the double wedding day of Menelaus's son and daughter, the father speaks much more of lamentation than celebration. "It is with no pleasure I am lord over all these possessions" (*Od*, 4.93), he tells the young traveler. It is largely by sacking Troy that he became lord of all those riches, yet he wishes the war had never happened. The predominant mood of his speeches is the wistful optative:

> I wish I lived in my house with only a third part of all
> these goods, and that the men were alive who died in those days
> in wide Troy land far away from horse-pasturing Argos.
> Still and again lamenting all these men and sorrowing
> many a time when I am sitting here in our palace
> I will indulge my heart in sorrow, and then another time
> give over, for surfeit of gloomy lamentation comes quickly.
> (*Od*, 4.97–103)

Despite the present goods he surrounds himself with, nostalgia for a lost past reigns over Menelaus's Sparta.

By all rights, Menelaus and Helen should have the most difficult reunion of all couples following the Trojan War. After all, Helen's elopement was the cause of the ten years of death and destruction to begin with. Instead of waiting patiently at home like other wives, she is active under the gaze and in the arms of the Trojan enemies. Regardless of her choice or agency in the matter, about which ancient sources disagree and which Homer leaves open to interpretation,[17] Menelaus's personal pride cannot have been undamaged by the high visibility of his wife's infidelity. Yet on the surface at least, the couple now lives in perfect harmony, prosperity, and luxury. Some readers go so far as to hold them up as a paradigm of Homeric marital happiness, embodying the *homophrosunē*—like-mindedness—that is the poem's ideal of marriage.[18]

Book 4 of the *Odyssey* never overtly claims that Helen and Menelaus have anything other than a model Greek marriage. Yet small details point to the very real tensions underlying their union.[19] Their strained relations come into sharpest relief when they take turns telling Telemachus stories about his father. In the first, Helen recounts an espionage mission Odysseus undertakes incognito among the Trojans. According to her tale, Helen immediately sees through the wily man's disguise and manages to seduce him with a bath and oils to divulge his secret plans (*Od*, 4.239–264). This story sets Helen up as a loyal supporter of the Greek cause and as Odysseus's match in wits and persuasiveness. Menelaus's tale, meanwhile, narrates the experiences of the Greek soldiers hiding inside the Trojan horse. He tells how Helen walks around the horse three times, stroking it and mimicking the voices of the wives of those within. Each of the Greeks is moved to shout aloud and go out to the wives they hear; only Odysseus knows better and holds them back from revealing themselves and ruining the stratagem by which Troy will be taken (*Od*, 4.266–289). This time it is Odysseus who sees through Helen's deception. Both tales portray Helen and Odysseus as a match for one another: they are in much more active *homophrosunē* than Helen and Menelaus ever manage to be. But in contrast to Helen's own asseverations about her loyalty to the Greeks, Menelaus's tale depicts a duplicitous and mocking Helen intent on luring the Greeks to their destruction.

Strikingly, it is the spouses' competing *recognition tales* that reveal the mistrust and resentment between them. Book 4 of the *Odyssey* has thus put its audience in the same position as Telemachus: only by listening closely to stories of recognition can he discern the state of friendship or hostility between the tellers. In this case, the agonistic anagnorisis stories reveal a hidden animosity underlying the husband and wife's relations. If Telemachus is to become a perceiver of *nous* as adept as his father, he must learn to read anagnorisis narratives.

The morning after Helen and her husband entertain Telemachus together, Menelaus approaches the young man by himself (*Od*, 4.306–624). He tells Telemachus the story of his own *nostos*. Significantly, Helen plays no part in it whatsoever. The tale does, however, provide an emblematic image for the kind of recognition that is characteristic of Menelaus, in stark contrast to the kind that Telemachus is supposed to learn from the model of his father.[20] At the center of Menelaus's *nostos* is the ordeal with Proteus. Menelaus is stuck in Egypt with no winds to move his homebound fleet and all its booty back to Greece. An impish sprite confides how he can find his way home by tricking her father and gives him the means and intel to pull it off (*Od*, 4.365–424). Menelaus's task is one of recognition—but a kind that the rather slow-witted Atreid can handle. All he has to do is hold on tightly to the squirming, polymorphous Proteus until he perceives the god's original form (which, interestingly, is revealed by sleep).

Recognition here is a desperate attempt to hold on to secure knowledge. This desire for security without the risk of one's own investigatory performance is embodied in the simple task to hold on tight, no matter what. If you cling tenaciously enough, the Other will eventually revert to his original form from sheer exhaustion. This vice-like grip on Proteus is an emblem for Menelaus's mode of recognition. His nostalgic longing to keep hold of the relations he has had with other people is akin to his drive to accumulate material properties, regardless of their use to him and his personal happiness. Even his wife is a thing among things: a trophy to be owned and possessed. People, to him, are objects to own or discard, and the proper action in regard to property is to grab on and hold.

The only time Helen's name is mentioned in Menelaus's entire *nostos* narrative is not from his own lips. The silence that shrouds Helen's return journey speaks volumes. This is the time during which she would have had to renegotiate her status with the cuckolded husband and establish some sort of normalcy in their relations. She would have known to do so by performing the part of one of Menelaus's many storied possessions. The unpersonhood of this forced relation is underscored by Menelaus's emphatic silence about Helen in his entire narration of their return from Troy. The only mention of Helen comes not from Menelaus but from Proteus. He assures Menelaus that he will not die but become a resident of the Elysian Fields. The sole reason for this reward, Proteus says, is "because you have Helen" (*hounek' ekheis Helenēn*; *Od*, 4.569). The critical verb here is *ekhein*: to have, to cling to, to possess. Keeping possession of his wife, in other words, is the key to Menelaus's immortality. By holding on to Helen, Menelaus will be able to hang on to life forever. If he was undecided about what to do with Helen before this encounter (according to some sources, he had originally intended to kill her),[21] Menelaus certainly has incentive to retain his grip on her now. As he proved with the Proteus ordeal, holding on is Menelaus's forte, and it is a fitting token of the mode of recognition he practices.

But the relationship between Menelaus and his restored wife belies this wishful parable of tenacity rewarded. Menelaus has certainly maintained an unshakable grip on Helen. And yet the luxurious life they lead is suffused with grief, resentment, and sorrow. Memories of the past, which indeed make up the fabric of this Spartan present, are so distressing that Helen dispenses drugs to ease the pain of remembering. Here, the iterative *re* in recognition does not just call for persistence in clinging to the past—Menelaus's heroic skill—but requires the anesthesia that Helen's numbing potion provides. The *algos* of this *nostos* has to be dulled with drugs so powerful that anyone who takes them can watch unfeelingly as a brother or son is murdered (*Od*, 4.225).[22] To act as if trauma, violence, and betrayal have changed nothing in the relations between the reunited persons, this retrieved past must be played out with deadened senses. The endless life Menelaus looks forward to is enacted by cleaving to death.

The two brothers responsible for the Trojan War thus represent two poles of danger in the sorrow of homecoming. Both are caused by their modes of recognition. Agamemnon carelessly assumes that things will be the same when he returns home. Menelaus takes great care to clutch an irretrievable past. The Atreidai are thus figures of the paradox of security.[23]

Etymologically, *secura* means without care. Yet if one is cavalierly carefree in dealing with friends and family, then one risks the fate of Agamemnon. Conversely, the cost of guarding against all conceivable threats is to forfeit any peace of mind. By keeping a death grip on the past, Menelaus reifies the people around him and stifles any chance of present life. Both extremes—Agamemnon's trusting braggadocio and Menelaus's objectifying hypervigilance—lead to homecomings bereft of true security.

The Atreidai's two modes of recognition can be seen as the Scylla and Charybdis of homecoming. Will Odysseus, master knower of *nous*, navigate between these dangers? Like Agamemnon, his household is beset with ill-meaning enemies. Like Menelaus, his relationship with his wife will need much repair after the long years of abandonment and suffering. Clearly Agamemnon's warning in the underworld puts Odysseus on guard to dodge the former fate by taking on the intrigues of disguise and testing for which the second half of the *Odyssey* is famous. But in his cunning machinations to restore his household, will Odysseus manage to avert the trap of Menelaus's overanxious opulence? If so, he will not do it alone. Penelope and Odysseus together perform a mode of recognition in stark contrast to the ones demonstrated by the Atreidai. Yet recognition is not a virtue in the Aristotelian sense of the word: there is no perfect Ithacan mean between the extremes of Sparta and Mycenae. It is often forgotten that Odysseus does not escape scot-free from Scylla and Charybdis. The only way to avoid being annihilated by one of the monsters is to skirt just close enough to the other for it to grab and kill a few men among the crew. Similarly, homecomings that evade slaughter on the one hand or petrification on the other are still liable to all the contradictions that attend any attempt to restore a past state. Even the most successful recognition will have its casualties. In charting the successful courses of recognition in the *Odyssey*, the chapters that follow will also register the collateral damage they bring in their wake.

NOSTALGIC RECOGNITION AND EPIC AFTERNESS

The structure of nostalgia signified by the name of *re*cognition (knowing *again*) informs the very mode and genesis of the epic form. Paul Fleming has shown with Georg Lukács that the theory of the epic only comes about in retrospect with the advent of the novel. Like Friedrich Schiller's category of naive poetry, which can only be conceived as such in light of its later opposite, the sentimental,[24] the epic as an object of theory does not exist until it has been superseded by a form that requires it as a limit. The novel is a modern answer to losing the totality of the world the epic inhabits. It is not that epic cannot be identified and described before the novel; clearly Aristotle and others have done just that. But prior to the twin birth of the novel and its theory, there is no "theory of the epic" properly speaking, and even then it only exists as a limit case for theory: the "degree zero of all theory."[25] The time of the epic—which can never be glimpsed from within the epic—is always too late.

I will take this claim even further and insist that the belatedness of epic theory is already constituted by epic poetry itself. Epic, at least as celebrated in the seminal works of the genre in Western literature (Homer and Virgil), is structured around the wishful restoral of lost time. Epic poems are always already obsessed with what has come before and aware of themselves as followers and successors of an earlier greatness. They are, in fact, prime examples of "afterness," as coined and explored by Gerhard Richter. For Richter, afterness is the defining figure of modernity, an era in which we increasingly live in memory of a past that was never truly present.[26] This diagnosis, however, also perfectly describes the world and characters of Homer's poems. The pervasively melancholic nostalgia of ancient epic poetry will either strike contemporary readers as remarkably modern or tempt them to recognize afterness as a universal phenomenon of humanity.

Virgil points to his own belatedness with every dactyl of his Latin hexameters. In trying to recreate the magic and totality of the Homeric world, the *Aeneid* is a carefully crafted monument to the supposedly natural genius of the earlier Greek poems.[27] Aeneas learns as much when he arrives in Carthage after fleeing Troy. In the poem's first famous instance of ekphrasis, Aeneas is awaiting Dido in the temple of Juno, where he beholds intricate wall paintings depicting scenes from the *Iliad* and other epic poems of the Trojan War.[28] Through his tears, Aeneas recognizes his countrymen, enemies, and even himself in the illustrated figures. Ekphrasis here is not merely Virgil's achievement of capturing painted images in poetic verse, but the paintings themselves are necessarily ekphrastic in the other direction: they are artistic depictions of linguistic reports that have traveled from the Greek world. Homer had clearly reached Carthage before Aeneas landed there.

But Homer's poems are also too late. The *Odyssey* seems to be a straightforward sequel to the *Iliad*. The latter narrates a major turning point in the Trojan War, and the former relates the fates of the returning soldiers. As Norman Austin writes, however, not only is the *Odyssey* the indispensable companion to the *Iliad*, but the *Iliad* itself is unthinkable without the supposedly later poem.[29] For Austin, as mentioned above, nostalgia is the central pathos of the *Odyssey*. For what, though, is the voice of the poem as a whole nostalgic, if not for a time before the *Iliad* took place? Odysseus longs to return not only to his home but also to the way it was before he left to join the Greek expedition against Troy. Many characters in the *Odyssey* curse the war. Even Achilles repents of his famous choice for early death and glory in the *Iliad*. In the underworld, he scoffs at Odysseus's praise and consolation, saying he would rather pull the plow as slave to a poor farmer than be king over the dead (*Od*, 11.488–491). Nostalgia for a lost antebellum innocence and social harmony seems to be the key that determines the tone of the entire poem. If the war had never happened, however, then neither the *Iliad* nor the *Odyssey* could have been sung. The trials of the war and its aftermath provide material for the plots, but the displacement and social upheaval caused by the conflict are the rhetorical occasions for most speech and storytelling within the poems themselves. Characters' dialogue, which makes up fully half of the poems' bulk, repeatedly laments present suffering and longs for past happiness. The founding wish of the epic, therefore, is for its own nihility.

Epic is already belated even in its first instance: as performed in Homer's poems, at least, epic poetry only comes about out of a longing for the world before the epic. The same lost mythic wholeness and totality that modern novels must posit—in order to repair, respond to, or reject—is already postulated as lost within epic poems themselves. In fact, epic comes about precisely because of this loss. The founding moment of the *Odyssey*, for instance, is the scene in which Calypso discovers Odysseus pining for home as he gazes out to sea through teary eyes. Though readers have to wait until book 5 for this first encounter with Odysseus, the late tableau of stubborn melancholy sets the entire action of the poem in motion.

The *Odyssey* is a poem of *nostos*—of returning home following the war—and hence it is unmistakably a tale of afterness, but the *Iliad* is suffused with sorrow for lost time too. Like Odysseus's choice for home and mortality over eternal life with Calypso in the *Odyssey*, Achilles's decision between homecoming and glory, as narrated in book 9, is the ultimate founding moment of the *Iliad*. Achilles must choose between *nostos*, the theme of the *Odyssey*, and *kleos*, eternal glory. It is his election for the latter that makes his wrath and deeds worthy of epic treatment to begin with. The choice for glory would seem to predetermine the poem to be a celebration rather than a dirge. Yet while the *Odyssey* laments an irretrievable past, the

Iliad grieves for an inevitable future. Achilles does not die in the poem, but his parents' grief frames the beginning, middle, and end of the *Iliad*. Thetis is already mourning as if she has lost her son from her first appearance in book 1 to her orchestrated threnody (with no fewer than thirty-three named Nereids) in book 18. Achilles's father's grief, meanwhile, enters the poem in the figure of Priam in the final book. Hector's father supplicates the murderer of his own son by presenting himself as a man like Peleus, Achilles's father. This encounter with his sworn enemy is the closest thing to a homecoming Achilles will ever have. By recognizing his own father in Priam, Achilles allows for the transformation of his original wrath into pity that brings the poem to its close. Without the nostalgia of recognition, these two foundational epics would not exist.

But the afterness of epic recognition is even more troubling when one thinks of the scenes of nostalgia that are most closely associated with anagnorisis: Odysseus is recognized in Phaeacia by the way he weeps when reminded of the past. Yet he reveals his identity not by shedding a tear over a swineherd's idyll of his distant, formerly unblemished homeland but rather by grieving over tales of the Trojan War. He is recognized by his homesickness not for home but for another epic, from the same cycle that includes the *Iliad*. Epic poetry is hence not only instigated by a longing for the pre-epic world, but simultaneously consists of nostalgia for the destroying wrath that inaugurates the first epic (*mēnin aeide thea*: "Sing, Goddess, the wrath"; *Il*, 1.1). It longs simultaneously for its nonconception and its inception. Like Franz Moor in Schiller's *Robbers*, it both curses and blesses the lamentable and beautiful moment of its necessary coming into being. Epic contains its own theorization by positing itself as a mode of longing for its own nonexistence. Epic celebrates this very yearning for negation in which its mode of being exists. Epic poetry, therefore, is the sentimental incursion of its own death wish.

This claim may become clearer by comparing the epic to another ancient genre, elegy, which is a much more obvious instantiation of afterness. By definition, elegies mourn the loss of a past state. In declaring nostalgic self-negation to be constitutive of epic form, I am not simply eliding it into elegy. Elegy is primarily descriptive, whereas the driving force of epic is narrative. Epic poems do not dwell on lengthy portrayals of irrecoverable idyllic states; their nostalgia is constitutive but not always overt. Instead, it is the reaction to loss that impels the *action* of an epic poem. The founding scenes of the *Iliad* and the *Odyssey* are responses to afterness: Achilles's choice for *kleos* and Odysseus's for *nostos* determine the general trajectory of the action in the respective poems. In the *Odyssey*, these actions manifest as types of recognition: Agamemnon's blithe presumption, Menelaus's deathlike grasp, Odysseus's playful disguise, and Penelope's artful dance are prime examples of the ways a character's attitude toward loss manifests itself in the poem's actions of recognition.

Aristotle's *Poetics* suggests two other dichotomies that can help us think through the *Odyssey*'s afterness in terms of recognition: one generic and one formal. For one thing, Aristotle's treatment of genre maps neatly onto the paradoxical belatedness of the novel to the epic. Aristotle holds Athenian tragedy to be the form of poetic creation that best fulfills its natural potential. In his teleological account of the literary arts, other poetic forms, especially epic, are stepping stones on the way to the emergence of tragedy. In Aristotle as in Lukács, therefore, two generic oppositions are presented as historical genealogies, with epic figuring as the earlier, simpler form. Just as Fleming showed that there is no epic theory before the theory of the novel, one could easily argue that epic poetry only received any attention in the *Poetics* because of Aristotle's predilection for tragedy. No systematic theory of poetry, epic or otherwise, is attested in ancient Greece before Aristotle's treatise, which was clearly motivated first and foremost by tragedy. Aristotle is so obsessed with the Attic practice of tragedy as the fulfillment of the natural form of poetic perfection that all other genres are defined and judged in relation to it. Homeric scholars have long felt the need to be a bit defensive of their object of study in response to the short shrift epic receives in the founding document of literary theory.[30] Epic does not receive its own dedicated chapters until book 23, and by book 24, the treatment is complete. The coverage of tragedy, in contrast, takes up books 6–22. The fact that many of the illustrations for terms conceived for the analysis of tragedy come from Homer bolsters rather than diminishes the text's valorization of the tragic genre. Finally, in both Lukács and Aristotle, the later form (novel, tragedy) determines the definition of the former (epic). Aristotle simply takes his carefully thorough definition of tragedy and tweaks it to apply to epic poetry, which "ought to have the same forms as tragedy" and which comprises "the same parts, except for meter and spectacle" (*P*, 24, 1459b). Both are imitations of serous actions, character, thought, and language. Both can be appreciated by reading as well as through performance. Both have the same aims in affecting their audience. Yet when the final book of the treatise asks which is the better form of imitation, tragedy wins the contest handily. Tragedy comes *after* epic, but epic theory is an afterthought to that of tragedy.

Despite these similarities, the two dichotomies are different in important ways. For Schiller, Hölderlin, Lukács, and other dialectical thinkers, the later form is structurally required for the conception of the earlier form. There is no naive without the sentimental; no undifferentiated, primal being (*Sein*) without discriminating, posterior judgment (*Urteil*); and no epic theory without the novel.[31] Aristotle, however, is no German dialectician. In the *Poetics*, epic is defined the same as tragedy—just less so. As far as Aristotle is concerned, the differences between them are accidents of genre, not constitutive features of both forms. Nevertheless, the contingent discrepancies between epic and tragedy in the *Poetics* are illuminating. In fact, two structural paradoxes of recognition can be deduced from the specific divergences Aristotle enumerates. It turns out that a necessary dialectical opposition can be drawn between the types of recognition demanded by the material constraints of their respective forms.

The paradox of tragic recognition was diagnosed in the introduction to this book. As observed there with *Oedipus*, recognition is always a discursive process but must be conceived of as a single moment in order to have the effect that tragedy demands. For Aristotle, the power of tragedy comes from its concentration: from its shaping of life's myriad happenings into a unified action that can be taken in at a glance. Although careful attention to the imitation of recognition in *Oedipus* reveals otherwise, tragic recognition—in order to be tragic—must be thought of as instantaneous and nonrepeatable. The before and after of tragic recognition must seem to be clear, decisive, and world-changing because the spectator's experience of the imitation of tragic action takes place within the couple hours traffic on stage.

The experience of epic, in contrast, is very different. Whether reading or listening, no one expects to take in the entire work within a single sitting. Rhapsodes performed over many nights, and the story they told had to be diffuse and episodic. Recognitions could take their time and involve many feints, diversions, and reversals. In short, the discursive, repetitive features of recognition are emphasized by the mediality of the epic form.

Both of these incompatible truths of recognition require each other: to be meaningful, recognition has to be perceived as singular, life-changing, irrevocable; to be lived in human experience, it must be a discursive process that is repeated in endless variation. In order to come to terms with the drama of interpersonal relations, humans must stress both the seriality and the momentousness of recognition. They must hold tragic as well as epic views of coming to know other people.

A second Aristotelian distinction that resonates with the logic of afterness is his classification of all stories as either simple or complex. On Lukács's model of novel versus epic or Schiller's of sentimental versus naive, the earlier, more "natural" form requires the emergence of the successor before the prior form can be conceived. Simple versus complex is a similar binary in which the first term only becomes thinkable with the emergence of the second. No one can classify a story as simple without first decreeing what makes a complex plot. For Aristotle, all stories, simple and complex, represent action and change. A story becomes complex when the action it represents sports a reversal or recognition (*P*, 10, 1452a, 12–19). This distinction suggests several interesting consequences. For one thing, the simple can only be posited in contrast to the complex. In fact, the simple is defined solely by the lack of the defining features of the complex. Simplicity, then, is not a positive feature of any action but rather a quality recognized only in comparison to complexity.

According to the *Poetics*, the *Iliad* is a simple story of suffering, while the *Odyssey* is complex because it is "recognition through and through" (*P*, 24, 1459b, 15). Aristotle's word for complex, *peplegmenos*, literally twisted or folded, is an apt description not only of the actions described in the *Odyssey* but also of its sophisticated narrative form. The *Iliad* proceeds in strict chronological order from the quarrel between Achilles and Agamemnon to the reconciliation between Achilles and Priam. The *Odyssey*, however, begins by narrating Telemachus's travels before returning to recount Odysseus's journey from Calypso to Phaeacia. Only there, in books 8–12, does Odysseus himself pick up the earlier thread of his adventures after leaving Troy by telling the stories of his wanderings prior to reaching Calypso's island. The second half of the book then returns to a chronological narration of Odysseus's homecoming on Ithaca. The narrative structure itself is twined in layers. Recognition is not only internal to the action of the poem but also necessarily external in the audience's relation to it. Only as both internal and external events does recognition bring about the division between simple and complex. *Re*cognition must be *re*duplicated, must be folded twice,[32] in order to create not only the complex plot of the *Odyssey* but also the simple plot of the *Iliad*. In this basic distinction too, the prior form only comes into being with its sequel. The complex recognitions of the *Odyssey* allow the simple form of the *Iliad* to come into view. The two most defining epic poems of Western literature are inseparable and utterly codependent through the *re*cognitive structure of afterness.

This point is further corroborated by the words for simple and complex, *haplos* and *peplegmenos*, which, like the Latin roots of our English terms, evoke folds in fabric. Though simplicity would seem to be logically and temporally prior to complexity, the folding of cloth simultaneously creates both the complex and the simple with one fell swoop. In terms of logic, first of all, this structure of retrogressive priority in simple and complex narratives maps onto the relation of Same and Other. The Same, implicit in the etymology of simple,[33] only becomes thinkable with the advent of the Other. The Other is cut from the same cloth as the Same. A pleat will match up identically with its bottom layer, but unless woven together and ceasing to be a fold at all, it will always remain different. The action of *re*cognition is evident here. Recognition emerges as a desire to duplicate the Same but can only function through the mediation of the Other. Division is implicated in every act of repetition. The Same is already folded into Otherness as soon as it is identified as such. There is no iron that can press out the original division that makes the desire of recognition impossible: the matching of two Sames can only function as an operation between Others.[34]

This problematic idea is central to both ancient and Idealist philosophy, as evidenced in Plato's late dialogue *The Sophist* and Friedrich Hölderlin's seminal fragment, *Urteil/Sein* (*Judgement/Being*). The former is framed as a drama of anagnorisis that never finds resolution. The principal speaker of the dialogue is introduced as a stranger (*xenos*), just as Odysseus appears in his own household on Ithaca. Socrates greets him by quoting the *Odyssey* and joking that "by Homer's account," he must be a god in disguise (216A).[35] The stranger's name and identity remain tantalizingly undisclosed throughout the conversation. The line of questioning, meanwhile, revolves around an attempt to recognize the sophist as opposed to the philosopher. This hunt for the sophist leads to an investigation into Being and Nonbeing that culminates with an analysis of Same (*tauton*) and Other (*thateron*). It turns out that Nonbeing—that Parmenidean chimeric bugbear—is entangled with Otherness, which is the principle that makes possible both separation and relation between things and people: "To show that the same thing is somehow other and the other the same . . . is the manifest late-born brainchild of somebody who's just gotten in touch with the things that *are*" (259D).[36] There is no Same without Other; no Being without Nonbeing. This paradox is a founding realization of Idealist thinking, as Hölderlin hammers home in his famous fragment.[37] Undifferentiated Being only becomes thinkable through the separation of judgment. Poetry and philosophy long for the original unity of Parmenidean oneness, the recognition of which is grounded in division and separation. Novalis encapsulates this insatiable nostalgia of recognition by diagnosing all philosophy as homesickness.[38]

In terms of temporality, finally, the priority of the Same before the Other, the simple before the complex, is equally unfeasible. Recognition is powered by a longing to recreate the past but is made possible by the unbridgeable difference between past and future. The desire to match the past, to bend the fabric of time back, is met at the ragged seam of the real. Fabric, in fact, is a faulty metaphor for the phenomenology of time. Time cannot be folded; it is unidirectional. Time must remain simple—and yet unrecognizable as such, since technically there can be no complex time.[39] Any conscious measure of time must be an utterly simple—and hence unrelatable—phenomenon.[40] In order to share tales and memories, one must construct a fictionalized time. Only fictions of time can be folded into complex relations of Otherness that allow the simplicity of temporality to become recognizable. Yet it seems impossible to disrobe human thinking about time from these draping metaphors. Every remembrance tries to stitch in a loop; every story is a ventured tesseract. Memories and narrations are always attempts to make wrinkles in time. The many dramatic recognitions of the *Odyssey* comprise a tangled tapestry of time-traveling twists and turns.

SELF-SIGNIFICATION AND THE NOSTALGIA OF SEMIOTICS

Memories herald a folding of time at several critical junctures of recognition during the *Odyssey*. Both Telemachus in Sparta and Odysseus in Phaeacia are recognized because of their tears in response to stirring tales of the past. Reactions to shared memories accompany every step during the long, drawn-out dance of recognition between Penelope and Odysseus. In the *Poetics*, Aristotle devotes an entire chapter to enumerating various types of recognition, and Odysseus's weeping in Alcinous court is his primary example for anagnorisis by memory. Although anagnorisis by sign is a different class of recognition for Aristotle, it is clear that Odysseus's tears signify something to Alcinous. I undertake a more thorough critique of Aristotle's taxonomy of recognition (book 16) in terms of semiotics and reading in chapter 3, but suffice it to say here that *all* the means of recognition listed in the *Poetics* prove to be kinds of signs. Tears function as a sign of memories; the evidence of memory works as a sign of identity.

The status of the sign is troubled—and not just because so much signifying force is expressed in serial bouts of weeping in the *Odyssey*. The relation of the sign and signified is implicated in the same problematic pattern that has emerged with the other binary pairs involved in the operations of recognition. For starters, signs are the means of recognition between persons: they are the medium through which people come to know one another. Alcinous recognizes the hero of Troy by the sign of his stifled sobs; Helen and Menelaus discern the signs of Odysseus's progeny in the looks and behavior of Telemachus; Odysseus corroborates the linguistic signs of his self-announcement to Eumaios with the signifying gesture of revealing his unique scar. Yet another act of recognition, however, is necessary to identify the signs *as such* in the first place. We never directly recognize a *person*; every felicitous intersubjective engagement is mediated by the recognitions of *signs*. Alcinous must first interpret Odysseus's genteel weeping as a mark of good breeding and then draw the connection to its occasion (Demodokos's tale of Troy) as an indication of what "hits home" for the stranger. The king's judgment becomes manifest only when he acts (in this case to call a halt to the rhapsode's narration), which in turn invites a responding gesture from Odysseus (to tell his own tale). Recognition never happens simply *within* one person *of* another; it takes place through actions in the world *between* people.

On the surface, this unavoidable mediality of recognition through signs does not seem to bother characters in the Homeric epics, though it will be a major stumbling block in more modern texts. The plot of the *Odyssey* is largely determined by how deftly or poorly the characters navigate the consequences of a world mediated by signs. This skill, in fact, is the enduring virtue that marks out Odysseus and Penelope as the heroes of the poem. Yet the narrator of the *Odyssey* nevertheless seems obsessed with paronomasia and the intimate connection of names to their bearers.[41] The etymology of Odysseus's own name, for instance, is recounted in an attention-grabbing digression at the climax of the recognition scene in book 19. The poem's recurrent return to the significance of names speaks to the structural desire of recognition—for signs to connect directly to the things and people they signify.

This brings us back to the opening clause of Aristotle's definition of anagnorisis: "just as the name itself signifies." This brief preamble attests to a nostalgic yearning for unencumbered access to others that exists at the heart of recognition. If signs are our only means of approaching one another, then the best signs will be those that partake in the essence of the persons they signify. Accordingly, sounds should have a natural link to the concepts, people, or things they represent. If Aristotle's aside here can be taken seriously, then anagnorisis should properly be understood as a natural rather than conventional signifier. With four words (*hōsper kai tounoma sēmainei*: just as the name itself signifies), Aristotle's formulation embroils the dramatic term in age-old debates about the nature of language.[42] Plato dealt with this dispute in the *Cratylus*, where Socrates referees an argument about whether names are determined by nature or convention. The issue has become pervasive in semiotic discourse since the eighteenth century, from Locke to Saussure and beyond, with the distinction between natural and arbitrary signs. As I will show, both Aristotle and Homer weigh in on this question with surprising results.

The structure of recognition seems to draw binary pairs into its conceptual orbit. As seen above, the oppositional and troubling logic of dyads—such as the novel versus the epic, sentimental versus naive, judgment versus being, complex versus simple, and the Other versus the Same—has been revealing of the paradoxes inherent in recognition. Finally, and most intimately, the semiotic distinction between conventional and natural names comes into focus. It turns out that the relation of nature to convention in signs shares the same perplexing coemergence as the other binaries. In all cases, a desired primacy of the Same is inextricable from that of the Other. Whereas the drive to make the Other into the Same in homecoming attempts to recreate an irrevocable past, the desire of recognition in communication is for the sign to match the signified without loss, remainder, or possibility of confusion. Names should be identical with meaning. Signs should be the same as the signified. Of course, if this were the case, they would cease to be signs at all, for signification only exists through difference.[43] If this longing were ever satisfied, then the need for communication and recognition in the first place would disappear. The preference for natural signs is only perceived from within the linguistic vantage point of arbitrary convention.

The logic of recognition then might seem to lead down a deconstructive rabbit hole of *différance* and endless deferral. The *Poetics* and the *Odyssey*, however, shed unexpected light into the burrow that manages to illuminate the problem without oversimplifying the contours of its labyrinthine warren. Rather than insisting on either a strict conventionalist or essentialist position, the texts invite interpretations that map out a briar patch of uncanny hominess.

Plato's stance on natural and conventional names is ambiguous; there is much debate about the extent to which Socrates's fanciful etymologies in the *Cratylus* should be read ironically, and in any case, Socrates steers a complex course between the two extremes. Aristotle, on the other hand, is quite clearly in the conventionalist camp. *De Interpretatione* opens with an assertion of the universality of ideas (*pathēmata tēs psukhēs*) and the arbitrariness of the names that signify them. As if to avoid any chance of confusion on this score, the definition of noun (*onoma*) includes an explicit stipulation that it is significant "by convention" (*kata sunthēkēn*). Aristotle glosses this clause a few lines later: "The limitation 'by convention' was introduced because nothing is by nature (*phusei*) a noun or a name" (2, 16a, 28).[44]

The treatment of language in the *Poetics* does not seem to offer any reason to cast doubt on this thoroughgoing linguistic conventionalism. There too, the sounds that make up words of all types are repeatedly denied any essential meaning. Over and over again in the definitions of the eight categories of wording (e.g., *lexis*, itself one of the six parts of any tragedy), the word *nonsignificant* (*asēmos*: without mark or sign) appears. Aristotle takes great care to withhold significance from the building blocks of language. Significantly, even the elements that make up the word *anagnōrisis* must lack meaning. It is no surprise that the individual syllables are nonsignifying, but so are the prefix *ana* and the preposition from which it comes. All conjunctions or joint words, which include prepositions, are "non-semantic sounds." Only with nouns, which are "semantic sounds," does meaning arise.[45] That significance, clearly, is not inherent in the sounds or elements of the words but is arbitrarily assigned by convention.

Hence a name (such as *gnōrisis*) comes to be a sign for an idea (such as "knowledge" or "acquaintance") through the ineluctable custom of one's language community. This kind of name is simple (*haploun*—the same adjective used to describe simple stories above), whereas names that include more than one kind of word are compound or double (*diploun*—*not* the same adjective used for complex stories, *peplegmenos*). *Anagnorisis* is hence a compound word comprising signifying elements (*gnōrisis*) and nonsignifying elements (*ana*). Taken together, by the logic of Aristotle's analysis, the double word still has to be a name that receives its meaning from social convention, not from any natural, intrinsic source. Yet the prefatory clause to Aristotle's definition of anagnorisis, "just as the name itself signifies," flies in the face of this necessary conclusion. If recognition is a noun like other nouns, then its name *cannot* signify on its own, but only as an arbitrary sign applied externally. For the clause to make sense, it has to contradict Aristotle's claims about the nature of human language.

I am certainly not trying to peg Aristotle as a secret linguistic naturalist on the grounds of this one wayward phrase, but it is worth the effort to think through the seeming contradiction in terms of his other claims about language. Two ways beyond this aporetic impasse present themselves with interesting consequences for understanding the semiotics of recognition. The first has to do with the taxonomy of propositions and the second with the workings of metaphor.

The last part of language Aristotle considers is the proposition or phrase—in effect, speech broadly conceived (*logos*).[46] He defines it as a composite of different words and then allows for two ways that this "many" can be considered as "one" (*heis*): a phrase of multiple words is a single unit either by referring to one thing or by connecting many things. For the former, Aristotle gives the example of the definition of a human being, and for the latter, he adduces the *Iliad*. These two examples are telling. Speech can be unitary as either a definition or a story. Definitions are statements of what it is to *be* something. They perforce deal with universals and, like the concepts they explain, are supposedly timeless. Stories, on the other hand, as imitations of *actions*, always involve time. This distinction among types of speech is therefore analogous to that between the only two types of words that Aristotle allows to have significance: nouns and verbs are differentiated by time. Nouns, remember, are nontemporal compound semantic sounds, while verbs are compound semantic sounds with a temporal sense.

Anagnorisis straddles these divisions with unsettling aplomb. The effect of the prefix *ana* (re) is to introduce an element of temporality into a timeless noun. The definition of the word, which by rights should be a concept unaffected by its arbitrary sounds, is therefore tainted with self-reference to its status as a sign. The concept of recognition requires the connective tissue of stories to be fleshed out. The definition of recognition is a unit both because it explains one thing and because it connects multiple elements. A unit doubly grounded from different perspectives is necessarily not one but two. Recognition is a timeless universal infected by the time of recurrence. Its definition elides into story. It is not the case that simply naming actions—making nouns out of verbs—is problematic; running, thinking, and eating are all concepts that do not invite paradoxical reflection. The action of recognition, however, itself ties temporality in the figure of recurrence to knowing. By definition, it converts what is ideally a holding fast to permanent truth (Aristotelian and Platonic knowledge) into a *change* (*metabolē*). As I will show in the next chapter, this destabilizing function of recognition as a specific type of change is constitutive to understanding it as intersubjective performance. "Just as the name itself signifies"—whether between natural and conventional signs, between noun and verb, between word and discourse, or between definition and story—recognition is always transgressing.

Transgression is a key function of a second observation regarding recognition afforded by Aristotle's analysis of language: "Metaphor is a carrying over [a transference] of names from one thing to another" (*P*, 21, 1457b, 7). It is clear that recognition is involved in both the creation and appreciation of metaphors. Aristotle's high valuation of the art of metaphor comes at the end of book 22 as one of the final observations he makes in the analysis of tragedy. He calls it "the most important thing. For this alone cannot be received from others and is a sign [*sēmeion*] of natural abilities, because to use metaphors well is to have insight into what is similar [*to to homoion theōrein*]" (*P*, 22, 1459a, 9). The skill in discerning likenesses—in seeing the Same in the Other—is another way of describing the art of recognition. A prowess in making metaphor, therefore, is tantamount to expertise in coming to know others. Certainly the deftest wielders of extended metaphors (aside from the narrator) in the *Odyssey* are the two greatest knowers of people, Penelope and Odysseus.

But the kinship between metaphor and anagnorisis extends even further. A conventionalist like Aristotle has to renounce the temptation to discern natural meanings inherent in the sounds of a word. Once he presumes the ineluctable arbitrariness of linguistic markers, he has to give up on the imaginative illuminations that etymology might afford.[47] Yet he does not forgo playing with words and their meanings. Instead of discovering the unifying source of meaning in a concept's sign, this is a game of discerning similarities in differences. Whereas linguistic naturalism aims to collapse signs into a singular, original Same, metaphor pays court to the Other. Usually, of course, metaphors link together palpably different objects and concepts: "old age," as Aristotle quotes Empedocles in his example, "is the sunset of life" (*P*, 21, 1457b, 23). In the case of recognition, however, the name itself can be seen as a metaphor for the concept it represents. Precisely because the word transgresses by signifying itself, by making itself doubly Other, the sign becomes a metaphor. The very act of metaphorization, in turn, makes the word *anagnorisis* bear its own significance at many levels, some of which have become discernable in the course of this chapter. Aristotle defines a riddle as "all made of metaphors." A riddle, moreover, "speaks of its subjects in words a hearer is incapable of connecting with them" (*P*, 22, 1458a, 26).[48] Recognition is involved not only in the actions of connection-forging riddle solvers but also in the very construction of its own riddling definition, which precisely names the procedure of anagnorisis as an impossibly self-signifying conundrum: a noun that is a verb, a word that is a phrase, a definition that tells a story, a natural and artificial sign, "just as the name itself implies."[49]

Just as Aristotle's nod to the significance of the word *anagnorisis* complicates his avowed conventionalism, the *Odyssey*'s play with paronomasia belies the thorough comfort with exteriority and mediality that scholars have claimed for Homer.[50] If names reveal the self, then not only is there an interior self to reveal, but certain outward signs have a natural affinity to what is within. Some names, at least, would not be arbitrary matters of convention. In a telling though likely unwitting allusion to Aristotle's aside on recognition, W. B. Stanford's technical term for the many instances of paronomasia in the *Odyssey* is "Significant Names."[51] The poem seems to be full of names that signify their bearers to the discerning observer. Many of them in fact play on the root *noos*: for example, Alcinous, Antinous, Noemon, Autonoe, Pontonous. Odysseus comes to know not only the *nous* of many people but many people whose names echo *nous*, the very organ at which he excels.

Odysseus invents Significant Names for himself as well at important junctures during the poem. Most famously, he introduces himself as *Outis* (no one, nothing) to the cyclops Polyphemus (whose own Significant Name, meaning "abundant speech," is already a wisecrack about this dimwitted brute). This sets up an elaborate pun that allows Odysseus and his men to escape the island after blinding Polyphemus without being chased down by the other cyclopes. When Polyphemus calls out in pain to his fellows, they ask who hurt him. He replies that Nobody (*Outis*) hurt him, and so they shake their heads and advise him to pray. The language of their reply is a further pun, since they use the negative pronoun reserved for conditionals and imperatives, *mē tis*, which is homophonic with *mētis*, the precise brand of cunning always associated with Odysseus: "If no one (*mē tis*) did this to you, then . . ." (*Od*, 9.409). The narrating Odysseus himself makes the wordplay impossible to miss by echoing it four lines later: "My dear heart laughed over how my name and my blameless design (*mētis*) had deceived him" (*Od*, 9.413–414). Norman Austin shows how this inadvertent joke is name magic at its most potent: "Odysseus *polymetis*, when he is exercising his *Metis*, then is he invariably *Outis*. His mask is Metis; the face it displays to the world is Outis. Odysseus negates himself *qua* Odysseus, either by remaining anonymous, or by adopting, together with a pseudonym, a fictitious unreal persona."[52] I would go even further: *outis* has the same relation to *mētis* as the series of opposing pairs taken up in this chapter prior to this section. The two negative pronouns are related to Odysseus's given name as natural signs to conventional signs. This trio of names suggestively ties together the semiology of recognition.

The lack of differentiation and distancing judgment that characterizes Schiller's naive poet, Hölderlin's *Sein*, or Lukács's epic is necessarily *outis*—no one, nothing—until it is discerned and brought into being by *mētis*—craft, design, wisdom. *Outis* is simple, but *mētis* folds it into complexity. *Mētis* is the Other that allows the unknowable Same to be conceived; without *mētis*, there is no *outis*. The Stranger in Plato's *Sophist* follows this line of reasoning to tie Not-Being inextricably to the recognition of Being: the Other is a necessary component of knowing the Same. In each case, *outis* is associated with the object of nostalgic desire and *mētis* with the alienating ground of yearning. This pattern would lead one to expect *mētis* to be related to the radical division between sign and signified and *outis* to align with the longing for natural names. Where nothing interrupts the union of sign with signified, signs become illegible; by collapsing into one thing, they become no thing. Not only can nothing be recognized without division, *nothing* itself can only be recognized with division. *Outis* presumes *mētis*, and *mētis* operates by means of *outis*.[53]

But Odysseus himself twists a further braid into this line of reasoning. *Outis* and, by extension, *mētis* are names he chooses and that clearly indicate his character in a much more distinct way than his given name. Hence they are *natural* signs—if not in a manner Cratylus would recognize, then at least in the Aristotelian sense of providing insight into Odysseus's nature. Yet Odysseus is not content to leave Polyphemus under the impression that he has been tricked by Nobody, no matter how clever a device that might be for his signature *mētis*. Even before he is safe from the stones hurled by Polyphemus, and against the urging of his companions, he yells, identifying himself as "Odysseus, sacker of cities, son of Laertes, whose home is in Ithaca" (*Od*, 9.504–505). Ironically, it is by revealing his given name, the conventional sign Odysseus, that he brings down on himself the wrath of Poseidon, Polyphemus's father, and sets in motion the long series of suffering that delays his return home. The hatred of Poseidon has long been considered to be the fulfilment of the prophecy implied in one reading of Odysseus's name, which the *Odyssey* itself explicitly links to the verb *odusasthai* (to hate). In other words, by insisting on his birth name, Odysseus ensures that it will become a Significant Name. He artificially makes a conventional sign natural.

Homer's poem itself alludes to the origin of the name Odysseus several times and then makes its etymology an explicit part of its construction by highlighting it at one of the most tension-laden passages of the entire poem. In the midst of book 19, just as Eurycleia recognizes the stranger and the nerve-tingling tightrope walk of recognition between Penelope and Odysseus seems to be ready to topple, the narrator veers back to recount tales from Odysseus's birth and youth. At the outset of this famous digression, Odysseus's grandfather, Autolykos (the wolf itself—a self-signifying name as self-devouring as the universal wolf that Ulysses diagnoses in Shakespeare's *Troilus and Cressida*), is called on to name his daughter's newborn son. Autolykos, "who surpassed all men in thievery and the art of the oath" (*Od*, 19.396), declares the following:

> My son-in-law and daughter, give him the name I tell you;
> since I have come to this place distasteful (ὀδυσσάμενος) to many, women
> and men alike on the prospering earth, so let him be given
> the name Odysseus, that is distasteful. Then when he grows up,
> and comes to the great house of his mother's line, and Parnassos,
> where there are possessions that are called mine, I will give him
> freely of these to make him happy, and send him back to you. (*Od*, 19.406–412)

This Homeric etymology of the title character's name has attracted a great deal of academic attention and speculation since antiquity. Some maintain that the verb should be understood in the passive sense, while others place it in the active. Scholars want to peg Odysseus as either the hater or the hated. W. B. Stanford begins his own essay on the question with the following lament: "It is unfortunate that Homer's only explicit reference to the etymology of the name Odysseus is ambiguous."[54] I would suggest that if Odysseus's name signifies anything, it is a celebration of this very ambiguity. As fitting for any moniker bestowed by a consummate thief, the Wolf Itself, it is open to both inspire and confer hatred. This art of hostility is central to Odysseus's conception of friendship and practice of recognition, as will be shown below (chapter 4). The playful uncertainty of name signification in the *Odyssey* is also emblematic of the hermeneutic kind of knowledge involved in Odyssean and Penelopean recognition (chapter 3). All these necessary indeterminacies hinge on the basic understanding of recognition as a kind of change, which I turn to next in chapter 2.

What the name of *recognition* signifies is fraught, but the construction of its linguistic designation—*recognition* no less than *anagnorisis*—signifies this vexation artfully. The nostalgia of epic is reprised in the very formulation with which Aristotle hopefully introduces his definition of recognition: "just as the word itself signifies" is an impossible claim that nonetheless signifies the unattainable yearning of recognition for secure knowledge of other people again, and again, and now yet again.

CHAPTER TWO

"Recognition Is a Change"

Performance in Motion

ARISTOTLE DEFINES *RECOGNITION* with one word: change (*metabolē*). The remaining clauses all serve to modify that term and specify what kind of change recognition is. Each consists of an explicit dichotomy: ignorance and knowledge, friendship or enmity, and good or bad fortune. The previous chapter showed how the preceding nod to recognition's self-signification also led to the reappraisal of a long series of dualities. The word *change*, however, seems to buck this reliance on binaries. It is the single fulcrum connecting the multiple pairs on either side of the equation. But like *anagnōrisis*, *metabolē* is a double word inviting the complicity of opposing ideas. *Bolē* comes from the verb *ballein* (to throw); *meta* is a preposition that can mean "among," "into the midst of," "after," or "next to." The ambiguity of this prefix is telling: change has to be a toss, but its direction, destination, and timing are a toss-up. The English word *change* hides its compound nature, but its logic requires a before and after, a here and there, that are necessarily different. At the same time, change cannot consist in either the before or the after but must be at work somewhere in between.

The present chapter will connect the betweenness of change to my claim that recognition consists in the intersubjective performances in which people participate. Oedipus only sees his incestuous identity through the act of presenting his own blindness to his uncle/brother and daughter/sister (see the introduction); Menelaus and Helen enact their tense remarriage through the agonistic rehearsal of memories dulled by drug-induced forgetfulness (see chapter 1). Relational knowledge only manifests in performance between people.

But wait!—before one can reply to the question "What is the action of recognition?" with the answer "Why, it is performance!" one must also be able to say what performance is. Reading many of the books and articles that purport to be part of the amorphous field of "performance studies" may well lead to despair of ever finding a de*fin*ition that has any *finis*, any limits, at all—*everything* becomes susceptible of being seen as performance.[1] If recognition is performance, and performance involves recognition, then what is recognition *not*?

The *Odyssey* is a perfect case in point: no one could deny that Odysseus is the consummate actor. Everything he does and says has an audience in mind, whether he is taking the place of the singer in Alcinous's court in order to perform the ultimate song of himself or playing the various roles he assumes once he arrives on Ithaca. Arguably, Odysseus is never without an audience for whom to perform in the *Odyssey*. The parts of his adventures in which he is alone are narrated by Odysseus himself *for the spectators* in Phaeacia. Even the tale of his lonely sea journey from Calypso's island is framed from the beginning with the Olympian gods as onlookers to his expressive sufferings. Not to mention, of course, that the poem itself only existed as oral performances for many generations before it congealed into a transmittable text. If the entire *Odyssey* is performance, and if it is "recognition through and through" (*P*, 24, 1459b, 15), then both terms seem so broadly pervasive as to become insignificant. Equating the two would be no more helpful than defining *poetry* as "words."

In four steps, this chapter endeavors to give more substance to the definition of performance and ultimately of recognition. The first section takes up accounts by contemporary scholars of the origins of Homeric poetry. Gregory Nagy's description of rhapsodic practice reveals how potential identities are enacted in mimetic actuality. This language, in the second section, invites a comparison with the keystone of Aristotelian physics, his understanding of change. The definition of motion in Aristotle's *Physics* can provide a template for thinking through the kind of change in which recognition consists: in short, recognition of others is the actualization of potential relations *as* potentiality. This formula might seem opaque at first, but it will prove a cogent and powerful account of interpersonal recognition. It furthermore lays bare a necessary contradiction in Aristotle's concept of anagnorisis: it must be—yet cannot be—an action. Third, the recognition of Odysseus through his performative crying in the *Odyssey* shows how the paradox underlying Aristotle's theory of anagnorisis unfolds in practice. Finally, the work of modern performance theorists and moral philosophers helps illuminate the stakes for recognition as outlined here. Aristotelian change has important implications for understanding the temporality (Richard Schechner, Rebecca Schneider) and ethics (J. David Velleman, Hilde Lindemann) of performance.

RHAPSODIC MIMESIS AND NARRATION

Narrativity is inextricable from performance in the *Odyssey*. Not only is narration the content of the poem's performance—for the external listeners of the rhapsode and for the internal listeners to characters—but performance is the medium of the poem's narration. Even the most hard-core narratological categories, such as focalization and metaphor—which would seem safe from the showiness of spectacle—function in the *Odyssey* through a consciousness of performavity. Narrative is necessarily representational, as it reports and describes what is absent, while performance, in contrast, aspires to presence. Yet these two aspects of the poem—narration and mimesis—are imbricated with one another, and it is precisely in the space of their codetermination that anagnorisis unfolds. The third section below will expose the performative structure of Homeric metaphor in recognition scenes. The present section shows how the performance of the *Odyssey* co-opts narrative focalization to enact recognition.

Thanks to the pioneering ethnographic work of Albert Lord and Milman Parry in Yugoslavia during the first part of the twentieth century, we have a better understanding of how long narrative poetry is produced by oral performers. They make a convincing case that the Homeric poems came into being in a similar fashion.[2] Rhapsodes took advantage of a toolkit of handy formulae and clear but flexible meter in order to improvise with great artistic sophistication the occasion's (or series of occasions') song. More recently, Nagy has followed the oral-formulaic hypothesis of the poems' genesis to trace further how they were disseminated and eventually crystalized into the texts we cherish today. He deduces the modes in which the Homeric poems must have been performed and perceived in the centuries leading up to their gradual solidification into textual forms. The ability to "maintain continuity through variety" is the phrase with which he characterizes the activity of Homeric rhapsodes. They have this virtue of continuity in common with the singing nightingale to which Penelope compares herself in her interview with the disguised Odysseus (*Od*, 19.518–523).[3] It is no accident that the metaphor Nagy lights on as an exemplum of rhapsodic performance comes from the most intricate dance of recognition in the *Odyssey.* This mode of creative rehearsal in the performance *of* the poem is a pattern for what I claim recognition is between people *in* the poem. Like the nightingale, both Penelope and the rhapsode choose from a limited set of ready-to-hand formulae and string them together into a performance that is simultaneously a reenactment of an identifiable role *and* a new creation.

Nagy takes advantage of Aristotle's notion of mimesis in order to explain how this is possible. Cutting through centuries of contentious debate about the precise meaning of mimesis, Nagy argues that it should not be understood as "imitation" in modern usage so much as "'re-enactment, impersonation' *in a dramatic sense.*"[4] He turns to Stephen Halliwell's incisive assessment of mimesis in the *Poetics* for support: "Aristotle's guiding notion of mimesis is implicitly that of enactment: poetry proper (which may include some works in prose) does not describe, narrate, or offer argument, but dramatizes and embodies human speech and action."[5] With this authority, Nagy continues by connecting this definition of mimesis as "re-enactment, impersonation" with the "mental process" expressed by Aristotle's "equation *houtos ekeinos*: 'so this is that!' (*P*, 1448b, 17)."[6]

Here it begins to become clear why I claim that an enactive concept of mimesis is important in an account of recognition. This *houtos eikeinos* formula, from book 4 of the *Poetics* about how deeply mimesis is part of human nature, is an example of recognition.[7] Aristotle admits as much in the explanation following his definition in chapter 11, when he says that anagnorisis can also be of things and actions. But the drama of recognition *between people* can never simply be a matter of a "mental process" in which one matches a this with a that. Aristotle insists that poetic recognitions and reversals are parts of the plot or story (*muthos*), which is the imitation of an action (*praxis*). This is why, although "a change from ignorance to knowledge" can take place "in relation to inanimate or chance objects," the ones "involving people" are "most suited to *muthos* and *praxis*" (*P*, 11, 1452a, 36–1452b, 5).

This goes a long way to explain why an understanding of mimesis as a copy or image of something, on the model of painting, is inadequate to account for Aristotle's use of the term. Halliwell convincingly argues that Aristotle favors an enactive mode of imitation that involves the direct reproduction of people's speeches and actions. Instead of slavishly attempting to reproduce a realistic likeness, as Socrates's attacks on mimetic arts in the *Republic* imply, mimesis for Aristotle is about rehearsing human actions. If the realization "this is that" (*houtos ekeinos*) is a passive cognition, then it is only so for spectators who discern what is being represented in the drama.[8] Within the drama or epic, recognition is a two-way street that requires active participation, input, and interpretation. In Sophocles's *Oedipus the King*, for instance, long before the ultimate recognition plays out in tragic reversal, Oedipus and Creon endeavor to rehearse roles of responsible king and loyal minister, respectively. Oedipus constantly reassesses the speeches and actions of Creon to determine if he is a friend or enemy, and Creon must react in kind. The very speeches by which Oedipus enacts his suspicions toward Creon are themselves formulae that indicate changing knowledge, uncertain friendship, and precarious fortune. This back-and-forth rehearsal of familial, political, and personal roles is, I contend, the kind of reenactment in which the performative action of recognition consists.

Nagy goes even further in his account of rhapsodic performance by likening the complementarity of his distinctive pair, performance and composition, to Ferdinand Saussure's *parole* and *langue*.[9] Just as the underlying laws and potentials of language only ever come into being in the form of actual speech, the formulaic creativity inherent in the composition of Homeric poetry is only actualized in its delivery by a particular rhapsode to a particular audience. We can have no experiential access to the system of rules that make up *langue*—only to particular instances of speech. The same relationship holds true for recognition, I argue: an individual's knowledge (or opinion)[10] of other people only becomes visible through reenactment in performance.

In the activity of this performance, Nagy argues, the singer *becomes* Homer. He maintains that the narrating "I" of the singer "is not a *representation* of Homer: it *is* Homer. . . . The rhapsode is re-enacting Homer by performing Homer . . . he *is* Homer so long as the mimesis stays in effect, so long as the performance lasts."[11] Similarly, the performance of knowledge in recognition is not the representation of knowledge (any more than speech is a representation of language) but rather its only avenue to actualization in the world.

The self-referential episodes in Alcinous's court in which a rhapsode tells stories (*Od*, bk. 8) are a natural place to look for clues about the oral presentation of Homeric poetry, and Nagy carefully combs through the entire book to elucidate his historical account of rhapsodic performance. Though Nagy has much to say about the rhapsode Demodokos in other respects, he does not take up a narratological analysis of the bard's stories.[12]

This is surprising because it is precisely through narration that rhapsodes "become Homer." In fact, the narrative technique of focalization allows Homer to become Demodokos, an ideal example of the process Nagy aims to elucidate. The narratologist Gérard Genette coined the term *focalization* to describe the mechanics of how perspective is conveyed through narration: even in the third person, a narrator often focalizes the storytelling through the limited point of view of a particular character.[13] Genette's terminology can help articulate how the perspective from which the story is being told subtly shifts at the outset of Demodokos's second tale about the erotic hijinks between Aphrodite and Ares. The narrator of the poem begins his account of this story in the third person:

> And he [Demodokos], playing the lyre, began (ἀνεβάλλετο) to sing beautifully
> about (ἀμφ') the love of Ares and sweet-garlanded Aphrodite,
> how (ὡς) [they] first lay together (μίγησαν) in the house of Hephaistos
> secretly; [he] gave (ἔδωκε) [her] much and fouled (ᾔσχυνε) the marriage
> and bed of the lord Hephaistos; to him there came (ἦλθεν) as messenger
> Helios, the sun, who had seen (ἐνόησε) them lying in love together. (*Od*, 8.266–271)[14]

In this passage, the narrator reports that Demodokos began singing, shares the song's theme ("about" the love of Ares and Aphrodite), and then relates a brief synopsis of the plot ("how" they did things). But the subjects of the verbs governed by *hōs* (translated as the relative adverb *how* or the conjunction *that* to introduce indirect discourse) are rather confusing. The first ("lay together") is plural, and must refer back to the philandering siblings. But the next verb ("gave") is singular and has no explicit subject or indirect object. Grammatically, there is no reason to assume that Ares is the intended subject of this and the following verb ("dishonored"). It could just as easily be Aphrodite who was generous and insulting, though cultural habits (ours no less than the Greeks') may account for the fact that all translations I have consulted make Ares the subject. Helios, meanwhile, has to be the subject of the next two verbs ("came" and "saw"). This ambiguity in syntax accompanies the gradual unmooring of narrative focalization here.

Narratively, this confusion is compounded by the question of whether these lines should all still be heard as a report of Demodokos's story in indirect discourse. In English, this would be clarified either by the repetition of the adverb (e.g., "He sang how they did this, how someone did that, and how someone else did something else") or by staggering the tenses (e.g., "He sang how they did this. Someone had done that, and someone else had done something else"). Lattimore availed himself of the latter option above by translating ἐνόησε with the past perfect (had seen), even though the verb form—like all others following "how"—is aorist. But in the Greek, one is left wondering whether the continued story is still governed by the "how" at all. Is the narrator still reporting about the story Demodokos told, or is the narrator now telling the story? There is no clear demarcation between the narration of the poem and the narration of the character. The focalization gets out of focus here and remains blurry until the next articulation point in the song after Ares speaks three lines to Aphrodite[15]:

> So he spoke (ὣς φάτο), and she was well pleased to sleep with him. (*Od*, 8.295)

By the time of this brief summarizing pause, the narration is fully focalized through the character Demodokos. Although the last articulation point began in external focalization with the bard starting his story (*Od*, 8.266), no one would hear or read this common formula, "so he spoke," and imagine that Demodokos is its subject and has suddenly gotten very lucky. There is no confusion that the blind rhapsode, and not Ares, is going to bed with Aphrodite. The narrator of the *Odyssey* is no longer describing *how* the bard sang but rather singing *what* the bard sang. The transition from indirect to direct discourse was hidden but is now complete. The narrator has *become* Demodokos.[16]

This performative enactment in which the narrator of the *Odyssey* slips into the role of the bard Demodokos provides strong internal evidence and an exemplary model for Nagy's claims about how rhapsodes in fact take on the identity of Homer in their performance of the Homeric poems. Interestingly, this performative enactment is effected by the techniques of narration rather than by any flourishing gesture, musical trick, or vocal inflection.[17]

The performative consequences of this conclusion become even more curious with the verb that introduces the passage to begin with: Demodokos *started* (*aneballeto*) to sing. One might assume that "to start" is something that can only occur at one point in time: at one moment, the bard is silent; at the next, he is singing. Yet the imperfect form of the verb here stands in stark contrast to the series of aorists that follow. It underscores the progressive aspect of the action: starting to sing is an ongoing and repetitive function. The "initializing" *prooimion*, despite Homeric scholars' efforts at precise demarcation,[18] bleeds on into the act of narration. This continuity of incipiency is appropriate to the long ambivalence in focalization with which the story opens.

This morphological feature of the verb's aspect is complemented by its lexical denotation. *Anaballein* is literally to "throw up" (directionally, not in the sense of *vomit*) and most commonly means to put off or delay. When used in the middle voice in the context of lyre playing (*phormizein*), it can also denote "to strike up, begin to play or sing."[19] The same verb can mean both "to start" and "to postpone." This word is very apt for the technique of a narrator of serial poetry—like the Homeric epics—whose strategy to keep the story going must fold "beginning again" into every pause and, conversely, imbue any resumption of narration with postponement. This dual meaning is equally necessary for people in playing roles for each other: each time they reunite, they must pick up where they left off and begin the dance of delayed recognition once again. Continuation requires both stopping and starting at once.

The noun form of this verb, *anabolē*, means both "a prelude on the lyre" and "a putting off, delaying." *Anabolē* is hence an amalgamation of recognition and change—*anagnorisis* and *metabolē*—in more ways than the obvious trading of prefix and root. Recognition is a performance that changes by staying the same, that stops by starting. As will soon become clear, anagnorisis is a matter of what Aristotle calls *entelecheia*, which is the continuity or persistence of an activity. This echoes the way Nagy depicts the action of the rhapsode's bringing-into-being of Homer: "We see here a model of songmaking that is ultimately patterned on its own goal, achieved by maintaining continuity through variety. To maintain this continuity is to keep on re-creating, which is the process of mimesis. In mimesis, every performance is a re-creation. To rephrase the words of Aristotle in the *Poetics*, the representing 'this' *re-creates* the represented 'that' (1448b17)."[20] This active re-creation is the change of performing. The poem's composition is its potentiality; when it is actualized *as* composition, performance happens. Homer comes to life for the recognizing audience.

CHANGE IN ARISTOTLE'S *PHYSICS* AND *POETICS*

The language of potential and actualization in Nagy's descriptions of composition and performance is reminiscent of common English translations for two of Aristotle's most important philosophical terms, which pervade all of his thinking about the world and which receive their fullest explanation in the *Physics*. The first three chapters of book 3 of the *Physics* are devoted to developing a definition sufficient to explain motion in all of its varied forms. Motion (*kinēsis*) for Aristotle is always a species of change (*metabolē*), the defining predicate in Aristotle's account of recognition. Recall that peripeteia and anagnorisis, the two elements that make a story complex in Aristotle's *Poetics*, are both kinds of change (*metabolē*). Peripeteia (reversal) is a "change to the opposite of the things being done," and anagnorisis is a "change from ignorance to knowledge" (*P*, 11, 1452a, 23 and 29). Hence change links the two most important elements of the best stories, and yet scholars of the *Poetics* have little to say about the science of motion and change in Aristotle. Why is it important to think of reversal and recognition as change? What kinds of change are they? How are they related to one another? To answer these questions, it makes sense to examine the central role that motion plays in Aristotle's thinking.

To understand Aristotle's definition of motion, it is necessary to say something about *dunamis* and *energeia* (the origins, by surprising philological twists and turns, of our modern English words *dynamic* and *energy*), which are usually translated respectively as "potentiality" and "actualization."[21] Aristotle concedes that these two terms are not definable in any usual way but can only be apprehended by analogy and example. The *dunamis* of any thing is its natural tendency to function in its characteristic ways; it exhibits *energeia* when it is actively fulfilling this proper function. The composition of the latter term helps suggest its meaning: *en*ergeia = at work (*ergon*). The analogical parallels of this pair with Nagy's composition and performance, or Saussure's *langue* and *parole*, should already be clear. The potency of Homeric poetry lies in its compositional elements; it is only actualized when at work in performance. The underlying structure, rules, and formulaic chunks of language constitute its *dunamis*; its *energeia* is only actuated in speech. To discern the relation of potential and actuality in recognition will require a bit more work. Aristotle's pair nonetheless provides a more helpful analogy for the relation of performance to knowledge that takes place in recognition than Saussure's or Nagy's pairs, mainly because it best explains how recognition is a change.

Aristotle begins to circle around an understanding of change by comparing motion (*kinēsis*) to *energeia*. Because the latter is an activity, it would seem to be synonymous with motion and change. At first thought, things seem to be active mainly when they are moving about and changing. But Aristotle's key insight, the linchpin to his entire system, is that motion *cannot* be identical with actualization. Motion, in its very essence, is incomplete (*ateles*). It is a process of change toward some goal, and hence, once something has reached a state of completion or perfection, it ceases to be in motion. *Energeia*, in contrast, is the work of something fulfilling its innate nature. It is complete: not a process but an activity. Happiness is Aristotle's prime example. Humans aim to be happy but achieve it only in the activity that actualizes their natural potential. Happiness is an active state of agency in fulfilling human nature, not a passive condition of fortune or pleasure.

Yet motion too has its own nature that can be actively engaged. The natural activity of motion is change. Change, as it pertains to any other thing, is never an example of *energeia*, but in respect to itself, change is the fulfilling activity of a potentiality *as* a potentiality. In that formulation, which Aristotle derives through many intricate steps of reasoning, I have stumbled onto the definition of change. This definition allows Aristotle to avoid the paradoxes of motion proposed by the Parmenideans, who held all change to be illusory. The definition furthermore propels his investigations through the *Physics* on to the study of being in the *Metaphysics*—and thus lays the impetus and groundwork for Aristotle's entire understanding of how the universe works. Let us look at its construction more carefully:

> ἡ δὲ τοῦ δυνάμει ὄντος <ἐντελέχεια>, ὅταν ἐντελεχείᾳ ὂν ἐνεργῇ οὐχ ᾗ αὐτὸ ἀλλ' ᾗ κινητόν, κίνησίς ἐστιν. (*Ph*, 3.1, 201a)
>
> (The fulfilment of what exists in potential, when, in its fulfilment, it is in activity not as itself but just as the potency to move, is motion.)[22]

In other words, motion is the *entelecheia* of a *dunamis* as a *dunamis*. The word I translate as "fulfillment," *entelecheia*, is considered by many scholars to be interchangeable with *energeia*. In fact, as Joe Sachs argues, it should be understood as the active completeness of *energeia* with the added idea of continuity or persistence.[23] Accordingly, to condense the definition to its simplest formulation, change is the continuous actualization of potentiality insofar as it is potential. When the nature of a thing ceases to be potential and has become actual, change is over. Only while the activity of potentiality itself persists does change occur. Aristotle's first example is building: as long as the bustle of construction is going on, before a house is complete, the buildable (i.e., the materials and capabilities that create a potential future house) is fulfilled *as* the process of building. That is motion. As soon as the house is standing and move-in ready (as the real estate agents like to say), the function of building stops and the house can actualize its being as a domicile. Aristotle gives this example in terse shorthand. One can spell it out by plugging it into the syntax of his definition:

> The fulfilment of building, not as the final house but as the potency to work in construction, is building.

Aristotle mentions other analogous examples of change: "learning, healing, rolling, leaping, ripening, and aging" (*Ph*, 3.1, 201a). The dramatic plot device of peripeteia, literally "turning around," can be explained with this model as well. Aristotle defines it as a "change to the opposite of the things being done (*prattomenōn*)" (*P*, 11, 1452a 22). Halliwell's helpful if freewheeling translation renders this as "a complete swing in the direction of the action."[24] For most of *Oedipus Tyrannos*, for instance, the "things being done" are headed in one definite direction: Oedipus's zealous investigation to find and punish the murderer of Laius. Intentions and actions are both directed straight ahead toward this one goal; there is no change. At the end, similarly, the action is unwavering: Oedipus is determined in his intent to live in exile and bear witness the consequences of his discovered guilt. Again, there is no change in direction when he is led off stage as the final chorus pronounces that no mortal should be called happy while yet alive. Between these two bearings—to seek and to suffer—a change must take place. This change in the action is peripeteia, which might be expressed in the language of the *Physics*:

> The fulfilment of altering course, not as the active new direction but as the potency to turn, is peripeteia.

The action of the plot in this sense is analogous to the dance of the chorus in Greek tragedy: if during the strophe they are headed stage left and during the antistrophe they are dancing stage right, then at some point between the two songs, they have to take steps that turn them around.

Peripeteia is not the rhythmic slapping of the feet on the stones in one direction or the other but their pivoting turn. Reversal is thus a phenomenon confined to a limited part of the plot of some stories. It is a change that is in effect only as long as the changing is going on, and it ceases once a new course in the action is established. It is easy to see how this is an action (*praxis*) liable to be imitated and enacted in poetry.

Recognition seems well poised to follow the same pattern. Learning (*mathēsis*) is specifically cited as an example of change (*Ph*, 3.1, 201a). The definition of anagnorisis appears to work equally well for learning: "a change from ignorance to knowledge." In the case of identifying *things*, this indeed conforms to the example set by building quite nicely. The end aimed for is knowledge, an active state of holding a justified true belief. Coming to know is an exertion for the sake of something else, and it ends as soon as the desired knowledge is attained. Recognition hence is a change insofar as it is in action *as* a potential. The action of recognition ceases when it spills over into knowledge. I see a snake, my heart is pounding in fear, and I move away. As I watch more carefully from a safe distance, however, I notice that the snake does not move. Curiosity competes with fear, and I pull in closer to observe and investigate. Recognition is at work in this active state of uncertainty and exploration. Finally, I poke the uncannily still snake with a stick and discover it to be a rope. Ignorance has been replaced by knowledge; the change is complete, and recognition has run its course. Now I can laugh in relief at my own willies.

This recognition as learning what something is (the famous *ti esti*) fits the formula of Aristotelian change easily:

> The fulfilment of learning, not as the attained knowledge of what something is but as the potency to learn about it, is learning.

If the object of learning is another person, however, things get complicated. People tend to tie knots into the lines of most definitions, and this one is no exception. Humans are not objects like ropes and snakes. Once correctly identified as such, a rope will never turn back into a snake and bite me. There is no guarantee, however, that an enemy newly classed as a friend will not do just that. Not only can any seeming resting place in the relations between people—marriage, sibling love, friendship—always erupt into its opposite, but even the relation itself must be kept alive with the constant rehearsal of retrieved behaviors. Being a husband or sister or parent is a daily chore—with daily sources of grievance and delight. When

I try to hold on to a fixed idea of an Other's relation to me, I end up treating her as a thing or possession. As observed in the last chapter, this Atreidian mode of recognition leads to tragedy—as with Agamemnon and Clytemnestra—or to suppressed trauma—as with Menelaus and Helen. In other words, whereas the recognition of objects is an action, the recognition of other people is an activity.

This difference between recognizing people and things inheres in performance. By invoking the term *performance*, I do not mean that interpersonal conduct is necessarily theatrical. Performing, understood in its technical sense as the deportment of actors in a theater, would be a kind of change insofar as it is an actualization of the potential of dramatic enactment as a potential. Again, one can express a definition of theatrical performance in terms of change:

> The fulfilment of performing, not as the complete drama but as the potency to work as a performer, is performance.

That is, the activity of performing is in motion as long as the action of the play is being actively rehearsed before an audience. The performed drama, meanwhile, can achieve actuality in itself and has its own potential ends—such as bringing about catharsis in the spectators. This explanation may be all well and good as a—perhaps unnecessarily formalistic—description of the dynamics of theatrical and rhapsodic performance, but how can any of this help clarify recognition? In fact, the payoff of slogging through all these Aristotelian technicalities is nigh when one considers performance *not* in its theatrical sense but in its most basic meaning of acting and speaking before others.[25] The work of recognition between people involves interpreting the words and behaviors of others while speaking and behaving in turn. Whereas theatrical performance can be viewed as an object or action and can potentially lead to a final "*houtos ekeinos!*" performance in its wider anthropological sense of behavior between people cannot rest in the confidence of such a declaration. It always remains subject to change.

To frame the problem in the terms of Aristotle's definition, the change in which recognition consists could be expressed as follows:

> The fulfilment of coming to know another person, not as the complete knowledge of her character but as the potency to interpret performance and perform, is recognition.

Here I have finally arrived at a formulation of interpersonal anagnorisis that captures the valence of its *metabolē*. With this definition, the radical consequences of taking recognition seriously as change come in to view. Recognition between people never ends.[26] Ethically speaking, this means that any assumption of fixed relational knowledge is an affront to human agency. Philosophically speaking, it means that interpersonal recognition is not strictly an action that has an end outside of itself but shares many features with *energeia*.[27] Like happiness, recognition is an activity. Recognizing someone as a friend or enemy is not a one-off event precisely because it is not a question of insight into another's (or one's own) internal disposition but can only be actuated in the continued repetition of certain behaviors. "Helping friends and harming enemies" was a common formula for virtue in the Greek world.[28] Being a friend is not the mere assurance of another's fondness but entails reenacted performances that must be reciprocated in some manner by gestures of gratitude, acknowledgment, or returned assistance.

The activity of this coming-into-being of knowledge as potency is illustrated well by Nagy's analysis of epic performance as reenactment. The rhapsodic delivery (and recreation) of the Homeric poems before an audience provides a perfect (but one-sided and hence simplified) model for the presentation of self and its acceptance by others. The rhapsode's combination of formula and creativity, of convention and reinvention, is a wonderfully apt metaphor for the way people are always already reenacting their social roles and their individual selves to those around them. This understanding of recognition as performance implies that there is no actual knowledge about other people *other than* as a potency: we never arrive at a perfected, complete knowledge of others but are always encountering them in the midst of a moving reenactment of our mutual responsibilities and relations. Recognition is always in motion, always at work, whenever people interact.

The consequence of applying the logic of change to the vagaries of human interaction leads to a perpetual motion machine of recognition that, like Solon's knowledge about human happiness, can only end in death.[29] Yet this endlessness of recognition flies in the face of the claim that it must be understood as an action (*praxis*) for Aristotle. It was the surprising realization that recognition must be an action that motivated this book's investigation into change in the first place. Now I am already forced to make a second reversal by identifying recognition between people as an activity. Action, especially as imitated in poetry, has a beginning, middle, and end.

Under praxis, Aristotle comprehends "not any and all human doings, but those deeds that begin with a choice, proceed through an in-between series of necessary or likely consequences, and end with the achieving or failing to achieve an end."[30] The ceaseless change that constitutes intersubjective performance would thus seem to rule out its candidacy as the action of anagnorisis.

Yet this contradiction is precisely what drives dramatic recognition. The desire to be sure of a friend or enemy demands a conclusion to stories of coming to know. The nostalgia for security in knowledge of other people, as diagnosed in the previous chapter, calls for viewing the endless work of recognition as a discernably self-contained event. This tension between the necessary incompletion and required containment of recognition underlies the drama of both epic and tragic anagnorisis. The *Odyssey* seems to end happily in a clear resolution of finalized reunions between estranged members of a household: husband and wife, father and son, master and servants, king and subjects. Yet the poem thematizes the insufficiency of these settled recognitions at several points, most notably in the prophecy Tiresias imparted to Odysseus that he would not rest at home but be forced to wander again on land and die at sea (*Od*, 11.121–136), which Odysseus repeats to Penelope during their first joyful embraces after twenty years of separation (*Od*, 23.248–284). *The Odyssey*, the most famous imitation of the action of recognition, acknowledges its own incompletion even at the climax of its conclusion.

This understanding of recognition as the actualization of knowledge-about-other-people as a potency, which takes place through mutual performance, is very broad. It certainly does not apply only to those instances of dramatic anagnorisis that interest Aristotle in Greek tragedy and epic. The explication of recognition as change proffered here can admittedly serve as a description of nearly *all* social encounters, not simply to those that produce turning points in good drama. Usually the activity of recognition is a matter of constant and minute course correction rather than radical about-turns in intersubjective relations. The specific kinds of recognition that for Aristotle are "most appropriate for a story" (*P*, 11, 1452a, 39) require the further clauses of his definition of anagnorisis: they "lead to friendship or enmity in people bound for good or bad fortune" (*P*, 11, 1452a, 30). It is important, however, to understand the dynamics of the whole category of changes in knowledge between people—which is what my performative definition tries to get at—before going on to examine what is at stake in the clausal modifiers Aristotle adds to delineate poetic anagnorisis. Such an elucidation is the task of the next three chapters, which analyze what effect recognition as change has in terms of epistemology (chapter 3), the ethics of friendship (chapter 4), and the fate of identity in fortune (chapter 5). These recognitions, to be precise, are the ones that effect a peripeteia, a "change to the opposite of what's being done" (*P*, 11, 1452a, 22). In order to be imitable as good epic or dramatic poetry, in other words, the activity of recognition must be misrecognized as the action of reversal.

CRYING FOR SHOW IN THE *ODYSSEY*

Weeping is a well-practiced art in Homer's epics. Tears drench so much of the action that ancient and modern commentators alike have felt compelled to impugn or defend the heroes' manliness with normalizing dams against the flood of gender disruptions.[31] Performative weeping, in fact, provides the fulcrum of a pivotal recognition scene in the *Odyssey* that can help reveal the paradoxical structure of anagnorisis as action and activity. At the close of book 8, Alcinous, king of the Phaeacians, finally demands to be told the name, origin, and identity of the stranger they have been hosting and feasting with for so long (*Od*, 8.536–585). The immediate cause of this abrupt—if overdue—request is Odysseus's reaction to the blind singer's tales of the final battle of the Trojan War. Aristotle's citation of this scene as an example of recognition (*P*, 16, 1455a, 1–2) is an express invitation to closer inspection, which reveals several important consequences. For one thing, it puts to rest any question that anagnorisis, for Aristotle at least, must transpire between individuals who had some close previous relationship (long-estranged siblings, parents and children, friends, spouses, etc.). Odysseus and Alcinous have no kinship or prior relation.[32]

Yet the incident can also be seen as an instance of recognition as change in its double aspect of action and activity. To the extent that noticing the stranger's behavior makes Alcinous suspect his noble and heroic identity, the recognition scene can be framed as an action with beginning, middle, and end: the king observes a strong reaction to Demodokos's tale of Troy's fall and the stranger's noble comportment, then uses these remarks to fashion a polite demand for his identity. Odysseus apparently completes this action of recognition at the beginning of the next book by announcing his name, patronage, and homeland. Yet the *Odyssey* makes clear that this action, even in so successful a dramatic recognition as that between Odysseus and the idealized Phaeacian court, cannot be so neatly contained. The ordeal of presenting himself before Alcinous and Arete in such a way as to encourage this favorable reception is the result of much preparatory work. From the moment of his encounter with their daughter, Nausicaa, on the beach, the nude, shipwrecked Odysseus had begun presenting himself in a manner that would capitalize on the ritualized host/guest relations of Greek culture. The princess helps Odysseus hatch an elaborate plan for Odysseus to perform a role that would elicit the approval of her parents (*Od*, bk. 6). Their plot determines the events of the next two books (*Od*, bks. 7–8), climaxing in Alcinous's courteous appeal. Odysseus does not rest with the announcement of his identity but proceeds to take the place of Demodokos as rhapsodic entertainer and perform a long autobiographical narrative (*Od*, bks. 9–12) to ensure that Alcinous makes good on his promises of copious gifts and a ride home. The king proves himself a friend to the stranger in the most emphatic way possible for traditional Greek morality (helping friends and harming enemies). Yet even after the Phaeacian sailors place the sleeping Odysseus on his native shore, he awakens to suspect that they have deceived him and played him false (*Od*, 13.209–215). Only by physically touching and counting up the booty that has been piled up on the beach can Odysseus know "whether they might not have gone, taking some of it with them in the hollow vessel" (*Od*, 13.215). Hence it is clear that the anagnorisis between Odysseus and Alcinous begins before they lay eyes on each other and is still uncertain long after they have parted. Although their recognition is most movingly emblematized in the action of Odysseus's tears, it is an activity that must be rehearsed over and over.

The passage in which Homer describes the telltale tears of Odysseus, moreover, points beyond itself in striking ways. It is worth reading in full:

> So the famous singer sang his tale, but Odysseus
> melted, and from under his eyes the tears ran down, drenching
> his cheeks. As a woman weeps, lying over the body
> of her dear husband, who fell fighting for her city and people
> as he tried to beat off the pitiless day from city and children;
> she sees him dying and gasping for breath, and winding her body
> about him she cries high and shrill, while the men behind her,
> hitting her with their spear butts on the back and shoulders,
> force her up and lead her away into slavery, to have
> hard work and sorrow, and her cheeks are wracked with pitiful
> weeping.
> Such were the pitiful tears Odysseus shed from under
> his brows, but they went unnoticed by all the others,

but Alkinoös alone understood what he did and noticed,
since he was sitting next [to] him and heard him groaning heavily.
(*Od*, 8.521–534)

If for Aristotle this weeping sequence encapsulates the long process of anagnorisis between Odysseus and Alcinous, its remarkable simile brings together a host of contradictions that are emblematic of the action of recognition in general. It equates opposites: man and woman, warrior and wife, vanquisher and vanquished.[33] The story of Odysseus's glorious victory results in tears of the unspeakable horrors of defeat.[34] Odysseus had himself requested the tale of the Trojan Horse, calculating, perhaps, that a heroic account of his brilliant stratagem could serve as an impressive preamble to the impending revelation of his identity as its author. Demodokos's song, however, emphasizes the carnage that followed in the "grimmest fighting" of house-to-house combat (*Od*, 8.513–520). Just as Odysseus had to face the victims of his warlike exploits in the rhapsode's song, the poetic space opened by the narrator's metaphor makes readers see and hear the voluble suffering of warfare's "most pitiful" casualties. Alcinous's subsequent speech questioning the stranger's identity culminates in a surmise that the song of Troy must have reminded him of some kinsman or companion who "perished before Ilion" (*Od*, 8.580). In fact, though, it is not the memory of a friend who sparks the tears that cause this recognition and friendship between Alcinous and Odysseus but rather compassion with the suffering of the enemy.

Even more pertinent to the workings of recognition, however, is the utter incongruity of the behavior of the two compared weepers. Scholars have not remarked on how the simile seems to misalign the tenor of their actions entirely. Although Odysseus's muffled sobs are discreetly hidden and go mostly unnoticed, the widow's wailing imposes itself on anyone within earshot. How can the paroxysms of twining limbs and shrieking voice be like the stifled groans that barely escape from beneath Odysseus's cloak? The claim to similarity made by this Homeric simile demands that the question be posed. The answer lies in the fact that pairing these two disparate acts underlines their shared valence as performance.

Objections to this claim may be on the tips of many tongues: how can the authentic, unprecogitated reactions of a grieving wife as she is dragged off to abject slavery be impugned with the conscious theatricality of performance? Surely she is not trying to impress an audience with the drama of her lamentation? Or if Odysseus attempts to *hide* his tears, then surely this is the opposite of performativity? Both objections can be met by clarifying the concept of performance. In the first case, however authentic one's grief, the precise forms that acts of mourning take are largely determined by codified behaviors in a given culture. To notice the culturally specific practices of grief does not diminish at all the genuineness of those feeling the emotion. In the example of the simile, for instance, it does not matter whether winding one's arms and legs around the slain husband was a commonly practiced convention of grief in archaic Greece or whether it was the individual improvisation of this particular wife. Both possibilities qualify as performance—though with potentially very different valences in the semiotic context in which they occur. Performance, again, is a broader category than theatricality and should be understood at its most basic simply as behavior before others, with or without an explicit consciousness thereof.

This brings us to the second objection: Odysseus seems to be attempting to avoid precisely that—making a show of his weeping. By concealing his tears beneath his cloak, surely he does not want to enact his grief before others at all. There are two ways to meet this criticism. For one thing, concealment is already in itself a behavior before others, regardless of the type of reaction disguised. In fact, the term *performance* in general still carries the stigma of duplicity for many, though the relation between dissimulation and authenticity is very fraught indeed, as the readings in this book hope to show.

Second, and most telling, Odysseus may well intend this specific act of deception to be seen through. His entire conduct since arriving at court has been choreographed in advance with Nausicaa, and his every act is aimed at persuading Alcinous and Arete to help him. Twice Odysseus manages to make Alcinous the sole perceiver of his artfully hidden tears while the rhapsode sings of Troy. The earlier description of Odysseus's cloaking his tears (in response to Demodokos's first tale of the quarrel between Odysseus and Achilles at Troy) is even more ostentatious: during the rounds of song, he veils his face with his sea-purple mantle, then uses it to dry his eyes with each pause, after which he pours a libation to the gods with a two-handled goblet. This pattern is repeated multiple times before Alcinous notices and calls off the singing (*Od*, 8.83–95). By the time Odysseus is melting in shrouded tears in response to Demodokos's third tale, Alcinous demands that the stranger reveal his noble heritage. The courteous gesture of a guest delicately concealing his distress from the host is the soft sell that closes the deal. The sight of Odysseus's lament adds a human touch to the stories he knows he will eventually be obliged to tell, and thus his tears pay off in the gold of the Phaeacians' impressed hospitality.[35]

These two suggestive incidents of well-targeted concealment are not the sole evidence for this surmise. Hidden weeping plays a role in the crucial recognition scene later between Odysseus and Penelope. In book 19, when Penelope interviews the strange beggar who has appeared in her home, she begins weeping at the tale he tells of having encountered her husband before. In reaction to her obvious suffering, Odysseus "in his heart felt pity for his wife as she mourned him, but his eyes stayed, as if they were made of horn or iron, steady under his lids. He hid his tears in deception" (*Od*, 19.210–212).[36] This passage reveals that Odysseus is quite capable of suppressing tears entirely when the situation demands. It is not because he is *more moved* at the singer's tales than by his own wife's misery that he lets tears fall for the former and holds them back for the latter. Rather, he performs his grief in manners suited to the occasion, considering the formulae of social protocols and the expectations and needs of his interlocutors.

Despite current common ideas about emotions, outward display in the *Odyssey* is not simply a yardstick by which to measure the magnitude of interior feelings. Instead, passions are functions of integrated scenes between people that must be evaluated and "read" on their own contextual—and intertextual—terms. The fact that Odysseus bawls openly in grief when alone staring out to sea on Calypso's island (book 5), muffles his sobs in Alcinous's court (book 8), and sheds no tears before Penelope (book 19) does not mean that his feelings vary in strength or that his anguish at beholding his wife's pain is less genuine than his sorrow on hearing tales of Troy. It is not only the emotion that determines the actions it elicits but also the requirements of the scene at hand.

Thus the full force of the simile equating the openly wailing widow with the discreetly sniffling actor becomes apparent: they are both examples of performance appropriate to their situations. Odysseus's tears, even when controlled and directed, are *like* the shrill cries and clinging limbs of the bereaved widow because they both are effective acts in the multiple valences of their respective scenes: the widow makes her unfathomable loss felt by the very soldiers who bereaved and now enslave her; Odysseus channels his nostalgia to portray the decorously grieving guest. They thus open up the potential for recognition with the persons beholding them. The woman playing widow and slave enacts her overwhelming grief and rage before the people who will control her fate;

Odysseus playing the silently suffering hero impresses the man who holds his own fate in the balance. The former invites potential sympathy; the latter, respect.

Both effect a change in knowledge that can be represented here emblematically as an action but that must be maintained as an activity. For the soldier's widow, the threnetic wildness of her performance may invite initial compassion, but that is no guarantee of enduring lenience. As the widows in Euripides's *Trojan Women* intimate, the enslaved woman will have to invent many and varied ploys throughout the years to come in order to mitigate the abuses of her bondage. In fact, the woman does not even escape the cruel blows of the victors' spear butts in the very simile in which her tears are so moving. Similarly, though he incites Alcinous's avowed generosity with his carefully staged weeping, Odysseus must continuously plot and act in order to maintain Alcinous's friendship. He does not rest assured of the Phaeacians' goodwill even after they have deposited him on Ithaca's shore. The performance of recognition may be epitomized as an action, but it never escapes the enforced rehearsal of activity.

This conclusion becomes manifest in the details of Homeric similes. Just as the narratological function of focalization does performative work in the rhapsode's identification as Homer (see above), the performance of recognition becomes visible through the poetic device of metaphor. In each case, the idea of performance must be stretched to include the mechanics of storytelling and poetry. The striking consequences of this lyrical narrativization of interpersonal performance will become clear in chapters 3 and 8 through 10 of this book. For now, it is important to see how it points toward the ongoing *activity* of recognition underlying its representation in the comprehensible magnitude of an *action*.

RECOGNITION IN PERFORMANCE THEORY AND MORAL PHILOSOPHY

Although this performative extrapolation from recognition is unorthodox as an interpretation of Aristotle, there is nothing novel in situating a theory of human behavior in performance. Adam Smith grounded his entire moral system in incisive observations of interpersonal performance arbitrated by an "ideal spectator" (*Theory of Moral Sentiments*, 1759). Exactly two hundred years later, the sociologist Erwin Goffman published an account of human interaction in even more explicitly performative terms (*The Presentation of Self in Everyday Life*, 1959). In the decades since, a veritable industry of performance theory has sprung up to account for every supposed human universal from gender to the environment. In order to test the utility and innovation of my reading of Aristotelian anagnorisis, it is helpful to put it in the context of some of these more recent theories of performance. Though many have interesting points of contact with the approach taken here, I focus on its implications for two performance theorists (Richard Schechner and Rebecca Schneider) and two moral philosophers (Hilde Lindemann and J. David Velleman). The work of performance theorists and moral philosophers has much to offer any study of recognition, and the present book is in debt to both. Aristotle's concept of change, in turn, invites helpful interventions in the two discourses of performance and philosophy. On the one hand, techniques of narratological analysis are necessary to understand performative scenes. On the other hand, the careful philology of superficial close reading is required for any responsible ethics. Performing recognition is always already a matter of telling stories and observing surfaces.

Richard Schechner is one of the founders of performance studies as a discipline. An innovative theater practitioner, Schechner worked closely for many years with the anthropologist Victor Turner to develop his approach to a broad spectrum of performance types from ritual to sports. His most influential theoretical contribution to the fields of anthropology and theater is the thesis that performance can best be understood as restored behavior: "Performance means: never for the first time. It means: for the second to the nth time. Performance is 'twice-behaved behavior.'"[37] In a later summary of this thesis, Schechner admits that *all* behavior is restored behavior: "all behavior consists of recombining bits of previously behaved behaviors."[38] It is the job of performance theorists to develop methods and terminology to analyze the ways that behavior is in creative dialogue with its earlier instantiations.

It is easy to see how Nagy's description of Homeric reenactment fits this bill. The rhapsode improvises with a battery of formulae to cut and paste an entirely new improvised performance out of previously rehearsed material. Yet Nagy relies on a structuralist paradigm to explain the working of rhapsodic reenactment: the rhapsode's performance is to the Homeric composition as Saussure's *parole* is to *langue*. By privileging the performance itself, Schechner would seem to reject this reliance on an underlying model of which individual performances are mimetic manifestations. Schechner's great achievement was to free theatrical studies from its obsession with authorial texts as originary sources. Performances should be judged and analyzed in their own right, which is always in the context of their iterative genealogies but without authoritative originals of which they are mere copies. Despite this radical potential, however, Schechner's language and diagrams still rely on a nondialogical notion of the self. He occasionally compares restored behavior to "natural events" and "natural behavior."[39] At the center of every one of Schechner's graphics illustrating his theory (which are decked out with all the diagrammatic trappings of scientific figures—from vector lines to mathematical subscripts) sits an omphalic "Me," the unmoved mover for the dynamics of his entire system.[40] Though Schechner eloquently insists on the essential "betweenness" of performance,[41] his meticulous account of the processual emergence of restored behavior lacks a theoretical grounding in intersubjectivity.

The understanding of performative recognition explored in the first two chapters of this book can help supply that lack. Performance as restored behavior is constituted on the fissure between anagnorisis and *metabolē*. On the one hand, recognition's self-signifying desire for an unattainable originary presence drives the move to trace the sources of any perceived behavior to begin with, whether in an authentic self, an original event, or a native homeland. The fact that all behavior is twice-behaved explains the need for *re*cognition, which in turn craves to grasp a Same amid the necessary Difference of new contexts. On the other hand, the recognitive structure of Aristotelian change determines the shape of Schechner's analysis of performance. Though claiming to resist the linearity and artificial wholeness of dramatic texts, Schechner's own astute ethnographic accounts of performances—from sadomasochistic participatory voyeurism to historical simulation—are inevitably linear and whole. He takes great pains to provide discursive descriptions of the deliberative and contingent processes involved in production, from workshopping ideas through rehearsals and from showtime to the after-party. Even to describe experiential ritual and nonlinear performances, Schechner narrates a dramatic arc with beginning, middle, and end. His analysis is thus caught in the paradox of recognition: it keeps turning ongoing activities into comprehensible actions.

Furthermore, though Schechner's work attempts to shake the structuralist paradigm of abstract system and concrete manifestation, if one takes restored behavior seriously as a dialogic phenomenon (as opposed to the journeys of "Me" sketched in the diagrams), one finds it more at home with the Aristotelian concepts of potency and actuality. The mutual interplay of restored behavior is the continuous actualization of potential scenarios *as* potentiality. The activity of recognition is a perpetual reenactment of nostalgic bits that can never fully rehearse an original wholeness. Enacting twice-behaved behavior in interpersonal performance hence folds the logic of recognition into the logic of change.

For Schechner, twice-behaved behavior drives home the ephemerality of performance.[42] Peggy Phelan developed this conclusion into an ontology of performance grounded in its radical impermanence. For Phelan, performance "becomes itself" through its very disappearance.[43] Rebecca Schneider, however, takes the same phenomenon of restored behavior as evidence for the dogged persistence of performance through time. Her insightful study *Performing Remains* suggests a temporality of performance that is remarkably in sync with the understanding of recognition offered here. In a series of readings of historical and theatrical reenactments, Schneider stitches together the complex intertextualies of performance. She explains that this kind of reading makes "restored behavior . . . available for recognition."[44] In doing so, she is "interested in repetitions, doubling, and the call-and-response of cross- and inter-authorships."[45] This call-and-response, which for Schneider can span centuries and even millennia, is the performative scene of intersubjective recognition. Even neolithic hand paintings by prehistoric peoples extend a gesture demanding recognition by future generations unimaginable to their creators.[46] The chronological durability of performance is multiplied, not diminished, by its evanescent iterations.

The "texts" that Schneider reconstructs—Civil War battle reenactments, the restoration of experimental Polish theater by an American acting troop, reperformances of art installations, sculpture, and photography—may seem altogether incommensurate with the texts considered here—archaic poetry and modern drama—yet her readings share a methodological kinship with this book. Schneider is acutely alive to the instructive inaccuracies in attempts at reenactment, and it is through these very misfirings that she is able to pry open windows to view the utterly strange congruities between people, places, and times. For instance, Schneider reveals lazy assumptions about gender and media at work in a famous art historian's reception of the photographer Cindy Sherman: "To get it right, that is to *recognize* Sherman, necessarily requires that the viewer labor to recognize the operations of misrecognition. And so again the question arises: what does the error, the missing, the not-quite-right get right about that which it strives to replay?"[47] This is precisely the question posed by Menelaus's misrecognition of Helen in the previous chapter and by the odd equation of victorious Odysseus with the vanquished woman above. For the former, it is the tension beneath the smiles, and for the latter, it is the mismatch of the simile that invites a reappraisal of the recognitions they perform.

In lived human relationships, the psychology of recognition consists in the continuous reperformance in endless variety of traumas, triumphs, put-downs, and affirmations. Aesthetic mimesis deliberatively reproduces this endless loop of reenactment in concentrated form as an artificial whole. Schechner called such miniscripts of restored behavior "bits." The temporal tenacity of recognition is constituted by the autopoietic replication of these bits. What Schneider does is fold and refold the textual fabric (or, to use Schechner's metaphor, the film reel) of performance bits in order to compare them more closely. Often, more can be learned from patches where the patterns are subtly off, where attempts at reenactment make a mismatch. Schneider calls these revealing moments "*what inadequacy gets right*."[48] To allow readers to recognize them, she builds a narrative frame around the circumstances leading up to, away from, and around the telling event. The temporality of performance, therefore, is tied to that of narrative. Together, they construct the durability of recognition.

The insights of both Schneider and Schechner thus emerge from the implicit work of narrative framing. The contribution of this book to performance studies, therefore, is not only to suggest the complementarity of Aristotelian change to theories of performativity but also to propose the necessity of narratology for the methods of performance scholars. This is evident in the ways that focalization and complex metaphors inflect the performance of recognition in the *Odyssey*, as explored above. The readings in the following chapters will expand on this. Especially the intertextual mismatches between recognition scenes in Plato and Shakespeare (chapter 6) and Kleist (chapter 10) provide moments of illuminating inadequacy like those that Schneider makes visible. They come to light only by the convergent tracing of performative, narratological, and philological patterns.

Explicit scholars of performance are not the only ones for whom it is helpful to think of recognition in performative terms. Two especially cogent analyses of human behavior as performance come from contemporary philosophers with no connection to the academic discipline of performance theory. J. David Velleman's *How We Get Along* (2009) and Hilde Lindemann's *Holding and Letting Go* (2014) offer explanations of morality based on the practice of improvisational theater. We are all actors, playing ourselves, with a limited but flexible repertoire of set pieces and retrievable behaviors. Sound familiar? Just as the rhapsode *becomes* Homer, we *become* ourselves through our performance of the role to others. Recognition, the perceived acceptance of that role through the reactions of those around us, is vital to our self-understanding. Both philosophers explicitly compare human behavior to the work of improv actors. In fact, both of them hit on commedia dell'arte as a good analogy for how people interact.[49] Yet despite this clear affinity between two prominent contemporary moral philosophers, they never cite each other or engage one another at all.

This mutual blind spot between two leading American ethicists points to a fundamental rift between the discourses in which they participate.[50] Velleman sees his book as a work of metaethics, while Lindemann designates her intervention as "naturalized moral epistemology."[51] Metaethics, in the tradition of Kant, attempts to uncover the fundamental metaphysics, semantics, and epistemology of morality. Naturalized ethics, for Lindemann, bypasses this gesture toward first principles in "a rejection of a priori, idealized judgments that have no connection with actual on-the-ground practices."[52] Metaethicists might see naturalized ethics as willfully ignorant of its own inevitable principles of knowledge and reasoning. Naturalized ethicists, in turn, accuse metaethics of idealism regrettably unmoored from the "real world." One way to characterize the divide would be as a focus on the ultimate source of ethical facts and concepts (metaethics) versus a kind of moral psychology that is interested in how ethical practices empirically work (naturalized moral epistemology).

Despite the cross-purposes of their starting places and goals, however, Lindemann and Velleman end up on remarkably similar terrain. Both analyze moral action as a performance space between individuals, and their descriptions of this space share uncanny echoes. Lindemann "liken[s] one's self-comportment in an ordinary social interaction to a theatrical improvisation, in which all the actors project facets of their identities that require uptake from the others on stage if the scene is to go smoothly."[53] Velleman also invokes theatrical improvisation to show how people enact identities: "As rational agents, you and I share a common stage, on which we improvise our own actions while viewing and seeking to interpret the actions of both."[54] Though the detailed mechanics of their analyses of human behavior have so much in common, the two philosophers draw different—to some extent incommensurable—conclusions. For Lindemann, the performance analogy supports an applied ethics of judging in specific cases when and how to "hold on and let go" of others' identities. For Velleman, the same theatrical account provides structural evidence for grounding ethical accounts in assumptions about agents' mutual reliance on practical reasoning in constituting actions, which leads to a skeptical but robust outline of the limits of normative ethics. Identical metaphors of theatrical performance thus provide one thinker with the metaethical foundation for morality and the other with case studies for applied ethics.

These two performative accounts of ethics are rich dialogue partners for the theory of recognition presented here. In fact, my reading of Aristotelian change provides a way to understand Lindemann's and Velleman's mutual neglect as an oscillating image of the paradox of recognition. On the one hand, Velleman's understanding of action as behavior plus reason[55] can be seen as closely linked to Aristotle's notion of praxis as grounded in choice and moving toward an end. Lindemann's account of the ethical necessity constantly to know when to hold on to another person's identity and when to let it go, meanwhile, is very much akin to Aristotelian *energeia*. It is an activity that requires continuous engagement. Hence Velleman and Lindemann stress different aspects of the paradox of performative recognition diagnosed above: the former highlights it as an action; the latter, as an activity.

Yet this theoretical emphasis is not reflected in their respective descriptive practices. Action, recall, is the only possible object of imitation in stories for Aristotle. Activity, in contrast, cannot be represented in its wholeness as a discrete motion with beginning, middle, and end. Yet Velleman, for whom interpersonal performance provides the theoretical basis for the primacy of *actions* in practical reasoning, claims that narrative storytelling can be a supplemental but not a necessary component of recognizing self and other; in practice, causal-psychological self-understanding will often exceed the confines of narration.[56] For Lindemann, on the other hand, storytelling is the primary modus operandi both of her own methodological procedure and for all selves performing their identities in the world. She begins each chapter with a finely crafted tale that serves as example and touchstone for the analysis that follows. Her earlier study, *Damaged Identities, Narrative Repair* (2001), moreover, is a fine account of the narrative construction of identity.[57] The two philosophers therefore always stand at opposite ends of the paradox of recognition, but they reverse their polarization when it comes to theory and practice. Lindemann theorizes recognition as an activity but practices it as an action; Velleman, vice versa, conceives of recognition as an action but admits its unbound activity-like character in practice. Together, they make up a moving image of the contradiction that drives dramatic recognition.

The philosophers' mirroring opposition comes into sharp relief when seen through the tears that Odysseus sheds (or holds back) in the *Odyssey*, discussed above. Weeping functions as an important instance in the works of both thinkers. Acts of crying make up Velleman's first and Lindemann's last example for the improvisational enactment of the self. A comparison of these tearful scenes reveals critical differences between the kindred accounts of performative recognition given by the two philosophers and the one offered here. For both thinkers, crying is interesting because it sits at the intersection between voluntary and involuntary behavior. Yet they take different perspectives on the scene of crying: Velleman observes it from the point of view of the weeper; Lindemann, from that of the one beholding the tears. Velleman compares the involuntary tears of initial shock to the fake wails of a child: "Between these extremes lies the authentic but also voluntary behavior of . . . sincerely expressing real emotion." For Velleman, this is an all-important example of how improvisation of self rises to the level of *action*. The weeping is "propelled by an emotion, but it is also shaped . . . into an *act of crying*." This allows Velleman to hold it up as a "model of agency."[58] Crying, therefore, is a pattern for how individuals can take the basic repertoire of emotional reactions and cultural signs and mold them into creative acts of self-presentation.

Lindemann takes the same situation and focuses on the responsibilities of the ones observing a crying person. In the final chapter of her book, Lindemann fills in "what it all means" by summing up the moral obligations people should feel to one another in her account of the performance and recognition of identity. She lights on the example of finding a friend crying. The weeper is not performing all her possible identities, "but she is performing a particular person in distress, and it's that to which you respond, drawing on your own sense of who you are in relation to her." A proper response may involve letting go of some of her identities (e.g., "drama queen") and holding on to others (e.g., the trusting, vulnerable confider). Either way, this model showcases the performative calculus arising from Lindemann's moral categories of holding and letting go: "However you respond, you are answerable to the moral norms arising from your and her identities."[59]

It is easy to see how these two analyses of weeping can inform a reading of the recognition scene in the *Odyssey*. The philosophers' examples complement each other perfectly by applying to different characters. In Velleman's model, Odysseus's tears in response to Demodokos's songs would be genuine acts of selfhood. Odysseus takes the very real grief he feels in being reminded of his experiences at Troy and shapes it into an expression of noble restraint that is in full accord with the character of himself he means to play. In Lindemann's example, Alcinous shows insightful moral acumen by noticing and responding to the stranger's tears. In the first instance, he stops the distressing song but allows his guest to hold on to his anonymity. In the second instance, Alcinous similarly cuts short the painful tale but takes the opportunity to call on the stranger to let go of his role of troubled mystery. He promises to embrace and hold on to whatever identity the stranger should reveal. Thus Odysseus and Alcinous exemplify the moral agency in Velleman's and Lindemann's systems respectively.

The same example demonstrates how my own understanding of recognition departs from that of the two philosophers. Lindemann carves up her account of performative personhood into four components: mental states, their expression, recognition of what is expressed, and response based on this recognition.[60] In her analyses of the vignettes she provides, these distinct steps are always neatly demarcated and identifiable. Performances involve two parties: one person feeling and expressing, and another person recognizing and responding. In both parties, a mental state (feeling/recognizing) is followed by a bodily action (expressing/responding). For Lindemann, the "'recognition' moment of personhood," like the other party's initial mental state, is a discrete, internal cognitive event.[61] The readings in this book, however, challenge precisely such a model of recognition. It is impossible to slice up the anagnorisis scene between Odysseus and Alcinous into such clear-cut components. The mental state of Odysseus, for instance, is entirely inaccessible to readers—and arguably to Odysseus himself—except through its expression in Odysseus's narrated actions of poorly hidden weeping. Alcinous's recognition of the stranger, similarly, is inseparable from—and in fact consists in—his responding words and actions. Lindemann's astute performative analysis of interaction relies on categories of interiority and exteriority that will prove to be more and more problematic with each successive reading in the present study, beginning with the recognition between Odysseus and Penelope (chapter 3) and culminating in the tragedy of the modern subject in Kleist's *Penthesilea* (chapter 10). In both cases, surface readings of narrative and performative language (rather than claims about deep meanings) make the ethical implications clear. In literature as in life, I argue, philology is an inescapable medium of morality.

A related supposition about the accordance between interior and exterior states is at work in Velleman's system. The primary difference between Velleman's explanation of these scenes of weeping and my own is his assumption of the possibility and desideratum of "authenticity."

Despite all the careful skepticism of his limited metaethics, Velleman still works within a framework in which he determines between authentic and inauthentic performance. It presumes a "true" interior self that either successfully expresses its internal states or fails to do so. Such a determination would spell the felicitous end of the action of recognition. If, however, interpersonal recognition consists in change that resists closure, then authenticity is an unattainable (if compulsory) desire. Anagnorisis, recall, is a change that can only be actualized in its character as potency. The unavoidable potentiality of interpersonal knowledge gives the lie to the desire for authenticity in modern ethics. In a behavioral universe that consists of the endless feedback loop of performance, the question of authentic versus insincere behavior becomes ultimately beside the point. In the next chapter, Penelope will be my guide in navigating the strange new world of this indeterminate legibility of other people.

CHAPTER THREE

"From Ignorance to Knowledge"

Penelope's Poetological Epistemology

ONE OF THE most perplexing problems in Homeric scholarship is "the Penelope question." When exactly, between the arrival of the disguised beggar at her doorstep (book 17) and her public embrace of him as husband (book 23), does Penelope suspect the identity of the stranger? Is there a gap between Penelope's recognition of Odysseus and her acknowledgment of him? The poem's reticence on this point has led to contentious debate and wildly different interpretations of Penelope's character. The present chapter will argue that the drawn-out illegibility of Penelope's anagnorisis is emblematic of the kind of knowledge that recognition between people entails. Further, the hermeneutical testing to which Penelope subjects her husband demonstrates the poetological[1] sensibility of interpersonal recognition. In fact, Penelope's actions construe a critique of Aristotle's taxonomy of recognition. Crucially, Penelope's epistemology is a function of poetics.

PENELOPEAN EPISTEMOLOGY (READING PENELOPE)

The question of what Penelope knows when has fascinated readers of Homer since antiquity.[2] It is one of the few controversies of classical scholarship that seems able to capture the popular imagination. As recently as 2011, an entire special issue of *College Literature* was dedicated to competing articles debating the question from opposing sides.[3] Scholars tend to take very strong positions about the question, and they fall roughly into four stances: Penelope recognizes Odysseus before or during their colloquy in book 19; she does not know him until the test of the bed in book 23; she suspects or subconsciously intuits his identity at some intermediate point; or the indeterminacy of her knowledge is subordinate to the narrative construction of the epic plot.[4] In recent decades, proponents of all these positions have claimed the mantle of feminism for their cause. They all rely on prior assumptions about Penelope's character and human nature to make their points.

Advocates of early recognition claim that to think otherwise amounts to a bias against female intelligence. Only if Penelope knows the beggar to be Odysseus during their long interview during book 19, they argue, can the two be seen in an equal partnership (or as equal as the social norms of archaic Greece allowed). For them, Penelope's decision to hold the test of the bow (*Od*, 19.572) is evidence that she has discerned her husband's identity and given him the brilliant means to defeat the suitors. They see these two masters of cunning and deception conniving together to secure the restoration of Odysseus's household. To assume that Penelope is blind to the clues of the beggar's identity, they claim, is to deny her agency, intellect, and virtue.[5] All these readings pivot around a recognition of Penelope's character as strong, insightful, and at least as resourceful as her husband. Recognition within the text is doubled by the reader from without and is an inevitable aspect of reading.

Other scholars make use of twentieth-century psychology to posit subconscious, intuitive, or repressed intimations of recognition for Penelope. Their glosses of Homer's text read almost like modernist novels with deep readings of Penelope's layered psyche. Despite this sophisticated (if perhaps anachronistic) psychological understanding, however, these critics still argue against early recognition from a traditional notion of literary character. Though circular, arguments based on the critic's prior convictions about Penelope's character are usually reserved for the rhetorically effective final punch: "Finally, Penelope's behavior in Harsh's interpretation is rather out of character."[6] These scholars' positive claims are also based in ad hominem (or rather *ad feminam*) judgments about the queen. Anne Amory, for instance, argues that "the true explanation of Penelope's behavior in Book Nineteen surely lies in the particular kind of perception which is characteristic of her." She sees Penelope as thinking "intuitively rather than rationally," and all of her subsequent textual arguments for understanding Penelope's recognition of her husband as "subconscious" derive from this prior recognition on her part as reader of who Penelope is.[7] These readings also rely on the characterization of intuition as a specifically feminine kind of mentality.[8] Though these critics, writing from the sixties to the eighties, present this instinct as a positive representation of women, it runs the risk of chauvinistically pigeonholing female knowledge as a kind of irrational feminine mystique.

The most persuasive proponents of late recognition, meanwhile, similarly use character judgments to make their case. Sheila Murnaghan's cogently and carefully argued rejection of both early recognition and Amory's "subconscious" knowledge, despite painstaking and thorough array of textual evidence, ultimately relies on her assessment of Penelope's character and the way she wants readers to view the heroine. She dislikes Amory's reading because it makes Penelope too weak: "It must be recognized that that characterization does diminish Penelope in terms of the most overt values of the *Odyssey*, for it denies her the kind of intelligence that is expressed in the exercise of *mētis*."[9] If, on the other hand, we imagine that Penelope knows who Odysseus is right away, Murnaghan counters that she would then gain too much control over her situation and destiny for readers to have the proper amount of compassion for the plight of her circumstances both individually as Odysseus's wife and generally as a woman in Homeric society: "What is lost in this . . . interpretation is the poem's awareness of Penelope as a victim first of her social situation, in which the role she chooses for herself—faithful wife of a man who is absent—is an impossible one, and further of her husband's defensive response to that situation, which serves to reinforce and perpetuate it."[10] Murnaghan argues eloquently for the poem's sensitivity to Penelope's untenable situation. Making her equal to Odysseus in knowledge would destroy the grounds for sympathy in her character.

If Murnaghan rejects early recognition because it threatens the audience's pity for Penelope, Helene Foley does so to preserve their admiration for her. Foley applies Aristotelian categories of moral choice to Penelope's situation (under the assumption of a late recognition) so as to see in her a model of ethical responsibility: "From this perspective, Penelope's choice [of setting the contest of the bow] is less dubious or irrational than tragic (by Aristotle's standards): the dilemma of a good person attempting to act correctly without full, in this case, critical knowledge of the circumstances (Odysseus' identity and fate)."[11] For Foley, to posit an early recognition is to put her in full control and knowledge of all her circumstances and hence to deprive her of the conditions of Aristotelian heroism. Like the proponents of early recognition, she wants Penelope to be strong, intelligent, and admirable; she only disagrees about what those character attributes entail.

Another strand of scholarship takes the Penelope question as an invitation to narrative theory. For one thing, most arguments against early recognition base their reasoning on assumptions not only about Penelope's character but also about Homeric storytelling. Scholars who "take Penelope at her word"[12] point out that there is no direct textual support for Penelope recognizing Odysseus before she says so in book 23 (i.e., nowhere does the narrator *say* that Penelope suspects Odysseus's identity). This argument implicitly buys into Erich Auerbach's famous judgment about Homeric style (in contrast to that of biblical literature) that Homer "conceals nothing"—that everything the characters think and experience is clearly and openly depicted by the narrative voice.[13] A disinclination to see Penelope as disguising her knowledge goes hand in hand with a desire for Homer to be straightforward and transparent.

Scholars for whom the *Odyssey* is a work of great narrative complexity and sophistication, in contrast, make Penelope's deviousness the principal showcase for their argument.[14] Marylin Katz, for instance, sees the indeterminacy of Penelope's character as integral to the narrative construction of the text. Penelope's radical unknowability becomes "a better representative of the spirit that animates the *Odyssey* than Odysseus even—a spirit of indeterminacy affecting both character identity and narrative form, and expressed principally as a refusal of closure, a persistence of uncertainty."[15] She goes so far as to draw universal conclusions about the instability of human subjectivity and reality based on her insightful observations about the narrative ambiguity of Penelope's recognition.[16] Lillian Doherty, meanwhile, marshals this same "openness" of the text in the service of a feminist interpretation that valorizes Penelope's circumspect navigation of the social constraints of her situation.[17] Her character's long evasion of interpretation is an act of resistance to the "ideological norms" and "androcentric values" that institute these constraints in the first place.[18] Penelope ultimately acquiescences to these norms, however, by accepting Odysseus as her returned husband. This narrative closure reaffirms patriarchal hierarchies and points to the limits of resistance. For both of these astute scholars, Penelope's textual performance ends up confirming positions they already hold. For Katz, Penelope's contradictions are deconstructive proof of the illusory fiction of the autonomous subject.[19] For Doherty, Penelope simultaneously challenges the prevailing ideology of gender norms and demonstrates the insidious strength of hegemonical social values.

As this brief survey of scholarly reactions shows, critics respond to the Penelope question according to how they perceive her character. Their interpretation of the text depends on a prior recognition of the person—as a strong and wily equal to Odysseus, as a mysterious and intuitive woman, or as an admirable or pitiable victim of social circumstances. Perhaps unsurprisingly, readers and scholars tend to discover in the pages of the *Odyssey* a Penelope who matches their understanding of the world and their desires for an ideal heroine. Whether this vision approaches the paragon of submissive, sincere feminine fidelity that many ancient and modern (male) readers apprehend[20] or whether it resembles a postmodern debunking of subjectivity, sexist authority, and naive realism, Homer's Penelope reflects the desires and intellectual tendencies of the reader.

As Georg Lichtenberg observed in the eighteenth century, "A book is a mirror."[21] But this is not to say that the *Odyssey* is fated only to be a sop for reader-response relativism. It is true that in determining when Penelope recognizes Odysseus, readers reveal a lot about themselves. Any act of reading (listening or spectating) always already implicates readers (auditors or spectators) in the demand for interpretation, with its attendant traps and dangers. But if they read carefully, Penelope is a mirror who talks back: her textual image refracts distortions and inconsistencies in whatever totalizing image one tries to impose on her. All the scholars discussed above noted passages that challenged their own positions. Though firm in their interpretive judgments, the scholars are alive to the recalcitrant provocations of the text.

The specific nature of this double bind is the main point of this chapter: in order to understand Penelope and responsibly evaluate her actions, a reader must decide when she recognizes Odysseus. Yet the text withholds any resolution of this question. The Homeric Penelope simultaneously refuses final certitude about the timing of her recognition *and* requires readers to determine it. Penelope both evades and demands interpretation. Hence her character is emblematic of the kind of knowledge in which interpersonal recognition consists. It is supposedly a change from ignorance to knowledge, but this change (as diagnosed in the preceding chapter) can never fully arrive at actuality except in its virtue *as potential*. Knowledge between people is always provisional but must be treated as complete in order for individuals to act. Interpretation is a continuous process, but circumstances require action as if it were fulfilled. This central feature of recognition in its double aspect of knowing and doing—an engine of hermeneutic circular motion that paradoxically propels forward—is what I am calling Penelopean epistemology.

This fate of recognition is multiplied within the *Odyssey* and replicated for its external audience. By allowing her actions to be interpreted in both ways, the poem's refusal to confirm or deny Penelope's early recognition leaves readers in the same position of judgment about her as Odysseus.[22] Should he see Penelope's decision to hold the contest of the bow as a sad capitulation to the demands of the suitors or as a brilliant stratagem she contrives in secret collusion with his aims?[23] In forcing listeners to recognize Penelope, the poem furthermore requires that they recognize the performance of recognition as such.[24] At what point do Penelope's actions begin to constitute a reenactment of the knowledge of who Odysseus is? In leaving this question unanswerable while simultaneously demanding an answer, the poem recreates the inevitable gap between performer and audience in any act of recognition. This claim does not simply reduce recognition to a black box model of subject-to-subject communication. Instead, anagnorisis inheres in the performative space opened up by the impossible demand for interpretation. This performance space is the best "knowledge" for which interpersonal recognition can hope.

This account of Penelopean epistemology shares similarities with some of the scholars' reactions to the Penelope question cited above, but there are also important differences. Foley's Aristotelian assessment of Penelope's tragic heroism is a formula of decisive moral action in the face of uncertain knowledge. The reader's interpretive dilemma likewise requires risky judgment of an ethical nature. But whereas Foley feels secure in positing Penelope's ignorance about Odysseus, my reading of the text refuses finality in this question. In fact, it places the reader in a position of ignorance evolving toward knowledge vis-à-vis Penelope's recognition.[25] This necessary indeterminacy resembles Katz's deconstruction of Penelope's character but without resting in resignation at the constructed illusoriness of all subjectivity. Foley's moral realism and Doherty's (and Murnaghan's) sensitivity to historical social determinations provide helpful counterweights to Katz's shrewd subversion of presence. The verses of the *Odyssey*, I contend, masterfully place listeners in the same position as Odysseus regarding the knowability of his wife's recognition, and they must participate with nearly as much input as he in the performance of its dynamic actualization. Interpretation becomes an exercise in moral imagination.

The form of this exercise is emphatically poetic. As Barbara Clayton and Gregory Nagy argue in strikingly different contexts, Penelope's weaving is the central metaphor for the composition of Homeric poetry.[26] Her character's paradoxical demand for interpretation in the face of incomprehensibility also makes Penelope a figure of hermeneutics. Hence she represents both the composition and the construal of poetry. Appropriately for the mutuality of recognition, she stands at opposite ends of the performative formula as both actor and spectator. The focus in this chapter so far has been on reading Penelope; now it turns to view Penelope reading.[27] The former operation leads to an explication of interpersonal knowledge based on the ethics involved in interpreting Penelope in Homer's text and results in a "Penelopean epistemology" of action in indeterminacy. The latter involves paying attention to the evidence of how Penelope herself interprets others. Penelope's mode of interacting with others is a poetological practice.

The resulting "Penelopean poetics" can take several forms. One promising direction is the thread Clayton follows by exploring the image of Penelope weaving and unweaving Laertes's shroud as a metaphor for the oral reenactment of rhapsodic poetry.[28] Clayton connects Penelope's deception to her artistry in order to present poetic work as a function of feminine *mētis*. Olga Levaniouk picks up a different strand in her masterful reading of book 19 of the *Odyssey*. She traces a complex web of intertextuality in the book's dialogue in order to show how Odysseus and Penelope engage in an agonistic performance of stunning subtlety and refinement. Levaniouk's Penelopean poetics amounts to a brilliant theater of self-referential myth-making.[29] Both scholars' studies are excellent models of how to learn from Penelope the art of hermeneutics. In the next section, I will study a different lesson in the same course by focusing on Penelope's means of reading others as a critique of Aristotle's taxonomy of anagnorisis.

PENELOPEAN POETICS (PENELOPE READING)

Aristotle enumerates several categories of anagnorisis in chapter 16 of the *Poetics*. The return of Odysseus supplies him with four different examples for his various classes—more than any other single myth. Noticeably absent from the catalog of examples, however, is the one that provides for the greatest drama and interest in Homer's epic: the long, drawn-out reunion of Penelope with Odysseus. This blatant omission underscores the difficulty of pinning down the timing of Penelope's recognition: without deciding when she knows her husband, it is impossible to assign her anagnorisis to one of Aristotle's classes. In fact, in the course of her extended testing of the beggar, Penelope employs all the means listed by Aristotle in his catalog of recognitions, almost as if the *Poetics* were a checklist. It is illuminating to consider Aristotle's categories in light of Penelope's glosses. The use to which she puts them can be read as an astute commentary on his classes of recognition. Penelope, with her very practical concern, sometimes shares his literary evaluations of the various types. Yet her actions offer a corrective taxonomy of anagnorisis by combining the circumspect care of philology with the creative daring of hermeneutics.

Chapter 16 raises more problems than it clarifies. Aristotle identifies five (or six, depending on how one counts) kinds of anagnorisis: recognition by sign, by the poet's invention, by memory, by reasoning, (by misreasoning), and out of the action of the story. To begin with, there is a basic mismatch between these types: some refer to the means by which characters within the story recognize one another (by sign, by memory, by reasoning), some to the author's techniques in plot construction (by the poet's contrivance, out of the events of the story), and one to the audience's reaction (by misreasoning). Any taxonomy based on such incommensurable categories appears hopelessly flawed. It is no wonder that commentators have had trouble with chapter 16. As Stephen Halliwell writes, after enumerating a different set of problems with the categories, "One is left with the impression that the chapter is the merest jotting of points which have not been adequately sifted."[30]

Part of the trouble comes from the convolution of qualitative and quantitative distinctions. Within the first ten lines of the chapter, the adjective *artless* (*atekhnos*) appears three times, inflected in quick succession in its superlative, comparative, and absolute forms. This trajectory from least artful to less artful to artless not only shows how inextricable Aristotle's prescriptive comments are from his descriptive analysis but also reveals artistry (*tekhnē*) as something specifically important for recognition. It is a matter of not merely passive perception but the skillful employment of intellect and action. Again, there is no interpersonal knowledge for Aristotle without a performative manifestation. This is true no less for ethical interactions between people than for poets constructing their plots.

Artistry is equally important to Penelope, master weaver and figure of the poet at work. To begin, toward the end of the epic, after the slaughter of the suitors has rendered further deception unnecessary, Odysseus finally sends Eurycleia up to announce his arrival to Penelope. He is revealing himself in the manner of the second type of recognition described by Aristotle. Such bare announcements are decreed by the whim of the poet, not necessitated by plot or mediated by tokens or proofs, and are therefore *atekhnoi* (inartistic).[31] As if in agreement with Aristotle's assessment, Penelope refuses to accept the claims of the stranger. After twenty years of abandonment, Penelope demands more from her husband than mere words.

Nor does she set much store by what Aristotle calls the "least artistic" means of anagnorisis, recognition by signs. This class of anagnorisis for Aristotle is limited to congenital marks or physical objects.[32] His prime example is Odysseus's scar, which Penelope never even bothers to inspect. It is the servants—the old nurse and herdsmen—who must content themselves with this base form of recognition. When Eurycleia tries to convince Penelope to acknowledge Odysseus, she tells her mistress about the scar: "But here is another proof (*sēma*: sign) that is very clear" (*Od*, 23.73). Penelope remains unconvinced, suggesting that a god could have faked such a thing. She shares Aristotle's disdain for mere corporeal features as a means of ascertaining identity. By extrapolation, modern fingerprints and DNA tests would be equally unsatisfactory. For Penelope, recognition must take place in performative interaction.

But the clear overlap between Penelope's judgments and Aristotle's ends with these inartistic modes of recognition. For one thing, Penelope's language levels a critique at the distinctions Aristotle draws. Her final test of Odysseus, which warrants her ultimate acknowledgment of him as her husband, involves intimate knowledge that only the two old lovers share. Odysseus had built their marital bed out of the trunk of a rooted tree. When Penelope slyly instructs her servant to go move this bed, Odysseus is enraged. She thus tricks him into revealing how precious the remembrance of their shared love is to him. This bed test would most accurately fit the class of recognition Aristotle calls "by memory." Yet Penelope twice refers to the memory proof as signs (*sēmata*; *Od*, 23.109, 206). This explicit designation underlines a further problem with the classes of recognition in the *Poetics*. Not only are some types incommensurate with others, but even the matching classifications do not correspond to fundamental divisions, as Aristotle's own treatise on *Categories* would demand. In the examples of recognition by memory and by reasoning, characters figure out others' identities based on outward clues. The locks and footprints of Orestes function as signs for Electra no less than the tears of Odysseus for Alcinous. These two types of recognition, by reasoning and by memory, respectively, are easily reducible to the more basic class, by signs. The remaining categories are also susceptible to this reduction. The language used by characters who announce their identities in the second type (by the poet's contrivance) is composed of signs. Even in the final type (out of the action), events themselves function as signs. Aristotle's example of Iphigenia giving the letter to her brother is a perfect case in point. As diagnosed in this book's first chapter, *all* recognition is mediated through signs, which would seem to make all Aristotle's categories here redundant.

What's worse, each of Aristotle's five main "types" are involved in every act of recognition he cites. In addition to signs (type 1), what recognition does *not* include verbal statements (type 2), memory (type 3), reasoning (type 4), and action (type 5)? Even Eurycleia's recognition of Odysseus, which Aristotle adduces as an example of anagnorisis by signs, could not take place without the other types: while the scar the nurse discovers is indeed a sign (1) of Odysseus's identity, it is at once accompanied by confirming speech (2). Without memory (3) and reasoning (4), no sign can function (and indeed the long digression of the backstory as well as Eurycleia's moving emotional reaction accentuate the importance of memory to this scene). Finally, the swift actions of Odysseus in throttling the nurse and of Eurycleia in agreeing to keep mum enact a restoration of their relations that comes directly out of the necessary actions of the plot (5). Recognition only becomes manifest in the actions characters take. Not only can all five of Aristotle's categories be reduced to one, but every act of recognition involves all five.

Though Penelope's word choice invites this logical conclusion, she adds some refined twists to her reading of signs. In book 19, she inquires of the Cretan stranger, who claims to have once met Odysseus, how her husband was attired. As with the bed, Penelope explicitly refers to this evidence as signs (*sēmata*; *Od*, 19.250). The request is ridiculous, of course: no one would be able to recall the clothes of an acquaintance one knew for twelve days two full decades ago.[33] Odysseus describes his own attire, however, with minute and improbable accuracy, and the answer cuts her to the quick. The sartorial signs by which Penelope tests the veracity of her visitor are spun of lies warped on a woof of truth that have been rotting at the bottom of the Mediterranean for years. The importance of this test, however, does not lie merely in its truth quotient—not in the bare fact that the stranger proves his knowledge of information that only Odysseus could realistically know—but more acutely in the personal significance of the objects he chooses to describe. Every article of clothing Odysseus details was a gift from Penelope's hands. They are special for the shared memories that they invoke.

Recognition by memory may not be a strictly logical category of anagnorisis per se, but it can helpfully be construed as a specific kind of *sign*. The signs through which recognition is inevitably performed are constructed in different contexts, trigger different reactions, and function in different ways. A more careful taxonomy would base types of recognition on the nature and context of the signs through which it comes about. Penelope thus offers a corrective for Aristotle's mismatched categories by first insisting on what they all have in common: recognitions occur through signs (*sēmata*). Yet the brief references to Penelope's performance and interpretation of signs thus far can already initiate a more stringent categorization of recognition's semiotic mediality. First, there are signs that attempt direct communication of information (e.g., "I am Odysseus!"), which do not much impress either Penelope or Aristotle. Second, there are the physical signs of the body or objects (e.g., "Here is my scar!"), which Aristotle and Penelope also disparage. Signs used in reasoning (e.g., "Only Odysseus can bend the bow; the stranger bends the bow—therefore, he must be Odysseus") and those required for action (e.g., the active collusion necessary for Odysseus's disguise and vengeful slaughter of the suitors) are appreciated by both thinkers. Aristotle calls the latter the "best" and the former the "second best" kind of recognition. Penelope, however, prefers the only class of signs to which Aristotle does not assign a qualitative modifier: those that evoke memories and scenes of emotion (e.g., "Go move our bed!"). She corrects the basis of categorization and rearranges the qualitative ordering of recognition. For Penelope, at least, the most important test of recognition is the one "through memory": not simply a confirmation of personal identity but a performance displaying that she and her lover still share strong feelings about the things most important to them both. Like birthmarks, necklaces, and scars, the signs of memory participate in a semiotic system of relations. Penelope's language here upbraids the sloppy logic of Aristotle's categories, but nevertheless the signs that prick remembrance *mean differently* than those that confirm identity.

The main feature that differentiates Penelope's cache of signs from those of other characters is the intimacy of the common memories wrapped around them. Her final test of Odysseus before running into his arms in unguarded joy involves the most private object the two lovers share: their bed. It is not enough that Odysseus has demonstrated his unique strength with Penelope's test of the bow or proven his same old mettle and ingenuity in battle with the suitors. He must also show that the personal nature of the bond between them is still intact. Penelope provokes him with a wry reminder of that edifice to their love that he erected with his own strong but gentle hands, and his outburst at the notion of its having been disturbed is exactly the proof she needs to reward him with her acknowledging embrace. This parallels Penelope's first probe for signs in book 19, where the physical reaction comes in the form of her own tears. This time, she triggers her husband's performed rage with the memory she suggests and, finally confident of his love, falls into his arms.

The tests share three important features. First, they are both provoked by objects of art. In the bed test, Odysseus was the craftsman; in the garb test, Penelope was the artist. The text details at great length the craftsmanship of these designs (*Od*, 19.224–240; 23.183–204). In fact, the passages are not bare descriptions of the objects but rather emphasize the artists' actions in creating them and the observers' reactions to them.[34] In the performance of recognition, both parties are equally artists and critics, authors and interpreters. Second, the two signs are not merely important for their artistic value; they were both fashioned as gifts for the spouse. In the Homeric world, social relations were largely functions of gift-giving.[35] Usually, a character's importance was measured by his largesse in the richness of materials and quantity of tribute. Rarely was the giver also the artisan. Penelope raises the stakes of this gift economy by targeting ones that were created by the giver for the recipient.

Third, both tests bring about dramatic emotional displays. In effect, these signs of memory facilitate recognition by staging a *scene* of passion. The resulting interactions are amenable to Aristotle's explanations of memory and emotion. As with his definition of recognition, it is surprising for modern readers how little interiority is at work in Aristotle's description of memory (*P*, 16, 1454b, 35).[36] Aristotle remarks only on the outward mechanisms of this third class of recognition: something triggers a memory that arouses a feeling that produces a physical reaction that gives someone away. Like the emotions it puts in play, memory is an interactive scene. As observed in the preceding chapter, Aristotle points to the example of Odysseus in Alcinous's hall, where the hero is induced into sad reveries by the minstrel's songs of the Trojan War. Odysseus's memories cause him to weep, and the *outward sign* of tears betrays his true identity to his host. Recognition by memory works through signs employed on a very specific stage of interrelations. It can thus best be understood as performance with the analytical tools offered in the previous chapter. Penelope's nostalgic tears, no less than Odysseus's steely eyes, are part of the drama of recognition the two enact whether they are playing the roles of host and guest (book 19) or husband and wife (book 23). Both before *and* after Penelope's public acknowledgment of Odysseus, the two are at work in an interactive play of changing knowledge about one another. As the next chapter will show, this necessarily incomplete epistemology of recognition invites a radical ethics of friendship.

Memory is not the only type of sign that Penelope artfully exploits. The fourth kind of recognition Aristotle mentions is by inference or by reasoning: *ek sullogismou*. What with all the portentous dreams, the reports of travelers, and the interpretations of augurs, Penelope has many clues about Odysseus's impending return. She is able to put two and two together from the moment she hears the commotion caused by the arrival of the stranger in her home and contrives an interview with him far beyond the bounds of intimacy expected between beggars and their female hosts (*Od*, 17.528–588). The lady who shares a whole stock of *-phrōn* (-minded, thoughtful) epithets with her wily husband will hardly fail to reason through the evidence before her. Soon after she learns about the presence of the drifter in her halls, she sends him an invitation to her private chambers, a surprising offer of trust and privacy. Even more shocking is the beggar's refusal to take her up on the invitation, as Penelope remarks (*Od*, 17.576–578). The daring prudence and savvy restraint displayed in the mendicant's admonishment of his host's generosity are the first signs that make Penelope wonder about the identity of her guest before she even lays eyes on him.

At the same time, however, neither will she let any amount of circumstantial evidence convince her on its own. Her hopes have been dashed too often before. The example Aristotle provides for recognition by inference is Aeschylus's famous scene from the *Libation Bearers* in which Electra reasons out Orestes's presence by the similarity of a lock of hair and footsteps to her own curls and feet. This kind of improbable but ultimately vindicated reasoning became a common topos in Greek tragedy and comedy. Euripides pokes fun at the far-fetchedness of such logic in his *Electra*, as does the Euripides character in Aristophanes's *Frogs*. Homer almost seems to be sharing in the joke several centuries in advance when Penelope stops herself from giving away too much while telling the nurse to wash the stranger's feet:

> ἀλλ᾽ ἄγε νῦν ἀνστᾶσα, περίφρων Εὐρύκλεια,
> νίψον σοῖο ἄνακτος ὁμήλικα: καί που Ὀδυσσεὺς
> ἤδη τοιόσδ᾽ ἐστὶ πόδας τοιόσδε τε χεῖρας: (*Od*, 19.357–359)

(But come now, stand up, circumspect Eurycleia,
wash your lord's—age-match. Odysseus probably
has such feet and such hands now.)[37]

One can almost hear the gulp a good rhapsode would have placed here at the line's caesura between "lord's" and "age-match." After the genitive *soio anaktos*, one naturally expects *podas*: "your lord's feet." By uttering *homēlika* (of like age) instead, Penelope saves herself at the last second from slipping up and revealing too much. Fitzgerald's translation makes the incident even more explicit:

bathe, bathe your master. I almost said,
for they are of an age, and now Odysseus'
feet and hands would be enseamed like his.[38]

The text does not reveal whether the irony here is Penelope's or Homer's. If the former, Penelope cannot reveal her real reasons for mistaking the beggar for her husband (namely, that she suspects he *is* her husband), and so she grasps midsentence for the flimsiest alternative: since the guest is the same age as Odysseus, his limbs must be similarly wrinkled. If the latter, the rhapsode crafts Penelope's speech to toy with the audience's expectations. The two options are by no means mutually exclusive. Either way, the strained logic is quite in the same vein of humor as Euripides's much later jokes about the implausible tropes of dramatic recognition. In staging anagnorisis by reasoning as a comic bit, Penelope's language both celebrates and cautions against the theatricality of syllogistic logic.

Homer in this scene also makes use of what Aristotle calls a "composite" kind of recognition, "from a false inference (*paralogismos*) of the audience" (*P*, 16, 1455a, 12–16). Aristotle expands cryptically on this category of misreasoning later, when he praises Homer as the master liar and cites the "washing scene" as an example (*P*, 24, 1460a, 25). Appropriately enough, there is no way to know whose recognition he is referring to here: Penelope's, Eurycleia's, or the audience's. Most commentators assume Penelope to be guilty of paralogism by believing the lying tale of the beggar.[39] As seen above, this requires a previous presumption of Penelope's ignorance. But two details speak against this interpretation. First, if *Homer* is praised as the master liar, why would Odysseus's supposed duping of Penelope be the best example? Recall that in the catalog of anagnorisis, paralogism was assigned to the audience (*tou theatrou*; *P*, 16, 1455a, 13). Why assume that

Aristotle suddenly turns back to two *internal* characters in the *Odyssey* to explain a phenomenon of Homer's paralogistic artistry on *external* readers?

Second, Aristotle refers specifically to the *washing scene*, which the beggar's tale precedes. If the poet Homer is the perpetrator of deception here, then it is precisely the nurse's recognition of Odysseus that invites the audience to reason falsely in this scene. Shortly after Penelope directs her to wash her "master's" feet, Eurycleia discovers the telltale scar. Listeners may well infer that the game is up. Odysseus's identity will now be publicly revealed to Penelope. In the same moment, Homer indulges in a seventy-line interlude describing Odysseus's birth and the hunting trip where he obtained the scar, which serves to heighten the suspense and to draw out the time that the audience must labor under the expectations of its false inference.[40] Penelope's actions during this narrative digression are telling. After discerning Odysseus's identity, Eurycleia

> turned her eye toward Penelope, wishing
> to indicate to her her beloved husband's presence,
> but Penelope was not able to look that way, or perceive him,
> since Athena turned aside her perception. (*Od*, 19.476–479)

Whereas in the caesura cited above (*Od*, 19.357) Penelope is complicit in encouraging paralogism, here she is prevented from perceiving the evidence that would transform uncertain inference to certain deduction.[41] The text remains painstakingly ambiguous about what Penelope knows or guesses about the stranger's identity at every stage. Here, divine interference is required to protect the narrative indeterminacy of Penelope's knowledge. By turning away Penelope's perception, Athena preserves both the audience's ignorance about Penelope's suspicions and the uncertainty out of which Penelope must act in order to attain heroic status.[42] It is directly after pointedly *not* being privy to this confirmation of the stranger's identity that Penelope suggests the test of the bow, the stratagem by which Odysseus will be able to regain control of his household.

In fact, Penelope's position in the text here clarifies one of the interpretative difficulties in Aristotle's chapter 16. It is unclear whether recognition by *mis*reasoning (para*logismos*) is meant to be an independent type or a subcategory of recognition by reasoning (sul*logismos*). Either way, the two are necessarily opposed to each other for Aristotle. The Greek prefixes specify this opposition: reasoning *with* (*sun-*) versus reasoning *apart* (*para-*). Penelope, in contrast, reveals how reasoning and misreasoning are inevitably interlaced. As Athena's intervention emphasizes, we are always condemned to reason *with* when we are *apart*: presence is imbricated by absence; syllogism can only operate from a position of paralogism. No one can ever command all the facts of a situation or escape the necessity of reacting despite ignorance. People must reason, choose, and act, no matter how dire the lack of certainty.

Precisely by amplifying the ambiguous relation between reasoning and misreasoning in recognition, Homer's Penelope is emblematic of the conditions of interpersonal knowledge. She is also a metaphor for the composition of Homeric poetry. These two figurations—Penelope as knower of people and as poet—are related. Storytelling is the art of paralogism, and narration is absolutely central to recognition. As Terence Cave noted, "Paralogism and anagnorisis seem to be hand in glove."[43] The previous chapter established the narrative dimensions of interpersonal recognition as performance. This chapter observes how Penelope demonstrates this brand of paralogistic knowledge at work.

Penelope is a master practitioner of storytelling and interpretation. In fact, she practices the latter by way of the former: not only does she extract and evaluate stories from the stranger, but Penelope tells her own stories as hermeneutical tools to test and measure him as well. The interview with the beggar in book 19 is a beautiful tapestry of such tales and countertales.[44] Penelope carefully gauges the stranger's reactions to the narration of her dream, for instance, as a final test before declaring that she will announce the bow contest. Here she explicitly demands an interpretation (*Od*, 19.535), but Odysseus's judgments, implicit in his responses to every story she tells, figure in her own evaluations of the man before her and determine how she will stage the next volley of narration. The act, finally, that solidifies Penelope's public acknowledgment of Odysseus as her husband is a supernaturally extended night of mutual storytelling. Athena must again intervene, in fact, to make the nighttime accommodate all that they have to tell one another (*Od*, 23.241–246). Paralogism and syllogism, fiction and truth, and narration and interpretation are all woven together as integral fibers of the activity of recognition.

This imbrication between Aristotle's categories of reasoning and misreasoning builds a bridge to his final class of recognition. The best anagnorisis, he declares, arises "out of the actions themselves" (*ex autōn tōn pragmatōn*; *P*, 16, 1455a, 17). Aristotle praises stories constructed so that the recognition comes about through the likely but shocking proceedings of the plot. The messenger naturally wants to make Oedipus happy, but his news forces the tragic realization of his parentage. Iphigenia naturally wants to send word to her brother and astonishingly puts the letter directly into his hands. One puzzle about this category is that whereas the previous types of recognition depended on the intelligence, actions, and choices of the characters within the story, this class seems to make the *poet* the agent of recognition and to render the characters passive puppets yanked around on the strings of plot. Oedipus's self-knowledge depends on the timing of the messenger's arrival; Iphigenia's discovery of her brother is at the mercy of postal custom. Anagnorisis ceases to be a means by which the audience can learn about the character of literary figures through the ways they come to know one another and becomes merely a clever plot device.

Penelope, however, shows how this class can also be construed as the character usurping the agency of the author. By announcing the test of the bow among the suitors, Penelope provides Odysseus with a ready-made scheme for a recognition that comes "out of the actions themselves." This scene could well have warmed Aristotle's heart, for it proceeds directly out of the natural probabilities of the plot, just as he demands. What is more likely than that Penelope should wish to select the strongest suitor, the one most like her old husband? The ruse works beautifully as a test because it not only requires that Odysseus be as powerful and as skilled an archer as once he was but also assays his wiliness, courage, and daring to apprehend and seize the opportunity presented by Penelope's proposal. If Odysseus comes up with the stratagem that allows the Greeks to take Troy, Penelope invents the scheme that allows Odysseus to take Ithaca. It is thus another proof of the extent to which this amazing couple deserves one another. Even if for Penelope's personal acknowledgment of her husband the test of memory looms larger, she is the one who furnishes the epic with Aristotle's "best recognition of all" (*pasōn beltistē anagnōrisis*), the central plot device by which Odysseus makes known his identity to his enemies and reclaims from them his household. In a very real way, Penelope is the author of the *Odyssey*'s happy ending.

Penelope's seizing of the authorial reins in turn allows a reappraisal of the Oedipus and Iphigenia cases. The messenger never would have arrived in Thebes with the devastating news of Oedipus's birth if the king had not relentlessly been seeking to learn. It is Oedipus's own choices and actions that bring the messenger to his gates. Iphigenia would never have had occasion to send her brother a message if she had not chosen to free one of the Greek prisoners in the first place. She creates the circumstances for the surprising unfolding of events by thinking quickly and acting daringly to begin with. Like Penelope, Iphigenia and Oedipus are agents of the actions out of which their recognitions transpire. Despite Aristotle's vaunted preference of plot over character, the two elements of tragedy and epic are causally and logically interdependent. Halliwell is absolutely correct to emphasize Aristotle's insistence on the primacy of action: "Reversal and recognition are features of the action of the play." Yet when he goes on to conclude that they therefore "offer only minimal opportunities for characterization in Aristotle's sense,"[45] he misses the potential for recognition to result directly from ethical actions. It is precisely in a figure's choices and deeds that her character is revealed. Since the best recognitions come out of events that (in the best stories) are the consequences of moral deliberation and behavior, they facilitate not only discoveries between characters within a story but also revelations about character to an outside audience.

In sum, Penelope's glosses on the six means of recognition enumerated by Aristotle amount to a collection of ways to deal with the conditions of interpersonal human knowledge. The first part of this chapter compared readings of Penelope in order to outline those conditions: the knowledge of others to which recognition aspires is necessarily incomplete, precarious, and indeterminate. The second part of this chapter observed Penelope reading others. Her hermeneutical techniques manage to navigate the unavoidable uncertainties of recognition with considerable aplomb. She is hyperaware of the ways that knowledge between people manifests in the mutual performance of signs. Linguistic signs that merely announce claims of identity are suspect, as are markers of physical identity like scars and tokens. She gives careful weight to signs that provoke memories, resulting in scenes of shared emotion. As a skilled teller and interpreter of identity narratives, she is alive to the casuistry of reason and the artistry of fiction. Finally, her manipulation of events and circumstances in the choices and actions that shape life with others make her a formidable coauthor of selfhood. These are the practices of poets and readers. Penelope's answer to the hermeneutic circle of recognition is to insist on the strictures of philology.

In his letter about the liberal arts, Seneca lists some of the many things philologists seem to argue over endlessly and fruitlessly:

> Why try to discover whether Penelope was a pattern of virtue (*pudica*), or whether she had the laugh of her contemporaries? Or whether she suspected that the man in her presence was Ulysses,

> before she knew it was he? Teach me rather what virtue (*pudicitia*) is, and how great a good we have in it, and whether it is situated in the body or in the soul.[46]

Seneca thinks a liberal education should consist in learning the virtues important for the good life rather than worrying over trivial questions such as when Penelope knows Odysseus. This chapter has argued, however, that the *Odyssey* displays the complex action of recognition in such a way that the Penelope question can be central to an investigation into knowledge and virtue. Penelope's example is strikingly instructive about the nature of human relations and the inescapable dangers of interpretation. Penelope can teach as much if not more than Plato or Aristotle about navigating the treacherous seas into which the circumstances of life and society throw us. Aristotle stresses the importance of the operation of recognition by placing it alongside peripeteia as one of the two most moving catalysts in the plots of literary texts. The *Odyssey* emphasizes recognition as an indispensable tool in life, not merely in art, and provides admirable models of respect for the artful workings of two canny performers finding a necessarily uncanny home again in each other.

Penelope's poetic sensibilities are a commendable answer to the indeterminacy of interpersonal knowledge that, as the previous chapter showed, is consigned to change by its contradictory impulses to action under the condition of activity. This chapter has adumbrated the hermeneutical uncertainty of knowledge in recognition; the next will take up the ethical consequences of this Penelopean epistemology. Despite Seneca's warnings to the contrary, philological attention to the Penelope question turns out to be the best guide to elucidating the contentious moral virtue of friendship.

CHAPTER FOUR

"Into Friendship or Enmity"

An Ethics of Authentic Deception

RECOGNITION AS DESCRIBED so far comprises strange paradoxes. It is a change that aspires to complete action though an ongoing activity (chapter 2), involves Others who long for an impossible Same (chapter 1), and includes knowledge that demands interpretation yet insists on indeterminacy (chapter 3). What kind of relationship might such a fraught operation bring about? The present chapter will address this question. Aristotle's definition of anagnorisis, which provided the impetus for the contradictions explored above, continues with the phrase "either into friendship (*philia*) or into enmity (*ekhthra*)" (*P*, 11, 1452a, 30). How can anything like friendship arise from the flux and inscrutability intrinsic to recognition as described above? In fact, it will become clear that the relationship of Penelope and Odysseus provides a model for an ethics of friendship that emerges out of precisely the performative brand of recognition under investigation.

Before interrogating the nature of friendship and enmity, however, the grammar of Aristotle's sentence poses a problem.

> ἀναγνώρισις δέ, . . . ἐξ ἀγνοίας εἰς γνῶσιν μεταβολή, ἢ εἰς φιλίαν ἢ εἰς ἔχθραν (*P*, 11, 1452a, 29–31)

(a) Recognition is a change:
(b) from ignorance into knowledge;
(c) into either friendship or enmity.

Does this latter disjunctive prepositional phrase (c) modify change (a) or knowledge (b)? Grammar alone does not answer this question, yet the difference is critical. Does recognition *bring about* friendship/enmity, or does it *consist in* the transition to one or the other? In other words, is the *metabolē* (change) of recognition two-pronged (into knowledge *and* friendship/enmity), or are the social relationships dependent on knowledge? Most translators opt for the latter interpretation by supplying a participle to specify the subordination of friendship/enmity to knowledge: "Recognition . . . is a change from ignorance to knowledge *resulting in* either friendship or enmity."[1] Here, the ethical relation is a result of coming to know. Few translators are willing to let stand the syntactic ambiguity present in the Greek.[2] Is knowledge logically prior to the practices of human sociability, or is knowing coeval with the activities of friendship and enmity? This question, forced by the syntax of Aristotle's definition, repeats the equivocal relationship between knowledge and virtue in Platonic ethics. It remains unanswerable in the *Poetics*, and this ambivalence feeds the understanding of interpersonal knowledge as both aorist action and imperfective activity advocated above. The contradiction at the heart of change inflects not only the working of knowledge and of ethical behavior, respectively, but even the causal relation between distinguishing friends from enemies and behaving as a friend or enemy.

The distinction between friend and enemy is absolutely central to ancient Greek morality. "To help one's friends and harm one's enemies" is the immediate answer Socrates's interlocutors give to his questions "What is virtue?"[3] and "What is justice?"[4] Although Plato challenges this common conception of morality in both dialogues in which characters trot out the familiar formula, its foundational status to Greek ethics is attested by the staggering number and variety of ways it appears in every genre of writing that has survived.[5] Even in Plato, though Socrates takes issue with the precept to harm enemies, it is clear that the philosophical enterprise is an exercise in friendship. When Socrates converses with adversaries, such as Thrasymachus or Callicles, they are inevitably stymied by aporetic ill will and resentment; only when he speaks with like-minded friends, such as Glaucon and Adeimantus, do the dialogues soar to heights of philosophical fancy. Though not unduly keen on the "harming enemies" half of the traditional bromide, Aristotle reaffirms the importance of "helping friends" to the virtuous life in the *Nicomachean Ethics*, fully one-fifth of which is devoted to *philia*. For Aristotle, the highest form of friendship is a matter of reciprocity in attaining virtue through common pursuit of the good. Recognizing friends is not only a matter of utmost importance to one's own life but also revelatory of goodness and character in others (*NE*,

1156b). Friendship is an integral part of any ancient account of morality, and it is clear that the best philosophers (friends of wisdom: *philosophia*) become such by being good friends.

In the modern world, however, friendship is problematic for moral philosophy. Kant's famous ethical conundrums, for instance, pit the demands of friendship against those of morality, and morality always wins.[6] Not only are modern conceptions of morality different, but even our notions of friendship have changed. Aristotle never expected his advice for living the good life to be applicable to all humans in all places and walks of life, but an ethics today that does not make universal claims (even if the universal claim is radical relativism) is considered parochial and invalid. Aristotle also considered the highest form of friendship to be between people united in the same virtues (*NE*, 1170ab). Friendship today, in contrast, is assumed to be a rather idiosyncratic affair. It is another's unique foibles and tics as much as—if not more than—her moral rectitude that win our friendship.[7] Thus while morality has gained in universality, friendship has become more particular. As Alexander Nehamas puts it in an excellent articulation of the problem, "Friendship . . . is a mechanism of individuality." Its "value lies [in] promot[ing] variety and differentiation." Friendship pulls "in a direction opposed to that of morality."[8]

Although the friend/enemy distinction, so central to ancient Greek morality, has largely disappeared from moral philosophy, it has not exited the stage of modern discourses. It has merely migrated from ethics to politics. The binary friend/enemy is the key decision for an influential strand of twentieth- and twenty-first-century political theorists from the Nazi jurist, Carl Schmitt, to left-leaning thinkers like Jacques Derrida and Giorgio Agamben. While the present chapter will concentrate on the ethical framing of the question as implied in Homer's *Odyssey*, its counterpart in the second part of this book (chapter 9 on Goethe's *Iphigenie*) will turn to the implications of the model sketched here for the realm of politics. For now, however, this chapter suggests that Derrida's reformulation of the moral imperative of Aristotelian friendship can provide a way beyond the impasse between friendship and morality and that Penelope's relationship with Odysseus offers an illustration of this solution at work.

Derrida's *Politics of Friendship* (1994) is a roller coaster of readings. Its twists and turns through Aristotle, Montaigne, Nietzsche, and Schmitt are replete with "ruptures" and "leaps" and "hauntings." The book, however, has remarkably little to say about what it is like to be a friend. In stark contrast to many writers on friendship (Aristotle and Nehamas, for instance),

Derrida offers few concrete examples from life or imagined thought experiments to illustrate his claims and interrogations. He is not so much interested in the lived experience of friends as in some shocking consequences of the linguistic representation of friendship theories. Every statement of Aristotle or Schmitt seems capable of signifying something aslant from what a first interpretation might suggest. If being friends with someone is at all like the experience of reading with Derrida, then it is an exhausting and anxious ordeal with constant traps, inevitable misunderstandings, and recurrent dangers.

Nevertheless, Derrida's account manages to bridge the seemingly incompatible demands of modern morality for universality and modern friendship for particularity. He does so precisely by avoiding concrete instances of friendship and dwelling instead on the underlying structural conditions necessary for friendship to be possible. For Derrida, the traditional model of friendship grounded in reciprocity and sameness requires the modern model based on dissymmetry and difference. The Greco-Roman friendship of equality is articulated in a rhetoric of bias and discrimination that prefigures the Nietzschean, crypto-Christian friendship of disparity—and vice versa.[9]

While insisting that accounts of friendship cannot escape this aporia, Derrida himself cannot help privileging the latter model. For him, the friend occupies a position of extreme asymmetry and exercises an immeasurable demand on one's responsibility.[10] This language echoes Levinas's ethics of alterity and the infinite claim of the other in the face-to-face encounter.[11] In effect, Derrida makes friendship the transcendental condition for morality as such as well as for the more limited phenomenon of politics. Friendship is a universal grounding for morality *precisely because* the friend, in the particularity of her unique otherness, commands one's hospitality, respect, and love.

In order to make this move toward an ethics of friendship as first philosophy, Derrida unmasks and then explicitly rejects Schmitt's emphasis on enmity in the friend/enemy distinction.[12] Schmitt takes the idea of the enemy to its logical extreme—a willingness to kill the Other—as the basis for politics. A truly ethical attitude, however, will take the friend as the basic value, leading to radical hospitality as the guiding principle of politics.[13] Derrida hence replaces murder with the gift as the foundation for political morality. The most powerful expression Derrida gives to this ethical maxim, however, reinscribes the friend/enemy decision back into the definition of a higher form of friendship: "To be capable of this friendship, to be able to honour in the friend the enemy he can become, is a sign of freedom."[14] This assertion ties together the ancient ethics of friendship with modern philosophy's preoccupation with freedom. It also is an ideal formula for the kind of friendship made possible by performative recognition as described in this book.

It may seem difficult to imagine how anagnorisis as glossed thus far—an inconclusive change into a radically indeterminate knowledge—could lead to any kind of desirably reliable friendship at all. Yet Derrida's formula encapsulates how this brand of recognition can marry goodwill toward the Other with respect for her autonomy. Respecting the enemy that the friend can become is precisely the way that Odysseus and Penelope approach each other during the long process of their mutual recognition in the second half of the *Odyssey*. Under the freeing cover of anonymity, they give each other space to enact any desired relationship with the old spouse, even if that should be rejection, betrayal, or neglect. This true form of mutual respect is at its highest during the interview between the stranger and the queen in book 19, when Odysseus masks his identity in order to test his wife and Penelope masks her knowledge in order to test her husband. Odysseus's disguise is crafted not only to evaluate Penelope's loyalty but also to perform *for her* his own appreciation of her suffering, prudence, and cunning. The text carefully stages Penelope's performance, moreover, so that readers are in the same position as Odysseus, who does not know whether she sees through the deception and is feigning ignorance.[15] The question is not only, Does she know? It is equally, Does he know that she knows? Or it can go further: Does she know that he knows that she knows? And the question drives even deeper: Does he know that she knows that he knows that she knows? It is a tense colloquy of recognitive brinkmanship. The entire interview can be profitably reread with yes/no answers to each question and works remarkably well as drama under all eight assumptions.

Two questions might be raised in light of the analysis of recognition offered thus far. First, does the audience share in the friendship/enmity distinction, as they do in the ambiguity of knowledge? As the preceding chapter argues, the text of the *Odyssey* brilliantly keeps all the possibilities of Penelope's cognizance alive, demanding the reader's interpretation while absolutely refusing any final confirmation. Like Odysseus, the audience is in a position of having to recognize Penelope in the face of radical indeterminacy. The reader's recognition conforms to all of the above conclusions around the definition of anagnorisis—its self-signifying nostalgia, its paradoxical change, its uncertain knowledge—up to the friendship clause. Being sympathetic toward a character does not make her one's friend. No matter how well disposed a reader may be toward Penelope or Odysseus, there is no danger of the character's enmity ever spilling over to threaten the life of the audience. Only Odysseus and Penelope themselves would suffer the consequences of one spouse's discovered hostility, and to them alone belongs the moral agency of respecting the enemy the other can become.[16]

Second, while Derrida's moral maxim for respecting the potential enemy in a friend might apply to the transitional episode of book 19, can it really account for the enduring friendship of Penelope and Odysseus beyond their accomplished reunion? The pregnant interview between beggar and queen has the aspect of an event in Derrida's understanding: it seems singular and unrepeatable. The layers of dissimulation and potency of this scene surely cannot extend into the daily and yearly ups and downs of long-term friendship. Yet Derrida's formula acknowledges the hidden tumult beneath every friendship's stolid appearance and converts what might seem a source of lamentable turpitude (the inevitable betrayals, large or trivial, that friends perpetrate) into a force for moral probity (acting in hope for friendship's promise while respecting the friend's prerogative to treachery). It depends on a structure of iteration: friends must constantly reenact the services of amity in endless variation in countless possible circumstances. Friendship, like recognition, is subject to the conditions of performance.

This book has been analyzing recognition as performance, and Derrida similarly articulates the scene of friendship into three performative "modalities." Responsibility takes on the "performativity of a prayer" in which one answers *for* a self, responds *to* another, and answers *before* an audience.[17] These three prepositions inflect the dissymmetry of the "question of response." The process of recognition between Odysseus and Penelope in the *Odyssey* affords a perfect vantage point from which to explore these three modalities that *Politics of Friendship* sketches in brief but suggestive outline. The Homeric pair offers both helpful illustrations of and challenging provocations to the dynamics involved in Derrida's scheme.

First, one must answer the other *before* a third figure, "a community of others, an institution, a court, a law."[18] The conventional distinction between recognition and acknowledgment in Penelope's anagnorisis of Odysseus at first seems to provide a clear and simple example of this dimension of response. Her recognition of Odysseus, whenever it might take place, is a private affair until she publicly acknowledges him as her husband after he passes the bed test. Telemachus, Eurycleia, and the remaining (surviving) household servants make up the audience for Penelope's embracing answer to the other's claim. Yet Penelope's long testing and the extended process of recognition are equally performed before others. Maidservants are present throughout the interview with the beggar, during which she treats him with even more generosity than the guest/host laws require.[19] Responsibility to the potential friend in the stranger precedes acknowledging him as a specific relation, just as respect for the known friend's potential to turn into an enemy extends beyond the initial public embrace, as will become clear.

Although Derrida admits that the "self" for which one answers in the next modality "supposes unity," it does not require the "concept of the *subject*."[20] This self is not an Aristotelian source of activity, nor the product of a Kantian transcendental unity of apperception. Derrida clarifies the unified self by saying that it is "memory [that] answers." The specific nature of Penelope's tests for the stranger certainly corroborates the importance of memory in the process of recognition. As discussed in the last chapter, "by memory" is her preferred means of anagnorisis. In book 19, she expressly switches from addressing the beggar as stranger (*xenos*) to friend (*philos*) after he describes her husband's clothes, made by Penelope, with loving accuracy (*Od*, 19.254). In book 23, she finally embraces Odysseus after tricking him into displaying the emotions evoked by memories of their bed. Memory may seem to be an autonomous locus for selfhood independent of the need for feedback or confirmation from others. But the fact that for Penelope it is a vital medium of recognition reveals the necessary input of others in the remembrances that make up the self. Though he does not say so, by grounding selfhood in memory, Derrida provides additional support for his claim that the next modality, responding to the other, is "more originary, more fundamental."[21] The memories that constitute the self must be validated, amended, or spurned by the friends who share them.

The primacy of the third modality, "response *to* the other," grounds the performative medium of friendship and recognition. Yet what kind of stage is this performative continuum? In Aristotelian friendship of reciprocity, the performance of friendship would take place in a horizontal plane among equals. In the Derridian model, the friend has an infinite claim on oneself.[22] This Levinasian ethics takes place in a near-vertical angle through which the self looks up to the dizzying height of the other person. The geometries of these two ethical worlds do not seem to share the same space. The former represents a flat plane where all players are on the same level.

The latter is a vertiginous stage where each player is the nadir of her own valley from which she gazes up at any other actor in sight. For Aristotle, equality is a necessary feature of friendship (*NE*, 1157b–1158a).[23] People in different stations of life or of differing mental and moral capacities cannot share the highest form of friendship because they cannot reciprocate the benefits they bring each other. In order to preserve friendship for modern ethics, Derrida has to reject the demand that friends be on equal footing. In fact, Aristotle's values of equality and like-mindedness (*homophrosunē*) run entirely counter to Derrida's account of friendship founded on asymmetry and difference. Only by repudiating equality among friends can Derrida rescue friendship from elitism and make it a universal risk, available equally to all.

These two versions of friendship seem utterly incompatible. Aristotle describes almost like an anthropologist the different types of friendly human relationships that can occur—for utility, for pleasure, for the good—and under what circumstances they flourish. Derrida provides a metaphysical grounding for the possibility of moral action: only by always encountering the other as a possible future friend with an illimitable claim on oneself can one hazard virtue. The former observes the variety of friendships as experienced in the world; the latter suggests an ontological basis for friendship that can only exist as a future potentiality, never as a present actuality. The reciprocity of Aristotle's *philia* appears radically incommensurable with the infinity of Derrida's *lovence* (*aimance*).[24]

Yet the relationship of Penelope and Odysseus suggests ways that the two opposing conceptions require one another to account for the same friendship.[25] Neither Aristotle nor Derrida alone provides an adequate description for the husband and wife bond enacted in the *Odyssey*. In fact, Odysseus and Penelope do not even qualify as friends according to the strictures of the two systems. For Aristotle, husbands and wives cannot be true friends because they are necessarily unequal. For Derrida, in contrast, the couple's equality, as evinced in their vaunted *homophrosunē*—their similar values, mutual acquisitiveness, and tacit acceptance of prevailing power structures—would prevent the eruption of potential friendship. The interactions of Penelope and Odysseus as portrayed in the epic, however, are simultaneously emblematic of the highest forms of friendship for each of the two contradictory accounts.

Technically, Penelope and Odysseus cannot be friends in Aristotle's system. The inferior social condition of women in ancient Greek society meant that they could never be equal with men, a necessary precondition for friendship based in virtue (as opposed to utility or pleasure). Yet the *Odyssey* repeatedly emphasizes the ways that Penelope is the only creature in the wide worlds of his roving journeys who is the mortal match and equal of Odysseus. Neither the immortal beauty of Calypso nor the innocent-natured bounty of Nausicaa can long tempt him away from the quest for Penelope's complement to his long-suffering, long-learning soul. Clytemnestra might be said to have proved herself a match for Agamemnon on his triumphant return from Troy; Penelope, in putting her spouse on trial, shows herself to be the only match, in quite a different sense, for Odysseus. The point of their probing each other in their painstaking process of recognition is not merely to confirm identity as a DNA test might manage today. Instead, their mutual testings more importantly serve as performative affirmation of the unique stature and bond of their relative characters.

Odysseus is well aware of her need to get to know him again, and he would respect her less if she did not test him as he tests her. Smiling and amused, Odysseus defends Penelope from their son's petulant charges of coldness after her silence on their first official meeting as man and wife: "Telemachus, let your mother test (*peirazein*) me in the palace as she will" (*Od*, 23.113–114).[26] But Odysseus also seems aware that Penelope's far-ranging mind will be at work even before he reveals himself. Prior to his interview with the queen in book 19, Odysseus tells his son, "I shall remain here in order to provoke (*erethizein*) your mother and the maids again. She, grieving, will ask me (*eresthai*) about everything" (*Od*, 19.44–46).[27] Robert Fitzgerald renders this with beautiful symmetry that formally echoes the equipoise of their actions:

> Here I stay
> *to test your mother* and her maids again.
> Out of her long grief *she will question me*.[28]

The last two lines of Odysseus's words to his son on the eve of the great event are emblematic of his relationship with his wife. His contrivance of the circumstances for their first meeting is balanced by the way she takes the initiative in both eliciting and giving information during their interview. Even before he sees her, Odysseus expects that Penelope will be the one asking the questions in their mutual interrogation. This knack for critical trial is in and of itself a remarkable characteristic of their union: only

Odysseus would be so duplicitous in his return to his hearth and family after so many years, and only Penelope would be so circumspect in taking him back.

> No other woman (*ou men k' allē . . . gunē*), with spirit as stubborn as yours,
> would keep back as you are doing from her husband who, after much suffering,
> came at last in the twentieth year back to his own country. (*Od*, 23.168).

"Who else in the world," Fitzgerald begins to translate Odysseus's wonder at his wife here, would act as Penelope does when her husband returns after twenty long, hard years? The answer, of course, is only Odysseus, which is precisely why they deserve one another. The formulation of this wonder is the mirror image of Athena's admiration for Odysseus's circumspect duplicity on arriving in Ithaca: "Any other man (*k' allos anēr*) come home from wandering would have run happily off to see his children and wife in his halls" (*Od*, 23.333–334). The very fact of their stringent testing of each other is a mark of their passing the trial of equality.

Read together, Athena's words about Odysseus and Odysseus's about Penelope simultaneously challenge and confirm Derrida's critique of Aristotelian friendship and its legacy of excluding women from the rhetoric of friendship for millennia. On the one hand, Athena and Odysseus still insist on the gendered nouns *man* and *woman*: they do not exclaim *allos anthrōpos* but *allē gunē* and *allos anēr*. On the other hand, they both use the adjective *other* (*allos*) to assert the character's uniqueness. It is by being different—*allos*—that Odysseus and Penelope are equal. This sameness stitches them together despite the opposed gender of the nouns the adjectives modify. The shared difference overcomes the exclusion of women from Greco-Roman friendship that Derrida laments. Odysseus prefaces his declaration of Penelope's radical alterity by addressing her as "Strange woman!" (*daimoniē*). Penelope replies with the same vocative: "Strange man!" (*daimoni'*). The xenonym becomes a dual autonym by repetition. Its echo of divine possession marks their matching difference, their *allos autos*. Recall that a friend, for Aristotle, is an "other self" (*esti gar ho philos allos autos*; *NE*, 1166a). The friend is the difference that makes identity recognizable. Odysseus and Penelope perform this function for each other despite the inequality of their social positions.

In Aristotle's noblest relationship, friends share their lives together because they make each other visible to themselves in a way that would be impossible alone. One comes to know oneself through long-term interactions with a friend. This happens through the contemplative view of one another's actions—that is, through sight—and through discussions of differences—that is, through speech. Both seeing and speaking are thus vital to the self-knowledge afforded by friendship, but Aristotle attaches the greatest virtue to *speech*, to coming to understand differences between people through dialogue, rather than to *sight*.[29] The recognitive faculty of friendship, moreover, is only actualized—only put to work—in the choice for friends to *live together*:

> The *energeia* of this [the choiceworthiness of the friend] comes to be in living together (*suzēn*), so friends quite reasonably aim at this. (*NE*, 1172a)

The entire arc of this description of the highest form of friendship matches perfectly with the action of Penelope's recognition of Odysseus in the *Odyssey*, and its fulfillment occurs in the scene of their exchanging stories and perspectives in bed through the night, which is lengthened by the goddess to let them keep speaking with each other.

> τὼ δ᾽ ἐπεὶ οὖν φιλότητος ἐταρπήτην ἐρατεινῆς,
> τερπέσθην μύθοισι, πρὸς ἀλλήλους ἐνέποντε (*Od*, 23.300–301)
>
> (When Penelope and Odysseus had enjoyed their lovemaking,
> they took their pleasure in speech, each one telling stories.)[30]

They accomplish this complementary relationship despite the fact that the realities of Greek society made it impossible for men and women ever to be equals, which Aristotle insists is necessary for true friendship.[31] Odysseus never meets an equal who can become a friend and help him learn to recognize himself in the *Odyssey*—other than his wife. Only together can Penelope and Odysseus unfold in performance the full range of their potential as masters of recognition.[32]

The couple meets Aristotle's conditions of friendship not only through their equality but also through their shared insistence on reciprocity. They are both shrewdly acquisitive and exceedingly generous. When the disguised Odysseus watches Penelope wheedle "glorious presents" out of the suitors, he is not jealous of her coquetry but instead admires how she "beguiles gifts out of them" (*Od*, 23.279–283). The "last word" Odysseus speaks to Penelope in the prolonged night of their mutual storytelling, before sweet sleep overcomes them, is of the many gifts bestowed on him by the Phaeacians (*Od*, 23.341–342). They are both meticulous observers of guest/host customs, whether as givers or recipients of the *xenia* gifts.

This same shared insistence on the equitable exchange of favors and gifts that fits so snugly into Aristotelian *philia* makes Odysseus and Penelope unfit for Derridian *amitié*. The aporia of the gift parallels that of friends, for the slightest hint of reciprocity annuls the gift as it does true friendship.[33] Paul Ricoeur echoes Derrida's distaste for reciprocal exchange in his account of three modes of recognition: of objects, of the self, and between others. Ricoeur makes the gift into an ethical category at the apex of a system that constructs an entire cosmos of human experience through these three levels. He bestows the honor of the highest form of mutual recognition, in which "alterity" between individuals is maintained, on the (symbolic) giving of gifts. This ideal recognition smacks of Derrida's elusive dream of friendship. For Ricoeur, only generosity, a "paradox of the gift" in which giving is not premised on reciprocity, can sustain human relationships that honor the dissymmetry between self and other.[34] Ricoeur stops short of allowing any mutual recognition to Odysseus and Penelope. The gift-giving that pervades the *Odyssey* is by no means done in the generous, reciprocity-free sense that Ricoeur admires; it is rather an openly shameless form of self-aggrandizement on the one hand and a nominal upholding of the sacred laws of hospitality on the other. Curiously, however, it is not this insistence on reciprocity on the part of Odysseus that prevents Ricoeur from reading the poem as presenting an instance of mutual recognition. He admires the interplay between husband and wife in the *Odyssey* and claims that it "comes close to yielding something like mutual recognition."[35] But Ricoeur's assumptions about the poem's apparent valorization of the revenge plot and about the unequal relationships Odysseus reestablishes with his recognitions on Ithaca (even with Penelope) keep the episodes from progressing beyond the level of "self-recognition" (i.e., a realization of one's own capacities that culminates in self-avowal) in Ricoeur's system.

Hence it would seem that the *Odyssey* cannot illustrate Derridian friendship or Ricoeur's mutual recognition. Yet Homer's epic problematizes these objections, rendering Ricoeur's dismissal too simplistic. The poem's vivid representation of the slaughter of the suitors and their lovers among the serving women (especially those who cry for mercy), which transpires with divine approval—nay, insistence!—at the behest of Athena, is forcibly juxtaposed with the entire epic's preoccupation with the sacred status of the guest. Regardless of their behavior and the length of their stay, the suitors remain *xenoi* (guests/strangers) even while Odysseus kills them—with no more mercy than "lawless" Polyphemus showed to Odysseus's own (thieving) companions in the cyclops's cave. At the very least, the poem does not blindly endorse the actions it depicts, but in fact it invites readers to question the justice of Athena's demand for the wholesale murder of the suitors and the execution of the maids. Second, although the social system in which they were embedded undeniably awarded husbands "mastery" over their wives, Odysseus and Penelope's mutual testing shows how Penelope nevertheless manages to demonstrate her *homophrosunē* with Odysseus in the face of these social constraints.[36] It is not Penelope's subservience to her husband that prevents them from achieving Ricoeur's ideal of mutual recognition but rather the precise nature of the equality she proves. Nothing makes this couple more alike than their joint concern for reciprocity: both of them care passionately about returns on their generosity to others.[37] If any characters in Homer are incapable of the highest form of love (*agapē*) Ricoeur advocates, or the *lovence* that Derrida hopes for, then it is Penelope and Odysseus, who match each other in their acquisitiveness and tit-for-tat attitudes no less than in their cunning and inventiveness.

Yet this same pair is the best candidate for the mutual ideal of Derridian friendship and selfless *agapē* among the *pananthrōpon* of Greek mythic heroes.[38] While they ostensibly insist on horizontal reciprocity and equality, Penelope and Odysseus also act in the near-perpendicular oblique planes of dissymmetry and infinitude demanded by Derrida's Levinasian ethics. If Odysseus's "last word" on the day of their public recognition is of past gifts, his first word to the newly recognized wife is of future betrayal. During the first moments of their reunion, while Penelope still "could not let him go from the embrace of her white arms" (*Od*, 23.240), Odysseus tells his wife that their troubles are not yet over and that that he will have to accomplish "unmeasured labor" and "difficult trials." He cuts short these vague, ominous warnings, saying, "But come, let us go to bed" (*Od*, 23.254). "Circumspect Penelope" is not having it: "You shall have your going to bed whenever the spirit / desires it . . . but / tell me what this trial is, since I think I shall hear of it / later; so it will be none the worse if I now hear of it" (*Od*, 23.257–262). He relates Tiresias's prophesy that he will undertake a long journey inland and then die at sea. Odysseus is admitting to his wife that he will abandon her again and that he will not grow old and die in her company. He confesses that she cannot expect him to remain as husband forever—his *philia* is temporary, not to be counted on.

Penelope's request prompts Odysseus again to declare her a "strange woman" (*daimoniē*), the third occurrence of this name between the couple. This time, however, Penelope does not reciprocate the endearing sobriquet. The symmetry of the previous exchange is gone: now Penelope accepts Odysseus's confession with demur understatement. "If the gods are accomplishing a more prosperous old age, / then there is hope (*elpōrē*) that you shall have an escape from your troubles" (*Od*, 23.286–287). This is not the "absolute hope" that Derrida mocks in Greco-Roman friendship, a trust that the friend should continue in sameness beyond death.[39] Instead, it is a hope with its limits clearly on this side of mortality. She does not say "I hope" but rather asserts the existence of hope for her husband escaping bad things. Penelope here embodies Derrida's maxim of the freeing spirit of friendship: she respects the enemy her husband may become while living in the expectation of a future friendship to come.

In the climactic scene of their reunion, therefore, Penelope manages to exhibit the infinite responsibility of modern friendship by giving her friend leave to betray her. Does Odysseus exhibit—I cannot say "reciprocate"—such dissymmetrical love? One could point to his rejection of bewitching beauty (Circe), delightful youth and riches (Nausicaa), and divine immortality (Calypso) as evidence of Odysseus's boundless commitment to Penelope. By choosing her finitude over the goddess's infinity, Odysseus's dedication to Penelope shares in infinitude. Yet this was never a choice *solely* for his wife: the yearning for his ancestral home, his son, and the glory accorded by his fellow men played no small part in his desire to leave Calypso's island. But Odysseus's decision to dangle dire hints of Tiresias's prophecy before Penelope in the moment of their initial embrace is itself a way of disclosing vulnerability to the potential enemy in the friend. He gives her a chance to rebuke or even rebuff him *before* they consummate their reunion. Most husbands would have waited at least until the morning after to share such unwelcome news, if they bothered to do so at all.

Yet perhaps the best illustration of Odysseus's limited respect for his wife's autonomy comes after their shared night of lovemaking and storytelling. He shares his plans for the day and says, "But I tell you this, my wife, *though you have your own understanding* (*pinutē per eousē*; *Od*, 23.361; emphasis mine)." *Pinutē* means "wisdom" or "prudence" as well as "understanding." Odysseus informs Penelope about his plans and reasoning without including her in his deliberations. At the same time, he gives her space to have her own thoughts. This level of respect for a wife's intellect may surpass that of any other attested husband in antiquity, but its limits become clear in Odysseus's final words to Penelope: "Then go to the upper chamber with your attendant women, / and sit still, looking at no one, and do not ask any questions" (*Od*, 23.364–365). Odysseus literally gives Penelope "room" to disagree. His wife is free to think whatever she may wish, but she must do so silently within the confines of her own chamber.

The dissymmetry of Derridian friendship is in full blossom during the interview between disguised beggar and inscrutable queen (book 19). At that point, the willingness of both parties to honor the potential enemy in the old friend before them is at its highest. After their public acknowledgment, the opportunities for *lovence* diminish as social hierarchies, gender norms, and the habits of marital life are reinstated. Yet they never wilt entirely. The key feature of the pregnant interview that animates its moral potency is its self-awareness as performance. The openly hidden performativity of the scene raises the ritualized, iterative patterns of interaction between the couple to the status of an event. Though the potential for eventness underlies all interpersonal exchanges, which are necessarily performative, in this scene it is clearly activated *in its very potentiality*. This is precisely the formula derived in chapter 2 for the definition of recognition as a change. Book 19 of the *Odyssey* shows the epistemological and moral dimensions of recognition at work in the highest form of friendship: one assiduously alive to a turn to enmity.

The medium of this form of recognition is performance at its most performative: dissimulation. The appropriateness of taking performance to this extremity to describe recognition between people can best be illustrated with another famous anagnorisis scene in the *Odyssey*. As Odysseus first approaches his home in the company of the swineherd, he is noticed by Argos, his old dog, who is lying weak and decrepit on a dung heap.[40] The dog immediately knows his master and musters up enough strength to wag his tail and pull his ears back (*Od*, 17.302). Here again, as in the washing scene with Eurycleia, Odysseus's disguise is in danger of discovery. But it would be impossible to pull Argos aside and threaten him with violence should he reveal his master's identity, as Odysseus did with the nursemaid. For the dog, there is no distance at all between knowing and acknowledging someone: Argos perceives his master and immediately wags his tail. Dogs are incapable of *Verstellung*: they cannot pretend. They do not wonder about the state of knowledge in the recognized other, and therefore there is no question of interpretation of the other's behavior.[41] People, however, can (and in the *Odyssey* often do) disguise not only themselves but also their knowledge about others. Lying and contending with lies are integral to people coming to know one another.[42] In the *energeia* of knowledge about other people (as a *dynamis*), people must play roles to and with each other: they must perform and decipher others' performances. This is a uniquely human endeavor. Hence the anagnorisis scene with Argos serves as a limit case for what counts as interpersonal recognition.

Odysseus must teach those who discover his identity in Ithaca (or those to whom he reveals it) to disguise this knowledge, to lie: Eurycleia, Telemachus, Eumaios. This duplicity is proof of their loyalty and is itself a performance of their recognition of Odysseus. He does not have to teach Penelope this lesson; she is an adept at deception all on her own. No amount of training, however, would manage to teach Argos to hide what his senses reveal.[43] Fortunately for Odysseus, the excitement of perceiving his long-lost master and the effort of signaling his joy with a wag of his tail are too much for Argos, and the old dog expires without letting the cat out of the bag. It is important to grasp the difference between this straightforward reaction of Argos upon perceiving Odysseus—the wagging tail and flattened ears—and the kind of performance I define as recognition. Both can be seen as operating within systems of signs, but the former is never subject to doubt about its reference.[44] The latter, however, involves countless layers of complexity and uncertainty introduced by the multiple rhetorical perspectives, utterly unknowable except through the mutual rehearsals and reenactments whereby they become part of the world in the negotiated space between people. Where there is no dissimulation, there can be no change and hence no recognition as defined above.

Derrida begins his study of friendship with the apocryphal Aristotelian paradox, "Oh Friends, there is no friend!"[45] The ethical motto for which Odysseus and Penelope supply an apt illustration—"to respect the potential enemy in the present friend"—is reminiscent of another ancient Greek maxim that reads like a Derridian aporia. The pre-Socratic sage Bias advises followers to "love like people who are going to hate and hate like people who are going to love."[46] Though Derrida extensively cites the authors who are our sources for this fragment (Aristotle and Diogenes Laertius), he never mentions Bias's advice. This omission underlines a major difference between the two similar apothegms. For Derrida, friendship demands that one honor the prerogative of the other to betray one's trust. This is a moral good in and of itself as it confers ultimate freedom to the other, relinquishing any claim on her and exposing oneself to extreme harm. Bias's advice, meanwhile, is an attempt to limit vulnerability. To protect oneself from undue trauma, it is best to treat friends as if they can always turn enemy and vice versa. Derrida makes openness to the vicissitudes of human agency the touchstone of morality; Bias attempts to build a firewall around the hazards of fortune. But what do the exigencies of chance have to do with the performance of recognition between friend and enemies, an action that proceeds from deliberative choice? The next chapter will set its sights on the role of fortune in recognition.

CHAPTER FIVE

"For Those Bound for Good or Bad Fortune"

Casualties of Recognition

ARISTOTLE'S DEFINITION OF anagnorisis ends in misfortune, like many of the tragedies it is meant to elucidate. As with the friendship/enmity disjunction, the syntax makes it unclear precisely which previous phrase governs the final clause and to what—or whom—the good or bad fortune should belong. Most translators and commentators assume it designates the class of people who undergo tragic anagnorisis: "Recognition . . . is a change from ignorance to knowledge into friendship or enmity *among those destined for good or bad fortune*" (*tōn pros eutukhian ē dustukhian hōrismenōn*; *P*, 11, 1452a, 31).[1] Here, the genitive participle (*tōn . . . hōrismenōn*) is the subject (albeit a middle/passive one) of the action: "among those [people] destined for . . ." The clause hence shows to whom the preceding phrases of the definition should apply. Alternatively, the clause could be a partitive genitive modifying the predicate nominative *metabolē*: "Recognition . . . is a change, *of those [changes] that have been defined by reference to good or bad fortune*, from ignorance into knowledge, either into friendship or into enmity."[2] In this case, it would further specify *what kind of change* recognition is rather than *among whom* recognition transpires.

There is no purely grammatical reason to choose one or the other of these interpretations. Persuasive cases can be made on both sides. Fortune either determines the nature of the change in which recognition consists or affects the people who recognize. Appropriately enough, fate's intervention in the definition of recognition is capricious. This ambiguity highlights two ways that luck can intervene in the agency of recognition. Fortune (*tukhē*) is either the uncontrollable circumstances that help or hinder a person's actions or a feature of the given world of social power structures in which people operate. Fortune is either a question of character or identity.

For Aristotelians, who hold actions to begin in conscious choice arising from the active condition of character and proceeding toward a desired end, fortune is the result of contingent events extraneous to the natural progression of action toward its conclusion. As Martha Nussbaum explains, "What happens to a person by luck will be just what does not happen through his or her own agency, what just *happens* to him, as opposed to what he does or makes."[3] Aristotle has a healthy respect for the role of contingency in human affairs, and Nussbaum sensitively explores the implications of this for moral life through exemplary readings of the *Nicomachean Ethics* and Greek tragedy.[4] Those who seek insight into the relation of fortune to Aristotelian character will learn much by studying *The Fragility of Goodness*.

The present chapter will focus on the second way that fortune constrains or subverts the agency of individuals coming to know each other: the negotiation of identity. Gerhard Neumann delineates three different types of recognition: anagnorisis between other selves; anagnorisis between sexes; and anagnorisis between cultures. Traditionally, gender and culture have been seen as ineluctable elements of one's identity and hence the province of fortune in identity formation. Though Neumann claims these categories originate in Aristotle's *Poetics*, his elaborations of them launch from scenes in modern literature. Neumann reads instances of "love at first sight" or accounts in travel documents and anthropological texts of "first contacts" between cultures as recognition scenarios. His categories neatly bring contemporary scholarly approaches such as feminism and postcolonialism into dialogue with more traditional poetics.[5]

Though Neumann presents his classes of recognition as an explanation of Aristotelian anagnorisis, his categories of identity are hardly derivable from Aristotle's text. His understanding of the workings of hamartia and catharsis is clearly indebted to Gerald Else's anthropological treatment of those terms as ritual formulae of guilt and expiation, but his proposal of the three types of anagnorisis is more original than he admits.[6] This unacknowledged originality, couched though it is in the mantle of Aristotelian authority, does not detract from the useful synopsis of currently prevailing cultural-historical conceptions of identity that the three classes provide.[7]

Neumann's categories can be applied to instances of recognition in the *Odyssey* with particular felicity. They become especially helpful in understanding the relation between anagnorisis on the one hand and new cultural historicist readings of the poem on the other. Several scholars have begun to read the *Odyssey* from a postcolonial perspective; they see Odysseus's various encounters during his travels as expressions of the fears and hopes of Greek colonists regarding the aboriginal inhabitants of their new homes.[8] Odysseus's interactions with the lawless cyclops, who not only disregards the sacred social norms of hospitality but even kills and eats the Greek guests, represent one extreme of colonial experience with natives, while his treatment by the Phaeacians, who shower him with gifts and beg him to settle among them, exemplifies the other.[9] Neumann's categories provide a framing perspective from which to view these colonial readings of the poem alongside other recent feminist approaches.[10] Think, for instance, of Odysseus's initial encounters with Circe and Nausicaa. Both of these scenes represent a falling together of all three of Neumann's classes of recognition: between selves, between sexes, and between cultures.

In the first, Circe is a triple threat: not only is she another person whose motivations are shrouded in mystery, but she also represents a powerful and hostile culture[11] that transforms the Greeks into beasts beyond recognition; on top of all that, she's a *woman*. Recognition in this episode is almost ritualistic in its performativity. Hermes instructs Odysseus precisely what words and motions to repeat in order to turn Circe from enemy to friend (*Od*, 10.286–301). The "change" in knowledge here is clearly one of learning *technē* of ritualized role-play rather than gaining insight into Circe's soul. According to Hermes's directions, the two must alternate between pretending to be friends and enemies. Circe will offer Odysseus refreshment (*philos*) but lace it with poisonous potion (*ekhthros*). After eating her food, Odysseus must draw his sword and "rush forward against Circe" as if he were "raging to kill her." In other words, after accepting the guest/host offering of sustenance to the stranger (*philos*), Odysseus must play the part of an ungrateful and unholy criminal (*ekhthros*). This performance of hostility will cause Circe to invite him to join her in bed (*philos*), where she will be able to make him "weak and unmanned" (*ekhthros*). Odysseus must accept this erotic invitation (*philos*)—but not before demanding that she swear a divine oath that she "has no other evil hurt that she is devising against [him]" (*ekhthros*). This is a classic example of a performative speech act in the sense of J. L. Austin. The very power of the uttered words effects a change in the relations between the two. Yet despite Austin's attempt to exclude the theatrical and fictional from speech act theory,[12] the oath in this case is only one step in a complicated ceremony of disguising role-play.

The episode thus reinforces Jacques Derrida's erasing of the difference between stage speech and real-world speech in his effort to show that all performatives are impure.[13]

Odysseus's carefully rehearsed confrontation with Circe is so strange partly because of the tensions resulting from it having to work as a recognition scenario on all three of Neumann's levels: the other self, culture, and gender. Hermes provides him with the know-how to deal with the "technological superiority" of Circe's foreign culture, but Odysseus himself must negotiate to (re?)establish a hierarchy between the sexes, which Circe's transformative allure and power destabilize from what a Greek audience would assume to be the norm. The transgressive potential of a strong woman getting the better of Odysseus is elided by the performative ritual of playacting both friends with evil intent and enemies with goodwill.

The second recognition scenario uniting all three of Neumann's classes occurs chronologically long after his adventure with Circe, but his encounter with Nausicaa is narrated earlier in the epic (*Od*, bk. 6). Although Odysseus is once again in the position of wanting help from a foreign woman, the roles he and Nausicaa play could not be more different from the situation with Circe. No god instructs him what to say or do this time. Odysseus is the naked supplicant with no other means at his disposal than the eloquence of his tongue; Nausicaa is in a position of power to give or refuse succor to the stranger. The potentially scandalous nature of their initial encounter, however, compromises and determines the tenor of her help. Their relation must first be hidden—and then reenacted in a rather adroit charade—in order for her, in all propriety, to perform the role of host he persuades her to take on. The recognition scenario with Nausicaa hence reveals the way that gender roles demand layers of deception and playacting at conscious as well as unconscious levels. In order to enact her choice to help Odysseus, Nausicaa must disguise the fact that she has the agency to make this choice in the first place and dupe her parents into making it for her. Gender identities to which societies assign subordinate positions, such as women in antiquity, are doomed to mask their agency as passive acceptance of fate.[14]

Nausicaa is both foreign and female, but Odysseus soon discovers her culture to be a kind of utopia epitomizing all the values of hospitality, honor, and social hierarchy to which the Greeks aspire. The contrast between the sordid reality of social values in the Greeks' households in Ithaca or Mycenae (or even the glossy, drug-induced haze of the Spartan court) and the fabled ideal of Phaeacia is too stark to overlook. In a way, then, Nausicaa turns out to be foreign because she is too perfectly Greek. The depiction of Phaeacian society, which is typified in the charming first contact scene,[15] could also inspire self-recognition in Homer's audience so it could potentially see the discrepancy between its ideals and its reality.[16]

A third passage in the *Odyssey* could also be construed as uniting Neumann's three classes of recognition—from opposing, incommensurable points of view. When Odysseus wakes up on the shores of Ithaca, he does not recognize his home: the place does not look familiar to him. He assumes that the Phaeacians have tricked him and set him down in another foreign land. His resulting lament encapsulates the fears and hopes of every first contact scenario between cultures:

> Ah me, what are the people (*brotoi*) whose land I have come to this time,
> and are they savage and violent, and without justice,
> or hospitable to strangers? (*Od*, 13.200–202)

So when he spies a young herdsman approaching, Odysseus assumes that he is in another encounter with an unknown and possibly hostile culture, and he acts accordingly. The shepherd, it turns out, is Athena in disguise. She is, of course, actually female, so that Odysseus is unwittingly involved not only in the recognition between cultures he assumes but also in a recognition between sexes. It is, in fact, Athena who masks both Ithaca and herself, thus causing the false inference in both cases. But Athena is a goddess, and so Odysseus's encounter here is not even with another mortal (*brotos*), as he naturally assumes. This is an example in which every class of recognition (between other *human* selves, sexes, and cultures) proves to be deceptive and false.

Yet this passage is one of the truest in the poem. In it, *nostos* and anagnorisis coincide at the structural and thematic center of the entire epic. Athena chooses precisely this moment of return in order to engage Odysseus in the colloquy that will reveal his character—will make known his essential identity—in an overt act of recognition. Odysseus has the gall to test Athena with his dissembling tales. The goddess smiles and caresses her pet, saying, "You play a part as if it were your own tough skin" and "Two of a kind, we are, contrivers both" (*Od*, 13.291–301).[17] The behavior in which Athena delights, however, and that demonstrates Odysseus's nature (his wariness, deception, disguise, and playacting) in this axial anagnorisis does not consist in a form of homecoming but rather its opposite: deliberate distancing from one's origins and denial of identity. Odysseus does not merely question the boy and devise sly tests of his veracity but assumes a disguise of his own; he constructs an invented character to impersonate for the young herdsman. Odysseus's encounter with Athena, at the midpoint of the epic, is quite literally *the* central recognition scene in a poem that is anagnorisis through and through: it occurs at the very middle of the poem, it is his first encounter on his return to Ithaca, it is the most overt statement and celebration of his unique character, and it establishes the model of disguise and testing that will determine Odysseus's actions throughout the rest of the poem. Recognition at its core is mutual role-play.

Despite Athena's obvious identification with Odysseus, however, she can never be a match for him in the way that Penelope is. The husband and wife are both mortal, and they risk their very lives in the dissembling gambit of their recognition trials. Like the dog Argos, the goddess Athena represents a limit of human recognition. The dog was incapable of dissimulation, which barred him from the veil of indeterminacy necessary for Derridian friendship. Athena is certainly a master of deception, but she is immortal, which bars her from the ultimate danger of death to which Derridian friends must open themselves by respecting the enemy the other may become. Athena is never exposed to vulnerability in her relations to Odysseus and hence cannot enact the kind of ethical friendship that Penelope models. If the goddess cannot suffer the consequences of a human's potential hostility, the acts of friendship are never the gift of freedom that Derrida describes.

In fact, Athena's goodwill, like Poseidon's ire, is much more akin to the favor of fortune for Odysseus than the mutuality of friendship. The fondness she feels for Odysseus is not due to his piety, though he is certainly careful to pray to her at every junction. She dotes on him because of his character: "Always you are the same, and such is the mind within you, / and so I cannot abandon you when you are unhappy, / because you are fluent, and reason closely, and keep your head always" (*Od*, 13.330–333). One is tempted to rephrase the question posed to Euthyphro. Socrates asks him about piety: "Is the pious loved by the gods because it is pious, or is it pious because it is loved by the gods . . . ?"[18] Instead, with the fortune attendant on recognition in mind, one wonders, Is a person who she is because of the gods' favor, or do the gods favor a person because of who she is? Athena is partial to Odysseus because of his shiftiness, discernment, and cunning—but because of her partiality, she is always giving him the means to hatch and carry out his disguises and crafty devices.

Character and fortune are thus inextricable in the poem, and the acts of recognition that reveal the former simultaneously bring about the latter. In this sense, character and identity are aligned. Sheila Murnaghan has shown that the *Odyssey* in many ways is Athena's poem. From the very beginning, Athena contrives to free Odysseus and bring him home. The plot of the epic is mainly her work. One might think that a story dominated by a powerful female goddess would be liberating and encouraging for feminists. Yet Murnaghan argues that the effect of Athena's intervention is ultraconservative.[19] She works tirelessly for the restoration of the male-dominated hierarchy and the subjugation and disempowerment of women. Athena is the good fortune (*eutukhia*) that accomplishes the triumph of Odysseus's identity as patriarch and ruling father, husband, and king. But of course that means that she is the misfortune (*dustukhia*) of anyone who stands in the way of this restoration. She demands the slaughter not only of the suitors but also of the twelve serving women who (arguably under the duress of the same chauvinistic social strictures Athena works to restore) have been sleeping with them. Athena's work in the poem is to reinforce the inescapable tyranny of identity. If for Heraclitus character is fate, Athena's plot shows that identity is fortune.[20]

These three instances of the full or partial convergence of Neumann's three classes of recognition in the *Odyssey*, *therefore*, present a progression through the possibilities of engaging the Other. In the episode of Circe, who is truly different in all three senses, the Other must be forcibly subjugated to Odysseus's understanding lest (via the perverting power of desire) she transform him beyond it. In the Nausicaa scene, the other culture turns out to be an idealized image of the Greeks' own. In the Athena encounter, meanwhile, the Other is so very alien that even the basic categories of recognition (between cultures/genders/selves) are no longer valid. The goddess functions as the grounding of a social order in which identity fully determines a person's realm of agency. The poem, in its movement from one multiclass recognition scenario to the next, thus offers an elaborate taxonomy of the structure of relations to the other with suggestive consequences for anthropologists and sociologists alike. Although Neumann's classes of recognition cannot be derived from Aristotle's *Poetics*, they nevertheless afford a shrewd perspective on how the fortune of identity plays into the performance of recognition in the *Odyssey*.

The last word of Aristotle's definition of anagnorisis in Greek is *hōrismenōn*. Whether translators render this participle as designating the characters "determined" for good or bad fortune or prefer it to show how the action of change is "defined," these Latinate English words both share semantically similar roots with the Greek. Like *horos*, *terminus* and *finis* mean "limit" or "boundary." The verb *horizein* is the source of English *horizon*. This word appropriately marks the end of the defining sentence, just as the fate of identity sets constraints on the range of viable performance in society. As observed in the examples of Odysseus's encounters with his old dog and with his patron goddess, there are important boundaries to the operation of recognition between people. The limit cases human/animal and human/god are represented by Odysseus's reunions with Argos and Athena. Yet there is a third limit constitutive of humanity that Odysseus explores in the *Odyssey*: death. Of all the many lands Odysseus visits, there is only one where recognition is not an extended process. In Hades, Odysseus encounters old comrades in arms from Troy, a recently dead shipmate, and his mother, and they all address him immediately by name or epithet without any evidence of doubt or deliberation as to his identity.

Though the shades in Hades do not engage in any kind of testing in order to recognize Odysseus, their acknowledgment of him does not come without a price. After digging a pit of precise dimensions, Odysseus pours it full of "drink offerings for the dead"—honeyed milk, wine, water, and sweet barley—and then "promises many things" (about the fat cow he would sacrifice to them upon his return home) to the "blurred and breathless dead" (*Od*, 11.26–39).[21] Finally, he pours fresh blood from newly slaughtered sheep into the delicious concoction, and suddenly he is surrounded by hordes of spirits that come swarming toward the pit of libations from every direction. With the exceptions of Elpenor (who had died recently and whose body is yet unburied) and Tiresias (who as a prophet presumably has special privileges),[22] none of the dead crowding around the pit speak to Odysseus or give any sign that they know (or are even aware of) him. Odysseus sees the shade of his mother among the dead, who "has not brought herself to look (*idein*) directly at her own son or to speak to him (*protimuthēsasthai*)," and he begs Tiresias to tell him how she might come to recognize him (*Od*, 11.143–144). The prophet explains the simple rule: any dead spirits he allows to approach the libation will speak[23] the truth; the others will go away. And sure enough, the moment Odysseus steps back to let his mother drink, "at once she knew me" (*autika d' egnē*), and she immediately begins speaking to him with lamentation (*Od*, 11.153). Throughout the rest of Odysseus's visit to Hades, recognition is never an issue (as a test, performance, or any other sort of process) after he gives them the bloody cocktail to drink. Agamemnon knows him at once after he drinks (*egnō d' aips' em' ekeinos, epei pien haima kelainon*), and like Anticlea, his first reaction is to break into lamentation (*Od*, 11.390); Achilles follows the same procedure: he drinks, knows Odysseus, and begins lamenting (*Od*, 11.471).[24]

On the face of it, the rituals Odysseus must perform to achieve recognition among the dead may seem similar to the elaborate rites through which he gains Circe's friendship. But there is a huge difference: with Circe, the back-and-forth of the scripted act *comprises* the process of recognition between the two. The shades, however, are entirely incognizant of Odysseus until they drink the libation, almost as if it were a light switch. Recognition among the dead is not a mutual performance in the way defined above.

For the dead, no homecoming is possible anymore. They can look forward to no return and have no need to test and probe their living visitor. No sign of recognition lights up the eyes of the shades in Hades. Where return is impossible, tests are unnecessary, and anagnorisis is nonexistent as a plot device or intersubjective process. Recognition and acknowledgment can be bargaining chips for power and happiness among the living. The dead no longer have anything to gain or lose by separation or connection to the living and dispense with the game of recognition altogether.

Three horizons delimit the performance of recognition as defined here. The dog Argos cannot dissemble. The goddess Athena is invulnerable. The dead have no hope. These three components are indispensable to interpersonal recognition: dissimulation, vulnerability, and hope. Recognizers enter onto a stage of mutually assured deception with a promise of friendship but exposure to trauma, subjugation, and death. To escape the constraints of this performance is to cross beyond the limits of what it means to be human. Animals, gods, and the dead are not subject to the conditions that make possible the promise and menace of human relationality. The activity of recognition may blossom in such finitely liberating friendships as that between Penelope and Odysseus, but recognition's many casualties crowd the fields of Hades.

Part II

Outing Interiority

Modern Recognitions

A visualization of the structure of this book:*

(1 & 6) (2 & 7) (3 & 8)

"Recognition, just as the name itself signfies, is a change from ignorance to knowledge, into either friendship or enmity, among those bound for good or bad fortune."

(4 & 9) (5 & 10)

*Key:
(Chapter #s)
interrogated term

PART I OF this book distilled five concepts whose workings are integral to Aristotle's definition of dramatic recognition: the self (*to auto*), change (*metabolē*), knowledge (*gnosis*), friendship (*philia*), and fortune (*tukhē*). Its chapters explored these root ideas through the lines of the *Odyssey*, in each case pushing both with and against Aristotle's system to uncover the performative gestures they rely on. Part II will take up each of these terms in turn again in the new environments, suppositions, and historical horizons of England around 1600 and Germany around 1800. Both of these times and places stage important turning points in the history of the self. Wherever they fall on the spectrum between the fragmented, contingent practice of self-fashioning and essentialist Shakespearean "invention of the human,"[1] scholars agree that early modern England marks a nodal point in representing how the self is constituted. The cusp between Enlightenment transparency of the internal subject and Romanticism's obscure interiority, meanwhile, can be seen as a perigee of the trajectory of selfhood inward since the Renaissance. Goethe and Kleist present, respectively, a celebration of the modern subject's potential and a dire warning about its dangerous instability.

Four texts will guide this interrogation of recognition in modernity: three plays and one biographical anecdote. Why these particular texts?

Each of them nods to an Odysseus figure, but that alone cannot motivate their choice. This book makes no attempt to be a comprehensive—or even adumbrating—survey of Odysseus reception.[2] Instead, at stake in these texts is the way they revisit and represent the terms of Aristotle's definition of recognition. Each chapter can thus be seen as a case study in Blumenbergian *Umbesetzung* (reoccupation). Like Hans Blumenberg's *Work on Myth*, this book challenges a common story of intellectual history. Blumenberg disputes the widely accepted development of human knowledge from *mythos* to *logos*, most cogently articulated by Ernst Cassirer.[3] The studies of the five terms from Aristotle's definition of recognition in the present book, likewise, offer provocations to the story of the rise and fall of the interiorized subject.

According to many scholars, the Homeric poems do not portray a self as we know it. The self was first theorized in classical Athens by Plato and Aristotle but did not begin to take on the *wholeness* and *depth* with which people today tend to imagine it until the early modern era. The cult of interiority reached its peak (or nadir, rather) with the Romantic subject around 1800. Modernist and postmodern portrayals of the subject, meanwhile, often clash with now popular assumptions of the self's integrity and inwardness, presenting selves that are both ruptured and constituted by external phenomena.[4] This nice circular story of the self's rise and fall thus ends in a return to Homeric discontinuity and fragmentation.[5]

The explorations of recognition in part I of this book challenged this exclusive denial of integrity, autonomy, and inwardness to the selves in Homer's *Odyssey*. The chapters of part II similarly question assumptions behind the prevailing narrative of early modern, Enlightenment, and Romantic interiority. They do so not to dispute the validity of historicizing intellectual concepts: indeed, one can effectively challenge one story only by adducing another. The readings in this book query the overdetermined, continuous arc of the history of the self by forging alternative and concurrent connections both backward and forward: Shakespeare's and Kleist's deconstruction of the trope of reflective self-knowledge is already intimated in its founding Platonic text (chapters 6 and 10). Goethe's morphology is prefigured in Aristotle's *Poetics* (chapter 7); recognition between selves in his *Iphigenie*, in turn, foreshadows important twentieth-century contributions to aesthetics (chapter 8) and politics (chapter 9). Shakespeare, Goethe, and Kleist are thus indebted to Homer, Plato, and Aristotle in ways not made clear before. Their reworkings of the Greek stories and ideas, moreover, have helped determine contemporary interpretations of antiquity no less than modern understandings of identity, selfhood, and politics.

The Aristotelian *self-signification* of anagnorisis in chapter 1 can never achieve its desire for the unmediated sign: the yearned-for unity always dissolves in a duality. Similarly, in chapter 6, the Platonic ideal of self-knowledge through reflecting dialogue is shown to be unsustainable and inaccessible by Shakespeare's *Troilus and Cressida* (ca. 1601). Ulysses gives Achilles a lesson about self-reflection derived from Plato's *Alcibiades I* that turns the purported doctrine of the soul inside out. It is almost as if Ulysses is delivering a Machiavellian commentary on Plato's advice to the aspiring young politician. With the emergence of the modern subject and in the wake of the revival of Neoplatonism in the Renaissance, Shakespeare's play unmasks the essentialist soul to reveal a radical theatricality of the self.

Aristotle's definition of recognition as change (chapter 2), meanwhile, turns up in a new form with Goethe's study of metamorphosis (chapter 7). In "Glückliches Ereignis" ("Fortunate Event"; 1817), Goethe narratively ties together recognition in poetry, science, and ethics. The paradox of Aristotelian recognition as simultaneously praxis and *energeia*, action and activity, turns out to be a central problem of morphology too, though it plays out under different terms. For Goethe, the operating conflict is between the types of vision that move from wholes to parts (and vice versa) on the one hand and between beholding the unifying *Urform* of a phenomenon "in the mind's eye" and seeing its manifold appearances in the world on the other. Inseparable from understanding change, for Goethe, are the organs that enable its perception. While collapsing poetical, ethical, and scientific recognition into the same dynamic (an archetype of anagnorisis, so to speak), Goethe's autobiographical sketch adds the changing subject to the changing objects involved in coming to know. This unifying simplification thus leads to dizzying complications that impugn the very possibility of stable knowledge.

Chapter 8 shows how interpersonal knowledge is navigated in Goethe's classicizing play *Iphigenie in Tauris* (1779–1786). In chapter 3, the problem of reading Penelope was emblematic of the inherent indeterminacy of knowing other people in the performative situation of recognition. Penelope's reading of others in turn provided poetological strategies for dealing with this human condition. In *Iphigenie*, the knowledge of self and others turns out to be intertextual as well as theatrical, demanding philology and a poetic sensibility. The effect of the play's recognition scenes within the drama, moreover, is to reveal a strikingly prescient critique of four interpretations of Aristotelian catharsis that will be proposed in the centuries following the play's premiere. Ultimately, *Iphigenie* extends the poetical epistemology of Penelope from interpersonal recognition to the aesthetics of effect as theorized from the nineteenth through the twenty-first centuries.

Chapter 9 offers another reading of *Iphigenie in Tauris* to show that the play foreshadows future developments in political theory. To do so, it picks up on the friend/enemy distinction explored with Odysseus and Penelope in chapter 4. *Iphigenie* has been read as a parable of recognition politics that champions freedom and multicultural identity in the vein of Charles Taylor and Axel Honneth. Yet the decision between friend and enemy in the drama challenges this optimistic vision and points toward the very different politics of Carl Schmitt on the one hand and Patchen Markell on the other. Iphigenie's final performance of recognition, however, moves beyond all these positions to prefigure the theories of Hannah Arendt. At each step, the theatrical text complicates and enriches the ideas of its descendants in political philosophy.

Commonly understood as a play about the tragic intransigence of gender and culture in human relations, Kleist's *Penthesilea* (1808) seems perfectly poised to continue the exploration of identity as fortune undertaken with the *Odyssey* in chapter 5. Instead, chapter 10 argues that the modern conception of selfhood itself compels the tragedy in Kleist's play. Penthesilea is a figure of Cartesian subjectivity taken to the extreme. She enacts the fate of recognition under the conditions of the radically interiorized self. In a fortunate symmetry, the play falls into two parts that echo the mirroring mode of self-knowledge (chapter 6) and the theatrical knowledge of others (passim). Kleist's drama thus offers a *reflectio ad absurdum* (to paraphrase Euclid) of the Cartesian self that is a fitting conclusion to the second part of this book, which opens with the infancy of the modern subject in early modern England. At the very height of interiorized subjectivity in Romantic Germany, Kleist's thought experiment clearly demonstrates the absurdity of its necessary fate.

CHAPTER SIX

Self-Knowledge between Plato and Shakespeare

Alcibiades I and *Troilus and Cressida*

THE BIT OF ancient wisdom that has resonated most profoundly through the ages is the Delphic injunction to "know thyself!" (*gnōthi seauton*). Michel Foucault has shown how the command meant something very different for its early audience than it does to its latter-day navel-gazing fans. Originally, it was largely understood as a matter of self-care, involving practices, exercises, and bodily regimens.[1] In the intervening centuries, it has taken on many different philosophical, religious, and mystic valences as the imperative to know oneself is interpreted according to the needs and concerns of each age. But what is the point of viewing self-knowledge, in any time or culture, through the lens of dramatic recognition? Even if the process of coming to know oneself fits the general species of "a change from ignorance to knowledge," it surely does not entail friendship or enmity, and if good or bad fortune is involved, it is only incidentally, right?

Yet the operation of recognition is always already one of returning to one's own, of coming to know the self (*to auto*). The first chapter of this book established that the semantic field of the word recognition comprises an endlessly repeated desire for the same. Plato's *Sophist* shows that being is impossible without nonbeing by demonstrating the codependency between the Same (*tauton* = *to* + *auto*) and the Other (*thateron*).[2] In short, the attempt to know the Other is inevitably self-directed. By the same token, coming to know oneself must transpire through engagement with the Other. In consequence, one may discover that one has been one's own worst enemy, as Oedipus does to his horror, or that one can be a better friend to oneself, as Socrates urges Alcibiades. The Platonic dialogue *Alcibiades I*[3] culminates with a beautiful scene of self-knowledge, in which one comes to know oneself only through reflection in a friend, as an eye sees itself in the mirror of another's eye.

The present chapter explores the implications of this interpersonal mirroring image as a recognition scenario by observing how it plays out in two dramatic scenes that explicitly appeal to its reflective imagery. The dialogue between Ulysses and Achilles in Shakespeare's *Troilus and Cressida* bears striking similarities to that between Socrates and Alcibiades, both in terms of the formal dramatic situation and in the specific content of their conversation. It turns out that the two discussions comment meaningfully on each other, and the modes of self-knowledge proposed by Socrates and Ulysses, though seemingly contrary, are actually mutually complicit.[4]

Foucault lectured on *Alcibiades* in one of his final seminars on the care of the self in the ancient world. For him, this dialogue is a turning point in the relation between the "care of the self" and "self-knowledge." For the first time, it makes the Delphic injunction to know thyself (*gnōthi seauton*) logically prior to the already ancient demand to take care of one's self (*epimeleia heauton*).[5] For Foucault, this was the first step on a slippery slope toward the modern predicament of assuming knowledge alone to be the key to truth, in contrast to the ancient attitude that knowledge is inextricable from practices and activities.[6] As my reading will show, however, the presentation of the formation of self through transformative interaction with a reflecting other in Plato's *Alcibiades* is already rendered suspect in the action of the dialogue. Plato's text does much of Foucault's critical work for him.[7] The precise form and wording of *Alcibiades*, meanwhile, are echoed and revealed to fall apart in Shakespeare's *Troilus and Cressida*. The interplay between Ulysses and Achilles repeats the performative structure of Plato's aporetic dialogues and questions the very possibility of following the Delphic injunction to know oneself.

PHILOSOPHY OR THEATER?

In *Alcibiades*, Socrates confronts the cocky young Athenian at the end of youth's bloom just as he is about to rocket into notoriety for political oratory, military daring, drawn-out defeat, accusations of sacrilege, treason to the Spartans, and double-crossing. In the dialogue, Socrates tries to convince his young friend to take time to learn about himself and virtue before embarking on a career in politics or war. By the end of the dialogue,

Alcibiades begs Socrates to be his teacher so that he may become virtuous. The climax of this dramatic reversal is the scene in which Socrates likens learning to know oneself with a person looking at her reflection in another's eye. The irony of this happy ending, of course, is that the dialogue's readers all know the impiety, treachery, and narcissistic posturing that await Alcibiades in the future.

Troilus and Cressida, meanwhile, is Shakespeare's send-up of Homeric epic and medieval romance. In it, a travesty of Chaucer's moving love story between *Troilus and Criseyde* plays out against the backdrop of a farcical version of episodes from Homer's *Iliad*. The pertinent storyline here is Achilles's loutish refusal to fight with the Greeks and Ulysses's machinations to get him back in battle. Like Socrates with Alcibiades, Ulysses uses the image of two people coming to know one another through reflection as a hook for Achilles. Yet Ulysses's philosophy does not have the (admittedly temporary) dramatic effect on his interlocutor that Socrates manages with Alcibiades.

Troilus and Cressida is in many respects the most openly philosophical of Shakespeare's plays. Usually Shakespeare couches great swathes of thought behind the characters he creates, which merely hint subtly at any philosophical doctrines that might stitch them together and join their seams. The stubborn flesh and spirit of recalcitrant people rather than didactic ideas animate his dramatic creations. In *Richard II*, for example, the competing political teachings of a king's divine right to rule versus his responsibility to serve his subjects are constantly, though rarely overtly, jockeying for position in a dramatic debate carried on by the gestures, words, and deeds of persons in the play.[8] Characters may suggest ideas and hint meaningfully and beautifully at their consequences, but it is always the interaction of the figures *as people* that drives a Shakespearean play and makes it jar us with immediate and urgent discomforting wonder or terrifying recognition.[9] Shakespeare rarely makes characters expound metaphysics or political theory onstage for us to yawn at intellectually. Instead, MacDuff and Othello and Brutus make us gasp and gawk in the theater and then bring us to think only in retrospect when we are at home afterward.

There are many points where *Troilus and Cressida* breaks with this technique of subtle philosophizing, as it pounds out arguments or presents mind-bending paradoxes with all the pedantry of a lecturer in logic. Ulysses's lengthy speech on degree (*TC*, 1.3.54–137) is certainly the greatest offender. It is an eloquent bit of rhetoric in and of itself and is deliciously full of irony considering who is speaking, the speaker's intentions, and his later actions, but this is all drama that one must think into the situation after the fact. Agamemnon and Co. sleep diligently through much of Ulysses's harangue in many modern productions, and the fact that most directors cut it severely shows that they fear audiences may do the same. The play is all talk. There is no real action until the battle scenes in the final act, and even they seem more the farcical results of desultory inaction than they resemble any kind of culminating denouement. Shakespeare's plots are usually driven by the immediacy of action, but this one is pushed along by the afterthought of debate. The difference between *Troilus* and the rest of Shakespeare is that when Hamlet is asked what he is reading, he answers Polonius simply, "Words," whereas Ulysses, when posed the same question by Achilles, actually gives a detailed exegesis of his philosophical text.

Just as some theatergoers might complain about the expansive verbal theorizing in *Troilus and Cressida*, many philosophers are at a loss to know how to deal with the theatrical aspects of Plato's dialogues. Instead of clear, uncomplicated access to arguments and lines of reasoning that can be easily identified with their author—as one enjoys with, say, Aristotle or Kant—Plato's texts confront readers with all the layers of irony and complex motivations involved in the specific dramatic situations that spark and determine the philosophical discussions between speakers. We have no access to Plato himself; at best, we can interpret and reason about the ideas of his characters.[10] Plato, in this sense, is very much akin to Shakespeare: both men are authors of some of the most potent ideas of human history, but readers can never be certain of the creators' attitudes toward these creations. One can no more identify Plato with his Socrates than Shakespeare with his Hamlet (junior or senior).[11] The dramatic structure of Plato's dialogues and Shakespeare's plays ensconces them in webs of hermeneutic complexity that serve both to sever the textual "orphans" from their parents and to force readers to participate more actively in the philosophical endeavor.

Despite Plato's supposed antitheatricality, he wrote very moving dramatic plays.[12] If the dialogic form is intentionally theatrical not only in an attempt to avoid the pitfalls of the texts Socrates slyly points out in the *Phaedrus*[13] but also because there is intrinsic value in dramatic structure, then one should expect them (the good ones, at least) to share some of the potential powers of drama that Aristotle identifies in the *Poetics*: they will imitate actions that involve dramatic reversals and recognitions and may produce a cathartic state of wonder in readers. Catharsis in this sense of awe—a state of open, questioning perplexity in the face of a surprising turn of events—is very much akin to the numbing aporia toward which Socrates often steers his interlocutors. The aporetic acknowledgment of ignorance is potentially the beginning of an honest philosophical endeavor.[14] If plays and dialogues share this common potential, and if one accepts their invitation to become wonderstruck, then one must read Plato's dialogues with an eye to their dramatic currents and watch Shakespeare's plays with an ear for their philosophical undertones.

MIRRORED DRAMATIC STRUCTURES

There is no way of knowing for certain how much Shakespeare knew of Plato. None of his dialogues had been translated into English by 1600, though Henri Estienne and Jean de Serres had dedicated their three volume Greek and Latin edition of *Plato* to Queen Elizabeth in 1578. Nevertheless, *Alcibiades* has been conjectured as a source of the mirroring eye image in act 3, scene 3. Due in part, no doubt, to Shakespeare's famously "small Latin and less Greek," David Bevington thinks Plato an "unlikely direct source" and mentions discussions of the same ideas in Cicero, Montaigne, and Sir John Davies as possible candidates for the transmission of what he admits to have been a "commonplace of the era."[15]

It is nonetheless surprising that no one has deemed it worthwhile to read the dialogue in close conjunction with the play. *Alcibiades* was considered one of Plato's most exemplary dialogues and usually the first (and often only) one read by students throughout late antiquity and the Renaissance, all the way up until its authorship began to be questioned in the nineteenth century.[16] Even if Shakespeare never read one of the Latin translations of the dialogue that would have been available to him, it is certain that he would have been familiar with the "Life of Alcibiades" in Plutarch's *Parallel Lives*, one of his favorite sources. Plutarch pairs Alcibiades with his biography of Coriolanus, which Shakespeare followed closely in his own eponymous play about the Roman general. Plutarch's *Alcibiades*, meanwhile, refers back to Plato's dialogue as one of its own sources. There is no way to judge whether the intertextual references between play and dialogue were intended by Shakespeare, but the question of intentionality is ultimately uninteresting compared to the wealth of edifying parallels the two texts reveal.

If Plato's *Alcibiades* is a source for the image of mutual reflection in Shakespeare's scene between Ulysses and Achilles in *Troilus and Cressida*, then it is a particularly devious one. *Alcibiades* was first impugned as spurious by Schleiermacher, and since then, most critics have followed his lead, the general consensus agreeing with the assessment of D. S. Hutchinson in the foreword to his translation: "The clearest argument against Plato's authorship is probably that Plato never wrote a work whose interpretation was as simple and straightforward as that of *Alcibiades*."[17] If this chapter accomplishes nothing else, I hope that its Ulyssian reading of *Alcibiades* will challenge the notion of the dialogue's simplicity.[18]

On the surface, the rhetorical situations of the two scenes share many similar features: in both, an older, more experienced man with a reputation for craftiness and wisdom (*mētis* and *sophia*) converses with a talented younger man who is wildly popular and stubbornly willful. Both Socrates and Ulysses, moreover, make use of the image of the eye seeing itself in the mirror of another's eye in order to drive home their points. Furthermore, for a play in which characters have been relentlessly poked and analyzed to yield up any possible satirical commentary on contemporary political figures,[19] it is not too far-fetched to carry the largely accepted parallels between Achilles and Essex to the further level of Alcibiades.[20] Like Alcibiades in Athens after his infamous Sicilian expedition, the brilliant and promising general Essex would return from the disastrous military invasion of a distant island (Ireland) to be arrested and convicted of treachery in his native London. Achilles, Alcibiades, and Essex were all charismatic figures possessed of an overweening confidence in themselves, their abilities, and their indispensability to the sovereigns for whom they had nothing but contempt.[21]

But all these similarities serve to draw our attention even more closely to the discrepancies between the two texts, both in terms of the general constellations of characters and in the precise words of the arguments. Shakespeare's scene turns Plato's on its head. Whereas Socrates begins the dialogue by accosting Alcibiades with an attestation of his love for the younger man (*Al*, 103a), Ulysses announces his departure and the end of their discussion with the same formula: "Farewell, my lord. I as your lover speak" (*TC*, 3.3.216). Socrates meanwhile saves the analogy of the eye seeing itself in another eye for the climactic clincher with which the dialogue culminates; Ulysses, in contrast, opens his conversation with Achilles by alluding to this "conceit." Whereas Socrates had to go to great lengths to explain the intricate image to Alcibiades, Achilles immediately picks up on the topos Ulysses is alluding to and even proceeds to gloss it to the older man.

Just as *Troilus and Cressida* thus seems to reverse the Platonic scenario structurally, the rhetorical aims of the characters are similarly turned around. Socrates wants to hold back Alcibiades, to restrain the eager young man from a precipitous entry into the political fray. Ulysses's intricate machinations, however, are all calculated to spur Achilles back into battle after a long bout of lethargic inaction. The very assumptions underlying the seemingly identical images are also radically different: Socrates holds that the activity of one soul looking for its reflection in another soul will lead the vision and attention of the seeing soul to "that region in which what makes a soul good, wisdom" (*Al*, 113b), and he has to convince Alcibiades that this activity should be prior to (in the senses of being a necessary prerequisite for and inherently superior to) political and military action. Ulysses, however, explains that the knowledge engendered by such reflection only comes about through constant public activity.

A closer look at the precise words and formulations used in the two conversations, however, proves that the differences are not quite as clear cut as they might seem at second sight. Prior to letting Achilles see him with the book, Ulysses directs his fellow generals in a bit of mummery for the brooding hero. The "Embassy to Achilles" in book 9 of the *Iliad*, in which Odysseus, Phoenix, and Ajax visit Achilles in his tent in an attempt to persuade him with gifts and soothing speeches to return to the battle and help the beleaguered Greeks, is one of the few situations in which we see Homer's Odysseus fail at something he undertakes. Book 9 is also one of the seven books that George Chapman published in the first English translation of Homer in 1598, which Shakespeare would have been able to read before the likely composition date of his play (1601–1602). If one thinks of the events in *Troilus and Cressida* as a kind of reworking of the Homeric scene, then one can imagine an amusing paradox of Ulysses learning from Odysseus's mistakes.[22] In the *Iliad*, Odysseus tries to rely on rhetoric and bribery to lure Achilles back onto the field. In *Troilus and Cressida*, Ulysses orchestrates a whole theatrical production with all his fellow generals as players. He instructs them carefully in their cues and parts as to how they should put on a show of indifference to Achilles and "pass strangely by him, / As if he were forgot" (*TC*, 3.3.39). René Girard has acutely and convincingly argued that this scene—and indeed the entire play—should be read as a theoretical exposition on the workings of mimetic desire, whereby the objects of human longing are constructed in a field of emulative mimicry: we most want those things we see other people wanting; we value what others hold in esteem.[23]

This model illustration of mimetic desire may be apt for a modern dramatist like Shakespeare, but surely it cannot be implicit in Socrates's teachings in the favorite introductory dialogue for Neoplatonists. Yet at the beginning of *Alcibiades*, Socrates has engineered a very similar situation:

> I was the first man to fall in love with you, son of Clinias, and now that the others have stopped pursuing you I suppose you're wondering why I'm the only one who hasn't given up—and also why, when the others pestered you with conversation, I never even spoke to you all these years. (*Al*, 103a)

Like Ulysses, Socrates waits until the many men who "used to bend, / To send their smiles before them" (*TC*, 3.3.71–72) no longer fawn and dote on Alcibiades before he approaches the younger man with an eye to teaching him a lesson. Socrates wishes to seduce Alcibiades to philosophy, to the love of a wisdom that should itself be proof and physic against the disease of mimetic desire (replacing the reciprocal imitation of desire with a true longing for the Good). Paradoxically, however, Socrates must take advantage of the mimetic nature of desire to make his seduction work: he can only bring Alcibiades into a state of honest introspection if the gazes of others have been removed, and he must replace them with a gaze of his own that always flirts while it teases, cajoles while it admonishes, and flatters in order to humble.

After his initial success in rousing Alcibiades's curiosity by demonstrating how well he recognizes the young man's secret ambitions,[24] Socrates makes several tactical missteps before finally alighting on a strategy that will win Alcibiades over. His initial dialectical arguments prove, always with Alcibiades's assent, that the young man does not know anything about the very matters (justice, generalship, etc.) necessary for the leader of a city and that those who might teach him are equally ignorant (*Al*, 106c–119a). But the mere admission of ignorance is only nominal: Alcibiades does not yet *feel* that he does not know. Although dialectic, knowledge, and philosophy are at odds with rhetoric, opinion, and sophistry, Socrates must now resort to rhetorical tricks to tempt Alcibiades toward an acknowledged aporia. He feeds on Alcibiades's vanity and ambition as an incentive to inspire a *felt desire* for more genuine self-knowledge (*Al*, 119–124).

MIRRORED SELVES

Structurally, therefore, Ulysses and Socrates have set the same scene in motion. Alcibiades will finally have the same reaction to the anxiety of no longer being recognized as does Achilles. "What mean these fellows? Know they not Achilles?" (*TC*, 3.3.70) he demands in perplexity of Patroclus before being taught by Ulysses to doubt whether he even knows himself. This formal similarity between the play and the dialogue may well lead one to wonder if *Troilus and Cressida* provides any counterpart to the philosophical content of *Alcibiades* as well. The central question of Plato's dialogue emerges in the wake of Alcibiades's final (and at first seemingly genuine) admission of his ignorance: "Well, Socrates, I swear by the gods that I don't even know what I mean. I think I must have been in an appalling state for a long time without being aware of it" (*Al*, 127d). Socrates quickly assures him that it is not too late to begin taking pains to cultivate himself, though that naturally begs the question of what self-cultivation (*sautou epimeleisthai*—to take care of yourself) entails.

It is surprising that in his extensive commentary on *Alcibiades*, Foucault never mentions a glaring logical gap in the dialogue's elenchus that occurs here. Socrates's aforementioned manipulative cajolery eventually leads to the key question that is the "only possible way . . . to find out what we ourselves might be": they must ask what itself is in itself (*auto to auto*, *Al*, 129b). This question—marked though it is with the "*ti estin*;" (what is . . . ?) formulation that introduces all of Socrates's great investigations ("What is justice?" and "What is virtue?"), and though expressly designated as vital to finding out who we are—is immediately lost and never investigated at all. Instead, it is subsumed into a different question: "What is a man?" (*ti pot' oun ho anthrōpos*; *Al*, 129e—a more emphatic and less scientific way of framing the "what is" question). This avoidance of the key query is too blatant to miss and must cause readers to view any result achieved without the answer with suspicion.[25]

Socrates sleekly reaches the conclusion that "if [man] *is* something, he's nothing other than his soul" (*Al*, 130c; original emphasis). While celebrating this heady conclusion, however, he still pauses to remind Alcibiades that they have cheated a bit:

> We skipped over, because it would have taken quite a lot of study . . . what we mentioned just now, that we should first consider what "itself" is, in itself. But in fact, we've been considering what an individual self is (*auton hekaston*), instead of what "itself" is. Perhaps that was enough for us, for surely nothing about us has more authority than the soul, wouldn't you agree? (*Al*, 130d)

It is almost as if Socrates is so nervous that Alcibiades's new aporetic willingness to philosophize may dissipate at any moment that he speeds to his high-blown conclusions with all the haste he can muster before his promising young friend loses interest. If being sure of what self-cultivation and self-knowledge entail is so vitally important, then one cannot help but distrust any conclusions reached by shirking the most essential inquiries only because they "would have taken quite a lot of study." In essence, Socrates's beautiful concluding image of two souls gazing into one another in mutual recognition is comprised—and compromised—by this glaring lack: a refusal to ascertain what the self is in the first place. The two souls admiring one another in reflection are necessarily empty at core until this work is done (if in fact such a thing could ever be discovered in the first place). Socrates's failure to complete the investigation with Alcibiades means that at the end of the dialogue, neither of the two men, lost in an exchange of flattering, erotic glances, can truly recognize himself or the other. Ancient readers were acutely aware that Alcibiades would go on to lead a life of self-aggrandizement, treachery, and double-dealing, and the apparent happy ending is already loaded with irony from this prior biographical knowledge. In calling readers' attention to this inadequacy, Plato builds Alcibiades's inevitable corruption into the construction of the very dialogue meant to represent Socrates's high hopes for the young man's future.

Although this aporia goes unremarked by Foucault, it nevertheless lends support to his diagnosis of a "paradox of Platonism." Foucault sees *Alcibiades* as a reflection of the irreducible tension between spirituality and rationality "in the history of European thought at least until the seventeenth century."[26] Socrates's evasion of the necessary but difficult rational argument here in his rush to reach the spiritual vision of the soul undermines his trust in both Logos and Eros. If the love that Socrates hopes will lead Alcibiades to self-knowledge and virtue can only climb Diotima's ladder by circumventing the logical work of elenchus, then neither reason nor love can hit the mark of their goals.

Troilus and Cressida is a demonstration of this failure, this rupture in the foundational possibility of self-knowledge, taken to its extreme.[27] Shakespeare gives Ulysses more speeches, and longer ones, than any other character in the play. Despite this, spectators hear less of what Ulysses actually thinks than they do from any of the other less eloquent and wordy characters. Ulysses never soliloquizes alone to himself on stage: he always has an audience—and the desires, weaknesses, or faculties of this audience determine the tenor and purpose of Ulysses's speech. Not once does

Shakespeare's Ulysses mention his longing for peace, for Ithaca, or for Penelope. It is impossible to construct any theory of Ulysses's motives on the basis of his own asseverations taken at face value, and what one can ascertain (by sifting through the varying strains of his conflicting dialogues in the play, playing a game of negation and reduction, and judging the actual results of his speeches in order to guess at his possible aims) is rife with conjecture. Shakespeare's Ulysses is the ultimate politician precisely because he is nothing but show. There is no secret or vulnerable core of the man that might betray the intended effect of whatever act he assumes. Homer's Odysseus is an endlessly fascinating figure because he is such a richly layered complex of worldly-wise, savvy, and deep-rooted loves and passions. Shakespeare's Ulysses is just as crafty but less complex. While Homer's hero has political *and* personal ends, Shakespeare's character consists only in his policy.[28] Any other motivations that might jeopardize his tactical plans—that might fill the hollow core of his machinations—have been removed. Strip away the stratagems from the man, and all you have left is an actor without any lines. Excise everything but the political from the character of Ulysses, and all that remains is theatricality: a consummate actor with no personal life for the tabloids to exploit. Shakespeare's play thus exposes the ultimately theatrical nature not only of politics but also of the constructed and performed individual.[29]

This was certainly not the first time that Shakespeare made his politicians supremely theatrical. Both Richards (II and III) are consummate actors who never cease to wallow in their performative genius. But they are also ultimately unsettled and even undone by the disparity between the roles they play and reality. Alexander Leggatt has located the "birth of tragedy" in Renaissance England in this general discomfort of the actor with the role. Modern tragedy, according to Leggatt, always springs from some dissonance between "role" and "self" (however tenuously constructed).[30] Ulysses in *Troilus and Cressida* avoids the danger of tragedy in that the text refuses to reveal any self that could chafe uneasily against the various roles he plays.

This glaring lack of a self in Ulysses is in itself a critique of the key thesis in Plato's *Alcibiades*. It has already been seen how impossible it is to pin the arguments espoused by Plato's characters on their author. It is difficult enough, in fact, to nail down any of the ideas to which Socrates's gives voice firmly even as the character's own true opinions. The arguments made by various incarnations of Socrates in Plato's dialogues often contradict each other. One must always take into account *to whom* Socrates is speaking and what Socrates's goal (stated or not) might be in any given situation with his interlocutors. Like Ulysses in *Troilus and Cressida*, Socrates only ever speaks to an audience; he never delivers a soliloquy, which might be read as a direct window to his true thoughts.[31]

The elusiveness of self in Ulysses is endemic to the entire play. Harold Bloom notes that "Shakespeare's art of characterization withdraws itself from *Troilus and Cressida*."[32] The interiorization of the self that he finds in a host of characters spanning the rest of Shakespeare's entire corpus is missing entirely from the figures in Troy and the Greek camp. The play thus picks up on a lack central to Socrates's doctrine of the self in *Alcibiades* and pushes it to its extreme.[33] Several passages throughout the play seem to deconstruct and dismantle identity (e.g., Troilus's denial of Cressida after witnessing her with Diomedes in the Greek camp [*TC*, 5.2] or the triple fugue of literary self-referential allusions before the consummation of Troilus and Cressida's lust [*TC*, 3.2]).[34] The analysis here, however, will limit itself to an examination of the conversation between Ulysses and Achilles that begins where Socrates and Alcibiades left off: with the beautiful image of an eye seeing itself in the reflection of another's eye.[35]

After staging his *Lehrstück* in mimetic desire for Achilles by engaging the acting services of the other generals, Ulysses remains behind to provide the interpretation for his didactic theater-piece so that the none-too-bright Achilles does not miss the point. The manner in which Ulysses decides to expound on this lesson, however, is itself quite revealing. He poses with a book within earshot of Achilles's first, untutored reaction to the "play." As it turns out, Achilles's unaided critical skills are incredibly apt.

> What, am I poor of late?
> 'Tis certain, greatness, once fall'n out with fortune,
> Must fall out with men too. What the declined is
> He shall as soon read in the eyes of others
> As feel in his own fall. (*TC*, 3.3.74–78)

The notion of coming to know one's own worth through the gazes of others is already so commonplace that Achilles does not need Ulysses to suggest it in a kind of directors' note. In fact, much of what Ulysses will expand on in the following passages is already contained in nuce in the lines of Achilles's initial reaction. He continues with the following:

> . . . for men, like butterflies,
> Show not their mealy wings but to the summer. (*TC*, 3.3.78–79)

The reflections to which Achilles is brought by the pageant (prior to the pageanter's exegetical tutelage) are a pale echo of Achilles's haunting speech in reply to Odysseus's embassy in the *Iliad*.

> For never had I benifite, that ever foild the foe:
> Even share hath he that keepes his tent and he to field doth go:
> With equall honour cowards die and men most valiant,
> The much performer and the man that can of nothing vant.
> No overplus I ever found when, with my mind's most strife
> To do them good, to dangerous fight I have exposd my life. (*Il*, 9, 318–322)[36]

Homer's Achilles is curiously wise in this passage, as he realizes that the human fate of mortality remains unchanged, whether a man remains inactive or fights bravely (think also of Falstaff's speech on honor).[37] Death makes all people equal. Shakespeare's Achilles meanwhile, in what is certainly his most reflective speech of the play, seems only partly aware of the consequences of this wisdom. It will be Ulysses's job in their subsequent conversation to keep Achilles away from this Homeric interpretation and steer him to the consequences of his own engineered reading. Again, Achilles goes on:

> And not a man, for being simply man,
> Hath any honour, but honour for those honours
> That are without him—as place, riches and favour,
> Prizes of accident as oft as merit;
> Which when they fall, as being slippery standers,
> The love that leaned on them as slippery too
> Doth one pluck down another and together
> Die in the fall. (*TC*, 3.3.80–87)

Like Socrates, Achilles already understands that attributes, possessions, and qualities of men are distinct from who they really are. A person is not valued for himself as himself (*auto to auto*) but rather only for those external belongings (social degree, material wealth, beauty, and esteem) he has accrued as often by chance as through any striving of his own. Achilles's puzzlement reaches a head in the very next words of denial he utters:

> But 'tis not so with me!
> Fortune and I are friends. I do enjoy
> At ample point all that I did possess,
> Save these men's looks, who do, methinks, find out
> Something not worth in me such rich beholding
> As they have often given. (*TC*, 3.3.87–92)

Achilles has not been deprived of the outward goods and qualities that had made men honor him before. Nevertheless, he has lost "these men's looks," and that fact alone robs all other riches of their value. There could be no clearer expression of the wonder and aporia to which Ulysses's theatrical trick has brought Achilles: his exclamations already contain the seeds of the interpretation Ulysses will provide. All it takes is a little push. The Ithacan has clearly been listening carefully to Achilles's reaction, and the "text" he then describes is nothing other than an exegesis and gloss of Achilles's own thoughts. Just as Socrates first tries to win Alcibiades's trust by revealing his knowledge of the youth's own secret ambitions, Ulysses can count on Achilles's agreement if he presents the soldier's private musings as the grounds for his further arguments. The difference is that whereas Socrates subsequently goes to great lengths to knock down Alcibiades's existing fallacious notions in order to construct an honest understanding in common dialectical effort to make Alcibiades a free agent in true knowledge of himself, Ulysses never goes beyond the rhetorician's trick of relying on his audience's existing beliefs, true or not, to persuade Achilles to be his tool and instrument in the wars.[38] Thersites, as usual, provides the keenest diagnosis of Achilles's servile role at Troy when he calls him and Ajax draught oxen yoked by Ulysses to "plough up the wars" (*TC*, 2.1.103)—an image that deprives their activity of valor and honor as well.

Ultimately, one might be tempted to consider the difference to be one of ends versus means: for Socrates, the lesson about knowledge of self and others afforded by the mirror analogy is not merely a rhetorical topos but the substantive reason for Alcibiades to follow his advice. Self-knowledge via intelligent observation of oneself in another's soul is Socrates's purported *end*: it is the express purpose for which Alcibiades ought to forgo public action. For Ulysses, however, the argument seems to serve only as a *means* to get Achilles back on the battlefield. A more careful consideration of Ulysses's position, however, proves to be not quite so simple. Since one cannot know (or even possess) what one is until one's attributes are reflected in the applause of others, one must be publicly active in order to achieve any kind of self-knowledge whatsoever. In Ulysses's logic too, therefore, his advice for Achilles to return to battle is a necessary means to the end of self-knowledge. In fact, Ulysses's cynical exposition of the argument can be seen to reveal something already inherent in Socrates's formulation. Ulysses reads the image not in airy terms of souls seeing souls but rather exclusively in language of material possession, of what man *has*:

> A strange fellow here
> Writes me that man, however dearly parted,
> How much in having, or without or in,
> Cannot make boast to have that which he hath,
> Nor feels not what he owes, but by reflection . . .
>
> . . . the author's drift,
> Who in his circumstance expressly proves
> That no man is the lord of anything,
> Though in and of him there be much consisting,
> Till he communicate his parts to others. (*TC*, 3.3.96–100; 114–118)[39]

Socrates too, immediately after explaining his analogy of the two eyes and the two souls to Alcibiades, makes the following claims:

> So if we didn't know ourselves and weren't self-controlled, would we be able to know which of the things that belong to us were good and which were bad? . . . And similarly we couldn't know that what belongs to us belongs to us, without knowing ourselves . . . And if we didn't even know what belongs to us, how could we possibly know what belongs to our belongings? (*Al*, 133c–d)

What follows is a long series of arguments based on the (lack of) knowledge about one's belongings and one's belongings' belongings. Despite these very deep complications about the self's complicity in its possessions or attributes, Socrates leaves the relation of the eye and the soul to the self (are they not also the self's "belongings"?) in the previous passage unexplained. Shakespeare's Ulysses simply dispenses with Socrates's tenuous assumption of the soul's primacy and autonomy in relation to the self and its belongings. His later glossing of the "author's drift" to Achilles, with all the haunting horrors of the "time" speech, is the logical conclusion of Socrates's position without this suspect soul.[40]

Even more shockingly, Ulysses's time speech can be taken as a reading precisely *of* Socrates's insistence on the soul. This is a classic case of what Blumenberg calls "reoccupation" (*Umbesetzung*): the demand for self-knowledge in Plato appears to take on a radical new meaning in Shakespeare, but in fact they are two responses to the same persistent question in varied historical contexts. Just as the failure to define and understand "itself itself" reveals an empty hole at the core of Socrates's vision of mutually regarding selves, so too is the very soul, which makes up the self, bereft—as it must be in Socrates's account—of every possession and quality that might distinguish it from another soul: a dangerously indistinct being. Girard diagnoses that "undifferentiation looms larger and larger in Shakespeare as desire 'ripens.'"[41] When Socrates equates the Delphic injunction to know oneself with the sensory imperative: "*ide seauton*!" (See thyself!; *Al*, 132d), which in effect amounts to two souls of indistinguishable substance leering lustfully at one another, we are not far from the paradox of narcissistic mimicry. Plato's dialogue already contains its own critique, which *Troilus and Cressida* makes explicit, since it displays the "paradox of the human self, the mysterious unity of self-centeredness and other-centeredness in all human beings"[42]

It may seem that Socrates's image of the reflecting eyes, leading as it does to a bright vision of interpersonal edification and the promise of attainable virtue and wisdom, is diametrically opposed to the dark, cruel world that the same trope points toward in Ulysses's speeches. In fact, however, the Ithacan merely takes elements already present in Socrates's argument and expounds on them to create the picture of a world where people can only know each other by constant motion, jockeying for fleeting glory, and theatrical self-display. With the hindsight of Alcibiades's actual career, one may well surmise this to be the Ulyssian lesson he in fact took away from all Socrates's hopeful efforts to the contrary. Ulysses, meanwhile, is ultimately no more successful in manipulating Achilles than Socrates is in educating Alcibiades, since it is the death of his friend and lover, Patroclus, rather than any rhetorical posturing that finally brings Achilles back to battle. The recognitions the two older men manage to engineer in their young interlocutors prove to be brief flashes "subject all / To envious and calumniating Time" (*TC*, 3.3.174–175).

Now that self-knowledge is revealed in its radical impermanence, it becomes clearer how it fits the definition of anagnorisis offered above (chapter 2). Coming to know oneself is a change that never ceases and occurs through the constant shuffling of interpersonal display. The necessity of repetition in the performance of recognition is not confined to acts of friendship between loved ones (chapter 4) but applies equally to self-knowledge. As long as knowing oneself depends on the perceived perceptions of others, it can never rest but exists through endlessly varied iteration. The Delphic injunction to know thyself hence is a process that can never reach completion. In fact, responsible self-knowledge takes on the aspect of the *practices* of self-care again, as Foucault would have wished (or as the "active condition" of Aristotelian *hexis* demands, for that matter).[43] Knowing oneself is a function of others' repeated acknowledgment of the roles one plays in the back-and-forth of the performance of recognition.

CHAPTER SEVEN

Metamorphoses of Recognition

Goethe's "Fortunate Event"

ODYSSEUS IS THE archetype for Goethe's image of himself.[1] The Greek hero accompanied three different kinds of recognition in Goethe's intellectual life. During his wanderings along the Mediterranean, Goethe became preoccupied with the *Odyssey* and began concrete plans to compose a drama based on Odysseus's encounter with Nausicaa.[2] It was while trying to concentrate on his readings of Homer in a lush garden in Palermo, which he mentally dubbed "Alcinous' Garten," that he discovered the *Urpflanze* (primal plant), the recognition of which would lead to his extensive botanical work and his invention of the science of morphology. This idea (or experience), in turn, would provide the central plot device for his autobiographical reflection, "Glückliches Ereignis" ("Fortunate Event"), which begins as a *nostos* (homecoming) tale with striking parallels to the *Odyssey*. Odysseus thus sojourns through Goethe's literary, scientific, and autobiographical writing, linking them together with the course of his passage.

In "Glückliches Ereignis," Aristotelian anagnorisis also ties together these three fields of activity in one dramatic moment. The short text is Goethe's account of an encounter with Friedrich Schiller in 1794 that changed the way the two men saw each other and led to the friendship that would permanently alter their lives. It functions as a conscious attempt on Goethe's part to come to terms with both the gain and the loss of his important friendship with Schiller, and the story's odd construction, organization, and wording—together with the context of its puzzling publication in a series of morphological journals—contrive the representation of three levels of knowledge vitally important to Goethe's understanding as a poet, scientist, and human being. This chapter follows the depiction of these modes of knowledge through the lines of "Glückliches Ereignis" and proposes that the figure of anagnorisis represents a paradoxical structure common to all three modes of knowing: theatrical, scientific, and ethical.

Aristotle's unique understanding of change (*metabolē*) is key to his *Physics* as well as to his dramatic term *recognition* (see chapter two). Goethe's studies of metamorphosis, meanwhile, are similarly crucial to both his scientific and literary imagination. In a way, one can plot the difference between ancient and modern conceptions of recognition by contrasting *metabolē* (meta + throw) with *Metamorphose* (meta + form/shape). For Aristotle, change is a complex operation at the threshold of actuality and potentiality that can have four basic types of causes (material, efficient, formal, and final)—only one of which proceeds from the form or shape of things and their relations, and the most important of which is teleological, that-for-the-sake-of-which. The efficient and material causes took on primary analytical power in the early modern era, meanwhile, as scientists began to explain the world in terms of mechanical forces and bodies acting on one another. Goethe's scientific endeavors were largely motivated by a reaction against this exclusively materialist mechanism. His thinking instead is dominated by attention to *form*. This may seem to be a throwback to a kind of Platonism, but in fact Goethe's *morphology* (a word that he coined) marks a radical shift in intellectual history at both the micro- and the macrolevel.[3] Just as chapter 2 of this book traced the logic of *metabolē* from Aristotelian physics to dramatic anagnorisis, this chapter will attend to the links that Goethe's concept of *Metamorphose* forges between the actions of recognition in his poetic, botanical, and ethical endeavors.

"GLÜCKLICHES EREIGNIS" AS ANAGNORISIS SCENE

"Glückliches Ereignis" tells the story of how Goethe and Schiller's initial enmity turned into a transformative friendship for both men. It was not published until 1817, some twenty-one years after the scenario described and twelve years after Schiller's death, and it conceals or glosses over several important details of the events leading up to and following the fateful meeting. Schiller, for instance, had already made generous overtures to Goethe in writing and through the intervention of mutual friends during the months preceding their first conversation in Jena. Goethe had in fact already agreed to contribute to Schiller's pet project, the journal *Die Horen*, though in the narrative the invitation and its acceptance occur as a result of the described encounter. Goethe also seems to conflate several different discussions that took place in Jena in July and September in the one episode he recounts. Even their meeting, which Goethe presents as spontaneous, unexpected, and coincidental, was prearranged by Schiller and his friends as a way to jump-start the intended rapprochement.[4] This is not to say that Goethe misrepresented the nature of his relations prior to and following the meeting in Jena—no one can deny that a real antipathy existed between the two writers in the years before 1794 and that a rich and productive friendship blossomed between them in the decade thereafter. As evident in carefully researched biographical accounts and primary sources, or even just the first few letters of Goethe's correspondence with Schiller, however, it is clear that the ill will, harbored grudges, and mutual suspicion dissolved slowly and that the friendship—though truly dramatic in its reversal—grew by faltering steps rather than in a momentary about-face. I suggest instead that "Glückliches Ereignis" strategically rearranges a few details in order to present the *process* of the change from hostility to friendship in the instant singularity of a tableau.

Goethe's account is a tale of sudden and fortuitous turnaround from extreme antipathy to deep and meaningful friendship and from artistic barrenness to fruitful productivity. The text records Goethe's disappointment and lethargy in the years directly following his return from Italy. He felt "paralyzed." The rapprochement with Schiller, however, sealed a cooperative "alliance that continued uninterrupted and brought about quite a bit of good for ourselves and others."[5] In emphasizing their estrangement previous to the encounter, Goethe writes that Schiller's "hateful" works "disgusted" him "utterly"[6]: "No association was conceivable."[7] He then frames their carefully arranged meeting as a fateful coincidence, by first recalling that he made a habit of attending Batsch's botanical lectures and then adding, "One time I discovered Schiller there, we *coincidentally* both left at the same time, and a conversation ensued."[8] Goethe even throws in the spice of tense precariousness at the moment of climax: after Schiller declares Goethe's presentation of the metamorphosis of plants to be an idea and not an experience, he narrates how much it irked him. He recalled some insulting lines from one of Schiller's essays, and "the old rancor wanted to rise up again." One imagines how easy it would have been for Goethe to withdraw behind his wonted coolness and distance, but he "pulled himself together" and came out instead with his famous quip: "Well, bully for me, then, that I have ideas without knowing it and can even see them with my own eyes!"[9] This one-liner combines in its harmonious fury and humor at once an expression of Goethe's very real frustration with Schiller's unwillingness to accept the relation of his experiences as such, a droll debunking of Schiller's Kantian pretentions, and a humble admission of the untenability of Goethe's own position. It is an invitation for the two men to laugh at themselves and to accept the trenchant difference of opinion as a stimulus—an *Anstoß*—rather than impediment to their relations. Precisely because of this engaged and passionate challenge to one another, they become fast friends and collaborators: thus, "by means of the greatest, perhaps never to be entirely reconcilable competition between object and subject,"[10] they forged a friendship that was a boon to themselves and others.

The structure of this narrative, as Goethe frames it in "Glückliches Ereignis," bears a striking resemblance to the classical drama of reversal and recognition as described by Aristotle. A peripeteia, recall, is "the change to the opposite of the things being done . . . in accord with what is likely or necessary." The definition of anagnorisis should be familiar to readers of this book by now. "A recognition is most beautiful," Aristotle says, "when it happens at the same time as a reversal" (*P*, 11, 1452a).[11] Every detail of the narrated account matches Aristotle's prescriptions perfectly. Goethe even manages to stress the events' accordance with "what is likely or necessary," which is a demand repeatedly linked by Aristotle to imitations of surprising plot twists. He mentions that his attendance at Batsch's lectures in Jena was habitual and that Schiller had just moved to Jena: the "chance" occurrence of Schiller's presence at the lecture and the equally "accidental" incident of their happening to strike up a conversation on the lecture's subject matter upon leaving the hall are natural and likely, even if at the same time the subject matter's fortuitous felicity in bringing the two men's differences to a point of harmonious contrast is remarkably surprising. This combination of the wonderful and the natural is precisely Aristotle's recipe for a well-made plot. The inclusion of reversals and recognitions, and especially the coincidence of both in the same scene, serves to make a story complex and, more importantly, to let a story move men's souls. In "Glückliches Ereignis," Goethe has fashioned his encounter with Schiller into the most beautiful type of drama, in which Goethe's reversal from poetic fallowness to creative ferment occurs simultaneously with his discovery that Schiller is not a foe but a friend.

Why does Goethe, consciously or not, go to such lengths to recast the remembered events into this moving plot structure? Surely it is not merely to make the brief account more dramatic and memorable (though it certainly manages to do this as well). One cannot answer this question without expanding one's view to other aspects of the text: the adroitly crafted theatrical anagnorisis (enemies become friends) is not the only type of recognition going on here. The narrative also dramatizes how the two men develop reflective and mutually influential views of one another. Goethe's account of his contrast with Schiller becomes most visible at the height of the very climax where anagnorisis and peripeteia converge, when Goethe is about to withdraw in frustration and their incipient friendship is in sudden danger of collapse: the irreconcilable difference between what Goethe claimed as "experience" and Schiller classified as "idea."[12] This meeting spawned the respective character sketches of themselves and each other, pictures that were never quite congruent but always mutually responsive and challenging.[13] Not only does the moment of peripeteia coincide with the foe-to-friend anagnorisis here, but it also occurs simultaneously with the genesis of a powerful explanatory model of understanding themselves and one another. Goethe's account expands the traditional trope of anagnorisis to include and crystallize the reflecting counterimage of the other, and in so doing, it utilizes the dramatic form of recognition to reveal the necessary relation of reversal and discovery with a kind of schematic and intuitive understanding of character: a picture of self-knowledge formed with and through recognition of the other.[14]

The recognition scene as a scene, as a dramatic unity, underscores the central paradox of recognition as such: one is forced to contain the living fullness and totality of another being in the limited picture of the imagination. Three such problematic objects of knowledge converge at the climax of Goethe's tale: the *Urpflanze*, the scientific and epistemological topic of their conversation; Schiller's and Goethe's schematic understandings of each other and themselves; and a synoptic view of the process whereby this understanding comes about—that is, the action of anagnorisis. This is not to suggest that these three orders of knowledge are identical by any means, but they share a very peculiar structure. All three types of knowledge are constituted by a process: a long and often difficult activity. All three, however, tend to be represented—to oneself or to others—as moments or flashes of insight. Contrast, for example, Goethe's chronicle of the slow, plodding *Werdegang* (gait of becoming) of his understanding of the *Urpflanze* in "Geschichte meiner botanischen Studien" ("History of My Botanical Studies") with the depiction in *Italienische Reise* (*Italian Journey*). In a later expansion of the former text (which significantly appeared together with "Glückliches Ereignis" in the first issue of Goethe's periodical *Morphologische Hefte* [*Morphological Notebooks*]), Goethe claims the following:

> Nicht also durch eine außerordentliche Gabe des Geistes, nicht durch eine momentane Inspiration, noch unvermutet und auf einmal, sondern durch ein folgerechtes Bemühen bin ich endlich zu einem so erfreulichen Resultate gelangt. (HA, 13, 167)
>
> (Not by an extraordinary gift of intellect, not by a momentary inspiration, unexpected and sudden, but rather by consistent effort did I finally reach such a pleasing result.)

In his *Italienische Reise*, meanwhile (whose initial publication in 1816–1817 took place within a year of the first issue of *Morphologische Hefte*), Goethe's account of his conception of the *Urpflanze* is strikingly different and can easily be construed as a "momentary inspiration, unexpected and in a flash," despite all claims to the contrary in "Geschichte meiner botanischen Studien." Descriptions of the (experienced) idea's genesis in the reconstructed diaries and letters published as *Italienische Reise* present a vision of Goethe wandering among the beautiful and exotic plants of Palermo, dreaming up a tragedy about Odysseus's encounter with Nausicaa, imagining himself in her father's garden, when he is struck by the sudden conviction that there must be an archetype, an *Urpflanze* uniting all the manifold variations of individual plants: "There must be such a thing! How else would I otherwise recognize (*erkennen*) that this or that object (*Gebilde*) is a plant, if they were not formed (*gebildet*) according to a single pattern?"[15] A little later, he adds that the botanical notion that thus possessed him drove away his poetical musings and transformed the world he saw around him: "My good poetical purpose was disturbed, the garden of Alcinous disappeared, a world-garden had opened up."[16] In a letter to Herder that was also included in the *Italienische Reise*, Goethe confides the "secret of plant reproduction and organization" with a description that is similarly sudden and transformative (HA, 11, 323).

This contradiction (the drive to represent ongoing, successive processes as singular moments, schematic formulae, or turning points) seems to be an inherent tendency. Yet instead of struggling to change or deny it, Goethe and Aristotle make the most of this curious feature of human cognition. Aristotle displays this quirk by identifying anagnorisis as an ongoing *action* whose depiction in a contained praxis is the greatest means to move men's souls (see chapter 2). Goethe also makes productive use of this paradox in all three fields brought together in his climactic tale: his scientific studies; his poetical efforts; and his self-reflexive life among men. To see how these three dramas of knowledge hang together, another return to the *Poetics* is in order.

RECOGNIZING ACTION: VISUALIZING STORIES

Chapter 16 of the *Poetics* presents a list of the various "kinds" of recognition, all of which, as shown in chapter 3, are reducible to the type of sign through which the recognition takes place. An alternative taxonomy of recognition can also be deduced from Aristotle's observations in the *Poetics*, which is perhaps more fundamental in its division of recognition according to its *objects* rather than its *means*. It is clear from the discussion following the definition in book 11 that the operation of recognition is not limited to discoveries of people but can also occur in relation to things or actions, even if these other types are not as dramatic as those between people. This admission lets one discern three distinct types of recognition (*P*, 11, 1452a, 36):

Types of Recognition

1. Of people
2. Of nonliving and random things
3. Of actions (i.e., whether someone has done something)

All three of these kinds of recognition play important roles in the text of the *Poetics* and, as will soon become clear, in both "Glückliches Ereignis" and readers' approaches to it. See these examples:

1. Goethe recognizes Schiller.
2. Scientists recognize the archetype of all plants.
3. Readers recognize the unifying action depicted in the narrative.

Before attending to these levels in the German text, however, it is necessary to pursue the action of recognition through the *Poetics* in order to show how *knowledge* on the one hand and *ethics* on the other converge in the action of recognition, regardless of its object.

The first incidence of recognition occurs already in book 4, in which mimesis or imitation figures as one of the most distinctive and important features of human nature. Aristotle traces the origin of the poetic arts back to two sources, both of which are aspects of mimesis. First of all, imitation is an inherent element of our behavior that both marks us as human and serves as a basis for our knowledge:

> For imitating is co-natural with human beings from childhood, and in this they differ from the other animals because they are the most imitative and produce their first acts of understanding by means of imitation. (*P*, 4, 1448b, 6)

Second of all, imitation is something in which we naturally take great delight. Both the pleasure and instruction provided by mimesis, however—imitation as entertainment and as a foundation of knowledge—participate in the same basic structure. They involve an act of learning in which philosophers and nonphilosophers alike can partake:

> What is responsible for this [delight in imitation] is that understanding [*manthanein* = learning, coming to know] is most pleasant not only for philosophers but for everyone else, though they share in it to a short extent. They delight in seeing images for this reason: because understanding [*manthanein*] and reasoning out [*sullogizesthai*; i.e., one of the means of recognition to be delineated in chapter 16] what each thing is results when they contemplate them, for instance "that's who this is." (*P*, 4, 1448b, 13ff.)

Both the joy and edification that imitation affords are the result of an act of recognition. It is the excited exclamation, "That's him!" (*houtos ekeinos*—literally "This one is that one!") in which the epistemological and pleasurable boons of mimesis bear fruit. The pleasure need not derive from imitations of human beings nor even of beautiful things. Even "contemptible insects and dead bodies" (*P*, 4, 1448b, 13) can provide the enjoyable "click" of recognition.

Hence one first sees anagnorisis in action in Aristotle's book on poetry at the very roots of the poetic art: it is an integral and necessary element of imitation. Then in books 11 and 16, anagnorisis makes its explicit entrance as a vital part of any story that should move men's souls. Immediately following book 16 on the types of anagnorisis, moreover, recognition makes a third appearance in the activity of poets or critics viewing a work of fiction. Before elaborating on this final model, let me propose another list of three different kinds of recognition in action in the *Poetics*. If Aristotle's own enumeration of five (or six, depending on one's interpretation) types of anagnorisis in book 16 is based on its *means* and my above division into three classes was derived from the *objects* of recognition mentioned by Aristotle, then the present distillation could be said to identify three separate *levels* of recognition:

Levels of Recognition

1. Audience recognizes character.
   The audience recognizes subject of depiction: "That's him!" (*P*, chaps. 4, 13, 15, 22; e.g., "The chubby one must be Goethe!").[17]
2. Character recognizes character (person recognizes person).
   Within the plot, this is "change from ignorance to knowledge leading to friendship or enmity among persons headed for good or bad fortune" (*P*, chaps. 11, 14, 16; e.g., Goethe comes to know Schiller).
3. Audience recognizes the action of recognition in the story.
   One character recognizing another in turn "moves the soul" of the audience (*P*, chaps. 6, 9, 22; e.g., Goethe's coming to know Schiller excites readers by its unexpected yet natural surprise. Secondarily, readers come to know that recognition is the central action of the text as a whole).

The schemata of these three levels of recognition, which can be seen as a kind of zigzag between the within and the without of the dramatic work and between audience/reader and play/poem, demonstrate how anagnorisis unites in one action both epistemology and ethics. The pleasing "aha!" moment of identification on the first level (present in every instance of recognition) is an operation of coming-to-know. On the second level, when regarding another person, this new knowledge leads to friendship or enmity and hence enjoins one to reevaluate one's relational responsibility to the other. The degree of attentiveness that one is called on to give to a story on the third level is itself a unification of the demands of knowledge and ethics in the first two.

Book 17 offers a model in nuce of the task of the poet and critic, and if one takes time to crack the nut, all three levels of anagnorisis make up layers of the shell. After having stressed the importance of beholding the general outline of a story in organizing and working out a play or a poem, Aristotle illustrates his point with plot synopses of two stories: one drama, *Iphigenia among the Taurians*, and one epic, *The Odyssey*. Recognition is at work in three vital ways here. The first level of anagnorisis has to work backward, so to speak, from its normal operation: instead of seeing an actor on stage and thinking, "Oh, that's Iphigenia!" we are urged to forget her particular identity for the moment and label her as "a certain girl."[18] On the second level, within the plot, we are led to see that both of these stories hinge on a recognition scene (or scenes, in the case of Odysseus) that, at least for *Iphigenia*, coincides with the peripeteia, the reversal or turning point, of the action. On the third level, the very operation Aristotle exemplifies with these two summaries is a kind of recognition: Aristotle has urged the poet "to put [the stories] before the eyes," since only thus can one distinguish the central action from mere episodes. True, this is not the kind of recognition that can be imitated for a soul-moving drama, a virtue book 11 has already reserved for recognition between persons, but Aristotle admits that anagnorisis "can happen in relation to nonliving and random things, or to recognize [*anagnōrizein*] whether someone has or has not done something" (*P*, 11, 1452a, 35). This is precisely what a poet must do before she can shape her material into a soul-moving work of art. All of these operations of recognition—the identification of "types," the encounters between persons resulting in changes in knowledge that lead to friendship or enmity, and encounters with objects resulting in the contemplation of actions as wholes—are vital parts of "Glückliches Ereignis" and readers' engagement with it as a dramatic scenario and a text.

Throughout this investigation, I will leap from viewing operations of recognition within the text and its action to observing myself view the account and try to behold the structure of recognition on the part of the reader. In this process, I will also take a cue from book 17 of the *Poetics*. We have already seen how Aristotle advises poets to recognize the central action of a story and how he closes the chapter with two examples of this exercise that amount, unsurprisingly, to the kind of central plot synopsis that one might find in any standard reference work on mythology. This is the predictable result of someone trying to set down the main idea or "general content" (*P*, 17, 1455b, 3) of a story: the skeletal outline of its central events. The method that Aristotle recommends for a poet to arrive at a view of the central action of a story, however, is quite surprising. Considering the etymological roots of words like *theory*, *synopsis*, *idea*, and so on in vocabulary of the physically visible, one might expect the poet or the critic to *step back* from her creation in order best to see its proper lineaments. Perspective and distance are generally held to be necessary for fair discernment of form. Instead, Aristotle encourages poets imaginatively to place themselves *within* their works: to place them before the eyes, yes, but to view them as if from within their midst:

> In order to organize the stories and work them out with their wording, one ought, as much as possible, to *put them before the eyes*. For one who *sees things most vividly* in this way, *as if he were among the very actions taking place*, would find what is appropriate and would least overlook incongruities. A sign of this is what Carcinus was blamed for . . . which he overlooked by not *visualizing* it. . . . As many things as possible ought to be *worked out with gestures*, for those who are *immersed in the experience* are the most persuasive from nature itself. (*P*, 17, 1455a, 22–28; emphases mine)

This is a process of distilling the central movement of the plot not through some intellectual operation arrived at by judicial observation from afar but rather in the very sensual activity of imagining one is seeing the story performed: of actively placing oneself in the physical presence of the actors and visualizing their gestures. One would think that, far from revealing the structural core of the plot, this method would lead poets to get caught up in the details of spectacle, which Aristotle seems to disparage.[19] But no—imagining its *performance* is the way to recognize the central movement of the story. And Aristotle does not stop with his deservedly famous demand that one place the story "before the eyes." He also suggests that one imaginatively work through the gestures and the other sensual affects of an experience in order to discern the true core shape of an action. He almost seems to condone a kind of proto-Stanislavskian "method" for the poet. But just as Stanislavski struggled throughout his career to find a balance between the loss of control that results from tapping the well-springs of the actor's emotional history and the control necessitated by an intellectual understanding of the character being portrayed within the larger framework of the drama, so too would Aristotle's method appear fraught with problems. Paradoxically, in order to identify the one action in a story that should serve as the organizing principle of the whole, an artist must project herself into the immediacy of a single scene. How can one "immersed in the experience" of all the physical sensations and emotional pulls of a story judiciously distinguish central action from mere episode? Standing naked and salt-encrusted with Odysseus on the beach of Phaeacia as he gazes at the bathing form of Nausicaa, any poet would be hard pressed not to be "persuaded from nature itself" to identify her story as the most moving and important part of the tale.[20] As if in acknowledgment of this difficulty, Aristotle closes the paragraph with one of his few jokes—harking back to Plato's *Ion* and setting the stage for Shakespeare's Theseus—saying that poets teeter precariously on the border between brilliant talent and insanity: "Hence, the poetic art belongs either to a naturally gifted person or an insane one, since those of the former sort are easily adaptable and the latter are out of their senses" (*P*, 17, 1455a, 28–30).

Yet this seeming paradox of methodology has guided me in writing this chapter (and indeed the entire book). I aim both to visualize as much as possible the action of Goethe's narrative (or drama) in all its immediacy on the stage of the imagination (or in all its concretion on the page) and to share the difficulties and rewards of trying to grasp this action "as a whole" (that is, to recognize it "in general"[21]), which is a task of both poet and critic. The simultaneous injunctions that one must see the story in its wholeness at a glance and that one must be immersed in the sensual experience of the story's details require readers to dip back and forth from within and without the text, to sink into close engaged reading and then to gasp for breath as one surfaces for air and a wider perspective. My effort will be to trace the acts of anagnorisis on all three levels along the fixed lines of text on the page and in the fluid dance of spoken word and spectacle in the mind's eye.

In insisting that the central action of "Glückliches Ereignis" is recognition, I would not seem to be making any new or revolutionary claim. After all, its version of the rapprochement between Goethe and Schiller, with the *Idee* versus *Erfahrung* (idea vs. experience) exchange, is the one anecdote about the two men's relation most often remembered and quoted. But although everyone gloms onto the story embedded at the center of the text, most commentators focus more on defending or debunking the accuracy of the iconic characterization of the two men and their relations as it was "canonized" in the text, or they concentrate instead on what it reveals about Goethe's scientific views.[22] No treatment of the encounter considers it as an anagnorisis scene or interprets the rest of the text in light of this central motif. In fact, the final four paragraphs of "Glückliches Ereignis" are almost universally ignored, although they offer some of the most fascinating reflections on the limits and potentials of our knowledge vis-à-vis other human beings.

The brief text consists of only fourteen paragraphs in all. Of them, only four (8–11) deal explicitly with the oft-repeated anecdote of the famous encounter: the "fortuitous event" itself. As seen above, it contains rising tension, a mounting climax, and a harmoniously tense resolution of the central story. While the first seven paragraphs partly manage the preparatory work for this embedded climax (again, as instanced above), much of their bulk and wording would be puzzling without tying them to the central thread of recognition. The final three paragraphs, which usually go uncommented and are in fact entirely lopped off of many anthologized versions of the text,[23] can only be properly interpreted through the lens of the moral demands and epistemic limitations of recognition.[24]

To begin with, however, the first half of the essay already opens up interesting vistas of anagnorisis. The opening sentence of the small text is a compact piling-on of conditionals that map out the structure of the tragedy[25] to be narrated with their intensifying layers of comparisons.

Protasis:

- *Genoß* ich die schönsten Augenblicke meines Lebens zu gleicher Zeit, als ich der Metamorphose der Pflanzen nachforschte, als mir die Stufenfolge derselben klar geworden,
- *begeistete* mir diese Vorstellung den Aufenthalt von Neapel und Sizilien,
- *gewann* ich diese Art das Pflanzenreich zu betrachten immer mehr und mehr lieb,
- *übte* ich mich unausgesetzt daran auf Wegen und Stegen;

Apodosis:

- *so* mußten mir diese vergnüglichen Bemühungen dadurch unschätzbar werden, indem sie Anlaß gaben zu einem der höchsten Verhältnisse, die mir das Glück in spätern Jahren bereitete. (HA, 10, 538; emphasis and diagrammatic presentation mine)

(Protasis:

- *If* I *enjoyed* the most beautiful moments of my life at the same time as I was researching the metamorphosis of plants, and their sequential development was becoming clear to me,
- *if* this imagined representation *inspired* me during my stay in Naples and Sicily,
- *if* I *became* more and more fond of this way of regarding the plant world,
- *if* I *gave myself practice* in it constantly as I made my way around [literally: on paths and footbridges];

Apodosis:

- *then* these pleasurable efforts had to become invaluable to me by providing the occasion to one of the most exalted relationships with which fortune favored me in later years.)

This complex layering of clauses encapsulates the beginning and end of the action to be imitated in the story to follow: "*If* I enjoyed the most beautiful moments of my life while I explored the metamorphosis of plants back in Italy (etc.), *then* these efforts became even more valuable by providing the occasion for my later fortune." It is important to note how the text begins by evoking the lost happiness of Goethe's Italian sojourn before linking it to the (by the time of writing) now equally lost happiness of his friendship with Schiller. There is an elegiac tone to this foreshadowing of a happy ending reflected already in the first sentence of the story. The text will return to this combination of wistfully impossible longing with hopefully expectant sanguinity in its closing paragraphs. It is also significant that the first sentence is composed of such an extreme series of conditionals. One almost has to diagram it (as above) in order to fully appreciate the force of the if-then clauses. This is no paradigmatic conditional construction, contrafactual or otherwise, that one might have encountered in Latin class.[26] The four main verbs of the protasis do not technically present a condition in which the fulfillment is necessary to determine the truth content of the apodosis. Instead, we meet with a series of intensifications: "*If* I enjoyed x, *if* x enthused my experience of Naples, *if* I came to love x more and more, *if* I practiced x constantly (all of which is tacitly understood to be the case) . . . *then* x was made even more invaluable by bringing about y." In other words, x (i.e., Goethe's ideas about the metamorphosis of plants) is doubly great for making both his time in Italy pleasant and for making his friendship with Schiller possible. Again, the contingent and tentative nature of the conditional structure contrasts the repeated heightening of positive clauses to create a contradictory mood: the sentence weaves the syntax of uncertainty with the lexical intensification of optimism. The second and final sentence of the paragraph then brings all three levels of knowledge mentioned in the first (and thematized throughout the text) into tight interdependence:

> Die nähere Verbindung mit Schiller [i.e., the recognition of another person] bin ich diesen erfreulichen Erscheinungen [i.e., the recognition of the metamorphosis of plants] schuldig, sie beseitigten die

> Mißverhältnisse, welche mich lange Zeit von ihm entfernt hielten [i.e., the action of dramatic anagnorisis] (HA, 10, 538).
>
> (I owe the closer relationship with Schiller [i.e., the recognition of another person] to these gratifying appearances [i.e., the recognition of the metamorphosis of plants]; they cleared away the poor relations that held distant from him for so long [i.e., the action of dramatic anagnorisis]).

In other words: "I owe the recognition of Schiller to the recognition of plants since it set in motion our recognition scene."

The second, fourth, and fifth paragraphs describe Goethe's return to Germany from Italy, where the very first sentence already stressed he had spent the "most beautiful moments" of his life (HA, 10, 538). It does so in the manner of every good and honest homecoming story ever since the *nostos* of Odysseus, who finally made his way back to Ithaca only to find his home beleaguered by hostile suitors for his wife's hand. What Goethe discovered on his return home "disgusted" him; the popular poets, wooing and winning the hearts of his countrymen, were "hated" by him; Schiller poured forth on his "Vaterland" the very juvenile excesses Goethe himself had learned to be ashamed of (HA, 10, 538). Indeed, Schiller and Heinse figure as the suitors vying for the love of Goethe's German public, whom he had abandoned to travel afar. The German readers prove not quite as faithful and patient as Penelope.

Both the returner and the land left behind have changed in the interval of absence. There is never any true homecoming: every *nostos* contains *algea* (pain), and there is an element of this estranged homecoming to every instance of recognition.[27] This *nostos* is uncanny because the suitors seem to Goethe to be earlier, less mature versions of himself. The fourth paragraph especially represents the nadir of Goethe's alienation after his return, the general approbation of the uncouth suitors: "that bizarre spawn . . . frightened me, for I believed all my efforts to be lost."[28] The disappointed and bitter tone of Goethe's description of what he found on his own return to the homeland (after nearly two years of imagining himself under the same sky and on the same seas as Odysseus) is fitting preparation for the way he recounts his most dramatic recognition scene—a more true and satisfying homecoming than Goethe's soured relations with his reading public (or with Charlotte von Stein).

If Schiller and Heinse are rapacious suitors wooing Goethe's readers away, then like Odysseus, by rights he will have to slay them. Instead, the third paragraph foreshadows (in its attempt to "excuse" Schiller for the bad taste of *The Robbers* [1781]) what will figure as the greatest challenge to true recognition in the final section of "Glückliches Ereignis": humans' ever-changing natures. People, it claims, cannot help but be active in terms of whatever stage of *Bildung* (development, education, culture, formation) they are in at any given moment: "This is why so many wonderful and ridiculous things spread over the world, and confusion develops from confusion."[29] The potential for misunderstanding caused by the challenge of comprehending another human in the flurried midst of her own (and one's own) metamorphoses is downright dizzying. The few reflections Goethe offers following the narration of his recognition scene with Schiller will provide the only answer he can give to the dangers alluded to here.

The sixth paragraph contains a critique of Schiller's essay "On Grace and Dignity" in which Goethe even recognized some passages as a parody of himself.[30] He accuses Schiller here of mistaken recognition.[31] More fundamental, however, is Goethe's criticism of Schiller's Kantianism, which also amounts to an attack on Schiller's mode of recognizing things in the world around him: "Instead of observing [nature] as independently, vividly, and lawfully generating from the depths to the heights, he took it from the perspective of a few empirical, human instincts."[32] The alternative Goethe praises, of viewing nature as "independent, living, and lawfully productive," turns out to be the very mode of seeing that Goethe recommends to the scientist. Despite the evident difficulties of seeing nature as a living whole, it is the only method he holds to be equal to the task of recognizing the true sources of the phenomena around us.[33]

The challenges of this approach to nature are similar to the ones faced by the reader in seeing the principle praxis of a story. It should now be clear, however, how the very problem of such a vision is refracted in its multitudinous manifestations throughout the text of "Glückliches Ereignis"—both in the introductory musings that make up the entire first half of the piece as well as in the central action of recognition imitated in the narration. In considering the third mode of knowledge represented in the text, that of seeing other people, the paradox of recognition in the final section of the text will become visible. First, however, let us look more closely at the kind of recognition Goethe recommends to Schiller as an antidote to the Kantianism of "Grace and Dignity."

RECOGNIZING THINGS: EXPERIENCING IDEAS

Ultimately, this poetical problem of recognizing a story's central action (both in its creative and critical aspect) is kin to the epistemological one of "intellectual intuition" (*intellektuelle Anschauung*) or, as Goethe preferred to name it, "intuitive judgment" (*anschauende Urteilskraft*), which was at once a bone of contention and the seed of friendship between Schiller and Goethe. It is indeed fortuitous that the *glückliches Ereignis*, the plot twist that brought about their recognition scene, took the form of a discussion about the very contradiction inherent in all instances of anagnorisis.[34] In the account the text offers, Goethe was enthused and encouraged by Schiller's dissatisfaction with the "fragmented (*zerstückelte*) way of handling nature" evinced by Batsch's lecture. In response, Goethe launched into an excited description of another kind of knowledge. He explained

> daß es doch wohl noch eine andere Weise geben könne, die Natur nicht gesondert und vereinzelt vorzunehmen, sondern sie wirkend und lebendig, aus dem Ganzen in die Teile strebend darzustellen. (HA, 10, 540)

> (that there can well be another way. Instead of taking on nature separately and individually, [one can] represent it active and alive, from the whole into the parts.)

This amounts to a precise description of the mode of knowledge that Immanuel Kant elaborates on in the *Critique of Judgment* (1790) as imaginable by but unattainable to humans.[35] For Kant, human understanding works discursively. Our knowledge requires two elements—a spontaneous conceptual faculty that bestows form on experience and a receptive faculty that receives the content of experience. He insists that these two elements can only ever be distinct in humans; for Goethe, this would doom us to a forever *zerstückelte* (fragmented, torn limb from limb) way of seeing nature. The tantalizing bait Kant held out with his vision of a "divine understanding" that could operate not discursively but intuitively was infinitely more appealing to Goethe, and what's more, the poet/scientist was convinced he had *experienced* just this mode of knowledge in his conception of the archetypical plant.

Schiller, as a good Kantian, refused to accept that his soon-to-be friend could "experience" the symbolic plant Goethe sketched for him in their fatefully fortunate encounter. He insisted that the insight was an "idea," to which Goethe quipped sarcastically that he was lucky to be able to *see* ideas with his own eyes.[36] This gibe discloses the foundation of true scientific knowledge for Goethe. He concludes that it "is not a conceptual unity that the understanding contributes, but a unity that is the object's own."[37] Good Kant scholar though Eckart Förster is, he refuses to condemn this seemingly ridiculous notion outright without taking the time and effort to replicate Goethe's many years of experience with plants.

It is worthwhile to examine another report of the encounter between Goethe and Schiller, because it is instructive in revealing what is involved in seeing wholes or archetypes in and through the partial appearances humans have access to. The following account was recorded by Johannes Daniel Falk after a conversation with Goethe in 1812:

> Nun traf es sich, daß beim Nachhausegehn die Rede auf die Vorlesung kam, wo ich bemerkte, daß man sich unaufhörlich mit den Generibus und Speciebus der Pflanzen herumquälte und darüber *das Allerwichtigste, die Verwandlung, den Übergang, die Metamorphose* vernachlässigte. Ich teilte ihm hierüber meine Ansicht mit, die er freudig auffaßte und hinzufügte, dies sei ja eine Idee, und ich möchte sie ihm ja nicht vorenthalten. Ob es eine Idee sei versetzte ich, das läßt mich völlig unbekümmert, die Data aber, die *meine Betrachtung* zu diesen Resultaten führten kann ich jedem *vor Augen legen*.[38]

> (Now it happened that on the way home we came to speak about the lecture, and I remarked that by struggling endlessly with the generibus and speciebus of plants, one neglected the *most important, the transformation, the transition, the metamorphosis*. I shared my view with him, and he joyfully took it in, adding that this was an idea, and that I could hardly deny him that. Whether it is an idea, I replied, is of no concern to me, but I can lay the data that led *my observation* to these results *before the eyes* of anyone.)

The highlighted portions of this excerpt point to two important aspects of the kind of recognition Goethe strives for. First of all, it is to the *transitions* that we must turn our attention. What plants have in common with the action of a drama or another human being with whom one comes into contact is the fact that all three of them live in *motion*: they play out their natures in processes of change and development, which, at least for individual plants, stories, and people, all have clear beginnings and ends. Hence to see a plant or an action as a whole, or in coming to know another person (or oneself), the understanding must move along with the transitions and metamorphoses they undergo. Förster lays out the two requirements of this kind of observation: "First, we must follow a natural process completely, from beginning to end. Second, this process must then be held together, as it were, and *viewed as a whole*, as a single phenomenon."[39] Not only is recognition an action, as Aristotle makes clear, but Goethe lets us see that its objects are also in motion. The problematic activity of anagnorisis involves getting one moving process in sync with another: of "molding oneself well" to a foreign process. This truly fits the job description Aristotle gave the poet: the "naturally gifted" (*euphuous*) who are "easily adaptable" (*euplastoi*). Literally, they are of a "good nature" and can "mold themselves well and easily." Seth Benardete translates the latter term as "easily take on any shape,"[40] and this precisely describes the characteristics of the scientist in her study of a phenomenon according to Goethe: her mind must mold itself to the object of her study.

If one hears the echo of Aristotle's demands for the poet in Goethe's requirements for the scientist, then it is no wonder that the madman is not far behind: "And an effect of nature that, as the idea demands, we should think at the same time as simultaneous and successive, seems to set us into a kind of insanity."[41] "Yet," Förster concludes, "this is what Goethe requires of an adequate attitude towards living nature."[42] It is also what Goethe and Aristotle both require of an adequate attitude toward moving plays and living people.

RECOGNIZING PEOPLE: MOVING TABLEAUX

A second point of interest in Falk's report arises from its alternate version of Goethe's reply to Schiller's doubt. Here, upon Schiller's insistence that the *Urpflanze* is an idea, instead of the challenge-contained-within-a-self-deprecatory-admission-disclosing-an-invitation of the famous quip from "Glückliches Ereignis," Goethe claims to have replied that he doesn't care if it's an idea but that he can provide evidence that will make anyone see it.[43] The facts that lead Goethe's *Betrachtung*—his view, inspection, or contemplation, as well as consideration—to the result (of what Schiller called an idea and Goethe an experience) can be *laid before the eyes*. As one scientist to another, Goethe is just saying that anyone can read over the recorded data of his experiments. But it is no accident that he uses the age-old rhetorical figure of "placing before the eyes" to say so. The insight that Goethe has into the nature of plants is sensible—it is "seen" with the organ he describes as the "mind's eye" (Auge des Geistes). As such, another person will only be convinced of its truth when she herself also *sees* it *physically* with the inner organ of sensible understanding. The means whereby such knowledge is shared will be largely rhetorical, a question of persuasion.

Goethe's enthusiastic description of the *Urpflanze* to Schiller is reminiscent of Wilhelm Meister's presentation of his Hamlet interpretation (i.e., his recognition of the central action of *Hamlet*) to Serlo and Aurelie.[44] In "Glückliches Ereignis," Goethe seizes pen and paper in order to make a visible sketch of his "idea" for Schiller; and in the novel, Wilhelm *performs* his version of Hamlet to make the siblings *see* Hamlet as he does. But Schiller is no more convinced by the impassioned diagrammatic evidence than Serlo is entirely won over by Wilhelm's histrionic mode of persuasion.

The dangers to the understanding and sanity involved in recognizing, or putting before one's own eyes—the central action of a story for Aristotle and of seeing the archetype of a class of natural objects for Goethe—are becoming clear. It is no wonder that attempts to convince others of one's own fragile and narrowly won insights, of putting one's own visions before the eyes of others, would be even more fraught with dangers and impediments. The third type of knowledge represented in "Glückliches Ereignis," that of coming-to-know another human being, compounds these difficulties. In it, one is faced with the challenge of envisioning a moving and living *object* outside ourselves, and one must respond to (one is *response*-ible to) her claims as a *subject*. I must take into account her own moving and evolving vision of herself (as far as it can be placed before the eyes) as well as her changing view of me (which also must be somehow communicated). All the while, it is also incumbent on me to represent to my interlocutor my own pictures of both her and myself. Here, the motions that must be brought in sync with one another are dizzyingly manifold (think of Ptolemy adding epicycle upon epicycle to harmonize the revolutions of heavenly bodies with human ideals of regular and circular motion, then quadruple the complexity): at least we never had to worry about plants' and stories' ideas of *us*.[45]

The madness to which Aristotle refers in the *Poetics* (about recognizing moving action) and Goethe in "Bedenken und Ergebung" (about recognizing nature) rears its head again in the final section of "Glückliches

Ereignis" (about recognizing another human), immediately following Goethe's narration of his supposedly successful recognition scene with Schiller. Here, he claims that the "prevailing difficulties" (*obwaltenden Schwierigkeiten*) involved in giving an honest and true account even of his own development should be obvious to every "*Kenner*" (literally: knower; also: connoisseur); they should "immediately strike the eye" (*sogleich ins Auge fallen*; HA, 10, 541). He goes on to compound the difficulties involved in such fair knowledge of oneself or another. It must be confessed "that something nearly impossible is undertaken whenever one attempts to depict the *transitions*, of which there must be thousands and thousands, in a clarified, freer, self-conscious state."[46] Again, it is to the *transitions* that one must pay attention, and the task looms as a near impossibility. He even gives up on seeing the metamorphoses as purposeful formative stages (as the third paragraph had hinted at): "One cannot speak of developmental steps (*Bildungsstufen*), but instead of wrong tracks, worn paths, and secret ways."[47] The insurmountable obstacles to recognition reach their fullest flowering in the next paragraph:

> Und wer kann denn zuletzt sagen, daß er wissenschaftlich in der höchsten Region des Bewußtseins immer wandele, wo man das Äußere mit größter Bedächtigkeit, mit so scharfer als ruhiger Aufmerksamkeit *betrachtet*, wo man zugleich sein eigenes Innere, mit kluger Um*sicht*, mit bescheidener Vor*sicht*, walten läßt, in geduldiger Hoffnung eines wahrhaft reinen, *harmonischen Anschauens*. Trübt uns nicht die Welt, trüben wir uns nicht selbst solche Momente? (HA, 10, 542; my emphasis)
>
> (And who can finally say that he always abides scientifically in the highest region of consciousness? Where one *views* the exterior with greatest mindfulness and with attention as keen as it is calm? Where at the same time allows one lets one's own interior prevail with intelligent circum*spection* [Um*sicht*] and modest *watch*fulness [Vor*sicht*]? Does not the world obfuscate [trüben] us; don't we obscure [trüben] ourselves in such moments?)

Is not every intuition of such knowledge illusory? Are not all such moments of recognition blind? A more disconsolate, pessimistic passage would be difficult to find in Goethe's works than this radically spiraling doubt in the possibility of knowing other humans. Yet the very next sentence is a declaration of stubborn hope:

> Fromme Wünsche jedoch dürfen wir hegen, liebevolles Annähern an das Unerreichbare zu versuchen, ist nicht untersagt. (HA, 10, 542)
>
> (We may yet harbor devout hopes; it is not forbidden to approach the inaccessible with love.)

Where does this sudden hope come from? What gives Goethe the right to insist on striving for responsible knowledge of others and himself despite all the undeniable difficulties? First of all, as with his idea of plants, Goethe feels he can trust his *experience* of mutually edifying friendship with Schiller. The evidence of their careful listening and responsive correspondence can give others a taste of this experience as well. But the text of "Glückliches Ereignis" points toward a more universal answer to this question: the only way in which this impossible project of mutual recognition between humans could ever be manageable is by cheating.

Two elements of this faithful betrayal, this true deception, can be distilled from the text. They are both related, and each has been explored above: one is the trick of seeing collections of parts as wholes, and the second is the tendency to represent processes as moments. The fictive narrative that Goethe composes of his anagnorisis moment with Schiller is a prime example, but the concentric rings of recognition scenarios that spiral out from around it provide more instances of the workings of these trickeries. It is the illusion of the tableau that is at work here: Goethe writes at the climax of the recognition story, when he and Schiller have their "Idea!"/"Experience!" exchange, that "the *point* that divided us was thereby indicated most exactly."[48] The same thing occurs in Goethe's report to Falk:

> *Dieser Punkt* ist recht geschickt zu zeigen, worin zwischen mir und Schiller die Übereinstimmung und die Abweichung bestand. Denn eigentlich sind wir über keinen Punkt von dem ersten Moment unsrer Bekanntschaft je zu völliger Übereinstimmung gekommen.[49]
>
> (*This point* is very adept to show what the agreement and divergence between myself and Schiller consisted in. For in fact we

> never came to more perfect agreement about any point from the first moment of our acquaintance.)

Of course, it would be foolish to believe that all the fullness and totality of the humans who were Goethe and Schiller, even in the limited context of their relations with each other, could be deduced from this stark tableau of *Idee* versus *Erfahrung*. Neither of the men would ever have insisted on doing so. And yet viewing such an illustrative still life or snapshot with the eyes of G. E. Lessing's pregnant moment[50] can allow the image to kip into a moving and productive vantage point from which honest interaction might blossom. The simplifying and fictionalizing operations of seeing parts as wholes and reducing processes to points are necessary to human interaction: they are, indeed, the only way to avoid being brought to a standstill by a kind of Zeno's paradox of motion in ethical relations.

The narrated anecdote is revealing about the workings of recognition between people at three distinct but interlocking levels. Goethe himself represents the scene as an anagnorisis moment that lets readers see "at a glance" the relationship between himself and Schiller "as a whole." It is quite appropriate that the opportunity for the life-changing recognition scene between these two people was generated by a difference over the possibility of recognition of objects. The problematic of the *anschauende Urteilskraft* in relation to plants is reduplicated in their encounter with each other. It becomes clear that this is what recognition aims at (*seeing* another person as a whole), as does the potential of such a simplifying but pregnant sight for both fruitful and tragic misunderstanding. Aristotle too realized this necessity of simplifying the totalities that make up human character in his insistence on unity in poems:

> A story is one, not, as some people suppose, if it is about one person, for many—countlessly many—things are incidental attributes of one person, with no unity taking in some of them. . . . For this reason every one of the poets who has made a *Heracleiad*, a *Theseid*, or other poems of that sort, has evidently missed the mark. (*P*, 8, 1451a, 15–36)

Homer avoided this mistake by organizing the *Odyssey* around a central action. Goethe too, in recognizing Schiller (and writing "Glückliches Ereignis"), does not conceive of a *Schilleriad* but rather hits on one central point of their difference and harmony, from which a multitude of further fascinating details might be deduced. If one strives to understand another person, one cannot help but do so in an image that is a whole, which by necessity must leave out many (possibly important) aspects of the other's life and character. That this *Bild* (image) is necessarily incomplete need not be a bad thing: it should, however, be responsible and suggestive in its unavoidable insufficiency. On the other hand, it can lead to tragic misunderstanding (tragic because it is largely innocent in its unlikely necessity—a true *hamartia*, a missing of the mark). The decade-long friendship between Schiller and Goethe was truly a mutually beneficial cross-pollination, despite—or rather *because of—the way* both of them tended to dramatize and, in a sense, fictionalize their differences. Schiller's essay "On Naïve and Sentimental Poetry" is his own version of the anagnorisis tableau between the two of them. Goethe's "Glückliches Ereignis," though equally suggestive in its productively simplifying representation of their differences, is even more blatantly dramatic, since in it a peripeteia coincides with the recognition scene in which the two men go from being guarded and distrustful rivals to becoming warm friends.

Similar anagnorisis moments between potential friends, however, can result in less-fortunate tableau-like understandings. Just think of the oft-retold encounter between Beethoven and Goethe in Teplitz. The (in)famous account of this meeting in Bettina von Arnim's published letters is much like "Glückliches Ereignis" in having more dramatic than historical truth in its depiction of the two men's recognition scenario. In it, Beethoven has long desired to meet the poet who stirred the high spirits of his youth with works of such passionate and unreserved flights of emotion as *The Sorrows of Young Werther*. He seems not to have read much of anything by post–Sturm und Drang Goethe, however, since he is very surprised not to find the anticipated friend and *Seelenverwandter* (soulmate) in the old poet when he finally finagles a meeting with his hero in 1812. Bettina von Arnim seems to have learned a lesson from her own (more complicated) adulation of Goethe with the almost certainly invented but nevertheless revealing anecdote of their encounter: Beethoven and Goethe are walking together along a promenade in Teplitz when they are approached by a group of high-ranking nobles. According to the tale, Goethe promptly doffs his hat, stands to the side, and bows while they pass by. Beethoven, meanwhile, boldly walks directly on through the gaggle of amazed nobility.[51] Despite the questionable veracity of the anecdote, it provides another deft example of how *every* dramatic tableau of characterization will necessarily be (a) a fiction and (b) a simplified picture that implies more than it literally says.

In the case of the pseudofiction of the Goethe-Schiller tableau, the crystallized pregnant moment points toward a potential for a complex, mutually challenging yet rewarding relationship. In the Beethoven-Goethe story, the pregnant moment leads to a telltale image of the two men's characters and results directly in the stillbirth of a burgeoning friendship, yet it also short shrifts the more complex and rewarding relation they might have had had they but listened and looked more carefully.

The fictionalization of events is an unexpected consequence of what Aristotle understood about the relation of history to poetry. Poetry is "more philosophical" because it represents probable potentialities as opposed to history's contingent actualities (*P*, 9, 1451b, 5–10). In order to raise the chance events of historical reality to a philosophical level of significance and universality, one must narrate and to some extent fictionalize them.[52] This conundrum is succinctly expressed in the title of Goethe's autobiography, *Dichtung und Wahrheit* (*Poetry and Truth*). As Goethe did with his encounter with Schiller, one must reshape historical processes—which far exceed even ten thousand Olympic racetracks[53] in the magnitude of their contingent causes and hence confound one's ability to "see them as a whole"—as manageable stories in order to grasp anything of use in them. So too must people recast their notions of others, whom they can never fully know in the totality (not to mention infinity) of their development, to fit into one comprehensible vision. For someone like Levinas, this attempt inevitably leads to an ethical betrayal of the sublime incomprehensibility of the Other; for Goethe, however, we have no choice but to make the attempt, and if we are in- (and ex)sightful enough, it is the only hope to engage in fruitful and ethically responsible exchange with another human.

"Glückliches Ereignis" represents in its complex construction the dramas of three different modes of knowing. In doing so, it reveals important structural kinships between these three different ways of representing knowledge: all of them share in the necessity of seeing scattered parts "at a glance" and "as a whole," all of them tend to represent the discursive processes of coming-to-know with a condensed flash of inspiration, and furthermore all of them uniquely combine in the *action* of recognition the claims of epistemology and ethics. Of course, significant differences are also manifest among the three types of knowledge, not so much in their structures as in the relation of ideas to objects. The archetype or idea of a plant, for Goethe, is fully present in all the individual manifestations and developmental stages of any given instance of a plant (rather like the Hegelian *Begriff* [concept], as Förster argues); experienced and practiced knowledge of the *Blatt* (leaf), therefore, amounts in itself to true botanical knowledge. The schematic and reflexive nature of a character sketch or tableau, however, is *never* fully commensurate with or explanatory of the living complexity of another human. At best, it can serve as a pregnant moment that impels people toward responsive interaction with one another; at worst, this shorthand template recognition of another can lead to tragic misunderstandings and terminal trauma. The recognition of a central action necessary for plot construction and analysis, meanwhile, is attended by all the essential differences (and kinships) that Aristotle noted in his pleas for poets not to confuse characters and actions. In a way, the differences could be summed up by comparing the *Nicomachean Ethics* (knowing people) with the *Physics* (knowing actions/objects). They come together in the *Poetics* (a treatise on objects imitating the actions of people) and show why reading fictional portrayals of recognition scenes, such as the *Odyssey* or "Glückliches Ereignis," can teach more about becoming responsible knowers of other humans than any number of ethical tracts by Aristotle, Kant, or any other philosopher.

CHAPTER EIGHT

Epistemologies of Recognition

Goethe's *Iphigenie auf Tauris* and the Spectacle of Catharsis

GOETHE'S AUTOBIOGRAPHICAL SKETCH, as explored in the previous chapter, stages the challenge of change or metamorphosis to the operations of recognition. This chapter will address the kind of knowledge that concurrent metamorphoses of human relations entail. The question of *gnōsis* (knowledge) in part I of this book led to a hermeneutics of and by the *Odyssey*'s Penelope: the challenge of reading Penelope turned into a lesson in Penelope's strategies of reading others (chapter 3). The corresponding inquiry into knowledge for modernity will look first to the internal workings of recognition within a single play by Goethe, before turning to broader questions of the effect of dramatic anagnorisis on spectators. The epistemology of recognition that emerges is a matter not of perceptual empiricism or a priori reasoning but rather of poetics. Whereas Penelope's poetical epistemology led to a taxonomy of interpretive and artistic techniques for dealing with the indeterminacy of interpersonal knowledge, Goethe's poetics of recognition is fundamentally allusive for characters within a text and potentially cathartic for the audience without. This chapter looks first at the performances of anagnorisis within *Iphigenie auf Tauris* (*Iphigenie in Tauris*, 1779–1787) in order to read them against Goethe's interpretation of Aristotelian catharsis (1827). In both instances, spectators are forced to ask unexpected questions about things assumed to be familiar. Instead of reinforcing justified true beliefs, the effect of anagnorisis is an invitation to investigate further: Goethe's poetic epistemology is the performative space at the threshold of philosophy.

SPIRALS OF INTERTEXTUAL PERFORMANCE

In order to show how one can recognize the central action of a story, Aristotle provides synopses for exemplary specimens of both drama and epic: Euripides's *Iphigenia among the Taurians* and Homer's *Odyssey* (*P*, 17, 1455b). While Euripides's play pivots on one single anagnorisis scene, Homer's epic thrives on a multitude of recognitions. In crafting *Iphigenie auf Tauris*, it is as if Goethe took the plot outline of the first work and projected it onto the second. The famous recognition scene between Iphigenie and her brother provides only one focus of the many concentric spirals of interlocking anagnorisis scenarios for Goethe's play, which reads as a complex meditation on the interior and social phenomena of recognition. Goethe makes the problem of anagnorisis into the central action of the play in a way much more fundamental than Euripides. In the Greek tragedy, the recognition scene between the siblings is the most stirring and beautiful fulcrum of the action, made even more effective by its coincidence with the reversal of fortune (in this case from bad to good). In Goethe's play, however, the anagnorisis between Orest and Iphigenie is only one of many recognitions in the drama, and it not only fails to coincide with the peripeteia (which itself is difficult to pinpoint in the play) but even declines to be contained within any one act, much less a single scene. Indeed, Goethe has taken the *Iphigenia* and made it, like the *Odyssey*, "recognition through and through" (*P*, 24, 1459b).

Recognition here is a process with an unclear beginning, middle, and end: an action that is difficult to see as a whole. In fact, a schematic look at the three major recognitions depicted in the play reveals that they correspond to the three levels of recognition derived from the *Poetics* above (chapter 7). In the first act, Iphigenie tells Thoas who she is. She does so by narrating the story of her family lineage and thus making herself a mythical character for Thoas as audience. Act 3, meanwhile, contains the staggered mutual recognition between sister and brother. In the fifth act, finally, Thoas becomes a spectator and witness to the recognition between Iphigenie and Orest and is subject to the effect of viewing anagnorisis. We can place these scenes in the scheme devised in chapter 7:

1. Audience recognizes character.
   Act 1: Thoas learns that his priestess is the character Iphigenie; he becomes audience to the narrated myth of her origins.
2. Character recognizes character.
   Act 3: Iphigenie and Orest recognize each other.

3. Audience recognizes the action of recognition in the story.
   Act 5: Thoas learns to see Iphigenie's recognition of Orest.

Detlev Schumann noticed how each of these three versions of emerging truth is an "intensification" (*Steigerung*) of a basic template of confessional scenes.[1] One can also picture the play's acts forming a spiral in which elements of each of the different levels of recognition are present and at work in all three, providing contrast with and instructive echoes of the dominant mode. This way of imagining the structure of the play borrows deliberately from Goethe's own identification of the "spiral tendency" in plant growth and formation.[2] Between the major recognition scenes of acts 1, 3, and 5 come episodes with Pylades that prepare the way and set in motion the three major changes in knowledge. He acts as a catalyst for the developing anagnorisis scenarios in vital ways by causing first Orest (act 2) and then Iphigenie (act 4) to withdraw from social interactions and the risk of recognition. Orest acknowledges the debilitating trauma of his guilt and abdicates to Pylades the prerogative to action (act 2). Iphigenie begins to doubt and hesitate in carrying through with Pylades's clever ruse for them to escape (act 4). In the succeeding acts, the siblings alternatively spring back into intersubjective encounters with all the more force. Their enacted self-knowledge, moreover, is determined by their limiting engagements with Pylades.

If the trajectory of the odd-numbered acts is an expanding spiral, then the even acts are movements in contraction. The alternating expansion and contraction mirrors the development of plants in Goethe's botanical writings. But a plant shrinks and grows into different forms of the same original phenomenon, the leaf, all on its own. Of course, external factors affect how a plant will thrive or wilt, but its essence is the internal motion of its growing and shrinking into various forms of the archetype. The development of people, on the other hand, as *Iphigenie* makes clear, is necessarily intersubjective. No individual human, planted alone on a strange shore, can grow through these spiraling rings of recognition. If the archetype of the plant is the simple essence of the leaf, then the *Urphänomen* (primal phenomenon) of humans consists in the plurality of subjects.

This condition of humanity in *Iphigenie* offers two points of interest for the dynamics of recognition. First, characters come to know themselves and others by interacting not only with one another, but also with mythic and textual templates. Second, the performative nature of recognition in this play reveals the unlikely primacy of *spectacle* in tragic recognition, contrary to its seeming denigration in the *Poetics*. As suggested in the scenes from Plato and Shakespeare (chapter 6), knowledge of self no less than of others comes about on the restlessly showy stage of interpersonal display.

INTERTEXTUAL INTERSUBJECTIVITY

Like Thoas in the first act, readers and spectators of *Iphigenie* must come to terms with the title character's identity within and against her mythic templates. A cursory examination of interpretations of Iphigenie's character from the eighteenth century through today shows that critics have had as much trouble achieving possession of her as Thoas did. From idealizing Iphigenie as a stylized representation of Winckelmann's "noble simplicity and quiet grandeur" formula for antique beauty[3] to seeing her as a bland everyman, "a human like you and I" (or worse yet, a "Weimaraner"),[4] Iphigenie's identity has proven a source of endless contention, and has often been the site of battles over German cultural identity itself.[5] Iphigenie first reveals herself to Thoas, however, simply by telling him the story of her family and by implicating herself in myth.[6] Every spectator of the play is in the same position as Thoas when he hears the tale and has to regard her in terms of her and others' versions of the legend. Thoas admits as much the moment she first names her ancestor:

> IPHIGENIE. Vernimm! Ich bin aus Tantalus' Geschlecht.
> THOAS. Du sprichst ein großes Wort gelassen aus.
> Nennst du *den* deinen Anherrn, den die Welt
> Als einen ehmals Hochbegnadigten
> Der Götter kennt? Ist's jener Tantalus,
> Den Jupiter zu Rat und Tafel zog. (HA, 5, 306–311)

> (IPHIGENIE. Hear then: my ancestor was Tantalus.
> THOAS. That was a weighty word, so calmly spoken.
> Are you of his race, whom the world remembers
> as one to whom the gods once showed high favor,
> That Tantalus whom Zeus himself invited
> To counsel him and sit at table with him.)[7]

At this first level, in which audience members recognize characters, Goethe's figures define themselves in relation not only to each other but also to intertextual templates. Thoas compares Iphigenie to stories he has already heard about the Tantalids. Modern readers compare this Iphigenie to a complex and muddled amalgam of what they know of the Greek legends. They may well compare her more concretely to Euripides's Iphigenia as well as to other characters to whom they hear clear parallels. George Steiner, for instance, recognizes Sophocles's Antigone in Goethe's Iphigenie, which leads him to an elegant reading of the play's problematic ethics.[8] Martin Mueller compares *Iphigenie* with Sophocles's *Philoctetes*, as both Neoptolemus and Iphigenie eventually reject the deception preached by Odysseus and Pylades, and they choose instead to tell the truth, regardless of the consequences. This comparison in turn leads him to identify Iphigenie as a secular version of Christ.[9] The intertextual feedback loop of identification is by no means limited to sources that predate Goethe's play. Later readers will see in Kleist's Penthesilea an anti-Iphigenie.[10] Anachronisms are inevitable in the layers of comparison recognition requires.

All of these cross-pollinating recognitions suggest comparisons that can be fruitful and instructive for readers trying to understand the play's figures and their relations. What also becomes clear, however, is that this level of recognition—whereby the audience comes to identify characters and place them in a comparative framework with the expectations created by other versions of similar characters—is also implicated in acts of self-recognition. Characters in the play define themselves by identifying with and against other characters. Orest points this out when he accuses Pylades of scheming and intrigue before they ever encounter Iphigenie:

> OREST. Ich hör Ulyssen reden.
> PYLADES. Spotte nicht.
> Ein jeglicher muß seinen Helden wählen. (HA, 5, 763)
>
> (OREST. I hear Ulysses talking.
> PLYADES. Do not mock me.
> We each must choose our own hero.)[11]

Pylades realizes that people become who they are through the models of characters from stories: Whom are you inclined to emulate—Achilles or Odysseus? Hector or Paris? In order to be recognized, heroes have to identify themselves with heroes. Pylades's choice of Odysseus goes beyond a mere penchant for trickery. The very details of the lies he tells to Iphigenie, for instance, read as if their speaker had studied Homer's *Odyssey*. Like

Odysseus's various autobiographical fabrications on Ithaca,[12] Pylades invents a tale that resembles the truth very closely. Aristotle praised Homer for teaching us to lie with precisely this Odyssean example (*P*, 24, 1460a). In his mendacious tales, Odysseus purports to be a noble veteran of the Trojan War fallen on hard times in his attempts to return home. Pylades similarly weaves true details into his fable: "my friend is fleeing the furies for blood guilt" (HA, 5, 836). Pylades even makes them both Cretans, Odysseus's favorite narrative disguise!

Goethe is not the first to rely on Odyssean templates for characterization in a version of this myth. In the opening monologue of Euripides's play, Iphigenia narrates how Odysseus devised the subterfuge that lured her to Aulis to be killed by her father. Later, when she inquires about the returns of the Greeks from Troy, she curses Odysseus. Yet it is Iphigenia herself who comes up with the deceptive stratagem by which the Greeks escape the barbarians. The word she uses to describe Odysseus's stratagem (*technē*), in fact, is repeated by Orestes for Iphigenia's clever ruse (*technē*) when she turns around and gloriously uses similar tricks to dupe Thoas (*Iph*, lines 24, 1032). There are also parallels between Odysseus's treatment of his crew and Iphigenia's instrumentalizing regard for her retinue of Greek slaves, who make up the play's chorus. Orestes calls on her to "find words of persuasion" (*Iph*, 1053) to convince the women to keep their secret so that they can escape. She delivers a fine rhetorical performance, enjoining their solidarity as fellow women and praising them for their loyalty. Notwithstanding the likely fatal ire sure to fall on their heads once Thoas learns of her betrayal, she further promises to let them "share" her "good fortune" if she gets safely back to Greece (*Iph*, 1067–1069). She does not mention how implausible any assistance she could offer them from afar would be. By abandoning the Greek slaves in her planned escape, she surrenders them to Thoas's vengeance for her own transgression.[13] Like her father Agamemnon, Iphigenia is quite willing to sacrifice those near her to achieve fair winds for her desires.

Euripides's Iphigenia, therefore, discovers her agency in a very Odyssean mode. Goethe's Iphigenie, in contrast, develops her distinctive identity by opposing this way of acting. In rejecting Pylades's Odysseus-like deceit, Goethe's Iphigenie also repudiates Euripides's Iphigenia. She hence rejects the earliest textual version of her mythic template. In so doing, she effectively complies with Aristotle's demands about the propriety of female characters, who should not be "manly or terrifying" (*andreian ē deinēn*) (*P*, 15, 1454a, 23), advice that Euripides's women, including

Iphigenia, often flaunt. In the same breath in which Orestes admires his sister's cunning, he uses the adjective "terrifying" (*deinai*) and marks it as gendered: "Women are frightening when it comes to inventing subterfuges" (*Iph*, 1032).[14] Aristotle's attempt to stifle feminine strength and wildness is too late, for even the heroine of one of his favorite plays does not conform to his prescriptions—not until two millennia later, that is. Goethe's Iphigenie has been tamed and domesticated, and she accepts a "virtuous" restriction of gender roles even while she famously rails against the constriction of women's place in society. She thus represents a peculiar breed of feminism that tacitly embraces a man's image of feminine virtue while objecting to its restraints.[15]

Goethe's play reveals that people come to know themselves through the identification with and rejection of these intertextual models, whether taken directly from the stories or secondhand, through the figures around them who assume their characters. Iphigenie's self-recognition and self-assertion only occur as a result of her rejecting Pylades and his Odyssean deceit. Insofar as Pylades and Odysseus represent Greekness, reason, and civilization, Iphigenie's condemnation is part and parcel of the play's ambivalence about cultural superiority. Odysseus hence turns out to be instrumental to Iphigenie's burgeoning self-recognition. Even a "pure soul" (*reine Seele*; HA, 5, 1583), as Pylades sneeringly names Iphigenie's reluctance to continue lying, is insufficient to know itself without the imposing blemish of another's example.

The most dramatic example of Odysseus's role in Iphigenie's self-recognition coincides with the turning point from deception to honesty in her final interview with Thoas. Iphigenie approaches the king well equipped with Pylades's lies, and she even offers a Hobbesian defense of the underdog's right to trickery with rhetorical flair (HA, 5, 1866–1872). When Thoas retorts that caution counters deception, however, Iphigenie rather lamely insists that a "pure soul" (*reine Seele*) does not need "it" (*sie*—it is unclear whether the pronoun refers back to caution or trickery, as both are grammatically feminine; HA, 5, 1874). This echo of Pylades's derisory name for her after parroting his justification for dishonesty ushers in a crisis of identity. She reveals her inner turmoil and admits that the strangers were Greeks. Then she launches into a heartfelt disquisition on the nature of heroism: "Are men alone entitled to do heroic deeds? . . . What is called great?" She immediately glosses this question about greatness with the repetitions of narration: "What lifts the soul, trembling, to the ever repeating storyteller?" (HA, 5, 1892–1896). The first example she mentions is revealing:

> Der in der Nacht
> Allein das Heer des Feindes überschleicht,
> Wie unversehen eine Flamme, wütend
> Die Schlafenden, Erwachenden ergreift,
> Zuletzt gedrängt von den Ermunterten
> Auf Feindes Pferden doch mit Beute kehrt,
> Wird der allein gepriesen? der allein? (HA, 5, 1898–1904)

> (When one man at night steals in like sudden fire
> Among the enemy, and in hot rage
> Attacks them as they sleep and as they wake,
> And then, when they are roused and press him hard,
> Can still escape, riding a captured horse
> And carrying spoils—does he alone earn praise,
> And only he?)[16]

The episode she describes here is uncannily similar to Odysseus's and Diomedes's night raid in the *Iliad* (book 10). In this episode, the two Greeks "heroically" kill a Trojan who has surrendered himself to their mercy, then use his intelligence to steal into an enemy camp, slit the throats of sleeping soldiers, and steal away horses and booty before escaping when they begin to rouse. This "Doloniad" sequence of the *Iliad*, named after the murdered Trojan spy, has been a contentious point in ethical debates about heroic behavior for millennia. For Euripides and other classical detractors of Odysseus, it is the principal evidence from Homer of the Ithacan's perfidy. Of course, it is impossible that Iphigenie, who has only just learned from Pylades that the Greeks won the war, could have read the *Iliad*. Yet by citing this particular Homeric episode at the crucial point when she introduces a new type of heroism, one based on truth-telling, Iphigenie underlines the role that rejecting characters and their intertextual templates plays in her self-discovery and self-assertion.

Fritz Breithaupt maintains that anagnorisis in *Iphigenie* is a function of discovering and feeling similarities and affinities between people.[17] This is certainly true, but it is only half the story. Equally necessary for Iphigenie's burgeoning self-knowledge is her heartfelt dissimilarity with Pylades and disgust for the Odyssean character of Greek deviousness that he represents. Iphigenie's self-consciousness blossoms as "revulsion germinates" (Widerwillen keim[t]; HA, 5, 1713) in her breast. Iphigenie's botanical metaphor shows how *Wiedererkennung* (*re*cognition) here is a matter of *Widererkennung* (*contra*cognition). Breithaupt's thesis should be amended on both its counts: anagnorisis works not only through empathy but also through antipathy, and one negotiates one's identities not only with flesh-and-blood people but also with an entire gallery of storied characters.

Thus a good decade before Johann Gottlieb Fichte's *Foundation of Natural Right* (*Grundlage des Naturrechts*; 1796), Goethe's *Iphigenie* has already demonstrated that the self is an interpersonal phenomenon. The play goes much further, however, than simply to posit self-recognition as a function of *Anerkennung* between living, autonomous beings. Instead, it is a layered process of identifying with and feeling disgust at textual representations from myth, art, and even literary criticism. Fichte's provoking "summons" (*Aufforderung*), which calls out a subject to realize her free but limited agency,[18] issues from these imagined figures, even when not spoken by a living person. Fictional images are inextricable from the acts of self-recognition that Goethe's play both valorizes and problematizes: recognizing oneself is a messy process of envisioning and judging other characters. Self-knowledge can only take place in reaction to other selves, who are always already (textual) images. As Jane Brown glosses the final scene in which Orest reinterprets the oracle's directive, "The act of representation is now explicit—Iphigenie's truth, her innermost self (*Innres*) is suddenly represented by a statue; to be fully understood her self must be externalized, indeed allegorized, onto the figure of the goddess, which is, however, consistently identified as an image."[19] Recognition is not just intersubjective; it is intertextual.[20]

INTERTEXTUAL SPECTACLE

This emphasis on the inter*textuality* of recognition might seem to exclude the category of performance. Yet the textual fabric on which selves are constructed in this play is a performative space. As Brown insists, *Iphigenie auf Tauris* deals "at bottom with *how to recognize and represent identity*."[21] She shows that the self in question here is theatrically constructed, a masquerade.[22] This is true not only episodically in *Iphigenie* as seen in characters' coming to know themselves and each other through one-on-one interactions but also structurally by the need to open these encounters to third-party spectators.

In Euripides's *Iphigenia*, the moving recognition scene between brother and sister alone marks the before and after of fortune's reversal and the siblings' freeing realization of their own agency. In Goethe's *Iphigenie*, however, the siblings' anagnorisis at the center of the play (act 3) is insufficient. The intersubjective recognition does not bring about Orest's cure or Iphigenie's revolutionary self-knowledge. Orest must stage a theatrical therapy session in a vision of Hades to free himself from the crippling trauma of guilt.[23] Iphigenie does not approach liberating self-consciousness until she *restages* the recognition scene between herself and her brother before Thoas as an audience (act 5).

The sibling's mutual recognition—and Iphigenie's gradual self-recognition—cannot be contained within the interactions between brother and sister: they spill over into the final acts of the play and culminate in Thoas's begrudging acknowledgment. It has become a commonplace of criticism to note that, in contrast to plays of antiquity, in which *plot* is of paramount importance over character, *Iphigenie* marks a shift to a kind of drama that centers on the exploration and development of *character.*[24] Yet character in this play is inextricably tied up with actions between people—that is, with plot. Spectators can only know characters, and characters can only know each other, through their actions. The process of Iphigenie's coming to know herself only becomes visible—indeed, only consists—in how she chooses to *act* in acknowledging others publicly. The specific nature of these actions that facilitate recognition of self and other, however, is telling. Anagnorisis is not effected by swordplay or intrigue but by conscious performance.

In Euripides's play, Orestes discovers Iphigenia's identity when she dictates a letter for her brother to Pylades, whom she has promised to release in order to deliver it. Aristotle praises this scene as an example of the "best" kind of anagnorisis because it unfolds naturally from the action of the story. In striking contrast, Goethe's Iphigenie and Orest simply announce their identities to each other in act 3. Aristotle would have condemned this "artless" kind of recognition as the mere fabrication of the author. As if to remedy this artistic deficiency, however, Iphigenie insists on rehearsing the entire thing, replete with reported tokens and signs, at the end of the play.[25] The process of recognition and acknowledgment is not complete until they have reenacted their reunion scene before the audience of Thoas.

What effect does viewing the siblings' reconstructed recognition scene have on its royal audience? In the king's last longer speech, he is still ready to defend with weapons the "goods" of his land from the marauding Greeks (HA, 5, 2095–2107). This threat is followed by Orest's hermeneutical dance in which he reinterprets the words of the oracle so as to allow the Scythians to keep their icon of Diana (he recognizes the "*Schwester*" of the god's speech as his own sister Iphigenie rather than Apollo's Diana). Iphigenie then picks up the show with her entreaty that Thoas let them leave. "Look at us!" (Sieh uns an!) is her central imperative in this speech, demanding that the king *look* at them. His terse response, "Then go!" (So geht!), does not satisfy Iphigenie (HA, 5, 2148ff.). She also desires his blessing and a public acknowledgment of their friendship ("Ein freundlich Gastrecht walte / Von Dir zu uns"; HA, 5, 2153) and even paternal kinship ("Wert und teuer / Wie mir mein Vater war, so bist du's mir"; HA, 5, 2155).[26] "*Oh turn around to us*!" (O wende dich zu uns!; HA, 5, 2168), she cries—again commanding the Scythian's active spectatorship. Iphigenie wants a public recognition scene with Thoas before she leaves. She literally demands his peripeteia.

Yet Thoas answers (and the play ends) with another brief two-word response: "Fare well!" (Lebt wohl!). Thoas's reaction to the parade of recognitions Iphigenie and Orest offer him, therefore, finally consists of a mere four words that, though acquiescing to the barest minimum of the Greeks' demands, do not indicate the state of mind or attitude of the speaker. The printed words of Thoas's response give no hint for hermeneutical conjectures about his emotions or thoughts as Iphigenie speaks, demands to be seen, and then departs. The indeterminacy of the king's mental state leads to two points about the performance and the effect of dramatic recognition.

First, the final conundrum of *Iphigenie* underscores the primacy of spectacle (*opsis*) in anagnorisis. Two passages in the *Poetics* clearly disparage the element of spectacle in drama (*P*, 6, 1450b; 14, 1453b). Aristotle insists that just hearing or reading about the actions imitated in tragedy ought to produce the effects of fear and pity. But much of the language of the *Poetics* reveals just how these effects are produced: by visualizing the events described in the mind's eye. The previous chapter showed that Aristotle's advice to poets requires them to imagine watching the scenes on stage. Just a few lines after declaring spectacle to be the "least inherent" element in poetry, Aristotle makes an argument about the proper magnitude of stories, and he concludes by saying that they should have the look or appearance (*idea*) of what he has described (*P*, 6, 1450b, 35). This visual language permeates all aspects of the *Poetics*. Spectacle underlies the theoretical foundations of Aristotle's ideas about poetry.

The end of Goethe's *Iphigenie* also demonstrates the indispensability of spectacle. The insufficiency of the words attributed to Thoas to convey an adequate idea of his attitude means that a reader must supply her own mental image of Thoas's gestures, posturing, and tone in this scene. Is Thoas resigned? Livid? Moved to tears? Stiff and reluctant? Does he take Iphigenie's proffered hand or ignore it with a forced "Lebt wohl" through gritted teeth? Are we left with a final tableau of the three figures embracing with heaving breasts? Or does Thoas remain aloof to one side, alone and betrayed? Only the details of staging—whether in a theater or in the imagination—can answer these questions. Spectacle informs one's reading where the wording and actions are indeterminate. The entire tenor of the theatrical success or failure of Iphigenie's performed anagnorisis—and hence of the whole play—can only be supplied by the actors' staging or the reader's visual imagination.[27] The taciturnity of Thoas at the end of *Iphigenie* is reminiscent of the impenetrability of Penelope's attitude toward the disguised beggar before her public embrace in book 23. Yet while Penelope's indeterminacy solidifies into acknowledgment in the epic's conclusion, Thoas becomes illegible in the final lines. Any comprehensive interpretation of the play will arise from the visual blocking and staging of these concluding silences.[28]

THE EFFECTS OF TRAGEDY

One evocative interpretation of Thoas's taciturnity would stage it as dumbstruck wonder. This reading suggests a second point about dramatic anagnorisis. If one imagines that Orest's explanations and Iphigenie's entreaties have brought Thoas to the point where he is no longer certain of his own assumptions about friendship and enmity, even if he is not ready to replace them willy-nilly with the Greeks' counterclaims, then Iphigenie—in addition to playing Antigone and Christ—will also have been playing Socrates. In the process of coming to know herself, she would also have managed to stun Thoas out of his own habits of thought, much like the numbing torpedo fish to which Meno compares Socrates. This scenario is only one among many possible interpretations of the final scene in *Iphigenie*, but it serves as a model for the potential effect that dramatic recognition can have on any audience, including the readers and spectators of Goethe's play. The necessity of construing Thoas's final reaction in *Iphigenie* is one example of the moving puzzles with which *Iphigenie auf Tauris* confronts readers. These questions (the inequalities and disharmonies that the "happy" ending fails to gloss over) are viscerally felt in the experiences of fear and pity readers of the play share, and they offer the chance to think further about the paradoxes underlying the drama's actions. The play itself does not necessarily give answers to the problems it poses, but the questions themselves can be an invitation to engaged and committed inquiry.

This state of wonder in bafflement at the spectacle of recognition is surprisingly close to a recent interpretation of Aristotelian catharsis. This central term in *Poetics* has a much more contentious reception history than that of anagnorisis, partly because it is mentioned only once in a vital passage of the definition of tragedy and never explained or illustrated. Joe Sachs's interpretation of catharsis ties it to a series of metaphors in the *Poetics* that develop an aesthetics of effect—from clearing or cleansing (*katharsis*) to knocking away (*ekplexis*), leading to wonder (*thauma*). For Sachs, Aristotle sees tragedy's defining effect in its potential to spur its audience toward philosophy by clearing away deep-seated assumptions about the world.[29] This description fits one reading of Thoas's reaction to Iphigenie's play-within-a-play. Open perplexity and wonder are also honest reactions of readers to the illegibility of Thoas's final words. Goethe's drama thus presciently exemplifies an important current understanding of Aristotle's *Wirkungsästhetik* (aesthetics of effect).

Yet Thoas is not the only character who anticipates later interpretations of catharsis. In fact, figures in the play and Goethe's own later commentary map out four of the most influential currents of the debate about catharsis in the nineteenth through the twenty-first centuries. All of them, moreover, take an anagnorisis scene as their point of departure. Interestingly, although the play repeatedly presents cathartic reactions to the recognition scenes it stages, it has no room for the leading figures in the already long history of catharsis reception that predates it: no characters find clear inspiration to stoical acceptance of fate's determinations (Opitz), ennoblement through admiration (Corneille), or a purification of emotions by means of pity (Lessing). Instead, the characters in the play prefigure major scholarly assessments of catharsis that will only come into vogue long after Goethe's death.

As much as the baroque and neoclassical interpretations differ from one another, they all make catharsis into a moral category. Remarkably, in all the later readings of catharsis that Goethe prefigures, morality is largely beside the point. They turn catharsis into a psychological, emotional, intellectual, or purely dramaturgical phenomenon. Before Goethe, tragedy was primarily meant to make people virtuous; after him, it is a device for protopsychotherapy, rational refinement, or *werkimmanente* plot construction. Intimations for all of these later developments are on view in *Iphigenie auf Tauris*.

The first cathartic reaction to recognition in the drama occurs in reaction to the central discovery between the siblings (act 3). Orest, tormented with guilt for matricide, refuses at first to accept that he has been reunited with his sister. He swoons, and after Iphigenie leaves to get help, Orest awakes into an imagined Hades. He acts out drinking from Lethe's water and greeting the shades he envisions around him. Orest envisions his father and mother arm in arm and begs them to look at him as their son. He enacts a scene of reconciliation in the underworld, and only this fantasy of death frees him from debilitating fear and guilt (HA, 5, 1258–1316). Scholars have noticed the resemblance between this famous healing of Orest and Freudian psychotherapy and *Wunschtraum*.[30] In fact, Orest's cure here is an example of psychotherapeutic catharsis, in which a patient is finally able to experience emotions associated with past traumatic events that have been repressed or ignored. Freud's deployment of catharsis, meanwhile, owes a debt to the work of the classicist Jakob Bernays, who happened to be his wife's uncle. In 1857, Bernays offered an influential interpretation of Aristotle's *Poetics* that turned to Greek medical terminology for help. Arguing for a metaphorics of medicinal purgation, Bernays renders catharsis as an "erleichtende Entladung" (alleviating discharge) of "Gemütsaffektionen" (affections of the mind).[31] This translation is a precise clinical description of how Orest's cure functions. In order to deal with the oppressive guilt and fears afflicting him,[32] Orest must arouse and increase these emotions by descending to Hades and confronting his parents and ancestors. Only then can he relieve the pent-up feelings, permitting an "Ableitung" (draining off).[33] At the beginning of his vision, Orest describes the initial draft of water from Lethe as "washing away the spasm of life from my breast" (Bald ist der Krampf des Lebens aus dem Busen / Hinweggespült; HA, 5, 1260–1261). After his return from the underworld, he again uses liquid images, but this time they dissipate his trauma: "My curse dissolves" (Es löset sich der Fluch; HA, 5, 1358) as gods "pour the long-prayed-for rain / In mighty torrents" (HA, 5, 1346–1347). In order to discharge the unhealthy fluids, Orest's treatment must excite the very passions to be purged.

If Orest's catharsis occurs in a raging flood at the center of the play, then Iphigenie's is a deep pool that becomes more transparent and rarified throughout. In each act, she undergoes a process of clarification about herself by means of her relations to those around her. While trying to follow Pylades's directions to trick Thoas in the final act, Iphigenie's justifying explanations for deception reveal to her the necessity for truth.[34] In a moving dramatic reversal, she discovers that to be true to herself she cannot lie to others. Yet instead of presenting this revelation as a private sentiment, Iphigenie immediately universalizes it into a general moral maxim:

> Es hört sie jeder
> Geboren unter jedem Himmel, dem
> Des Lebens Quelle durch den Busen rein
> Und ungehindert flie-ßt. (HA, 5, 1939–1942)

> (Everyone born under every sky,
> can hear it [i.e., the voice of truth and humanity]
> if the stream of life flows through their breast pure and unimpeded.)[35]

Iphigenie's image of the deep spring of pure, clear water in the soul of every person (she immediately follows up by addressing the king's "tiefe Seele" [deep soul]) is an effect of her emotional self-realization in this scene. This language prefigures that of several late twentieth-century scholars of the *Poetics*, for whom catharsis is a matter of "intellectual clarification" (Golden), "conscious . . . alignment" between emotional and cognitive attitudes (Halliwell), or "clearing up" of moral confusion (Nussbaum).[36] Iphigenie's emerging self-recognition in the play could serve as a model for the cathartic function of tragedy for these classicists.

Both Orest's and Iphigenie's experiences of catharsis, as different as they are from one another, are central to the main action of the drama. In each case, the catharsis heralds the conclusion of a major plot strand: the story of Orest's healing and the story of Iphigenie's coming to know herself. They thus conform to Goethe's own interpretation of Aristotelian catharsis that he published more than fifty years after his first engagement with *Iphigenie*. Goethe makes it quite clear in his *Nachlese zur Aristoteles' Poetik* (*Afterthought on Aristotle's Poetics*; 1827) that the theater can have no lasting edificatory effect on the audience. He grounds this opinion with a new translation and interpretation of the definition of tragedy from chapter 6 of the *Poetics*.

> Die Tragödie ist die Nachahmung einer bedeutenden und abgeschlossenen Handlung, die eine gewisse Ausdehnung hat und in anmutiger Sprache vorgetragen wird, und zwar von abgesonderten Gestalten, deren jede ihre eigene Rolle spielt, und nicht erzählungsweise von einem einzelnen; *nach einem Verlauf aber von Mitleid und Furcht mit Ausgleichung solcher Leidenschaften ihr Geschäft abschließt*. (HA, 12, 342–343; emphasis mine)

> (Tragedy is the imitation of a meaningful and completed action that has a certain extension and is presented in graceful language, namely by separate figures, each of whom plays its own role, and not narratively by a single individual; *but [that] concludes its business after a process of pity and fear with the balancing of such passions*.)

Goethe wants the definition of tragedy to be confined to the characteristics of the aesthetic object itself. In attributing all of the listed traits to the *Handlung*, to the plot as enacted on stage rather than to the play as it appears in imitation, he insulates the *energeia*, the being-at-work of tragedy, within the limits of the stage. All other interpretations of catharsis require that the tragic play has an effect and accomplishes something in the world. Goethe, however, translates that a tragic plot "brings its business to a close *with the equalization of such passions*" (*mit Ausgleichung solcher Leidenschaften* ihr Geschäft abschließt). It sounds almost as if catharsis rings the five o'clock bell that announces the end of a shopkeeper's workday. The purely internal workings of a tragedy determine its closing in time. The implications are clear: Goethe is removing any action of the play from the realm of the audience. If tragedy wraps up its business with catharsis—that is, when catharsis takes place—then one has a purely analytical definition that relies on no outside factors or purposes for its truth content. A play that does not include catharsis as part of its makeup will simply not be a tragedy for Goethe by definition.[37]

Goethe rejects outright that plays can have any lasting effect on spectators, and he is determined to find a definition of tragedy that will be valid even if there are no spectators to watch it. Catharsis in his understanding then is necessarily very different from the audience-centered definitions of critics before and after him. Goethe renders catharsis as *Ausgleichung* and later comments that "by catharsis, Aristotle understands this reconciling rounding out [*aussöhnende Abrundung*], which is in fact demanded from every drama, and even from all poetical works."[38] The *aussöhnende Abrundung* seems to be nothing other than the resolution of conflicts at the end of a story, as marriages tie up all the loose ends in a comedy. The tragic catharsis is a kind of human sacrifice: someone must die or at least suffer in order to draw the tensions and rivalries in a tragedy to a close. This interpretation is surprisingly near to that of Gerald Else, who more than a century later claims that catharsis is "not a change or end-product in the spectator's soul" but "is accomplished by the whole structure of the drama."[39] Else's commentary on catharsis was the most widely taught authority in North American drama programs in the latter half of the twentieth century.[40] In this late essay, Goethe prefigures a fourth future interpretation of catharsis.[41]

The elder Goethe's assessment of tragedy is a cynical repudiation of the notion that a play can have any efficacy outside the formal confines of its own dramatic action. Yet the essay's language concedes an effect that is actually very close to the experience of discombobulation that Thoas may be feeling at the end of *Iphigenie* and that the ambiguity of Thoas's reaction invites in readers. Though Goethe's *Nachlese* rightly criticizes those who expect too much didactic impact from drama, it allows tragedy (and tragic novels) a very special power.

> Wer nun auf dem Wege einer wahrhaft sittlichen inneren Ausbildung fortschreitet, wird empfinden und gestehen, daß Tragödien und tragische Romane den Geist keineswegs beschwichtigen, sondern das Gemüt und das, was wir das Herz nennen, in Unruhe versetzen und einem vagen, unbestimmten Zustande entgegenführen. (HA, 12, 345)
>
> (Whoever progresses on the path of a truly moral inner education will feel and admit that tragedies and tragical novels in no way soothe the spirit, but instead set the soul [*Gemüt*] and what we call the heart in turmoil [*Unruhe*] and lead to a vague, uncertain condition.)

This description of tragedy's effect, which Goethe places just a few lines above his dyspeptic claim that spectators "go home not a jot better than they arrived," is precisely the condition of wonder. The unrest or disquiet (*Unruhe*) that Goethe names is like "the sudden loss of the sense that we understand what is going on" that Joe Sachs claims is "characteristic of wonder."[42] It is this experience of wonder that is the completion of Aristotle's account of the *telos* of tragedy, which began with the word *catharsis*:

> In the next-to-last chapter of the *Poetics*, Aristotle uses the adjective *ekplektikos*, having the power to know something away from us, as a description of the end of the art of poetry itself, without which it misses its mark (1460b 22–26). It follows that producing wonder is not some sort of occasional consequence of tragedy, but the very thing at which it aims; and Aristotle says exactly this in Chapter 24 (1460a 11–12). That claim amounts to nothing less than the long-delayed completion of the definition of tragedy that began eighteen chapters earlier. The *katharsis*, the washing away, is more aptly described as *ekplexis*, a knocking away, and the state in which we are left is wonder.[43]

In the very essay in which Goethe tries to make Aristotle say that catharsis is a mechanical operation within the tragedy, confined to what happens onstage, his own description of tragedy's effect is a dead ringer for Sachs's catharsis as the effect and purpose of poetry: it is the experience of *Unruhe* in which one's sense of justice and rightness is thrown into confusion. This is indeed by itself no kind of betterment or education of the soul; instead, it is an opening for further reflection. Whether an audience member or reader will make use of the chance depends on factors beyond the playwright's control. Drama provides *opportunity*, not any kind of twelve-step self-help program. The peculiar nature of the action inspired by good drama, like that of a conversation with Socrates, is that of a confrontation with an impasse, with *aporia*, which may or may not lead to contemplation, which may or may not lead to a change in behavior. The aim of tragedy is not to teach a lesson but to awaken the desire to learn one.

The future interpretations of catharsis intimated in Goethe's work thus come full circle. Within *Iphigenie auf Tauris*, Orest and Iphigenie exemplify catharsis as purgation (Bernays, 1857) and moral clarification (Nussbaum, 1992), respectively. Goethe, however, explicitly limits catharsis to the confines of the drama itself: it is a function of the dynamics internal to the tragedy, and not an effect of tragedy on external viewers (Goethe, 1827; Else, 1957). By staging her act of truth-telling fiction before Thoas, however, Iphigenie makes him the first audience to her drama of recognition. If the catharsis of her play-within-a-play does indeed spill over to affect its spectators, then one must question Goethe's own interpretation of Aristotle's definition of tragedy. The wording of Goethe's essay further suggests that this effect should be characterized as a troubling sense of perplexity and a wish to learn more.

Goethe provides further support for this account of the effect of drama in a short essay, "On Didactic Poetry" (1825). Here, he writes that "all poetry should be edifying, but unnoticeably; it should make people aware of what is worth learning; they have to draw the lesson from it, as from life, themselves."[44] The play itself does not instruct nor improve its readers or spectators. Yet it may open up a realization of the need to learn or become better. Recall the effect of Rilke's sonnet about the "Archaic Torso of Apollo": "Du musst dein Leben ändern!" (You must change your life!).[45] But how? The aesthetic experience brings one to acknowledge one's deficiency and desire change: it does not provide instructions for a self-improvement regimen. Thus recognition of a lack of knowledge is the poetic effect of moving anagnorisis scenes. The epistemology of recognition is a visceral feeling of ignorance.

According to this understanding, the effect of a drama in the third level of recognition can, when the tragic story represents a striking anagnorisis, lead to a rejection of assumptions about recognition revealed to be indefensible and insufficient. It is an invitation to think about why one feels unrest and to instigate a search for a more satisfactory understanding. It is impossible to know if Thoas himself is experiencing such an aporetic state of wonder when he utters his final farewell. But he is a spectator to Iphigenie's stunning performance of recognition, and the very indeterminacy of his reaction can be a model of tragedy's impact for the external audience that is disturbed into unquietness by his silent spectatorship.

CHAPTER NINE

Politics of Recognition

Friends, Enemies, and Goethe's *Iphigenie*

WHEN GOETHE'S IPHIGENIE confronts the king of the Taurians, she makes a demand to be accepted in the role of several identities that contradict his desire to make her his wife: as a priestess, as a Greek, as a woman, and finally as a sister to Orest and a daughter to himself. Hence it is easy to understand the temptation to read Goethe's *Iphigenie auf Tauris* as a perfect drama to model the ideals of recognition politics. Beginning with champions of multiculturalism like Charles M. Taylor and refined by third-generation Frankfurt School figures such as Axel Honneth, the Hegelian notion of recognition (*Anerkennung*) has been held up as the most legitimate way to underpin just relations between different sections of society.[1] Only if people come together and affirm each other in their (chosen or given) identities, they reason, will society achieve harmony and justice inclusive of difference. Goethe's play seems tailor-made to showcase how such recognition between cultures, genders, and individuals can come about.[2]

Yet though the drama gives rise to this desirable fantasy of recognition, it also contains its critique. In fact, just as *Iphigenie* anticipates future aesthetic theories (chapter 8), it also foreshadows important political theories of the twentieth century. This chapter charts the ways *Iphigenie* prefigures and comments on recognition politics (Honneth), its critics (Markell), authoritarianism (Schmitt), and pluralism (Arendt). The drama casts a long shadow over all these political thinkers and closes with a theatrically inflected, endlessly deferred promise of recognition.

Let's rehearse the recognition plot again: A Greek woman has spent years as a priestess of Diana among northern barbarians. Through her influence, they have suspended their traditional practice of killing all foreigners in a sacrificial rite. Despite the lurid violence of her own origins—her ancestors are guilty of kin-slaying and cannibalism, and her own father, Agamemnon, sacrificed her for the sake of his Trojan expedition—Iphigenie yearns for her family and homeland. In the opening act of the play, she finally reveals her story and identity to the king of the Taurians, Thoas, as a way of avoiding his insistent marriage proposal. The king's desire to possess Iphigenie breaks the liberalizing equilibrium achieved by her cultural influence, and he reinstates the edict to kill foreigners, beginning with two men who have just been captured. Iphigenie is charged to sacrifice them to Diana but soon discovers that they are Greek—in fact, they are her brother, Orest, and his friend, Pylades. Their conversations eventually lead to Orest's cure from the furies tormenting him for committing matricide (he killed Clytemnestra, who had killed Agamemnon, who everyone thought had killed Iphigenie). Pylades hatches a brilliant plan for them all to escape with the statue of Diana that the two men had come to Tauris to steal: Iphigenie should inform Thoas that the holy statue has been defiled and must be taken to the shore for cleansing. After some pangs of conscience, Iphigenie instead decides to tell Thoas the truth, endangering all of their lives. She stages a scene of persuasion, and Thoas finally allows them to leave.

Walter Erhart convincingly argues that the drama demonstrates the "struggle for recognition" that aligns dramatic anagnorisis with Honneth's political *Anerkennung*. "Pathologies of recognition" (*Anerkennungspathologien*) characterize relations between figures in the first part of the play:[3] Thoas misrecognizes Iphigenie in terms of gender and personal autonomy; Orest misrecognizes the crippling shame of his own responsibility; Greeks misrecognize the Taurians with dehumanizing assumptions of cultural superiority. These pathologies are slowly overcome through the mutual interplay of both autonomy and subjugation between characters. Erhart shows how the play maps out Honneth's three levels of recognition with almost formulaic precision.[4] The first level of love, friendship, and family is put to rights by the anagnorisis between brother and sister. This enables Orest's healing vision of the underworld, which brings order to the second level of right and justice. Finally, it is Iphigenie's act of truth-telling that invites Thoas (and Orest) to recognize her for her own achievements, as demanded by Honneth's third level of recognition, the granting of social esteem. In the last scene, Erhart writes, Iphigenie "plays through a complete register of modern forms of recognition."[5] Erhart admits that the play leaves open the extent to which the last recognition scene "works" but concludes on a hopeful note with a normative call for modern literature to "simulate social pathologies and conditions of recognition." This in turn would allow literary theory to "win back its social-theoretical potential," presumably lost to decades of deconstruction and historicism.[6]

This tall order, for all of Erhart's circumspect caveats, is a return to nineteenth-century trust in the edifying power of art to forward the ideals of humanistic *Bildung*, best exemplified in classicizing readings of Goethe's *Iphigenie*.[7] It rests on an implicit trust in the ability of literature faithfully to mirror social conditions in a representation that allows for scientific diagnosis (or at least for some kind of truth-revealing augury). If myth, as Hans Blumenberg suggests, is the wishful answer to the terror of living,[8] then trusting any adaptation of a mythic template to "simulate" sociological relations, as statistical models purport to do, is suspect. But what such work on myth *can* do is reveal the structures of desire that rise up as hopeful solutions to the changing problems and fears of living together. It is in the service of examining these mythic therapies that this chapter will return to read recognition in Goethe's *Iphigenie*: not as an experimental field in which to test sociological theories empirically but rather as an idealizing image that might reveal the anxieties it seeks to assuage. What are the questions to which *Iphigenie* is an answer?

Some of these questions have already been articulated in the previous chapter: How, for instance, can identity be an intertextual performance? The potential catharsis staged at the end of the play suggests that *Iphigenie* itself forces more questions than it provides comforting assurance for. This chapter will turn from individual identity and the cathartic effect of drama to the negotiation of recognition on the political stage. First, Patchen Markell's pointed opposition of recognition and acknowledgment must be addressed. A comparison of his cogent analysis with the very different account of recognition offered in this book reveals two aspects of recognition that Markell neglects. On the one hand, Carl Schmitt's definition of the political as the decision between friend and enemy must be taken seriously in its connection to anagnorisis. The friend/enemy distinction in *Iphigenie* turns up with a strange new face that shows how its ethical imperative, unmasked in chapter 4, assumes the figure of the political. On the other hand, the performativity of Iphigenie's final promise to Thoas illustrates Hannah Arendt's theory of action as a political scene of recognition. By repeating itself so often, the dramatic trope of recognition in Goethe's drama becomes a talisman both for and against the instability of the theatrical self and the encroachment of politics into ethics.

BETWEEN RECOGNITION AND ACKNOWLEDGMENT

Both Erhart and Markell want to save recognition from assumptions about the autonomy of the subject, but the former does so *with* Honneth while the latter does so *against* Honneth and other recognition theorists. For Erhart, *Iphigenie* is not the "drama of autonomy" that an influential reading from the 1970s would make it.[9] Rather, it is a drama of recognition that demands a conception of the subject as "doubled: as autonomous and as heteronomous, as free and dependent, as universally 'human' and as differentiated by gender."[10] In other words, Erhart reads the *Iphigenie* as displaying the intersubjective processes of mutual recognition on which any kind of independence must be founded.

Markell's rejection of the desire for autonomy is more radical. He cleverly and persuasively demonstrates that aiming for the mutual affirmation of recognition—the goal of identity politics and many latter-day Hegelians—renders its own worthy ideal of autonomous subject formation impossible. Clinging to the desideratum of recognition, in fact, can help sustain the very social dynamics of oppression that it is meant to overcome.[11] As a preferable alternative to the inevitable failure of political recognition, Markell urges subjects to realize the extreme fragility of human agency. He calls this awareness of the nonsovereign character of action "acknowledgment."[12] One should soberly acknowledge that the plurality of agents and the utter uncontrollability of the future will open a space for misunderstandings, objectification, and subjugation, despite all efforts to the contrary.

Markell strictly differentiates recognition (*Anerkennung*) from acknowledgment.[13] Neither of these concepts corresponds to the account of recognition as performance that has been developed in this book. Markell's *Anerkennung* is always an attempt to found sovereignty through an intersubjective process of mutual affirmation. It is an idealized version of Hegel's master/slave dialectic, in which neither party must lord over the other in order to achieve a (soon to be proven insufficient) validation of autonomous subjecthood. Instead, both parties perform validating functions for one another. For the political theorists of recognition with whom Markell is in dialogue, *Anerkennung* is a basic "good" of human society.[14] His "acknowledgment," in contrast, is never mutual but can only be a one-sided realization that seeking autonomy through *Anerkennung* is impossible.

Like Markell's *Anerkennung*, the performance of recognition as developed in this book is an intersubjective process, but the readings conducted thus far show it to be anything but an unmitigated "good." Instead, they suggest that recognition is the inescapable social situation into which people are thrown. They cannot help but construct their own identities in performative collusion with those with whom they interact—sometimes with objectifying (Menelaus and Helen, Creon and Antigone, Goethe and Beethoven), sometimes with affirming (Penelope and Odysseus, Iphigenie and Orest, Goethe and Schiller) results.

In a nuanced reading of Sophocles's *Antigone*, Markell shows how Creon's and Antigone's stubborn insistence on being recognized as agents in the spheres of the *polis* and the *oikos* (city/state vs. home/family), respectively, leads directly to her death and his remorse in the end. He marshals Aristotle's *Poetics* to argue that anagnorisis should be understood not merely as intersubjective recognition of identity but rather as a lesson on the limits of agency: "Tragic anagnorisis . . . is the acknowledgment of finitude under the weight of a (failed) effort to become sovereign through the recognition of identity." He goes so far as to call this an "ontological discovery" that enlightens characters, and presumably perspicuous spectators, about the "real conditions of one's own existence and activity."[15] This statement amounts to realizing the role of contingency in all human designs: because of the plurality of subjects, actions and intentions will inevitably cross, cancel each other, and go astray. Anagnorisis becomes an acknowledgment of fortune's (*tukhē*) might. This interpretation of anagnorisis enables Markell to offer a powerful reading of *Antigone* that goes beyond a simple conflict between the claims of state and family. It could also help illuminate anagnorisis in some other Greek tragedies. In learning about his own identity, for instance, Sophocles's Oedipus certainly comes to acknowledge the horrors resulting from his reliance on the subject's ability to control its own actions. Markell himself brilliantly glosses Aeschylus's *Eumenides* to show how the seemingly harmonious ending is made suspect by the constraints of recognition.[16]

Yet by equating anagnorisis with awareness of nonsovereignty, Markell is quick to elide the *effect* of some anagnorisis scenes with the central *action* of dramatic recognition. For one thing, many Greek tragedies sport *anagnoriseis* that have different, even opposing consequences for the characters involved. Most notably, in Euripides's *Iphigenia among the Taurians*, the recognition between the siblings leads directly to a veritable celebration of Iphigenia's agency in outwitting and escaping Thoas and his men. In this tragedy, anagnorisis transforms *tukhē* from crippling fate into blessed opportunity. Before discovering his sister, Orestes identifies so thoroughly with ill fortune that he takes *Dustukhē* (misfortune) as his rightful name (*Iph*, 500). After their reunion, this fatalism becomes a conviction that fortune favors the brave (*Iph*, 909–911). Recognition here effects a reversal in acknowledgment from Markell's avowal of human finitude to a hymn of human agency.

This play's anagnorisis, in fact, is mentioned and praised by Aristotle more often than any but *Oedipus Tyrannos*, and both are given as examples as the "best" kind of recognition (*P*, 16, 1455a, 17). Admittedly, one can pick out threads of Markell's acknowledgment in the fabric of *Iphigenia*. In a move that stresses the contingency of the happy outcome, for instance, Athena intervenes at the end to ensure that the Taurians do not pursue the Greeks' ship: their good fortune could easily unravel. As Martha Nussbaum drives home in *The Fragility of Goodness*, Aristotle and the Greek tragedians always evince a healthy respect for the role of chance in human life. Taken whole cloth, however, the effect of anagnorisis in *Iphigenia* is to cover up, if only briefly, human vulnerability to fate. It is hard to see how the "best" tragic recognition in *Iphigenia* could push either characters or spectators to a profound realization of their limited sovereignty. Markell's conflation of anagnorisis and acknowledgment would unduly limit the great variety of effects and purposes that Greek tragedy displays.

Markell's acknowledgment attests to the undisputable fact that the subjects of recognition are never sovereign masters of their actions, as my exploration of fortune in recognition in this book (chapter 5) also concludes. Yet dramatic anagnorisis, no more than the performance of recognition, cannot be reduced to an abdication of sovereignty in the pursuit of *Anerkennung*. The plurality of human subjects means that desires, expectations, and assumptions will always be at odds (often even within a single actor), and the ongoing intersubjective performance of recognition will often lead to deplorable oppression or mild discontent despite the best intentions of all parties involved. This risk is reflected in the final clause of Aristotle's definition of anagnorisis: "among those bound for good or bad fortune" (*tukhē*). By equating it with acknowledgment, however, Markell boils anagnorisis down to one person's change from ignorance to knowledge *about tukhē*. As Aristotle admits, many things can be the object of recognition: things, actions, and presumably severe truths such as Markell's eloquent articulation of acknowledgment. Yet *dramatic* anagnorisis—the kind imitated in tragedy and poetry—Aristotle goes on, will be the kind that happens between people (*P*, 11, 1452a, 27–1452b, 8). The one-sided, sobering wisdom of acknowledgment may be a part of that intersubjective process, but it does not make up the many valences along the entire arc of the action of recognition.

In some ways, acknowledgment, as Markell parses it, is more akin to the philosophical reaction to tragedy to which catharsis can lead (see chapter 8 in this book) than to recognition per se. Yet Markell's articulation of acknowledgment is a nuanced philosophical stance with a clear propositional attitude toward the world. Tragic catharsis in Sachs's interpretation, meanwhile, *knocks away* assumptions and unreflected worldviews; it does not offer replacement theories on its own. Poetry can be a *beginning* of a philosophical journey; Markell's acknowledgment is one possible *destination*. Catharsis is thus an opening up of the mind to the world, whereas acknowledgment is a defensive closing off due to the conviction of the world's penchant for catastrophe.

Although Markell's acknowledgment may be a very appropriate reaction to the contingencies involved in the process of recognition, Honneth and Taylor's *Anerkennung* may still seem the best hope for it. Even if it is ultimately impossible to achieve perfect autonomy, surely people should still strive for mutually affirming recognition, with a healthy dose of respect for the limitations of sovereignty as outlined by Markell, right? Yet for Markell, anagnorisis and acknowledgment are utterly incompatible with *Anerkennung*: "The pursuit of recognition *is* the failure of acknowledgment."[17] Goethe's *Iphigenie* throws down a challenge to this claim, just as Euripides's *Iphigenia* questions the equation of acknowledgment and anagnorisis. By freely choosing to reveal the truth to Thoas in full awareness of the risk to herself and her brother, Iphigenie pursues *Anerkennung* while acknowledging her lack of control of the outcome. In order to evaluate whether her gambit escapes the vicious circle that Markell draws for all *Anerkennung* attempts, it is necessary to recur to an aspect of recognition that neither Markell nor Erhart stresses: the distinction between friend and enemy.

THE EXCEPTION OF FRIENDSHIP

Anagnorisis for Aristotle involves a change *into friendship or enmity*. The example of Penelope and Odysseus showed how this disjunction opens up a space for ethics in recognition (chapter 4). Notoriously, however, the decision between friend and enemy is the criterion that defines the concept of the political for Carl Schmitt, *Der Begriff des Politischen* (*The Concept of the Political*; 1927–1932).[18] Schmitt makes it clear that by enemy (*Feind*), he means the public enemy, not a personal rival or hated adversary. In fact, he tries to clarify the term with Greek: he means *polemios*, not *ekhthros*.[19] This explanation would seem to spare anagnorisis from having any political valence in Schmitt's system, since it leads to either *philia* or *ekhthra*. But the distinction between *ekhthros* and *polemios* is not as clear as Schmitt would like to have it.

First of all, *polemios* is a very specific term: it is the adjectival form of the word for war (*polemos*), so its basic meaning is "of or belonging to war" or "warlike." In its substantivized form, it refers to enemy soldiers but mainly in the specific context of war. *Ekhthros*, meanwhile, can refer to a wide variety of hostile relationships, including enemy combatants in war. It is the umbrella term for adversaries of all stripes, just as *philos*, the general word for close ties, covers many more valences than the English *friend*.[20] Second, Aristotle's definition sets up its disjunction between the abstract concepts of friendship (*philia*) and enmity (*ekhthra*), not between discrete friends and enemies. The conceptual nouns corresponding to *polemios*, meanwhile, do not refer to an abstraction of the enemy combatant: *hē polemikē* is the "art of war"; *ta polemia* is "war and its business."[21] Hence not only does *ekhthra* include the notion of the public enemy that Schmitt invokes, but there is no other way to refer to *öffentliche Feindschaft* in Greek than with that very term.

Just because *ekhthra* does not exclude the political enemy, however, does not mean that anagnorisis entails a political decision in Schmitt's sense. A further criterion is necessary for the friend/enemy distinction to become political—its degree of intensity:

> The political can derive its energy from the most varied human endeavors, from the religious, economic, moral, and other antitheses. It does not describe its own substance, but only the intensity (*Intensitätsgrad*) of an association or dissociation of human beings. . . . The political entity (*Einheit*) . . . is always the decisive entity (*maßgebende Einheit*).[22]

The friend/enemy decision becomes political at the moment it intensifies to the existential magnitude of being ready to kill in its name. Friendship and enmity gain their conceptual force from "the real possibility of physical killing."[23] This willingness to take the life of the enemy in armed conflict is what makes the political distinction, the "decisive" (*maßgebend*) human unity.[24] Quite literally, it is the unit (*Einheit*) that provides the measure

(*Maß*) for human communities. The English translation does not reflect Schmitt's orthographic intensification of the two key terms in this paragraph: *Intensitätsgrad* and *maßgebend* are both italicized. Nor does the translation bring across the mathematical flavor of the language here: *Einheit* would be better rendered as "unit," as in the magnitude of the basic "one" necessary for counting and measuring. *Maßgebend* literally means "giving the measure," an important function that "decisive" does not suggest at all. *Intensitätsgrad* is not simply "intensity" but *degree* of intensity. The terms highlighted by Schmitt are reminiscent of book 5 of Euclid's *Elements*, which deals with magnitude and commensurability. The political for Schmitt offers a standard unit of measurement that makes all human groupings commensurable. The existential measure of man is his readiness to take the life of another human.

Hence Schmitt supplies the criterion that would make anagnorisis political. Not all recognitions lead to a readiness to exterminate the potential enemy in armed combat; most, in fact, fall far short of this measure. Penelope's declarations of the disguised beggar as her friend and then husband, for instance, proceed according to other criteria; at no point is she willing to order her servants to kill him. Neither does she have the power to command combat with the suitors besieging and depleting her household. Goethe's initial antipathy for Schiller, however hated (*verhasst*), never tempts him to consider murder. Though not all anagnorisis scenarios fulfill the criteria for becoming political, all political decisions that turn friends into enemies (or vice versa) *do* fit the definition of anagnorisis. When Odysseus tests the Ithacans in his household, he has every intention of trying to kill those he discovers to be enemies rather than friends. The restoration of Odysseus's household and kingship in Ithaca takes place through a series of recognitions that coincide with fatal political decisions.

Even in today's democratic (and not-so-democratic) societies, politicians exploit the dramatic logic of recognition in their rhetoric to persuade or explain. They cast political decisions about friends and enemies as causal narratives replete with reversals and recognitions. Think of Donald Trump's frequent recitation of "The Snake" during his 2016 campaign rallies. In the lyrics by Oscar Brown Jr., a woman takes in a needy serpent only to be bitten by it in the end. Before she dies, she is forced to recognize the hostile nature of the snake. Trump used this recognition scene to argue against the acceptance of Muslim immigrants. In his address to the United Nations Leaders' Summit on Refugees on September 20, 2016, President Obama also told a recognition narrative—but one aimed at urging lawmakers to take in more asylum seekers. In Obama's "true story," based on a letter sent him by a six-year-old boy, an American child saw a photo of an injured Syrian boy and realized that they are just alike. He wanted the president to invite the Syrian child to come live with his family and be his brother.[25] In the former story, a welcomed friend turns out to be an enemy; in the latter, a supposed enemy is seen as a friend. Rare is the political platform that is not based on a fable of recognition. For anyone wishing to understand persuasive discourse in historical or current rhetoric, it is imperative to examine the mythic templates underlying political speech about allies and enemies. This chapter claims that Goethe politicizes recognition in his reworking of Euripides's *Iphigenia*. The play, which is about a refugee in a society that spurns all foreigners, provides a perfect laboratory to investigate the narrative dynamics in Schmitt's distillation of the essential nature of the political.

During the long history of its reception, the story of *Iphigenia among the Taurians* has most often been retold as a play about friendship. Yet for more than two millennia, the ideal friends at the drama's center were Pylades and Orestes rather than brother and sister. From Cicero and Ovid to Gluck, whose opera *Iphigénie en Tauride* premiered the same year as Goethe's drama, the most moving scene takes place between the two men. After Iphigenia decides to let one of the Greeks escape to carry her letter, Orestes and Pylades are left alone on stage and keep trying to outfriend one another by each insisting that he himself should die while the other lives. In these popular versions of the story, Iphigenia is marginalized and discounted.[26] Although Goethe's Iphigenie is markedly different from Euripides's Iphigenia, the two women are at least the central focus of their respective dramas. The political, however, appears with remarkable contrast in the two plays.

The anagnorisis scene in Euripides's *Iphigenia among the Taurians* is not political. Even though Iphigenia is ready to prepare Orestes for death before recognizing him as her brother and chooses to let him live afterward, the political decision that classifies him as enemy in the first place is not hers to make. The scene takes place against a political backdrop, however. The Taurians kill every foreigner who arrives on their shores. They have taken the cultural distinction of "us and them" and intensified it to the existential extremity of organized murder. All strangers have been made into public enemies. At this point, according to Schmitt, the cultural custom—or the religious rite—has been rendered political. Thoas represents the epitome of the political decision: he declares that *every* Other is an enemy who must systematically be put to death. The Taurian state thus maintains a level of social order that resembles a Nazi fantasy of cultural purity.[27] This background of unmitigable mortal threat adds suspense to the siblings' discovery and escape plot without complicating their motives or compromising their actions. The Taurians are straightforward goons like the bad guys in an *Indiana Jones* adventure. The romance genre, which has its stage debut in this Euripidean drama, is an apolitical escapade amid extreme political scenery.

Goethe takes this romance plot and politicizes it. In one of his play's first major departures from Euripides, Thoas has suspended the practice of killing foreigners in Tauris due to Iphigenie's persuasion. Not even the goddess Athena has a civilizing mission to the Taurians in Euripides's tragedy. In her concluding deus ex machina, she commands Thoas not to pursue Orestes's ship and to free Iphigenia's chorus of Greek slaves, but she does not attempt to abolish the practice of human sacrifice. Instead, she commands Orestes to import a vestige of this violent ritual to Greece. He is to build a temple to "Taurian-faring" Artemis near Athens:

> This is the custom you must establish: when the people keep the feast, to atone for your sacrifice let them hold a sword to the neck of a man and draw blood: thus will piety be satisfied and the goddess receive honor. (*Iph*, 1458–1461)

The bloody laceration is a token of the Taurian practice of executing all foreigners. Far from making the barbarians more like the Greeks, she imports to Attica a violent reminder of the Taurian radicalization of the political decision.

No gods appear in Goethe's drama, but the human Iphigenie has managed to fundamentally change the Taurians' culture and laws. Her influence, in fact, brings about a state of exception to the normative law of the land. One might think that the play hence prioritizes some other social distinction over the political friend/enemy criterion: Iphigenie, after all, invokes the gods (religious antithesis: holy/unholy) and a universal morality (ethical antithesis: good/bad) in her rhetoric against human sacrifice. The play is commonly read as a drama of civilizing tolerance and enlightenment. Yet since Schmitt's definition of the political trumps other social grouping distinctions as soon as the friend/enemy decision reaches the extremity of killing, any temporary release from the execution of foreigners will necessarily be political as well.

In fact, the moratorium on killing strangers aligns with another important term in Schmitt's conceptual arsenal. As with the political, Schmitt provides an existential definition of sovereignty: whoever can effectually decide on the state of exception (*Ausnahmezustand*) is sovereign.[28] Thoas's abrogation of the Taurian death sentence invokes a state of exception to dismantle the political decision defining all strangers as enemies.[29] The ease with which Thoas reinstates the original law, after Iphigenie rebuffs his amorous advances, indicates the exceptional nature of its rescindment (HA, 5, 503–521). The relatively "open society" that flourished in the interim is hence revealed to exist at the personal whim of the political sovereign.

Structurally, therefore, Goethe's drama begins with a reversion to the extreme rule of Taurian law after years of a liberalizing emergency. It ends with a return to exceptional authority when Thoas is persuaded to allow the strangers to depart with their lives. Whereas one might reasonably expect a theatrical play to take place within the hiatus of an exception, the action of this one coincides with the temporary *return* to legality after years of emergency. The play flips the common view of exceptionalism, which is usually at the behest of totalitarian dictatorship, on its head. Instead of an established liberal order under threat of subversion by extralegal *auctoritas*, the tolerant society itself is the product of authoritarian fiat.

It is revealing to compare the nature of Iphigenie's influence on the sovereign decision in the first and last instances. The initial edict takes place years before the action of the play. After Iphigenie refuses his marriage proposal, Thoas blames the "friendliness" (*Freundlichkeit*) with which Iphigenie had "chained [him] with magic bonds" for charming him into decreeing the exception against the will of the people. In fact, Thoas now perceives his temporary policy of extrajudicial tolerance as a sorcery of recognition:

> Nur du hast mich mit einer Freundlichkeit
> In der ich bald der zarten Tochter Liebe,
> Bald die stille Neigung einer Braut zu sehn
> Mich tief erfreute, wie mit Zauberbanden
> Gefesselt, daβ ich meiner Pflicht vergaβ. (HA, 5, 511–515)
>
> (You alone bound me with a friendliness
> In which at times the sight of a gentle daughter's love,
> And then the quiet affection of a bride

Deeply gratified me, as if with magic chains
So fast that I forgot my duty.)[30]

The state of emergency rescinding the rule of law that condemns strangers to death coincides with the incestuous move from recognizing Iphigenie as a surrogate daughter to a potential bride. Only while Thoas sees Iphigenie as kin (*philia*) does he exercise his sovereignty to welcome strangers as friends rather than kill them as enemies. From Thoas's point of view, the insinuating blandishment of kinship, first paternal and then erotic, convinces him to instate the exception. Familiarity (in the sense of *family*) breeds clemency. It is excessive friendship that convinces the sovereign to suspend the extremity of the political in Tauris.

In the second case, during the play's final act, the audience is privy to the means of persuasion Iphigenie employs to convince Thoas to make an exception. Three stages of this process are important here. In the first, before Iphigenie makes her pivotal decision to tell Thoas the truth, she is still struggling with the Schmittian/Hobbesian system that Pylades schools her in (act 4). In fact, when Thoas tries to fob off responsibility for reinstating the death sentence for all foreigners by blaming the "ancient law" rather than himself, Iphigenie sets him straight. She reminds him that he is the sovereign who chooses which laws to enforce or exempt.

THOAS. Ein alt Gesetz, nicht ich, gebietet dir.
IPHIGENIE. Wir fassen ein Gesetz begierig an,
Das unsrer Leidenschaft zur Waffe dient. (HA, 5, 1832–1835)[31]

(THOAS: An ancient law, not I, commands you.
IPHIGENIE: We grasp eagerly for a law
When it serves our passions as a weapon.)[32]

By Thoas's own admission, after all, it was his desire for Iphigenie that led to the original abrogation of this ancient law. This exchange emphasizes the location of sovereignty in the will of the one who decides the state of exception.

Later on, Iphigenie begins a defense of trickery and betrayal for those condemned to die. This argument could come directly out of Thomas Hobbes's *Leviathan*. Despite Hobbes's trenchant absolutism, he firmly upheld that "no man can transfer or lay aside his right to save himself from death, wounds, or imprisonment."[33]

Auch ohne Hülfe gegen Trutz und Härte
Hat die Natur den Schwachen nicht gelassen.
Sie gab zur List ihm Freude, lehrt' ihn Künste . . .
Ja der Gewaltige verdient daß man sie übt. (HA, 5, 1868–1872)

(And nature has not left the weak defenceless
Against rude force. She taught them to enjoy
The exercise of subtlety and cunning . . .
Such arts are what the violent deserve.)

The powerful "deserve" to be tricked by those whom they threaten with violence. Yet it is while articulating this Hobbesian worldview in defense of her actions that Iphigenie comes to reject the very justification she is uttering. As seen in the previous chapter, her identification of the clever trickster with Odysseus leads her to repudiate him and Pylades's version of Greek cultural supremacy. To paraphrase Kleist, this is truly an instance of the "gradual formation of the self while speaking," and it leads to the second phase of Iphigenie's art of persuasion: universal moral law.

Iphigenie's move here has justifiably been compared to Kant's ethics of autonomy and the moral law. Her refusal to lie despite endangering herself and her friends prefigures Kant's critique of "the Supposed Right to Lie for Philanthropic Reasons" (*Über ein vermeintes Recht, aus Menschenliebe zu lügen*; 1797).[34] In its grasp for universal validity ("Everyone born under every sky can hear . . . the voice of truth and humanity"; HA, 5, 1938–1940), Iphigenie's decision to tell Thoas the truth betrays the particular Greek morality of "helping friends and harming enemies."[35] It is equally an attempt to replace the totalitarian logic of the Taurians' radical Schmittian politics, the very defense of which eventually leads her to this alternative. While Iphigenie's rhetoric may support connecting her truth-telling to Kantian morality, however, her actions suggest another explanation.

Iphigenie has unnecessarily politicized the private recognition between brother and sister. In telling Thoas the truth, Iphigenie puts the decision about the validity of her relation to Orest into the power of the state: recognition has gone from a familial affair to a matter of politics. Far from a move toward moral autonomy, this seems to be craven acquiescence to the will of the sovereign. Although she could have gotten away scot free to live in freedom with her brother, she feels compelled to let Thoas have the last say on whether to legitimate their *philia*. This act is an effective consent to the sovereign's political decision between friends and enemies.

Thus characterized, Iphigenie's decision is a kick in the face to the universalist, proto-Kantian ethics she is supposed to invent in this scene. It is possible, however, to read her choice in these political friend/enemy terms yet still *against* the logic of Schmitt's conclusions. In Jacques Derrida's critique of the *Concept of the Political*, he upholds the necessary jointure of the existential enemy with the idea of friendship, but he finds fault with Schmitt's prioritization of the enemy.[36] The political for Schmitt is founded on the willingness to murder. A hoped-for future politics with friendship at its core, in contrast, would have to be founded on the willingness to be killed by the enemy one respects in the friend.[37] This is precisely the vision of friendship that guides Iphigenie's decision to open up to Thoas. She twice explicitly and implicitly throughout invites her own death at Thoas's hands with this act of gratuitous revelation (HA, 5, 1936, 1944). Iphigenie is the embodiment of Derrida's promise of a politics of the future. She replaces a politics of readiness to kill the enemy with one of willingness to be killed by the friend.

Iphigenie's action in this scene is an attempt to solve a central contradiction of ethics and politics. On the one hand, the friend/enemy distinction is inevitable in politics (according to Schmitt, it is *constitutive* of politics). On the other hand, the friend/enemy distinction is anathema to universally valid ethics. A just politics cannot aim to further its own ends and those of allies at the expense of enemies or play rivals off against one another. Even designating another state as the enemy betrays the ideals of perpetual peace.[38] By treating Thoas as a friend while opening herself to his reaction as an enemy, Iphigenie subverts the logic of this contradiction and embraces the ideals of Derrida's future politics, which he himself dared not propose as a foundation to adhere to.[39] If Thoas's edict to kill all strangers is the epitome of Schmittian politics, then Iphigenie's invitation for him to kill her is exemplary of Derrida's dream of a friendship free from fraternal ties.

Yet the voices of reason, renunciation, and self-sacrifice fail to bring about Thoas's acceptance of the anagnorisis between Orest and Iphigenie and his own recognition of Iphigenie's right to self-determination. The final phase of Iphigenie's persuasion must follow the inability of enlightened human universals to do the job. As suggested in the previous chapter, Iphigenie's direction of this scene takes a decidedly theatrical turn: "Sieh uns an!" "O wende dich [a literal peripeteia!] zu uns" (HA, 5, 2148, 2168). This stage business coincides with a return to the traditional anagnorisis between *philia* and estranged kin. Iphigenie calls for a "friendly law of hospitality" (*freundlich Gastrecht*; HA, 5, 2153) to prevail between them. In fact, using a third-person imperative, she demands that this law of friendship emanate "from you to us." But instead of resting on the rhetorical laurels of this articulation of Derridian ethics as politics, Iphigenie follows it up directly with a reminder that she sees him as a father (HA, 5, 2155–2157). It was Thoas's move from loving Iphigenie as a daughter to desiring her as a wife that jeopardized the state of exception allowing the liberal order in the first place. Now instead of demanding a genuine recognition of herself as an autonomous subject with independent ends, Iphigenie resorts to stressing the daughterly aspects of their former relations. Knowing Thoas's proclivities, the erotic is not far behind paternal desire. She reinsinuates the familial into the universal. Her very last sentence requests his right hand as a sign of their "old friendship" (HA, 5, 2173). It is only this recurrence of recognition as filial anagnorisis that seals the deal and manages to elicit the curt "fare well" that concludes the play and reinstates the state of exception.

In three steps, Iphigenie's desire for recognition from Thoas has traveled full circle. First, by articulating a justification for deception in the Hobbesian worldview of Pylades, in which Thoas's recognition would be unnecessary, she comes to reject the particularism it implies. Second, the universal moral values she proposes instead amount simultaneously to a demand for recognition from Thoas and a submission of her life to him. This double move actualizes the hope for a future politics based in friendship without recourse to fraternity as envisioned but not pursued by Derrida. Yet it fails to win Thoas's immediate blessing of her autonomy, and she returns to the strategy of anagnorisis by invoking kinship.

As emphasized in the preceding chapter, Thoas's terse reply to this ploy renders indeterminate the nature of his recognition. No stage direction indicates whether he extends the friendly hand that Iphigenie asks for. Is his farewell an acknowledgment of Iphigenie's right to personhood? Is it a response to her appeal to him as a father figure? At stake is the distinction between recognition *of* and recognition *as*. Does Thoas recognize Iphigenie in her singular individuality, or does he recognize her *as* a surrogate daughter? This difference aligns with what Hannah Arendt calls saying *who* versus *what* someone is. This is the "curious intangibility that confounds all efforts toward unequivocal verbal expression" in the disclosure of the self and its recognition.[40] The paucity of Thoas's response to Iphigenie's involved action in speech is emblematic of the fate of interpersonal recognition on the political stage of the decision between friend and enemy.

THE PROMISE OF POLITICS

Thoas's hidden disclosure is not the only way that Goethe's play illustrates Arendt's ideas. Arendt's understanding of the dynamics of action has much in common with the account of recognition developed throughout this book. Iphigenie's final speech offers a poignant capstone to the potential promise of politics in human affairs. For Arendt, human action has two unavoidable sources of misfortune: its irreversibility and its unpredictability. One cannot know in advance what consequences one's speech and actions will have in the world, and one can never take them back when they turn out contrary to one's intentions. The only remedies for the inevitable regret that action will cause are forgiveness and promise. "The function of the faculty of promising," she writes, "is to master this two-fold darkness of human affairs"—namely, unpredictability and irreversibility. Promise is "the only alternative to a mastery which relies on domination of one's self and rule over others; it corresponds exactly to the existence of a freedom which was given under the condition of non-sovereignty."[41] Promise poses a challenge to Schmitt's location of sovereignty in the one who decides on the exception. Arendt calls any claim to sovereignty "by an isolated single entity" spurious. "Sovereignty resides in the . . . limited independence from the incalculability of the future" that is enabled by the "faculty itself of making and keeping promises."[42] In fact, morality can only be grounded in limited autonomy granted by the political goodwill to forgive and to promise.

In her final speech to Thoas, Iphigenie offers a model of this action of promise against the unknowable future:

> Bringt der Gerinsgste Deines Volkes je
> Den Ton der Stimme mir ins Ohr zurück
> Den ich an euch gewohnt zu hören bin,
> Und seh ich an dem Ärmsten eure Tracht;
> Empfangen will ich ihn wie einen Gott,
> Ich will ihm selbst ein Lager zubereiten,
> Auf einen Stuhl ihn an das Feuer laden,
> Und nur nach dir und deinem Schicksal fragen.
> O geben dir die Götter deiner Taten
> Und deiner Milde wohlverdienten Lohn. (HA, 5, 2158–2167)

> (Let even the least of your people come
> And bring back to my ears the sound, the speech

I have grown used to hearing here among you,
Let me see Taurian costume on the poorest
Of men—I will receive him like a god,
I will prepare a bed for him myself,
Invite him to sit down at our fireside
And ask no news but of how you are faring!
Oh may the gods reward as they deserve
Your deeds and your great generosity.)

This remarkable passage yokes together two kinds of recognition. In the first place, the imagined scenario she describes opens with her identifying a stranger as a Taurian. This *houtos ekeinos* (this is that) is accomplished by the senses of hearing and sight: she will note the distinctive language and clothing that mark the stranger as from Tauris. These signs of recognition function at the level of sensory shorthand that Aristotle in the *Poetics* and Penelope in the *Odyssey* both disparage (see chapter 3 in this book), but they are the conditions of identification that make theatrical representation possible. Here, they classify the imagined stranger as the cultural Other in general and as Taurian in particular.

In the second place, Iphigenie describes a political recognition that accepts and welcomes the stranger. This amounts to a rhetorical strategy of modeling the behavior she wants to encourage. It goes hand in hand with the final two lines that praise the desired action *as if* it were already accomplished. Both are manipulative. The former even implies an underhanded cultural rebuke of the Taurians: the kind treatment of the strangers Iphigenie describes is in stark contrast to their own practice of murdering foreigners. Think of present-day Germans offering to model a *Willkommenskultur* (culture of welcome) for neighboring countries reluctant to accept refugees. It is difficult to make a show of one's own enlightened virtue without denigrating others as xenophobic bigots. The implicit cultural superiority in this rhetoric, which Theodor Adorno effectually characterizes as Iphigenie bullying Thoas,[43] is an example of the way Markell sees the pursuit of recognition resulting in the failure of the just equity it aims for.

But Iphigenie adds one more important detail to this tableau of recognition: she stresses the stranger's poverty and low social class. She will treat "the least of these . . . like a god." This is a clear echo of Jesus's words in the parable of the sheep and the goats: "When you fed and clothed the least of these, you fed and clothed me" (Matthew 25:31–46).[44] Iphigenie here combines Greek *xenia* laws with Christian morality. The Greeks demand hospitality for strangers because they might be gods in disguise; Jesus commands his followers to serve the poor and downtrodden because they *are* God. Iphigenie does not merely promise to fulfill the duties of the guest/host relationship. By evoking Jesus in the context of future encounters with her captors, Iphigenie also implies—for post-Reformation German audiences, at least—the act of forgiveness. For Arendt, Jesus was the "discoverer of the role of forgiveness in the realm of human affairs."[45] This promise of recognition, then, is framed as a tableau of forgiveness, binding together the two remedies for action's infelicities in the drama's final speech.

Iphigenie's connection to Christ[46] hints at another way she provides a Derridian answer to Schmitt's political decision. Schmitt tries to inoculate his friend/enemy distinction from the command to love your enemies (*agapate tous ekthrous*; Matthew 5:44) by insisting that Jesus's enemy is a purely personal opponent.[47] Yet as argued above, *ekhthros* includes the political enemy. Arendt, moreover, folds the personal love that demands absolute forgiveness in Christianity into the political value of "respect": "What love is on its own, narrowly circumscribed sphere, respect is in the larger domain of human affairs. Respect, not unlike the Aristotelian *philia politikē*, is a kind of 'friendship' without intimacy and without closeness; it is regard for the person from the distance which the space of the world puts between us."[48] This transmutation of love into respect, in turn, makes Jesus's injunction fit Derrida's formula for the friend: to respect the enemy your friend may become. Forgiveness, therefore, is a retrospective version of this friendship: an attitude of respect for the enemy your friend has proven in the past. By promising a future forgiveness in the present, Iphigenie's temporality here is a veritable Augustinian image of eternity.

Significantly, Iphigenie's promise of friendship is not to Thoas himself. She vows to welcome the foreigner who will tell her *about* Thoas. The wandering Taurian *represents* Thoas in her fable of promise and forgiveness. Iphigenie thus subverts another Schmittian hobbyhorse: representation. For Schmitt, the figure of the sovereign must properly represent the state in order to bring about political unity.[49] The public declaration of friends and enemies for a group thus has its source in the unavoidably personal decision of the sovereign. Yet in Iphigenie's speech, the common citizen will represent the sovereign, and *she* has already decided to befriend him. Iphigenie turns the dynamics of representation and sovereignty upside down. The friendship she promises is both public and private; it is political by definition *and* a matter of personal morality.

Iphigenie's promise ties together dramatic anagnorisis and political *Anerkennung* in a markedly different way than Markell does. Instead of equating anagnorisis with a realization of the doomed fate of *Anerkennung*, which Iphigenie never concedes, her speech weaves together theatricality with narration in an idealized scene of recognition. Iphigenie tells how she will sit the stranger by the fire and "ask only about you and your fate" (HA, 5, 2165). Iphigenie's promise is to listen to stories about Thoas. The scene she imagines is the theatrical convention of the messenger's report. This age-old device for representing previous, offstage action is crucial to both ancient and modern drama. The bulk of the last section of Euripides's *Iphigenia among the Taurians*, for instance, consists of a messenger's report about the escape of the Greeks (*Iph*, 1284–1419); the final act of Goethe's *Iphigenie* also opens with Arkas's confused report of the same thing. The messenger's report marks the scene of recognition as emphatically theatrical.

At the same time, the messenger's report is the staging of *narrative*. For Arendt, the action of a human life can only be disclosed—and hence is only accessible to the understanding—as a *story*.[50] By soliciting stories about Thoas, Iphigenie expresses a desire to continue to know who he is. Stories are the disclosure of action: the only way one can come to know another person is by carving out a discrete narrative with beginning, middle, and end from the endless series of acts and speeches that take place: "*Who* somebody is or was we can know only by knowing the story of which he is himself the hero—his biography, in other words."[51] The imagined scene of recognition in Iphigenie's promise thus brings together the two media in which actions can be communicated for Arendt: narrative and drama.

Drama is a representation of the intertwining web of stories and actions, plural, in their complex interplay. If narrative aims for the biographical project of recognizing another person, drama is an imitation of the actions of recognition between people. This renders it, willy-nilly, political: "Theater is the political art *par excellence*; only there is the political sphere of human life transported into art. By the same token, it is the only art whose sole subject is man in his relationship to others."[52] In bringing together narrative and drama, Iphigenie's visionary promise joins anagnorisis and *Anerkennung* in a scene of recognition that is at once poignantly personal and stridently political. She would thus seem to be the quintessential Arendtian heroine.

The fact that Iphigenie's promise is dependent on a messenger's report introduces two elements of adversity into the rosy picture. First, she does not make a positive promise: only under the (unlikely?) contingency of encountering a Taurian traveler will the recognition scene be enacted. Second, the recognition conferred by a messenger's report is always deferred and one-sided. Iphigenie will learn news of Thoas, but the information will not pass the other way around. Thoas himself does not figure in the exchange. The only mutuality their recognition will attain is in the present moment of the promise, which is by its very definition a deferment of fulfillment. The scene Iphigenie describes of the stranger sitting by the fire, almost like the ekphrasis of an imaginary painting, is a tableau within a tableau. The configuration of the three characters on stage at the end of Goethe's play culminates with the chimerical vision of an implausible future theatrical device, the messenger's report, which is itself the figuration of absence. Anagnorisis, which can only take place *between* subjects, will always be *offstage*. The fulfillment of recognition in *Iphigenie auf Tauris*, therefore, is a celebration of recognition's endless deferment.

A celebration is not a dirge or elegy. This deferral of recognition does not yet amount to Markell's acknowledgment of the futility of pursuing *Anerkennung*. If any character in Goethe's play comes to acknowledge the frailty of recognition, it is Thoas. When Iphigenie urges him to take her hand in a sign of peace, he replies that she is making a great demand in a short time.

> IPHIGENIE. Um Gut's zu tun braucht's keine Überlegung.
> THOAS. Sehr viel! denn auch dem Guten folgt das Übel. (HA, 5, 1989–1990)

> (IPHIGENIE. To do good no deliberation is needed.
> THOAS. Yes, much! for evil follows good deeds too.)[53]

This formula amounts to a "theory of tragedy" in the vein of Markell (or Nussbaum). Despite one's best intentions to do good, evil may well follow. Goethe's play does not indicate what transpires in Tauris after the Greeks leave. Goethe originally planned to compose a sequel, *Iphigenie auf Delphi*, but this abandoned project would have dealt with a dramatic anagnorisis between Iphigenie and Electra rather than continuing the story of Thoas as Iphigenie envisions in her final promise. Because of Thoas's and Arkas's hints about popular unrest, however, one can easily imagine an "evil" that follows Thoas's "good" act. Perhaps the Taurian mob, after learning that their king allowed the foreigners to escape, will oust him in a coup and then forcibly reinstate the practice of human sacrifice. The singular instance of exceptional recognition that Thoas allows in Iphigenie's case could well lead to the bloody murder of innocent travelers for generations to come.

Does Iphigenie manage to escape the tragic fate of *Anerkennung* after all? The play's and Thoas's concluding silence prevents a final decision on this question. Goethe famously called his Iphigenie "verteufelt human" (devilishly humane),[54] and it is remarkable how she elides any conclusive judgment about the *Teufelskreis* (vicious circle) of humanizing hope for recognition. Goethe himself, much later and in the rather oracular mode of aphorisms, will weigh in on *Anerkennung*:

> Toleranz sollte eigentlich nur eine vorübergehende Gesinnung sein: sie muß zur Anerkennung führen. Dulden heißt beleidigen.
>
> —
>
> Die wahre Liberalität ist Anerkennung. (*Maxime und Reflexionen*, HA, 12, 385)
>
> (Tolerance should in fact be a temporary attitude: it must lead to recognition. To tolerate means to insult.
>
> —
>
> True liberality is recognition.)

Taken alone, these pearls of wisdom seem to be glorious confirmation for Goethe's approval of liberal ideals, and the heirs of Fichte and Hegel in political philosophy love to quote them in support of their own liberating theories.[55] Yet the maxims appear in a series of aphorisms that disparage majority rule, lambast proponents of freedom of the press, and then maintain that neither ideas nor concepts can be liberal.[56] Goethe says that liberality should be sought in the sentiments or attitudes (*Gesinnungen*), which arise directly out of the individual and her closest relations and needs.[57] Liberality is emphatically not a matter of pure self-determination but one that depends on a person's disposition and—crucially—the *people* with whom one relates and the *requirements* of a situation. If true liberality is *Anerkennung*, recognition can attain the authority of neither an idea nor a concept, but it consists rather in an interpersonal web of relations, needs, and sympathies that happen (rarely) to yield room for acceptance and affirmation rather than tolerant sufferance. Thoas and Iphigenie model different approaches to this fragile network of mutual esteem. On the one hand, Thoas protects a fantasy of autonomy that masquerades as inscrutability (Thoas can only be interpreted in performance). On the other hand, Iphigenie addresses the chaos of the future by making promises that endlessly defer recognition but imply forgiveness.

Promise and forgiveness, as Arendt reminds us, are hopeful ways to deal with the inevitable infelicities of action. Iphigenie may fob off any intimacy with Thoas, but the respect into which she transmutes his love confronts the fragility of human action and the uncertainty of the future with resolve and hope. The Derridian friendship with which Penelope welcomes Odysseus (chapter 4) expands to a politics of hospitality with Iphigenie. As seen in chapter 8, Iphigenie's navigation of the recognition of self and others proceeds by way of intertextual role-play. The limited success of her performance is due to her flexibility in playing parts and imagining pretend scenes, such as the concluding tableau of the final act. Iphigenie's recognitions thrive in conscious make-believe. In the following chapter, an anti-Iphigenie will demonstrate the misfortune of recognition for a character who cannot play pretend.

CHAPTER TEN

The Fate of Recognition

Kleist's *Penthesilea*

THE ODYSSEUS FIGURES linking the plays and poems gathered together in this book increasingly function on the fringes and sidelines of the dramatic action—they rarely take up the mantle of the principle character in the work at hand. The Odyssean Pylades in *Iphigenie auf Tauris* acts as a foil against whom Iphigenie must learn to recognize herself (chapters 8–9). In all Goethe's works, meanwhile, the Odysseus-figure is displaced from within the work of fiction and assumes the imaginary position of the author without (chapter 7). Ulysses in *Troilus and Cressida* manipulates events from behind the scenes and at one point explicitly takes on the role of a theatrical director trying to produce an effect by engineering a recognition in his targeted audience (chapter 6). And Odysseus himself in the Homeric epic proves less instructive about the agency of anagnorisis than his recognizer, Penelope (chapters 3–4). From this perspective, Penelope is the most interesting Odyssean figure in the *Odyssey*.

Just as Odysseus takes on an ever-more-marginalized role in the succession of dramas read here, so too does the action of recognition—clearly central and pervasive in the *Odyssey*—tend to slip away into other scenes: *immer ein anderer Schauplatz*.[1] The simple anagnorisis between friends or enemies is always bleeding over into other figures: realizations about whole or part, self or other, interiority or externality, audience or character, and reflection or performance. This chapter stages a reading of a text that itself weaves together these latter two recurring threads that the readings in this book have braided: reflection and performance. In Heinrich von Kleist's drama *Penthesilea* (1808), Odysseus is again a minor figure, but he frames the entire play from its first scene as a question of performing signs of recognition in the context of the mirroring trope familiar from Plato. The play brings together these two actions of recognition only by tearing apart a new notion of subjecthood that had become widespread by 1800 and still prevails today.

The three orders of recognition that helped clarify new understandings of fate in the *Odyssey* in chapter 5 of this book (recognition between selves, between genders, and between cultures) originally derived from a reading of *Penthesilea*.[2] Like Odysseus's encounters with Circe and Nausicaa in the *Odyssey*, the Greeks' first contact scenario with the Amazons in Kleist's drama brings together all three of these orders of recognition in one scene. But whereas the Homeric examples provide a complex template of parallels inviting an exploration of the ineluctable aspects of identity, the tragic fate of recognition in *Penthesilea* is not determined principally by gender or culture. Instead, this chapter argues, it is the modern conception of subjecthood, entirely foreign to the world of the Homeric poems, that compels the tragedy of Penthesilea.

Scholars of the past thirty years have discovered a surprising number of new languages and discourses in *Penthesilea*. The drama has been the source of a "rhetorics of feminism" (Jacobs), a "queer notion of language" (Pahl), and an original aesthetics (Chaouli).[3] It has also been read to prefigure discourses that would not emerge until more than a century later, notably French poststructuralist psychology and politics.[4] Other scholars, in contrast, have admired the play's radical deconstruction of the means of communication.[5] For Carol Jacobs, it both destroys conventional language and gives birth to new ways of speaking at the same time. She never spells out what the "Rhetorics of Feminism" announced by the title of her eloquent reading consist in, but it is probably connected to Penthesilea's "new poetry," which "is a language that disintegrates the order of metaphor and literality."[6] These readings of the text convincingly demonstrate the play's powerful creative and destructive potential in many disparate directions.

This chapter argues that the play not only demolishes old discourses or presages new ones but also engages constructively in ancient conversations. The first half of the drama cites the Platonic topos of attaining self-knowledge through reflection in another person, while the second half enlists the tradition of Aristotelian anagnorisis.[7] These intertextual performances do not merely serve to deconstruct the orders of meaning in the traditional topoi. Instead, their development and constellation in the dramatic structure of the play invite a productive contribution to the Platonic and the dramatic-theoretical conversations from which they emerge.

The text accomplishes this intervention, moreover, not in an ahistorical universalist vein, but at a very specific juncture in the history of the subject around 1800. The inside/outside dichotomy as a paradigm of selfhood for the phenomena of consciousness and emotion arose in the seventeenth century, yet it did not take hold of the popular imagination until the end of the eighteenth with the ascendency of the Romantic subject. In the case of consciousness, the input/output model of cognition quickly spread with the advent of Cartesian representational epistemology.[8] In the case of the emotions, passions in antiquity were generally understood as exterior forces or interactive scenes (as, for instance, in Aristotle's *Rhetoric*). Descartes's *Passions of the Soul* (1649) for the first time considered them as having hidden sources within the subject.[9] With Kant's conception of the passions as a basic faculty of the individual, the long process of interiorization in philosophical psychology was complete.[10] The turning point in this understanding of subjectivity coincided with what Foucault calls the "Cartesian moment," after which the subject is supposed to access truth via direct knowledge rather than through a host of external intermediary practices.[11] This immediation effectually isolates the subject and renders her ultimately inaccessible to others. Kleist's Penthesilea, I contend, is the perfect illustration of the interior Cartesian subject.[12] As Prothoe exclaims about her, "What force may preside in her, only she can know, / And every breast that feels is an enigma."[13] In the new era of interior subjectivity, every bosom must be a riddle.

The play tells the story of the Amazonian warrior queen, Penthesilea, who brings her army to Troy to fight both Trojans and Greeks in order to take captives for ritualistic breeding to propagate her tribe. Against her people's precepts, the queen falls in love with Achilles and wants to conquer him for herself. They take turns hunting each other in a confused and confusing mixture of desire and hostility. In shocking contrast to the Homeric sources, Penthesilea ultimately kills and mutilates Achilles out of a misrecognition of his submissive intent. On realizing her mistake, she commits suicide by an act of will.

It is easy to see why this play has rightly been held by critics to stage the difficulties of understanding other genders and cultures. In these readings, which lead to productive interventions in a number of pressing discourses, the Greeks stand in for the male-dominated Western hegemony and the Amazons for the unsublimated Other (e.g., Wolf, Neumann).[14] The text provides rich material for powerful interpretations seeing it as a as a pointed deconstruction of the entire Western tradition from Homer to Goethe and Kant (e.g., Jacobs, Gallas, Phillips).[15]

But what if, far from being an Other thoroughly alien to Western ways of thought, as many have assumed, the Amazonian queen represents a way of thinking about consciousness that is constitutive of Western modernity? This chapter argues, in fact, that she can be seen as the epitome and limit case of the interiorized subject. The drama thus stages the failures of recognition by insisting on the possibility of representing and recognizing internal states of knowledge. The language and action in *Penthesilea* move from a series of mirroring scenes that cast light on images of self-understanding to a climax highlighting performance and the capacity for knowing others. The analysis here will concentrate on these two recurrent motifs in the play: the repeated recourse to images of mirroring in the first half of the drama and the staging of theatrical anagnorisis scenarios in the second half. In this play, self-knowledge and knowledge of others are doomed to fail only in the assumed conditions of the interiorized Cartesian subject. Successful recognitions transpire through a model of intersubjectivity that surprisingly relies on dissimulation and pretense rather than a strict insistence on authenticity.

It is quite fitting for the reading of *Penthesilea* offered here that Foucault characterized the "Cartesian moment" in the introductory remarks to his 1982 lectures on the care of the self in Plato's *Alcibiades*, the dialogue that closes with the famous image of the soul coming to see itself in the reflection provided by another soul.[16] Foucault's reading of *Alcibiades* provides a helpful rubric within which to frame the first part of Kleist's text, but the play also points toward difficulties in Plato's text that Foucault does not consider. In this way, *Penthesilea* both confirms and challenges Foucault's archeology of the subject. Similarly, the second part of Kleist's play, with its metatheatrical recognitions, invites a return to pre-Enlightenment understandings of Aristotelian anagnorisis. This chapter will unpack these claims by comparing the two parts of the play with Plato's *Alcibiades* and Aristotle's *Poetics* in turn. In short, I claim that Penthesilea goes through the *motions* of ancient practices under the *conditions* of the modern subject.

THE MIRRORED GAZE

The scenes of mirroring in the first half of *Penthesilea* have buttressed the arguments for a series of psychological readings of the play that persuasively show how Kleist's text prefigures Lacan's critique of the subject, its construction through language, and the three orders of the imaginary, the symbolic, and the real.[17] But these reflecting scenes don't merely look forward to Lacan's mirror stage; they also trigger the traditional topos of coming to know oneself in the reflection provided by another's eye. As made evident above, the image of seeing oneself in the mirror of a companion's eye became a commonplace by the Renaissance, and was a favorite conceit in Shakespeare's poems and plays. The Greco-mania and Shakespeare-philia that overtook German writers in the late eighteenth century would ensure Kleist's familiarity with this conventional image.[18]

As seen in chapter 6, Foucault reads *Alcibiades* as a first step toward replacing the "care of the self" with "self-knowledge." This move anticipates the modern dilemma of locating knowledge in a directly accessible "truth" rather than in a necessarily mediated series of repeatable practices. *Penthesilea* supports this diagnosis in surprising ways. Foucault elaborates on three aspects of the long tradition of *epimeleia heautou* (care of the self) that are already present in the Platonic dialogue: the exercise of power; the question of pedagogy; and the concern with erotics.[19] The play's four scenes of reflection successively illuminate this analysis of practices of self-knowledge and then culminate by opening up an aporia in Plato's *Alcibiades* that Foucault neglected.

The Burning Blush. Each of the mirroring scenes in *Penthesilea* is an instructive misfiring of the expectations raised by the topos of the reflecting gaze. Once again, Odysseus functions on the margins of the drama, but he introduces the central motifs that will recur throughout the play. In the play's very first scene, for instance, Odysseus describes at length his initial encounter with Penthesilea. The Amazons have confused Greek and Trojan alike by attacking both factions indiscriminately. He is unable to comprehend their behavior and expresses the impossibility of finding a category of understanding to fit their actions into his ordered cosmos: "As far as I know, in nature there is only / Force and counterforce, and no third power besides."[20] The Amazons' refusal to fit clearly into this bifurcated formula is indeed a threat to the Greeks' political, ethical, epistemological, and aesthetic categories.[21] Critics have rightly pointed to Odysseus's words as the perfect example of the limits of rational language and Western, patriarchal attitudes when facing new cultures. Gerhard Neumann, for instance, compares the encounter Odysseus describes to Georg Forster's protoanthropological account of "first contact" scenes with native peoples, in which universalist assumptions about values and what constitutes a sign become destructive hindrances to understanding.[22] Odysseus simply cannot fathom what is going on when the Amazons attack both Greeks and Trojans—he insists on perceiving their actions and imagining their motives from within the framework of a Greek understanding of how the world works. This inflexibility leads to a miserable failure in interpreting the Amazons' motivations and renders powerless the famous Odyssean persuasive rhetoric that usually lets the character get what he wants.

In the midst of Odysseus's narration of his encounter, however, his desperate struggle to find *some*—any!—interpretable sign culminates in the unusual image he chooses to describe Penthesilea's blush. He and Achilles have approached the queen with an embassy to offer an alliance (recognition as friends), and she appears to them as devoid of all expression, utterly unreadable:

> von Ausdruck leer . . .
> Hier diese flache Hand, versichr' ich dich,
> Ist ausdrucksvoller als ihr Angesicht. (*Penth*, 1, 63–66; 7)
>
> (void of expression . . .
> This bare flat palm has more expressive features
> Than were displayed upon that woman's face.)

Her imperviousness lasts until her glance falls on Achilles, and her face lights up in a flaming glow "as if the world surrounding her were leaping into flames."[23] After some time, she turns red again when she finally recalls that she owes Odysseus an answer:

> Drauf mit der Wangen Rot, wars Wut, wars Scham,
> Die Rüstung wieder bis zum Gurt sich färbend,
> Verwirrt und stolz und wild zugleich: sie sei
> Penthesilea, kehrt sie sich zu mir,
> Der Amazonen Königin, und werde
> Aus Köchern mir die Antwort übersenden! (*Penth*, 1, 97–102; 8, mod.)
>
> (Then with the red of her cheeks, whether from rage or shame,
> Staining her harness again crimson to the waist,
> Confused and wild and proud at the same time: I am
> Penthesilea, she turns to me,

> Queen of the Amazons, and shall
> Send you answer from my quivers!)

The final moment of the recognition encounter is thus framed by Odysseus with the image of Penthesilea's blush reflected in her armor. He does not say, "Her cheeks were red"; he says, "Her armor colored with the red of her cheeks." Odysseus thankfully grasps the reddening of her face and its hyperbolic augmentation in the glow of the armor as a sign, but he simultaneously admits that he cannot know what it is a signal for.[24] The implied disjunctive, "wrath or shame," drives a syntactic wedge into the grammatical construction between the cheeks' red and the mirroring breastplate. Both options are unverifiable, and there is no reason to rule out other possible signifying emotions. At the same time, a potential symbolic order is introduced and its terms of relation are made undecipherable. Instead of the scene of a passion as described in Aristotle's *Rhetoric*, in which the constellation of figures, triggers, and reactions can be clearly mapped out, Odysseus is confronted with the expression of an unknowable emotion whose source is hidden. Penthesilea's blush heralds the entrance of Cartesian interiority on the stage of external Greek selves.

Several important scenarios converge in this rhetorical flourish: the anagnorisis tableau (i.e., recognizing friend or foe) together with the problem of signs and their interpretability are artfully reproduced in a very unlikely mirroring—an act of mimesis collected and refracted by the convex surface of the burnished iron. The illegibility of her face—the impossibility of recognition—seems to resolve itself in the moment when she announces her identity (recognition *of*: "I am Penthesilea") and her intentions toward the Greeks (recognition *as*: "and I will send you my arrows as reply!"—that is, "I am your enemy."). Yet it will turn out that the answering arrows are not necessarily a sign of enmity after all: they are, in fact, the means whereby the Amazons secure their lovers.

Like Socrates with Alcibiades, the encounter with Achilles brings about a reflection of Penthesilea. The sign of the mirrored blush that is so mysterious to Odysseus, moreover, intimates the erotic desire that drives Penthesilea's attitude toward Achilles. This echoes the eroticism Foucault identifies in *Alcibiades* as a lasting feature of *epimeleia heautou*.[25] Yet here the reflection is observed not by the blushing lover or the beautiful beloved but by a bewildered third party, Odysseus, for whom it figures as a sign in a political calculus alien to the mirrored interlocutor.

Mirrored Conqueror. The play's fifth and Penthesilea's first *Auftritt* (entrance/scene) presents us with a triumphant and victorious queen who wants to hear nothing about her triumphs and victories. Instead, she insists on returning to battle to confront the fleeing Achilles once again. She fantasizes seeing him in the dust at her feet and immediately responds to the reflection of her own image in his imagined armor:

> Ist das die Siegerin, die schreckliche,
> Der Amazonen stolze Königin,
> Die seines Busens erzne Rüstung mir,
> Wenn sich mein Fuß ihm naht, zurückspiegelt? (*Penth*, 5, 642–645; 31, mod.)
>
> (Is this the conquering Queen, the fearsome one,
> Who's mirrored back, when my foot approaches him,
> By the steel harness covering his breast?
> This, the proud empress of the Amazons?)

Once again, a moment of recognition is heralded by warlike armor casting a reflection of Penthesilea. If the mirrored glow of her face's flush in the first scene accompanied the announcement of her name and hostile intentions to others, this vision of her features reflected in the armor of a vanquished foe presents a crisis of self-recognition in Penthesilea herself. Achilles should be her present foe and future lover by the law of her tribe, and this ambiguity alone might be enough to confuse most, but for Penthesilea, against the express injunction of her people's law, Achilles is also at once her chosen beloved and enemy in the individuality of his narrated (textual) and physical (beheld) self. Thus the imagined encounter with his defeated body is deflected to a question of self-knowledge: "Is that me?"

This tableau brings aspects of eroticism in Foucault's analysis of *epimeleia heautou* to bear on that of power: "The care of the self . . . always has to go through the relationship to someone else who is the master."[26] *Penthesilea* takes to the extreme the agonistic hierarchies implicit in Platonic love. The relationship between Socrates and Alcibiades is never equal. Before the dialogue, the older man waits patiently while richer and more attractive lovers lavish their gifts on Alcibiades for scraps of his attention. Now that Socrates sees his chance, he maneuvers the younger man into a position of acknowledging ignorance and begging for Socrates's guidance. The beautiful vision of a soul coming to know itself in the reflection provided by another soul is necessarily one of lopsided dominance. Penthesilea's fantasy of seeing herself in the mirror of the vanquished Achilles at her feet reveals the power dynamics implicit in every act of self-revelatory love.

Mirrors Do Lie. In the ninth scene, meanwhile, after Penthesilea has been rescued from a disastrous battle with Achilles, in which she ended up in the dust at his feet rather than the other way around, she refuses to be persuaded to flee with her companions and in fact curses them all.

> —Die Hand verwünsch ich, die zur Schlacht mich heut
> Geschmückt, und das verräterische Wort,
> Das mir gesagt, es sei zum Sieg, dazu.
> Wie sie mit Spiegeln mich, die Gleisnerinnen,
> Umstanden, rechts und links, der schlanken Glieder
> In Erz gepreßte Götterbildung preisend. (*Penth*, 9, 1259–1264; 58)

> (—I curse the hand that for the fight today
> Adorned me, and the deceiving tongue that said
> It was for victory, I curse them all.
> How they stood round with mirrors right and left,
> The hypocrites, praising my slender limbs'
> Divine proportions cast in shining bronze.)

The mirrors here are not only the ones held in the hands of her servants but also the ones formed in the language of their descriptive and encouraging utterances. Even the word Penthesilea chooses for "flatterers" or "hypocrites" carries with it a sense of reflecting shine: *Gleisnerinnen.*[27] This scene evokes Foucault's third aspect of self-care: pedagogy. The syntax invites multivalent readings that play with contradictory meanings of *Bildung*: the physical shape of a body part and visual image of gods. First, the reflecting servants stand around her with mirrors and praise the divine form (Götter*bildung*) of her slender limbs. But like Cassius for Brutus, the Amazons also act as their queen's "glass" in which she apprehends—and comprehends—herself in the "divine image" (Götter*bild*ung) they form in speech. What's more, this godlike image is either imprinted on the bronze armor—rather like the mirroring breastplates of the previous two scenes—or this selfsame image is itself being pressed into the queen's arm- and shin guards along with the slender limbs it reflects. Together, these conflicting interpretations conjure the ideal of German education and self-cultivation, *Bildung*, which is mired in contradiction as soon as it is thought.

This passage's implicit critique of the scene of self-care and its pedagogical guise is even more pointed than Foucault's.[28] Penthesilea curses the inadequate education that necessitates renewed care for the self in the first place by attacking her flatterers. In Plato's dialogue, as shown above, the education of Alcibiades proceeds by way of flattery. Instead of leading Alcibiades to philosophy through superior arguments, Socrates relies on the techniques of seduction. A pedagogy of self-knowledge founded on erotic flirtation and blandishing praise is necessarily suspect, as Penthesilea's retrospective rejection of the mirroring flatterers confirms.

In all three of these instances of mirroring, an image of Penthesilea appears not in the eye of her interlocutor, as the original Platonic topos would demand, but rather in some part of her or another's armor. Armored plates make for a strange mirroring surface: their essential function is to guard and shield what is hidden beneath them. They form a protective shell but also a concealing cover for the human self inside. By the same virtue that armor repels blows, however, its burnished surface also reflects images with the potential to reveal as well as conceal. Displacing the mirroring scenario from the mutual gaze to the glancing armor underscores the new kind of self that is trying to participate in the ancient scene of self-knowledge: it is sealed off from any engaged contact with others and hidden from even its own view.

Armor is also a traditional locus for poetics and aesthetics to meet in narrative representation. The ekphrastic description of Achilles's shield in the *Iliad* has long been a touchstone for reflections on the differences between visual and narrative imitation. (Think of Lessing's *Laokoon*.)[29] The images depicted on Achilles's shield would be impossible to reproduce on any actual artifact of human design: they are pictures only made possible by the power of language. The reflections in armor presented in *Penthesilea* are equally absurd in any medium but that of words. The optic tricks required for Odysseus's description of the pervading, fiery reflection of Penthesilea's blush in her breastplate are entirely implausible outside of the world he creates as he speaks. Like the bucolic scenes of cosmic harmony on Achilles's Homeric shield, the mirror images on Penthesilea's and Achilles's Kleistian armor exist only in the discursive unfolding of *narration* and never appear in the present moment of dialogue.

Muddled Reflections. Only one of the four mirroring scenes does not involve warlike armor as a reflective surface. If the previous passages demonstrated the necessary interplay of power, pedagogy, and erotics in the armor-plated scene of self-care, the fourth episode brings an aporetic conclusion to the attempts to involve sovereign modern subjects in intersubjective reflectivity. Shortly before scene 9 closes, Penthesilea announces that she intends to roll the Ida Mountains up Mount Ossa and calmly set herself on top. Her companions, worried for her sanity, ask what she would do if she could accomplish this "work of giants" (*Penth*, 9, 1379).

> PENTHESILEA. Blödsinnige!
>   Bei seinen goldnen Flammenhaaren zög ich
>   Zu mir hernieder ihn—
> PROTHOE. Wen?
> PENTHESILEA. Helios,
>   wenn er am Scheitel mir vorüberfleucht!
>   . . .
> PENTHESILEA. *schaut in den Fluß nieder.*
>   Ich, Rasende!
>   Da liegt er mir zu Füßen ja! Nimm mich—
>   *Sie will in den Fluß sinken, Prothoe und Meroe halten sie.* (*Penth*, 9, 1383–1388; 64)

> (PENTHESILEA. Imbeciles!
>   I'd take him by his flaming hair of gold
>   And pull him down to me—
> PROTHOE. Whom?
> PENTHESILEA. Helios,
>   As he comes soaring close above my head!
>   . . .
> PENTHESILEA. *looks down into the river.*
>   I must be mad!
>   Why, there he lies, right at my feet! Take me—
>   *She tries to jump in the river, Prothoe and Meroe hold her back.*)

It is no wonder that a concerned Prothoe has to ask her queen whom she means to pull down to her by his flaming golden hair, since there has been no masculine noun that might serve as antecedent to the possessive "sein" in Penthesilea's answer. The identity of the image Penthesilea sees reflected in the river in this scene is furthermore thrice ambiguous: it could simply be a reflection of the sun—the very Helios who soars overhead. On the other hand, Penthesilea may also be seeing Achilles, who has been repeatedly compared to the sun throughout the play and whom the queen, as we have seen, has often enough envisioned at her feet: “Da liegt er mir zu Füßen ja!” This might explain her command to the image, “Nimm mich—,” and her desire to sink down to it: the self-subjugating erotics of domination. A third possibility, however, is that Penthesilea is ready to drown in the mirrored reflection of her own image. It may seem absurd that she should be suffering from narcissism at this low point in her self-esteem, when we have heard her curse the servants who had painted her picture so flatteringly, but what other image is she likely to see when she looks down from a bridge into the water below than her own, crowned perhaps with the glittering sun’s, which she mistakes for Achilles, or Helios, or both?[30]

The ambiguity of the image perceived in this sole instance of Penthesilea seeing a reflection in a nonarmored, nonlinguistic surface points toward the unknowability of the modern interior self. The scene also hearkens back to a feature of Plato’s *Alcibiades* observed in chapter 6: Socrates claims that the only path toward self-knowledge is by asking what the self itself (*auto to auto*) is (*Al* 129b). He then skips over this difficult question “because it would have taken quite a lot of study” (*Al* 130d) in order to jump directly to the more attractive conclusions that man is his soul and that souls come to know one another through mutual reflection. Foucault does not remark on this glaring aporia at the macular core of *Alcibiades*, even though it could have lent support to his suspicion that the seed for the future Cartesian self was already planted in this dialogue, which turns the question of *epimeleia heautou* into the imperative of *gnōthi seauton* (know thyself).[31] As soon as the practices of self-care are subordinated to the desire to know the self, an inaccessible space is hollowed out at the center of the self. This empty blind spot is the *auto to auto* that Socrates avoids examining and that prefigures the impervious interiority of the modern subject.[32]

The first half of *Penthesilea* dramatizes the movement of this incipient subjectivity in the practices of the ancient world. The queen goes through the self-caring motions of power, pedagogy, and erotics, only to end up staring at a reflection that is utterly unrecognizable. None of the drama’s mirrorings occurs between characters present on stage. The first (Penthesilea’s reflected blush at the sight of Achilles) is reported by Odysseus’s narration; the second (Penthesilea seeing her reflection in a defeated Achilles’s armor) is an imaginary scenario that never takes place; and the third (Penthesilea cursing the flattering Amazons) is interpreted into past events in hindsight. Only the fourth (Penthesilea beholding an image in the water) takes place in real time on stage, yet the reflecting situation does not involve any other character than Penthesilea herself. The mirroring topos as staged in Plato and Shakespeare certainly reveals the contradictions and difficulties inherent in coming to know self and other through interpersonal reflections in language, but at least they *do* involve interactions between people. Penthesilea is a character for whom other people simply do not serve as reflective aids to attaining self-knowledge. She is utterly inaccessible to others—as Prothoe remarks, she is an enigma. Prothoe is overly optimistic in saying that what is going on inside her "only she can know": in fact, as these scenes show, Penthesilea does not even know herself. The character of Penthesilea embodies the post-Cartesian "problem of other minds" at its radical extreme. It is not just that attempted recognitions between her and others are deflected or refracted in unforeseeable and unintended ways, as is the case in Shakespeare. Rather, Penthesilea never even manages to come into reflecting contact with another person in the first place.

PLAYS WITHIN PLAYS

As mentioned, Odysseus's description of the Greeks' meeting with the Amazons has been compared to Georg Forster's accounts of his travels around the world with Captain Cook and the "first encounter" scenarios of the European explorers with various native peoples. Neumann has convincingly shown how the play stages the "recognition between cultures" in terms of the then budding science of anthropology[33]—as well as the "recognition between the sexes" in terms of current notions of feminism and gender studies.[34] His analysis is very enlightening in putting this first scene into context and providing the play with a rich thematic background. But it does not account for the utter collapse of Penthesilea's capacity to negotiate human relationships—whether as a warrior or as a lover, enemy or friend—in her ensuing dealings with Achilles, other than as an instance of universal barriers to communication inherent in symbolic systems such as language, especially when they are called on to bridge the gaping abysses between genders and cultures.[35]

For one thing, however, it is not the case that Greeks and Amazons in general are entirely alien and incomprehensible to each other in the play. The Amazons function within a societal structure that is strictly hierarchical and no less subject to manipulation, hypocrisy, and ambitious political maneuvering than that of the Greeks. Once the fundamental laws and origins of their society are explained to him, Achilles "gets" the Amazons very well. He might pass disapproving judgment without sufficient justification, but the principles on which the Amazon state are founded are not beyond his conceptual framework. Prothoe equally has no problem understanding and communicating with Achilles. It is not an incommensurability between women and men or between Greeks and barbarians that leads to the horror at the heart of the play—the Amazon women are unanimously shocked and disgusted by Penthesilea's behavior in slaughtering and feeding on Achilles. What is it, then, that makes Penthesilea uniquely incomprehensible to all those around her and to herself?

All the mirrorings observed above occur without Achilles and Penthesilea exchanging a single word. When finally they encounter each other, the stage is set for them to play out a scene of mutual reflection. The queen crowns Achilles with roses and directs her gaze admiringly toward him:

> PENTHESILEA.—O sieh, ich bitte dich,
> Wie der zerfloßne Rosenglanz ihm steht!
> Wie sein gewitterdunkles Antlitz schimmert!
> . . .
> Sprich! Dünkt's dich nicht, als ob sein Auge glänzte? (*Penth*, 15, 1784–1791; 87–88, mod.)

> (PENTHESILEA.—Oh look, I pray you,
> How well the melting flush of roses suits him!
> How they light up the storm clouds in his face!
> . . .
> Speak! Do his eyes not seem to alight to you?)

The reflecting sheen of Achilles's face echoes in the luster of the crowning roses and in the shimmer of his countenance. When Penthesilea remarks on the gleam of his eye, we are well primed for the mirroring gaze to unfold. Instead, she follows up by questioning Achilles's identity: "I swear, you'd almost doubt, to see him this way, that it is he."[36] What comes next is a bizarre recognition scene between two characters who know full well who the other is. This remarkable exchange comes out of nowhere. Penthesilea has been addressing Achilles as Achilles throughout this and the previous scenes. Interestingly, the doubt about Achilles follows immediately on the heels of a remark on his eye (Achilles's heel, one might say, is his eye). In fact, Penthesilea does not even state this observation in the indicative but frames it in a typically Kantian-Kleistian "as if": "Didn't it seem to you *as if* his eye shone?—Indeed, one would almost be inclined, when he appears that way, to doubt that it is he" (*Penth*, 15, 1792–1793; 88, mod.). The incipient anagnorisis thus begins with a *potential* scene of the reflective gaze. The possible intersubjective mirroring scenario of learning about herself, however, is immediately deflected to a question of the identity of the other.

The stage history of dramatic anagnorisis parallels the transition in locating consciousness within an interior subject. In ancient Greek and Renaissance plays, characters make surprising discoveries about one another through a wide stockpile of contrivances, signs, and actions. In Euripides's *Iphigenia among the Taurians*, for instance, Aristotle praises the device of the letter Iphigenia wants to send to her brother as the plausible but striking means for her discovery to Orestes. By the time Goethe adapts this play for a post-Enlightenment audience, he dispenses with such theatrical gimmicks (see chapter 8 in this book). Iphigenie and Orest come to know each other and their own true natures by introspection. Kleist's Penthesilea is often read as an anti-Iphigenie,[37] and the unexpected anagnorisis scenario that she engineers here is remarkable for colliding ancient plot-driven recognition with a modern character-based model.

In the middle of the play, Penthesilea has been injured and taken prisoner by Achilles. While she is unconscious, her companion Prothoe speaks with Achilles. He reveals to her that he is in love with the queen and wants to make her his wife. Prothoe beseeches him to hide in the bushes before Penthesilea wakes up so that she can prepare her gently for the news that the queen has been defeated and is a captive to the Greeks. What follows is pure pageantry: Prothoe pretends to Penthesilea that the queen has, in fact, beaten Achilles, who is now her prisoner. Convinced by watching the two women speak that Penthesilea will never accept any lover who has not been conquered by her sword, Achilles emerges from the bushes and plays along, gamely taking on the role of her captive. This bit of metatheater is marked as a recognition drama on multiple levels. In the first place, the whole charade revolves around the problem of how a change in knowledge can lead from enmity to love, which is at the core of Aristotle's definition of anagnorisis. Prothoe also signals the nature of the act she is playing from its very beginning, when Penthesilea first regains consciousness. The queen asks, "Where am I?" and Prothoe does not answer this question but instead asks another one: "Do you not recognize the voice of your sister?"[38] By deflecting a simple and natural query about her location into an unsolicited assurance of personal identity, Prothoe heralds the opening of a recognition play in which two actors play fake roles in order to help a nonactor cope with reality.

This mise en abyme comes to a climax several pages later, after Penthesilea has adorned Achilles with the garlands of flowers that male prisoners of the Amazons wear in the traditional *Rosenfest* before they can be paraded to the women's beds. She speaks the lines quoted above that should trigger Platonic mirroring scene but then shifts to doubt whether the beautiful man is really Achilles. He protests:

ACHILLES. Ich bin's.
PENTHESILEA. *nachdem sie ihn scharf angesehen*:
Er sagt, er sei's.
PROTHOE. Er ist es, Königin;
An diesem Schmuck hier kannst du ihn erkennen.
PENTHESILEA. Woher?
PROTHOE. Es ist die Rüstung, sieh nur her,
Die Thetis ihm, die hohe Göttermutter,
Bei dem Hephäst, des Feuers Gott, erschmeichelt. (*Penth*, 15, 1791–1804; 88, mod.)

(ACHILLES. I am the one.
PENTHESILEA. *after scrutinizing him.*
He says it's he.
PROTHOE. It is he, Queen;
You can recognize him by this ornament.
PENTHESILEA. How so?
PROTHOE. Because, see here, this is the armor
That Thetis, his immortal mother, won
By flattery from the god of fire, Hephaestos.)

Prothoe points out a token—his famous armor—as proof of who Achilles is. This is a scene straight out of ancient or baroque recognition drama, in which tokens or marks are produced in order to corroborate the discovered identity of characters.[39] But what is it doing here, where there has been no separation and no disguise? The scene continues in its almost comical imitation of romance recognitions:

PENTHESILEA. Nun denn, so grüß ich dich mit diesem Kuß,
Unbändigster der Menschen, mein! Ich bin's,
Du junger Kriegsgott, der du angehörst;
Wenn man im Volk dich fragt, so nennst du mich.
ACHILLES. O du, die eine Glanzerscheinung mir,
Als hätte sich das Ätherreich eröffnet,
Herabsteigst, Unbegreifliche, wer bist du?
Wie nenn ich dich, wenn meine eigne Seele
Sich, die entzückte, fragt, wem sie gehört?
PENTHESILEA. Wenn sie dich fragt, so nenne diese Züge,
Das sei der Nam', in welchem du mich denkst.—
Zwar diesen goldnen Ring hier schenk' ich dir,
Mit jedem Merkmal, das dich sicher stellt;
Und zeigst du ihn, so weis't man dich zu mir.
Jedoch ein Ring vermiss't sich, Namen schwinden;
Wenn dir der Nam' entschwänd, der Ring sich mißte:
Fändst du mein Bild in dir wohl wieder aus?
Kannst du's wohl mit geschloßnen Augen denken?
ACHILLES. Es steht so fest, wie Züg' in Diamanten.
PENTHESILEA. Ich bin die Königin der Amazonen . . .
Und mich begrüßt das Volk: Penthesilea. (*Penth*, 15, 1805–1824; 88–89, mod.)

(PENTHESILEA. Then I salute you with this kiss, of human
Beings the most unbridled nature, mine! It is I,
Young god of war, to whom you now belong!
And when the people ask, you shall name *me*.
ACHILLES. Oh you who come to me, a dazzling vision
Descended from above as from the realms
Of ether, unfathomable being, who are you?
How shall I name you when my own soul asks
In ravishment to whom she now belongs?
PENTHESILEA. When your soul asks you that, name her these features [Züge]:
These be the name by which you think me.—
For though I give to you this golden ring,
Whose every mark can lend you full assurance,
And people will, if you but show it, lead you to me,
Yet a ring goes missing, names fade away;

If you forgot the name, or lost the ring:
Would you still find my image in yourself?
Can you still think it when you shut your eyes?
ACHILLES. Engraved as firm as facets [Züg] in diamonds.
PENTHESILEA. I am the Queen of Amazons . . .
Myself the people call: Penthesilea.)

In short order, Penthesilea provides an evaluation of the various methods of recognition. After Prothoe provides the token to prove Achilles's identity, Penthesilea quizzes him about her own. He begs her to tell him who she is—"Incomprehensible one, who are you?" In response, she suggests three different means by which he can recognize her in the future. She gives him a ring—perhaps the most common cliché of all anagnorisis tokens. She recounts to him her titles and her name. And she demands that he emblazon an image of her physical features in his memory. Object, word, and image—these three, but the greatest of these, for Penthesilea, is the mental image, which most people would consider the most transient and incommunicable of them all. She does not mention a fourth possibility suggested by her own deeds—namely, the kiss she bestows on him in salute. In addition to things, names, and images, she could have listed performative *actions*.

The passage deserves a closer reading. After the kiss, the action that significantly does not rate consideration by Penthesilea as a locus of recognition, she declares, "Ich bin's." This is a direct echo of Achilles's own answer to her initial question of his identity ten lines earlier. But whereas Achilles's self-assertion was self-sufficient, Penthesilea's requires a subordinate clause in the next line. Achilles answers, "It's me." Penthesilea declares, "It's me . . . to whom you belong. When someone among the people asks you, then name me." As a culmination of her interrogation of Achilles's identity, Penthesilea here is giving Achilles the means to be recognized among others: her own name. Her acknowledgment of his recognition will be witnessed among the populace by Achilles's invocation of Penthesilea as his owner—that is, "Who are you?" "I belong to Penthesilea." At its outset, therefore, Penthesilea frames the recognition of Achilles in terms of a master/slave relationship. At no point does she express distress at the resulting unfree nature of Achilles's acknowledgment of herself—in fact, when she discovers that he is *willingly* acting the part of her captive (a potentially liberating resolution of the master/slave paradox), she is mortified. Penthesilea thus seems quite at home in the subject-object relation between subjects. In Hegelian terms, she remains firmly entrenched in the Cartesian subject's necessary regard of others as objects.[40]

Just as Penthesilea's "Ich bin's" was a reverberation of Achilles's words with unexpected overtones, Achilles's answer echoes Penthesilea's: "O you, a shining vision [*Glanzerscheinung*] to me." Both see a potentially reflective *Glanz* in the other. And indeed Achilles frames his question in a way that is responsive to the fiction he is playing and that opens up a playful space for intersubjective coming-to-know as suggested by the gleaming eye: "How do I name you when my own *soul* asks *itself* (sich) to whom it belongs?" Penthesilea's answer, however, subtly misconstrues and reframes the question: "When *it* asks *you* (dich)." Her replacement of the reflexive pronoun with the second person is very revealing: For Achilles, the soul and the self are identical; for Penthesilea, the self is separate from the soul.

The elaboration of her answer takes three steps to move from the knowledge of the soul (15.1814–1815) to that of others (15.1816–1818) to that of the self (15.1819–1822). In the first instance, the queen commands, "When the soul asks you, then name these features [presumably indicating her own face or body]; that's the name in which you think me." Already it is a mental image that provides the grounding of representational thought. It's not the *word* but the *image* of the facial features that the self thinks in representing other people. In her reframing of Achilles's question, Penthesilea elides care for the soul into concern for a representational structure of knowledge that bestows extraordinary power on thought. She does not say "think about me," with a prepositional phrase but rather makes herself the direct object of thought: "think me." Moreover, this thinking replaces language with mental pictures. One is reminded of the extraordinary power ascribed to thought in Descartes's second *Meditation*: "But what then am I? A thing that thinks."[41] This thinking thing never perceives objects directly: "What I thought I had seen with my eyes, I actually grasped solely with . . . my mind."[42] In these two lines, Penthesilea takes Descartes's representationalism to its logical conclusion in interpersonal relations.

Penthesilea's next remarks avoid the logic of Achilles's question entirely. He had asked how he should identify her to his soul. Penthesilea now tells him how to identify himself to other people: "I give you this golden ring . . . guaranteeing your safety." Achilles's identity here consists again in her mastery over him. The scene of recognition is displaced away from any interaction between Penthesilea and Achilles. Instead, it would be the deictic action of other people who validate and construct the relational subjecthood of the two parties. With the introduction of the physical token of the ring, Penthesilea turns Achilles's desire for personal recognition (anagnorisis) into a question of social identity (*Anerkennung*). She would seem to be turning from Cartesian interiority to Hegelian intersubjectivity. Yet this outward sign was introduced with a caveat *zwar* that qualifies and limits its validity.

The third step in Penthesilea's analysis of recognition returns to the mental image as the only reliable mode of knowledge: "But rings go missing; names fade away." Penthesilea rejects both linguistic signs and physical signs. She now asks, "If the name slipped away from you and the ring got lost, would you find out my picture [Bild] within you again?" The formulation of this question emphasizes a complex interiority: "fändst du mein Bild in dir wohl wieder aus?" It is as if the image of Penthesilea were a relic that had to be unearthed from an archeological site.

In place of language and objects, Penthesilea places all her trust in interiorized imagination. This fetishization of the mental picture here amounts to a radical version of Foucault's Cartesian subject, for whom ethical practices have been replaced by internal knowledge. Penthesilea's exoticism and unknowability (as Achilles wonderingly addresses her, "Unbegreifliche") derive not from her foreign upbringing, alien socialization, or unconventional gendering but rather from her uncompromising commitment to "the idea" at the heart of classical representation in the Western philosophical tradition.[43]

This entire sequence of cognitivist analysis announces itself blatantly as a theatrical anagnorisis scenario, and it occurs despite the lack of any dramatic need or plot motivation for recognitions at this point in the story. We might call it a case of gratuitous recognition. The very presence of the scene, which comes at the center of the play that Achilles and Prothoe stage for Penthesilea—it is, in effect, a play within a play within a play—serves to underscore the true essence of the action of recognition: it is *performance*. This is what happens when people come to know each other: they play roles and act as spectators to the roles of others; the response they give as audience is then in turn calibrated into the others' performances and vice versa. This constant feedback loop of role-play and gauged reaction makes up the action of recognition: the changes in knowledge manifesting in deeds of friendship or enmity. Recognition is not a flash of insight revealing the secret inner core of one person to another; recognition consists in the entire *system* of interactions that constitute a performative scene between people.

The brilliance of the scene in *Penthesilea* in revealing the performative dynamic of recognition lies only partly in the self-referentiality of the sequence as a gratuitous theatrical device at the center of a mise en abyme. The nature of recognition as performance is also displayed by the complete failure of Penthesilea to play along. Even the most honest and truthful recognition scenarios take place through role-play and pretend. One need not be an Odysseus or a Penelope to test loved ones by a bit of—perhaps even unconscious—playacting. This fact becomes clear in Kleist's drama precisely because of Penthesilea's inability to pretend or to understand when others are "just" pretending. Toward the end of the play, an Amazon describes the final encounter between Penthesilea and Achilles, who had decided to allow the Amazon queen to vanquish him in single combat so that she could lead him away in triumph.

> MEROE. Doch jetzt, da sie mit solchen Greulnissen
> Auf ihn herangrollt, ihn, der *nur zum Schein*
> Mit einem Spieß sich arglos ausgerüstet. (*Penth*, 23, 2626–2628; 126–127, mod.)

> (MEROE. But now that with such terror-breathing menace
> She thunders in on him, who, *just for show*
> Came armed, unsuspectingly, but with a spear.)

Penthesilea fails to register the *Schein* of pretense.[44] Instead of playing along and winning the love of the man she desires—or, alternatively, berating him for his insincerity in a bile of insulted pride—Penthesilea descends on him with her dogs and rends his flesh from his limbs with her teeth. Perhaps the most famous line of the entire play is Penthesilea's lament, after realizing what she has done, that "kisses" and "bites" (*Küsse, Bisse*) rhyme, so that "one who truly loves with all her heart can easily take one for the other."[45] The mistake is not simply a neural flaw or a cognitive deficiency within Penthesilea's brain. The problem instead lies very much in the action of recognition in the world, between people, as they necessarily playact and imaginatively spectate the playacting of others. Love bites, as most will probably agree, can be incredibly moving and delicious because they are *pretend* and do not result in actual cannibalism. Feigned violence can be tender caresses; deeds of love are playacts.

In fact, it is not the case that communication never succeeds in the play: Achilles and Prothoe understand each other very well despite the culture and gender gap that divides them. Achilles, the Greek *andros*, and Prothoe, the Amazonian warrioress, *play* together: they manage to interact and coordinate a complex and sustained fiction for the sake of Penthesilea. Achilles even acts in Prothoe's proposed performance with a minimum of explicit (linguistic) stage directions from her: they live and communicate in an enactive continuum, not in the hermetically sealed, inscrutable interiority of Penthesilea. It is her fellow female, Amazonian Prothoe—and not the male, Greek Odysseus—who decries Penthesilea's inscrutability. Prothoe's universalizing follow-up attribution of the queen's indecipherability to all humans ("jeder Busen . . . ein Rätsel") is precipitous. Instead of deploring *every* feeling breast as a riddle, she might have confined her conclusion to the unique phenomenon of Penthesilea. Not only is the queen a conundrum to all those around her, Greeks and Amazons alike, but she is even an enigma to herself, as observed through all the skewed instances of reflection above. As long as Penthesilea lacks the capacities required to perform in intersubjective role-play, she will no more achieve self-knowledge through the mirroring actions and words of others than she will come to know and be known by those others.

Recent cognitive scientists and philosophers of consciousness have begun to challenge the notion—common since Descartes and overwhelmingly prevalent among both neuroscientists and the popular imagination today—that perception is something that happens *inside* a passive brain that processes information within a kind of black box of mind. This is what Susan Hurley calls the input/output picture: sensory information is input from the world to the mind, behavior is the resulting output from the mind to the world, and thought is the mediating process in between, to which other minds can have no access (except by making inferences in their own thoughts based on the sensory input they receive of others' actions). She and Alva Noë, in contrast, argue that perception is a person's very active engagement with the world around her—that consciousness is not confined to the brain but rather occurs in and through a person's interactions with her environment. While critiquing the input/output model of consciousness in the figure of Penthesilea, Kleist's drama offers an alternative model in the interplay of other characters.

The theatrics through which Prothoe and Achilles engage with each other illustrate the ongoing construction of their identities through performative acts, whether conscious or not. This recognition work takes place through a back-and-forth of performance and its acknowledged acceptance that consists of further performances. Judith Butler provides an excellent model for this performativity as an alternative to Penthesilea's essential selfhood.[46] The superfluous recognition scene in Kleist's play shows how this model is already implicit in Aristotle's claim that anagnorisis is part of the action (*praxis*) imitated by the plot. The action of recognition is necessarily histrionic. *Verstellung* (disguise and dissimulation) is often treated as if it were the antithesis of recognition and discovery. Characters must overcome role-play in order to reach the authentic self beneath the performance. In fact, *Verstellung* is the inescapable medium and element of knowledge between people in this play. It is because she cannot dissimulate, *sie kann sich nicht verstellen*, that Penthesilea fails to participate in a felicitous recognition scene.[47]

The danger in this reading of recognition in *Penthesilea* is that it may take the moment of Enlightenment optimism for knowability of Self and Other implicit in the negative example of the queen's exceptionalism too far. Of course even "successful" recognitions are always fraught with unexpected barriers, inevitable misdirections, and perilous opacities. The performance of anagnorisis is always displacing itself, spilling over onto *andere Schauplätze* (other scenes), to borrow Freud's suggestive formula. In Kleist's play more than elsewhere, the intractable distortions of language and bodies become manifest as the ineluctable medium of any communicative endeavor. There is no way to dismiss these material barriers to recognition between people. At the same time, however, the character of Penthesilea does embody a special type of incomprehensibility that arises directly from a radical, Cartesian dichotomy between mind and world—and more specifically, between mind and mind. She lacks a specific capacity for interacting with others: a facility of playacting, of engaging in mutual performance.

None of this is to suggest that the tragedy of *Penthesilea* can be reduced to her incapacity to pretend or recognize pretending.[48] But this particular feature of the drama—Penthesilea's blindness in interpreting and participating in role-play—does help identify the action of recognition as dissimulating performance. This conclusion is tied to the claim that Penthesilea herself *becomes* the impossibility of a post-Cartesian model of consciousness rooted in a strict division between mind and world. When Descartes reaches the worst-case scenario in his method of radical doubt, he imagines an evil demon, "supremely powerful and clever, who has directed his entire effort to deceiving me." He fancies "all external things" to be "bedeviling hoaxes" and "snares for my credulity."[49] This vision of omnipotent dissimulation is the extremity out of which Descartes gives birth to the cogito. Only by limiting its self-awareness to the fact of being a "thinking thing" can it wall itself off from the vulnerability to deception. Hence Descartes's strict dualism has its source in a fear of illusion, the description of which is reminiscent of antitheatrical diatribes common in the seventeenth century. Penthesilea's anathema to playacting is thus the flipside of her inaccessible interiority. The figure of Penthesilea is a *Sinnbild* (emblem; literally, sensory/sensible image) of the tragedy that results from taking the inward subject literally rather than figuratively or playfully.

In this trajectory from a series of deflected mirror scenes to a farcical anagnorisis scenario, Penthesilea is the ultimate modern subject trying to carry through ancient practices of recognizing herself and others. Her drama does not merely illustrate contemporary discourses but in fact shows how some of their root concerns are already implicit in Plato and Aristotle. The play performs a *reductio ad absurdum* of classical representation and the interior subject. Positively, it suggests that playful dissimulation is the inescapable medium for the action of recognition. It may seem that Socrates's image of the reflecting eyes, leading as it does to a bright vision of interpersonal edification and the promise of attainable virtue and wisdom, is diametrically opposed to the linguistic and epistemological collapse that the same trope points toward in *Penthesilea*. Yet Kleist's text makes visible the fundamental chasm cobbled over in Plato's dialogue, which in turn throws into relief the inadequacy of Penthesilea's Cartesian subjectivity.

Many critics have written about how *Penthesilea* stages the collapse of human communication by revealing the unbridgeable gaps between sign and signified—inner and outer—hence showing the failure of language as a representative system. This is certainly a viable and powerful reading of the text, but the play only demonstrates the breakdown of language and communication based on the input/output model. Penthesilea herself *becomes* the impossibility of this post-Cartesian model of consciousness rooted in a strict division between mind and world. In her, readers can recognize the embodied blind spot of input/output models of consciousness and their ultimately unbridgeable disassociation from other people and the world. The play not only points to the tragedy inherent in such a concept of subjectivity but also suggests that framing epistemological questions in the subject/object dichotomy itself leads into a blind and bloody alley.

Some of the most beautiful meditations on *Penthesilea* focus on the breakdown between literal and figurative language in the final scene in which the queen manages to commit suicide by forging a dagger within her breast.[50] The present chapter has shown how this incisive linguistic feat is a result of taking Cartesian consciousness literally. If internal, "clear and distinct" cognitions become truly sharp representations, they will slice interiority wide open so that it collapses on itself. Only by dulling and blurring the distinction between inner and outer can communication and knowledge become possible. Goethe, in one of his own many attempts to ground a non-Cartesian epistemology that transcends the radical division between world and mind, once wrote, "A person only knows himself in so far as he knows the world, which he only perceives in himself, and himself only in it. Every new object, if well observed, opens in us a new organ."[51] In the understanding of recognition offered here, the "new organ" opened up by encounters with other people consists of the capacity to perform and spectate in negotiated interaction. This organ is *not* exclusively internal but instead develops between subjects and objects. Penthesilea is in part a tragic figure because she lacks or never develops this organ of recognition. She never learns to play pretend.

Concluding Reflections

Signifying Silence in Blumenberg and Kafka

THE METAMORPHOSES OF recognition unfolded in these pages could gainfully be traced much further, even following the narrower spoor of Odysseus figures, up to the current moment. Adaptations of the *Odyssey* and of Odysseus's character cannot help but enact notions of how recognition plays out. No study of the transformations of Odyssean recognition would be complete, for instance, without readings of modernist novels, latter-day epics, and contemporary novellas (e.g., James Joyce's *Ulysses*, Nikos Kazantzakis's *Odyssey: A Modern Sequel*, and Margaret Atwood's *Penelopiad*). Nor could any such study get away without spectating Odysseus's appearances on the modern stage (e.g., Tadeusz Kantor's production of Wyspianski's *Return of Ulysses*, Heiner Müller's *Philoktet*, Botho Strauss's *Ithaka*, and Derek Walcott's *Odyssey*). Much of worthwhile interest would emerge from focused attention to these and other great reworkings of the myth. But this book does not pretend to be a comprehensive survey of Odyssean anagnorisis through the ages.

In fact, the turns that recognition takes in Homer's *Odyssey*, Shakespeare's *Troilus and Cressida*, Goethe's "Fortunate Event" and *Iphigenie auf Tauris*, and Kleist's *Penthesilea* already point toward the major possibilities for recognition's iterations in the last two centuries. Chapter 5 intimated the Homeric poem's potential for exploring issues of postcolonial identity, which Walcott's play (as well as his epic poem *Omeros*, which takes characters from the *Iliad* and places them in an *Odyssey*-like setting) actualizes with striking beauty and incision. Margaret Atwood's *Penelopiad* also explicitly takes up the feminist critique implicit in Homer's poem, which chapter 3 articulated as the radical indeterminacy of Penelope's recognition. Atwood, however (along with all other modern adaptations I have seen), removes any doubt from when and how Penelope knows her husband. Thus, though the novella lends Penelope agency in other forms, it robs her of the specific power she has at the heart of the Homeric poem.[1]

Kantor's, Müller's, and Strauss's plays all diagnose in different ways the debilitating effects of war and political oppression on people's capacity to know one another. Yet their "anti-Aristotelian" stagecraft and even their destabilizing depiction of human subjecthood and agency are powerfully prefigured in Shakespeare's *Troilus and Cressida* (chapter 6) and Kleist's *Penthesilea* (chapter 10). The Odysseus figure in Müller's reworking of Sophocles's *Philoctetes* moreover, is particularly evocative of Pylades in Goethe's *Iphigenie*: impatient with all the sympathetic moral soul-searching that in all likelihood will result in more death and suffering. Deception, in both Goethe's reworking of Euripides's play and Müller's of Sophocles's, has its own moral logic.

The fullest flowering of Goethe's Odysseus figures, meanwhile, is his own *Faust*. Tracing the forms of recognition in the two parts of that tragedy of knowledge would require its own book.[2] The modernist experiment of Joyce's *Ulysses* shares many features with the playfully comprehensive rehearsal of the history of Western literature in all its forms, genres, and allegories that is Goethe's *Faust*. If Joyce's *Ulysses* follows in the footsteps of Goethe's experimentation with form, then Kazantzakis's *Odyssey* plays with the Faustian inheritance in plot and character. The restless adventurer, insatiable for new experiences and knowledge, who is the hero of Kazantzakis's epic, shows (with Dante and Tennyson) how any "modern sequel" to Homer's poem will be a Faustian tale.

Instead of continuing this study with an endless analysis of recognition in the rich tradition of literary receptions of the *Odyssey*, I shall limit these concluding observations to two appearances of Odysseus in the twentieth century that pick up on aspects of recognition explored in this book and push them further. The trajectory forward becomes clearest if I take them up in reverse chronological order. First, Odysseus and Goethe make an important dual appearance in what turns out to be an analysis of recognition in Hans Blumenberg's *Work on Myth* (*Arbeit am Mythos*; 1979). Second, Kafka's reworking of Odysseus's adventure, "The Silence of the Sirens" ("Das Schweigen der Sirenen"; 1917/1931), closes with a formula that suggestively ties together the two threads of recognition that weave their way through this book: performance and reflection.

In investigating why the power of myth has such tenacity despite (and alongside) other explanatory practices, such as science, dogma, and mysticism, Blumenberg lights on myth's capacity to endow events, coincidences, objects, and persons with "meaning." He calls this quality *Bedeutsamkeit* (significance)[3] and goes on to analyze "the means of operation with which significance 'works,' and with which the work on significance is done."[4] Though Blumenberg does not mention recognition, the list of functional operations he puts together could serve as a taxonomy of narrative strategies for anagnorisis: "simultaneity, latent identity, the closed-circle pattern, the recurrence of the same, the reciprocity between resistance and heightened existence, and the isolation of a thing or action."[5] This list can be easily deduced for effective plot construction techniques[6] under the assumption of Aristotle's definitions of peripeteia and anagnorisis and his postulation that the best stories are the ones where reversal and recognition happen at the same time (*P*, 11, 1542a, 33).

To illustrate these functions, Blumenberg first gives an extended reading of an episode from Goethe's life before turning to the *Odyssey*. The first case is the "famous necklace story" of the conning of Marie Antoinette by Cagliostro in 1785, which Goethe turned into a musical comedy in 1791 and continued to mine in his autobiographical writings until the 1820s. Blumenberg pulls together a variety of epistolary, autobiographical, and anecdotal evidence to show how Goethe attributes great historical and personal meaning to a series of coincidences, deceptions, and revelations. All this serves as an illustrative example of two operations for generating significance: "latent identity" and "closed circle."[7] The discovery of Goethe's hidden identity as both a disguised visitor to Cagliostro's family in Sicily and their secret benefactor later on is anagnorisis on the world stage. The pay Goethe received for publishing the *Groß-Cophta*, the comic opera based on the Cagliostro affair, is intimated to be the source of the money he conveys to them, which brings the wide-ranging events of the episode full circle. Goethe comes to see his fascination with the necklace story as a premonition of the French Revolution and all its tragic repercussions. Recognizing these connections imbues them with significance for Goethe and raises them to myth-like proportions according to Blumenberg. Both the work *of* the myth and the work *on* the myth require the operations of anagnorisis.

"Fictional materials cannot achieve this suggestion of meaning," Blumenberg notes, which is why it is important for these narrated incidents to be tied to reality.[8] For a shortcut to myth, one must inscribe the tale as a "true story." Yet a representation of "true" events, as seen above with Goethe's pregnant account of his friendship with Schiller (chapter 7), relies on strategies of fictionalization rather than strict accuracy in order to take on meaningfulness. Events themselves are not meaningful: only their representations generate significance by forging striking connections and dramatic patterns. Fictions, in order to gain meaning, must masquerade as fact; reality, to seem significant, must take on fictional forms.

After denying significance to pure fictions, Blumenberg goes on to explain why myths nevertheless seem meaningful: "The significance of myth is not recognizable as something fictional, because it has no nameable author, because it comes from afar and does not lay claim to particular chronological position."[9] This opens the way for him to turn to the *Odyssey* as an example of further operations of significance with the "reciprocity between resistance and heightened existence" and again the "closed circle." The accomplishment of Odysseus's homecoming and recognition despite great odds and with monumental effort affords meaning and value to the Homeric epic.[10]

Later reworkings of the Odysseus myth choose different strategies to attain significance. All of them, despite widely different motivations and forms, can be seen as operations of recognition. Blumenberg writes about three main movements in this "deformation [*Verformung*] of the plan of the *Odyssey*."[11] First, Neoplatonic work on the myth imbues it with meaning by discovering in it all manner of allegorical interpretations: they recognize hidden truths behind the adventures and their representation in language. Second, Dante's Ulysses must be punished for his deception and his desire for knowledge, the two sources of his glory and success in Homer. The "closed circle" of Odysseus's *nostos* must be "broken open"[12] to accommodate a different kind of recognition: Dante's acknowledgment of the limits of human knowledge. The figure of Ulysses shows that trying to learn about the world on one's own, without divine help and revelation, is sinful and doomed.

Finally, Blumenberg turns to the "modern despisers of the 'happy ending.'"[13] Joyce's *Ulysses*, which represents the events of one arbitrary day, also dispenses with the "closed-circle pattern" and in fact makes a show of its "refusal of meaning" (*Sinnverweigerung*).[14] Yet this move itself takes on mythic significance. It is only secured by requiring "the appended work of philology" (*philologische Nachträglichkeit*) from the reader: "Such contingency demands the irony of the mythical vis-à-vis the factual: It could also be any other day—and it will be every other day. This reversal restores the mythical quality."[15] The invitation to recognize multivalent connections between ordinary life and Homeric epic becomes an endless significance-generating machine of meaningful meaninglessness. The recognition scene between husband and wife provides Blumenberg with the "most insidious form" of this denial of meaning. Because of the Homeric template, readers see that Joyce's Molly/Penelope is contemplating an infidelity with Dedalus/Telemachus even while she lies in bed next to Bloom/Odysseus. Here, the son Odysseus brings home is the incestuous object of desire for his estranged Penelope. "Its irony is only recognizable, in the countermove to the mythical superelevation of the closing of the circle," by taking events from Joyce's biography into account.[16] This modernist *Odyssey* has thus returned to the "latent identity" operations of significance established by Goethe's interweaving of *Poetry and Truth* in his autobiographical writings. Blumenberg's analysis, moreover, has "closed the circle" in its own minidrama of recognition.

For Blumenberg, myth and reality undergo the same operations of anagnorisis in order to acquire the sheen of significance. Recognition is an effective and recurring feature of stories because it makes them seem meaningful, and the experience of significance is a way to ward off the frightening "absolutism of reality." This explanation for the importance of recognition is the precise opposite of Aristotle's, for whom good stories contain anagnorisis scenes because recognition is a consequential activity in the world and good stories imitate serious, momentous actions. Either recognition is meaningful because it is a decisive event in human life or recognition is pervasive because it lends phenomena the meaningfulness of events.

This book cannot provide a conclusive solution to this quandary; in a way, literary scholarship gains its own sense of "meaningfulness" in the open cleft between the two possibilities. Like a good Platonic dialogue, when faced with this impasse over the source of recognition's power, I will resort to a final myth. This one is not of my own making but from the ultimate craftsman of myths for modernity. Kafka's short vignette, "The Silence of the Sirens," takes an episode from Odysseus's first-person narration of his adventures to the Phaeacians and recasts it with a devious third-person narrator who introduces major differences in plot, characterization, and narrative technique. Homer's Odysseus relates that Circe informed him how to listen to the Sirens' song without succumbing to their deadly pull: he must stop up his crew's ears with wax and make them tie him to the mast. Kafka's Odysseus comes up with the means (*Mittelchen*: a diminutive "little plan") for surviving the Sirens on his own: he is fastened to the mast *and* plugs his own ears with wax. The Homeric device allows Odysseus to be audience to a performance so beautiful that it is fatal: art with the ultimate *Wirkungsästhetik* (aesthetics of effect). The Kafka tale seems to remove the performative aspect from the encounter altogether: Odysseus merely wants to survive sailing past the Sirens; he does not attempt to hear their song.

Far from avoiding performance, however, the story renders even silence performative. Kafka's most striking innovation is the disclosure of the Sirens' silence. The narrator insists that it is even more terrifying than their singing: "Though it has never happened, it is perhaps conceivable that someone might have saved himself from their song, but from their silence, certainly not."[17] The danger of the Sirens' song has been described as the "allurement of losing oneself in the past." Their music offers knowledge of "everything that has happened, they demand the future as its price, and their promise of a happy homecoming is the deception by which the past entraps a humanity filled with longing."[18] The song of the Sirens is myth at its most overpowering: listeners drown in the unfathomable deepness of significance. Thus their silence is an abrupt withdrawal from this enticement of meaningfulness. To speak with Blumenberg, the silence of the Sirens is *Sinnverweigerung*: a beautiful myth that refuses to fulfill its promise of meaning. Significance withheld is much more deadly than insignificance.

Kafka's reimagining of Odysseus's encounter with the Sirens is emblematic of the ambiguities inherent in every recognition scenario. On the face of it, Kafka's vignette seems like a dizzying expression of the radical doubts about other minds resulting from a post-Cartesian worldview. Limited to an input/output model of understanding, the increasing levels of uncertainty about who knows what—and who knows who knows what—that build up in the successive paragraphs are logically unavoidable. The penultimate sentence seems to confirm the existence of an impenetrable interiority of selfhood that can never be accessed by others: "Odysseus, they say, was so full of guile, was such a fox, that even the goddess of fate could not penetrate into his innermost interior [*Innerstes*]."[19] But the progress of the narration belies the reality of any such privileged *Innerstes* that is separate from the mode of Odysseus's acting in the world. Though the narrator seems to make claims about what Odysseus (or the Sirens, or the gods) think, feel, and experience, these claims are soon explicitly cast into doubt with contradictory speculations. Only the gestures and expressions that the parties see in their brief encounter with each other remain unimpugned by the narration. The engagement consists of the external actions of the parties involved: Odysseus stopping up his ears, binding himself to the mast, sailing past, and surviving; the silent Sirens with "the turns of their necks, the deep breathing, the tearful eyes, the half-open mouth."[20] Intentions can only be a matter of speculation, no sooner suggested than doubted and replaced with alternatives.

The narrator sets himself up as an arbitrator of recognition but can come to no definite conclusion: in the story's short page and a half of text, the word *vielleicht* (perhaps) modifies three of the narrator's claims; three more sentences are in the subjunctive. The indeterminacy of recognition culminates in the final sentence:

> Vielleicht hat [Odysseus], obwohl das mit Menschenverstand nicht mehr zu begreifen ist, wirklich gemerkt, daß die Sirenen schwiegen, und hat ihnen und den Göttern den obigen Scheinvorgang nur gewissermassen als Schild entgegengehalten. (301)
>
> (Perhaps, though it is beyond the comprehension of human understanding, [Odysseus] really did notice that the Sirens were silent, and held up the aforementioned scene of pretense simply as a shield.)

For one thing, this formula—and the narrative performance of the entire text—makes a show of the impasse between Aristotle's and Blumenberg's explanations of recognition: Is it the representation of a real and decisive action or is it an operation of myth that confers the sense of meaning? The narrator's inquiries into motives and the status of knowledge between figures impose the logic of this question onto the event described. Yet the narration abdicates any responsibility to answer it. This situation reenacts Joe Sachs's interpretation of Aristotelian catharsis: the literary text can be an invitation to think philosophically, but it does not itself provide any easy answers to the questions it poses. Literary art resides in this space between Blumenberg's operation of myth and Aristotle's imitation of action. Therein lies its fascination and power.

More pointedly, however, Kafka's final sentence brings together the two components of recognition explored so suggestively in *Penthesilea* and hearkened back to so often in the pages of this book: the *Scheinvorgang* (process of seeming) of performance and the *Schild* (shield) of reflection. The *Scheinvorgang* that Odysseus is imagined to be holding up amounts to the performance of identity or self that constitutes one half of any recognition scenario as described in this book. The fact that Odysseus holds it up as a *shield* constitutes the other half. On the one hand, this shielding performance protects the subject from the blows and volleys of others; on the other hand, it *re*flects at the same time as it *de*flects. The projection or performance of self is simultaneously a defense of self. As in *Penthesilea*, the shield here provides a mirroring function for intersubjective encounters. By covering up the subject, the shield of performance reveals her to the other. By deflecting others' projections, the performative shield reveals the other to her. Together, to speak with Goethe, this pretense and this mirror make up the "organ" of recognition.

In the midst of their allegorizing reading of the *Odyssey*, Max Horkheimer and Theodor Adorno identify "the organ of the self" that allows it to survive as "cunning" (*List*), by which it "throws itself away in order to preserve itself."[21] This wily craft of deception is the same *mētis* with which Odysseus lied to identify himself truly to Polyphemus: he became no one (*outis*)—"throwing himself away"—in order to remain himself (*mētis*).[22] Dissimulation is the organ of self-preservation, yet it is simultaneously a mode of self-disclosure. Thus Odysseus and Penelope reveal their characters through bolts of fabrication. By misdirection, Socrates endeavors to steer Alcibiades on the right path; Ulysses stages a reading of introspection to goad Achilles on to the outward theater of war. Goethe tweaks historical accuracy to give a "truer" image of his own and Schiller's characters. Even Iphigenie becomes herself by lying—a little—in order to tell the truth more theatrically to Thoas.[23] Penthesilea fails truly to "connect" because she cannot tell a lie. The organ of recognition is a faculty of performance.

This book has shown how the organ of recognition emerges *between* subjects whenever they come into meaningful contact. Whether this meaningfulness is a function of myth (representation) or action (that which is represented) remains an open question. Yet these staged readings have, hopefully, demonstrated the devious interdependence of representation and its object: the latter cannot be recognized without the necessary distortions of the former. The final sentence of Kafka's work on the myth of Odysseus thus encapsulates the productive aporia for the sake of which this book has been written.

ACKNOWLEDGMENTS

LIKE THE WORK of recognition explored in these pages, the production of this book has been an intersubjective and collaborative affair. Conversations with many people have influenced the thinking that resulted in this book, though its final form may surprise, disappoint, or dismay them. Relationships with family, friends, students, and teachers have shaped my understanding of recognition even more than the texts explored in these pages, and I am indebted to them for contributing to my ideas and, most fundamentally, to who I am.

This book began as a dissertation at Johns Hopkins and Yale Universities. At both institutions, it benefited from the advice of my *Doktorvater*, Rüdiger Campe, who is masterfully adept at helping students come to see the form and import of their own ideas. He truly holds up a mirror of self-recognition for others in dialogue. His generosity in time and careful thinking helped foster any virtues the theoretical arguments of this book may contain, whereas the weaknesses and inconsistencies of the claims are all my own. I have also been fortunate in receiving encouragement from Carol Jacobs, criticism from Kirk Wetters, and inspiration from both. Other teachers have also been incredibly generous and helpful: Gerhard Neumann, who regaled me with tales of recognition at the oyster bar in Baltimore's Lexington Market; Rainer Nägele, whose seminar on Leaving and Returning inspired the first essay on the *Odyssey* around which my dissertation grew. Sincere thanks are due to Paul North, Henry Sussman, Glenn Most, David Scott Kastan, Stephen Johnson (and his 2007 class at the University of Toronto Drama Centre), and Elinor Fuchs for galvanizing discussions and advice. Discussions with Eric Downing and Christopher Wild during a German Studies Association panel on anagnorisis also helped sharpen my thinking about the problems of recognition.

Tutors at St. John's College (SJC) played midwife to my longest lasting ideas about texts and reading. I am particularly grateful to Gisela Berns, who reawakened my excitement about the topic (after it had begun to pall as endless academic drudgery) with brilliant suggestions full of intellectual delight. Adam Schulman's sophomore Greek tutorial planted the seeds for my thinking about Odysseus and political action. His reminder as my senior essay adviser that we should focus on what we can learn *from* books rather than prove *about* them has remained a guiding light for all my work. Joe Sachs was very generous in taking the time to engage in a stimulating email discussion about the meaning of anagnorisis in Aristotle's work. Michael Comenetz first posed the Penelope question to me when we read book 19 of the *Odyssey* in his freshman language tutorial. Most recently, Philip Chandler, leader of the Puget Sound SJC alumni seminar, has been keenly helpful: I hope this book avoids the pitfalls of jargon he justly scorns. Kathleen Blits in freshman math and Grant Franks in junior lab were the best writing teachers a student could wish for. Brother Robert introduced me to the joys of studied *wonder*.

Without the support of the University of Washington (UW) and my colleagues here, it would have been impossible to turn the dissertation into the book it has become. Jane Brown is the most admirable model of writing and scholarship imaginable. She sat down to go through one of the *Iphigenie* chapters line by line with me, resulting in improvements that make me feel embarrassed for the rest of the book. Ruby Blondell read what was originally one chapter on the *Odyssey*, and—though it may well horrify her to discover it—her incisive feedback is responsible for it multiplying by five. Richard Block makes Denny Hall scintillate with intellectual brilliance. I'm especially grateful for his generous thoughtfulness and ingenious ideas about titles. Thank you to Colin Marshall for setting me straight about contemporary schools of moral philosophy. My colleagues Brigitte Prutti, Sabine Wilke, Jeffrey Fracé, Michael Rosenthal, Olga Levaniouk, Adair Rounthwaite, Walter Erhart, Helmut Ammerlahn, Rick Gray, Eric Ames, Jason Groves, and Kye Terrassi have all been wonderfully supportive. I'm also thankful to the UW graduate students who gamely discussed recognition for an entire course and to the Performance Studies Research Group, which was generously supported by the UW Simpson Center for the Humanities. Many thanks to the group's organizers, Stefka Mihaylova and Scott Magelssen, for stimulating conversations and valuable feedback on a draft of chapter 2. Finally, the UW Royalty Research Fund made possible a much-needed quarter free from teaching in order to complete the revision, and anonymous reviewers on the award committee gave helpful suggestions about an early proposal draft.

Versions of chapters 7 and 10 of this book were published as "Dramas of Recognition: The 'Fortunate Event' of Recognition," *Goethe Yearbook* 17 (2010): 203–222; and "Reflecting and Performing Selves: The Fate of Recognition in Kleist's *Penthesilea*," *Germanic Studies Review* 41.2 (2018): 253–274, respectively. I am obliged to the Johns Hopkins University Press for permission to publish the latter and to Camden House for the former. The North American Goethe Society and its book series, New Studies in the Age of Goethe, made this manuscript become a book. Thank you to Karin Schutjer for believing in the project (and for all the considerate virtual hand-holding throughout!) and to Nicholas Rennie for being its first reader and thoughtful reviewer. I owe thanks to all the people at Bucknell University Press who helped this book find its way into print: Greg Clingham, Pam Dailey, and Sam Brawand. Finally, thank you to the editors at Rutgers University Press and Scribe Inc. for their careful copyediting of the manuscript.

Conversations with friends have been equally important to shaping my thoughts—they are too numerous to name in all, but I should mention Grant Edmonds, Sasha Newton, Barbara Rieger, Tully Rector, John Bova, Ansgar Mohnkern, Arne Hoecker, Raimund Lippert, and Wolfgang Müller-Molenar. Thank you to Anne Flannery for slogging through chapters and for the dockets. I owe a huge debt of gratitude to Brian Parkinson for agreeing to be my taskmaster in the dark year of 2016: he wielded the whip with firm grace.

Most importantly, none of this would have been possible without the love, support, and spiritual and intellectual inspiration of my family. My sister, Rebekah Wiggins, is more brilliant than she knows. My wonderful parents, Woody and Susan Wiggins, are shining beacons of recognition at its ethical best. Thalia and Felice have grown into recognizable subjects during the writing of this book, and learning the dance of recognition with them has been the greatest joy of my life. Most of all, I am grateful to my wife, Sara Khor, who has had to put up with me for far longer than anyone deserves and whose healthy skepticism about literary mumbo jumbo keeps me humble.

NOTES

Introduction

1. George Lucas, with Leigh Brackett and Lawrence Kasdan, *The Empire Strikes Back*, dir. Irvin Kershner (Los Angeles: Twentieth Century Fox, 1980).

2. Lucas, Brackett, and Kasdan.

3. *P*, 11, 1452a, 30; *P*, 6, 1450a, 35. *Anagnōrisis* and other oft-repeated Greek terms will henceforth appear unitalicized.

4. See Judith Butler, "Performative Acts and Gender Constitution: An Essay in Phenomenology and Feminist Theory," *Theatre Journal* 49, no. 1 (1988): 519–548.

5. Nancy Tilman, *I'd Know You Anywhere, My Love* (New York: Feiwel and Friends, 2013), 4–6 (emphasis in the original).

6. One hilarious fan video presents a résumé of these unanswered questions that manages to shoot out a round of 109 queries (I counted) in rapid-fire succession about the show in four minutes (College Humor, "Unanswered Lost Questions," posted May 24, 2010, http://www.collegehumor.com).

7. Lostpedia, "06x17 End," accessed March 19, 2011, http://forum.lostpedia.com/06x17-end-questions-theories-discussion-t58202p2.html.

8. See Wikipedia, "Critical Reception," in "The End (*Lost*)," accessed May 25, 2010, http://en.wikipedia.org.

9. Interestingly, critics' responses, like those of fans, were much more positive in the initial afterglow of the show's credits than it became after time had passed for reflection. This changing reaction over time corroborates my claims below: as the emotional punch of anagnorisis knowledge fades, the lack of factual knowledge is harder to ignore. I would even claim that if the final episode had eschewed anagnorisis in favor of explaining all the plot's riddles, the result would have been a theatrical and emotional dud: witness the anticlimactic but answer-laden twelve-minute "Epilogue" released with the *Lost* DVD. J. J. Abrams, Jeffrey Lieber, and Damon Lindelof, *Lost. The Complete Sixth Season: The Final Season* (Los Angeles: ABC Studios, Touchstone Home Video, 2010).

10. Wikipedia, "Anagnorisis," accessed April 12, 2016, http://en.wikipedia.org.

11. Aristotle does not use a noun one might translate as "moment" or "instant" when describing anagnorisis. He thus never speaks of a "recognition moment," though that has been a common formulation in nearly all modern treatments of the subject. To cite an example nearly at random, "[Oedipus] was heroic at the moment of recognition, and he sustained his courage before the gods and his enemies to the end" (Diana Culbertson, *The Poetics of Revelation: Recognition and the Narrative Tradition* [Macon: Mercer University Press, 1989], 41).

12. Aristotle claims that in *Oedipus*, the recognition happens at the same time (*hama*) as the peripeteia (*P*, 11, 1452a, 32).

13. *P*, chaps. 7 and 8; *Ph*, bk. 1.

14. This paradox will be explored more closely in chapter 7.

15. Robert E. Sherwood, *The Best Years of Our Lives*, dir. William Wyler (Los Angeles: Samuel Golden, 1946).

16. Sherwood.

17. Hannah Arendt, *The Human Condition* (Chicago: Chicago University Press, 1958), 236–247. Arendt's understanding of action will prove important to the one proposed in this book. Her ideas of forgiveness and promise are explored in chapter 9.

18. Terence Cave, *Recognitions: A Study in Poetics* (Oxford: Clarendon, 1988).

19. See Paul Ricoeur, *The Course of Recognition*, trans. David Pellauer (Cambridge, Mass.: Harvard University Press, 2005).

20. Patchen Markell, *Bound by Recognition* (Princeton: Princeton University Press, 2003).

21. Especially evident in Markell's readings of Hannah Arendt and Stanley Cavell (Markell, 9–25, 32–38).

22. Carl Schmitt, *The Concept of the Political*, trans. George Schwab (Chicago: University of Chicago Press, 1996); Jacques Derrida, *Politics of Friendship*, trans. George Collins (New York: Verso, 1997); Giorgio Agamben, "The Friend," in *What Is an Apparatus? And Other Essays*, trans. David Kishik and Stefan Pedatella (Stanford: Stanford University Press, 2009), 25–37.

23. Peggy Phelan, *Unmarked: The Politics of Performance* (London: Routledge, 1993), 148.

24. Gregory Nagy, *Poetry as Performance: Homer and Beyond* (Cambridge: Cambridge University Press, 1996), 59–86.

25. Richard Schechner and Victor W. Turner, *Between Theater and Anthropology* (Philadelphia: University of Pennsylvania Press, 1985), 36.

26. Rebecca Schneider, *Performing Remains: Art and War in Times of Theatrical Reenactment* (London: Routledge, 2011).

27. J. David Velleman, *How We Get Along* (Cambridge: Cambridge University Press, 2009); Hilde Lindemann, *Holding and Letting Go: The Social Practice of Personal Identities* (Oxford: Oxford University Press, 2014).

28. Alva Noë, *Out of Our Heads: Why You Are Not Your Brain, and Other Lessons from the Biology of Consciousness* (New York: Hill and Wang, 2009), 24.

29. For an excellent account of this narrative, see the introduction by Rüdiger Campe and Julia Weber in their edited volume, *Rethinking Emotion: Interiority and Exteriority in Pre-modern, Modern, and Contemporary Thought* (Berlin: De Gruyter, 2014), 1–20.

30. Cave, *Recognitions*. As Cave remarks on the very last page of his tome, "Recognition is *par excellence* the vehicle of nostalgia" (497). This book thus picks up where Cave's study leaves off.

31. Arendt, *Human Condition*.

32. Sophocles, *The Theban Plays: Antigone, King Oidipous, Oidipous at Colonus*, trans. Ruby Blondell (Newburyport: Focus, 2002), 153.

33. Arendt writes that a responsible understanding of a person's life only becomes possible with her death (*Human Condition*, 192), and hence one could say with equal justification that the *beginning* of recognition is death.

Part I

1. See, for instance, Axel Honneth's recurrent revisions of his sweeping claims for the universal moral value of recognition in response to criticisms of the original *Struggle for Recognition* (1995): *Redistribution or Recognition?* (2003), with Nancy Fraser; *Reification* (2007); *The I in We* (2012); and *Recognition or Disagreement* (2016), with Jacques Rancière. Think too of classicists' conflicting interpretations of Aristotelian *anagnorisis* as a "mere" plot device (Richmond Lattimore, O. B. Hardison), as an anthropological category (Gerald Else, Simon Goldhill), and as a philosophical concept (Seth Benerdete, Michael Davis).

2. Peter Gainsford, "Formal Analysis of Recognition Scenes in the *Odyssey*," *Journal of Hellenic Studies* 123 (2003): 45.

3. For example, see Sheila Murnaghan, Simon Goldhill, or Peter Gainsford.

4. For example, see Paul Ricoeur, Axel Honneth, Patchen Markell, or Gerhard Neumann.

Chapter One

1. *P*, 11, 1452a, 29 (my emphasis).

The word translated here and in most English editions of the *Poetics* as "itself" is *kai*, which is the copulative conjunction (*and*) as well as an emphatic intensifier (*even*). The Greek word for self or itself (*auto*) does not appear in the definition, but it is logically implied: "as even the name signifies" requires that the name *by itself* already carries its own meaning. A synonymous formulation *auto to* x (e.g., *auto to agathon* [the good itself]) was commonly used by Aristotle's teacher, Plato, to call attention to the meaning of words. Aristotle himself uses this formulation elsewhere (cf., *tounoma auto huposēmenei* [the name itself implies], *NE*, 1122a). This elided implication of the self is emblematic of the function of *itself* in recognition, as will become clear in this chapter.

2. For example, Aristotle, *De Poetica*, trans. Ingraham Bywater, in *The Basic Works of Aristotle*, ed. Richard McKeon (New York: Random House, 1941), 1465; Aristotle, *On the Art of Poetry*, trans. T. S. Dorsch (London: Penguin Books, 1965), 46; and Aristotle, *Poetics*, trans. Joe Sachs (Newburyport: Focus, 2005), 34.

3. Martin Heidegger, *Sein und Zeit* (Tübingen: Max Niemeyer Verlag, 1993), 219.

4. See, for instance, Patricia Huntington, *Ecstatic Subjects, Utopia, and Recognition: Kristeva, Heidegger, Irigaray* (Albany: State University of New York Press, 1998); and Lauren Freeman, "Recognition Reconsidered: A Re-reading of Heidegger's Being and Time §26," *Philosophy Today* 53, no. 1 (2009): 85–99.

5. See Michael Davis, introduction to *On Poetics*, by Aristotle, trans. Seth Benardete and Michael Davis (South Bend: St. Augustine's Press, 2002), xx.

6. The common words for "ignorance" are *agnōsia* or, as in Aristotle's definition for anagnorisis, *agnoias*. I have been unable to find any other instances of double alpha privatives like the one Davis proposes. It is unclear whether the Greek ear would even hear such a doubling of privatives as a positive. Considering the sheer number of *ana* prefixes in Greek (there are fifteen pages of such words in the Middle Liddell; see *LS*, 61–65.) It is

improbable that the privative rather than the prefix would be heard in constructions where both readings might be possible.

7. Thanks to Joe Sachs for this observation (private email correspondence, summer 2007).

8. It would be interesting to read these epiphanic accounts in light of dramatic recognition and, vice versa, to think through Greek tragedy and epic in terms of Levinasian ethics or Joyceian interiority. These latter two projects have attracted takers. Scholars of anthropology and psychology have given conflicting Levinasian readings of the *Odyssey*. François Hartog tries to rehabilitate Homer's texts for Levinasian morality (*Memories of Odysseus: Frontier Tales from Ancient Greece* [Chicago: University of Chicago Press, 2001]). Leswin Laubscher, though, finds the biblical Abraham a far more responsible moral agent than the self-aggrandizing Odysseus ("Of Odysseus and Abraham: Nostalgia, Heimweë, and the Ways [of] Home," *Peace and Conflict: Journal of Peace Psychology* 18, no. 3 [2012]: 214–224). Joyce himself, meanwhile, provided a modernist reimagining of the *Odyssey* with his novel *Ulysses*, in which Homeric recognitions are transformed into internal stream-of-consciousness epiphanies at every turn.

9. Interestingly, *enemies* as well as gods could make sudden epiphanies. See *LSJ*, 669.

10. Paul Ricoeur compiled an elegant catalog of meanings for *reconnaissance* in the introduction to *The Course of Recognition* (Cambridge, Mass.: Harvard University Press, 2005), 1–22; and the uses of the English *recognition* hew quite closely to those of the French. This suggestive ambiguity does not carry over into German. There, one must choose between *wiedererkennen* (recognize as to know again, the common translation for *anagnorisis*) and *anerkennen* (recognize as to acknowledge). This bears mentioning because the Hegelian *Anerkennung* is translated as "recognition" in English scholarship, which invites an ambiguity that the German verb lacks. The root verb *erkennen* is itself composed of an inseparable prefix *er* (usually: up, fully) + *kennen* (to be acquainted with) and retains some of the ambiguity that the additional prefixes dispel.

11. Svetlana Boym, *The Future of Nostalgia* (New York: Basic Books, 2001), 3.

12. Norman Austin, "Homeric Nostalgia," *Yale Review* 98, no. 2 (2010): 45.

13. Douglas Frame, *Myth of Return in Early Greek Epic* (New Haven: Yale University Press, 1978), 28–33.

14. Boym, *Future of Nostalgia*, 8.

15. All three of the great Attic tragedians would go on to offer agonistic versions of this family's tragic recognitions, from Aeschylus's *Oresteia* to Sophocles's and Euripides's *Electra*s.

16. For a good account of these parallels, see Norman Austin, *Archery at the Dark of the Moon: Poetic Problems in Homer's Odyssey* (Berkeley: University of California Press, 1975), 179–182.

17. See Ruby Blondell, *Helen of Troy: Beauty, Myth, Devastation* (Oxford: Oxford University Press, 2013).

18. See Austin, *Archery*, 188–189.

19. For an excellent analysis of their troubled relations and for the unsettling threat of female beauty and agency in the Homeric world, see Blondell, *Helen*, 73–95.

20. In the end, Telemachus shows that he has learned that possession of beautiful things alone is no model for the son of Odysseus. He politely declines Menelaus's gift of three fine horses with the excuse that Ithaca lacks the wide plains that would allow their possession to be a delight (*Od*, 4.600–608). Acquisitiveness in itself is not a problem—both his parents take pride in accumulating great wealth—but after witnessing the rigid dolefulness of Menelaus's rich hall, Telemachus only wants presents that will bring genuine pleasure.

21. See Euripides's *Trojan Women* (1036–1042), in Euripides, *Trojan Women, Iphigenia among the Taurians, and Ion*, trans. and ed. David Kovacs, Loeb Classical Library 10, vol. 4 (Cambridge, Mass.: Harvard University Press, 1999).

22. For a suggestive account of this drug's links to the dangers of forgetting and the power of poetry, see Blondell, *Helen*, 79–81.

23. For an elegant exploration of this paradox, see John T. Hamilton, *Security: Politics, Humanity, and the Philology of Care* (Princeton: Princeton University Press, 2013).

24. See Peter Szondi, "Das Naïve ist das Sentimentalische," in *Lektüren und Lektionen: Versuche über Literatur, Literaturtheorie und Litertatursoziologie* (Frankfurt am Main: Suhrkamp, 1974), 47–102.

25. Paul Fleming, "Belatedness: A Theory of the Epic," *MLN* 129, no. 3 (2014): 531.

26. Gerhard Richter, *Afterness: Figures of Following in Modern Thought and Aesthetics* (New York: Columbia University Press, 2011), 36.

27. The afterness of the *Aeneid* is also manifestly political. Augustus's empire, with its extensive bureaucracy and legal administration, is fully severed from the *oikos*-based political order of the Aegean Bronze Age, yet it longs for the legitimation of a heroic founding that can only be constructed fictionally in formal imitation of Homer. The *Aeneid* distracts from the new empire's immediate republican prequel by pointing even further back to posit Rome's "true" Trojan heritage.

28. Virgil, *Aeneid*, trans. Robert Fitzgerald (New York: Vintage Classics, 1990), bk. 1, lines 453–493.

29. Austin, "Homeric Nostalgia," 42.

30. See Andrew Ford, "Epic as Genre," in *A New Companion to Homer*, ed. Ian Morris and Barry Powell (Leiden: Brill, 1997), 104.

31. Nietzsche's *Birth of Tragedy* works with the same logic: there would be no original Dionysian force without the later Apollinian impulse.

32. The grammatical term for this construction (*peplegmenos*), with its doubled initial consonant, is the—seemingly redundant, but in retrospect quite apt—"reduplicated participle."

33. Fr. Lat. *simplex*, fr. *simil-*, as in Gr. *hama* (same, together with) + *plo* (fold; *LS*, 94).

34. For an eloquent meditation on the way that modern conceptions of the world, the self, and history are implicit in the figure of the fold, see Gilles Deleuze, *The Fold: Leibniz and the Baroque* (Minneapolis: University of Minnesota Press, 1993). The importance of Otherness to my account of the supposed identity-matching game of recognition is also reminiscent of Deleuze's insistence on a "philosophy of difference" (see *Difference and Repetition*, trans. Paul Patton [New York: Columbia University Press, 1994], 127–128). In a Deleuzian reading, the account of recognition I offer could be construed as an event:

it must be conceived as a singular dividing screen between two utterly different worlds of knowledge, yet tendrils of prehension stretch from the postevent relations (friendship or enmity) back, making the notional moment of the division necessarily fictitious (cf., *Fold*, 76–82).

35. Plato, *Plato's Sophist*, trans. Eva Brann et al. (Newburyport: Focus, 1996), 15.

36. Plato, 71 (original emphasis).

37. Friedrich Hölderlin, "Urteil und Sein," in *Sämtliche Werke* (Frankfurt am Main: Insel-Verlag, 1961), 947–948.

38. Novalis, "Philosophie ist eigentlich Heimweh," *Das allgemeine Brouillon*, #857, in *Schriften* (Stuttgart: W. Kohlhammer Verlag, 1960), 3:434.

39. I speak of profane time. To conceive of complex models of time, such as Christian eschatology, Hindu *kāla*, or Hegelian moments, for instance, a double take and recognition are necessary, just as fictional representations of time in memory or narrative require recognition to function.

40. See Henri Poincaré, *The Measure of Time*, in *The Foundations of Science (The Value of Science)*, trans. George Bruce Halsted (New York: Science Press, 1913), 222–234, https://en.wikisource.org.

41. See Norman Austin, "Name Magic in the *Odyssey*," *California Studies in Classical Antiquity* 5 (1972): 1. See also Simon Goldhill on naming and recognition, *The Poet's Voice: Essays on Poetics and Greek Literature* (Cambridge: Cambridge University Press, 1991), 26–36.

42. As mentioned above, Aristotle does not use the word *itself* (*auto*), but *kai* (*and*, here in the sense of *even*) carries the same emphatic force: "as even the name signifies."

43. Plato already drives home this point in the *Sophist*, but Derrida's many meditations on signs press the paradox further. Most seminally, see "Différance," in Jacques Derrida, *Margins of Philosophy* (Chicago: University of Chicago Press, 1982), 1–28.

44. Aristotle, *De Interpretatione*, in *Basic Works*, ed. Richard McKeon, Lifetime Library (New York: Random House, 1941), 40.

45. All references to the *Poetics* in these paragraphs are from bks. 20 and 21, 1456b, 20 through 1458a, 19.

46. Considering the various lengths this term must indicate, from a single phrase to the whole of the *Iliad*, Joe Sachs helpfully suggests thinking of it as *discourse*. See *P*, trans. Sachs, 50n53.

47. Aristotle does sometimes investigate the history of lexical change, as for instance in his review of ideas about the origins of Greek *drama* in book 3. Even there, though, he is careful to attribute etymological claims to the speakers of various dialects, which are often at odds with each other. His formulation is telling: "[The Megarians] make the names [comedy and tragedy] a sign [for their Megarian origin]" (*poioumenoi ta onomata sēmeion*; *P*, 3, 1448a, 36). The word for "make" here is *poien*—the same verb from which *poetry* derives. Aristotle does not write that the Megarians discern, discover, or come to understand the words as valid evidence for the true origin of drama but rather says that they compose, invent, or devise the names as signs. Even their habit of making etymological arguments is a conventional assignation of signification by common assent.

48. *P*, trans. Sachs, 56.

49. Ricoeur criticizes Aristotle for miring the study of metaphor on the level of words rather than discourse. For Ricoeur, living metaphors can never be constrained in the lexical register of defined terminology but always point beyond to the activity of language (*The Rule of Metaphor: Multi-disciplinary Studies of the Creation of Meaning in Language* [Toronto: University of Toronto Press, 1977], 9–43). By the logic of Aristotle's own text, however, the word *recognition* is a metaphor that is not merely a name. It always involves a verbal action. This transgressive reading of the recognizing metaphor in the *Poetics* aligns Aristotle more closely with Ricoeur's rule of metaphor than the Frenchman allowed.

50. See, for instance, Georg Lukács, *Theory of the Novel*, trans. Anna Bostock (Cambridge, Mass.: MIT Press, 1971), 30; and Bruno Snell, *The Discovery of the Mind: The Greek Origins of European Thought* (New York: Harper, 1960), 1–22.

51. Austin, "Name Magic," 1.

52. Austin, 16.

53. The seminal study of the role of Metis in Greek culture is Marcel Detienne and Jean-Pierre Vernant, *Cunning Intelligence in Greek Culture and Society*, trans. Janet Lloyd (Hassocks, U.K.: Harvester, 1978). Even though they have a long, involved analysis of the Cyclopes (68–92) and concede that, of all humans, Odysseus is the "very embodiment" of *mētis* (22), they surprisingly do not consider this episode from the *Odyssey* at all.

54. W. B. Stanford, "The Homeric Etymology of the Name Odysseus," *Classical Philology* 47, no. 4 (1952): 209.

Chapter Two

1. Though many of these studies include brilliantly suggestive ideas, formulations, and conclusions, they often prove resistant to careful delimitation. See, for instance, the introductory remarks in Richard Schechner's trailblazing book, *Performance Theory* (London: Routledge, 1988). There, he admits in succinct understatement, "Performance is an inclusive term" (xvii). Or, as Barbara Kirschenblatt-Gimblett writes, "Performance Studies sets no limit on what can be studied in terms of medium and culture. Nor does it limit the range of approaches that can be taken" ("Performance Studies," in *The Performance Studies Reader*, ed. Henry Bial and Sara Brady [London: Routledge, 2015], 25).

2. See Albert Lord, *Singer of Tales* (Cambridge, Mass.: Harvard University Press, 2000), 141–157.

3. Gregory Nagy, *Poetry as Performance: Homer and Beyond* (Cambridge: Cambridge University Press, 1996), 59.

4. Nagy, 58 (emphasis in the original).

5. Stephen Halliwell, *Aristotle's Poetics* (Chicago: University of Chicago Press, 1998), 128, quoted in Nagy, 4.

6. Nagy, 55.

7. The *houtos ekeinos* formula will become important in understanding the levels of knowledge implied by recognition (see chapter 7 in this work).

8. Even this assumption of a passive audience may be the product of modern theater practices imposed retrospectively. Spectators at Greek theatrical events were in fact participants in an elaborate ritual with rich social and cosmological significance. As Stephen Halliwell argues, however, Aristotle's own downplaying of the religious aspects of Greek tragedy in the *Poetics* anticipates the future secularization of the theater (introduction to

Aristotle's *The* Poetics *of Aristotle: Translation and Commentary* [London: Duckworth, 1987], 12–14).

9. Nagy, *Poetry*, 1.

10. In the formulations below, I will often relinquish the tiresome repetition of "or opinion" after each instance of "knowledge" that would technically demand it. Clearly many instances of recognition cannot be said to attain the status of "knowledge" in a either a Platonic or an Aristotelian sense, but only result in "opinion." Despite my omission, "knowledge about other people" in these cases should always be understood to imply the disjunction "knowledge or opinion."

11. Nagy, *Poetry*, 61.

12. See Gregory Nagy, *Homer the Preclassic* (Berkeley: University of California Press, 2010), 79–102; and Gregory Nagy, *Masterpieces of Metonymy: From Ancient Greek Times to Now* (Washington, D.C.: Center for Hellenic Studies, 2015), pt. 4. Nagy's approach proceeds mainly through lexical rather than syntactical or narratological analysis. He builds his historical argument about the performative residue in the Homeric text by reconstructing the significance of key words.

13. Gérard Genette, *Narrative Discourse: An Essay in Method*, trans. Jane E. Levin (Ithaca: Cornell University Press, 1980), 161–211.

14. Lattimore's translation has been modified to show verbal and pronominal forms more literally.

15. "Articulation point" is Mark Edwards's term for the summarizing minibreaks in continuous Homeric narration. For a good explanation of how these pauses work, see his *Sound, Sense, and Rhythm: Listening to Greek and Latin Poetry* (Princeton: Princeton University Press, 2009), 38–61.

16. Scott Douglas Richardson calls this passage a "narratorial anacoluthon" and concludes that it marks the "usurpation of Demodokos's song by the narrator" (*The Homeric Narrator* [Nashville: Vanderbilt University Press, 1990], 86).

17. This is not to say that these or other displays may not accompany a rhapsode's transformation.

18. See Nagy, *Homer the Preclassic*, 88–94.

19. *LS*, 52; Georg Autenrieth and Robert P. Keep, *Homeric Dictionary for Schools and Colleges* (Norman: University of Oklahoma Press, 1958), 26.

20. Nagy, *Poetry*, 57–58.

21. This practice, as Joe Sachs argues in his fine translation of the *Physics*, renders Aristotle's fundamental definition of motion "scarcely intelligible" (*Aristotle's Physics: A Guided Study* [New Brunswick: Rutgers University Press, 1995], 78). Sachs prefers "potency" and "being-at-work." Especially helpful are his introduction (*Aristotle's Physics*, 1–31), his commentary on book 3 (78–80), and his glossary (224ff., 249, and 242). Despite the admirable fidelity to Aristotle's thought that makes Sachs's translation preferable for any student of the *Physics*, in the present book, I largely resort to the traditional terminology of Aristotelian scholarship in English. Formulations such as "thinghood" and "being-at-work-staying-itself" would be off-puttingly obscure to readers who have not worked their way through Sachs's translations.

22. Compare Sachs's translation: "The being-at-work-staying-itself of what *is* potentially, whenever, being fully at work, it is at work not as itself but just as movable, is motion" (*Aristotle's Physics*, 74).

23. Sachs, *Aristotle's Physics*, 245. He renders it "being-at-work-staying-itself."

24. Aristotle, Poetics *of Aristotle*, 42.

25. The specific distinction between theatricality and performance is by no means agreed on by all scholars. In this book, I follow Erika Fischer-Lichte's general disambiguation. *Performance* is the broader term: any activity done *for* or *before* others. *Theatricality* is the subset of performances undertaken in the context of an aesthetic frame (which will vary from culture to culture). See Erika Fischer-Lichte, *The Semiotics of Theater* (Bloomington: Indiana University Press, 1992), 139–140; and Fischer-Lichte, *The Routledge Introduction to Theatre and Performance Studies*, trans. Minou Arjomand (London: Routledge, 2013), 99–110.

26. Assumptions to the contrary are the stuff of tragedy.

27. I should once again stress that these pronouncements about recognition, with their positivist and even normative ring, emerge directly from a juxtaposed reading of Aristotle's *Poetics* and *Physics*. They are an interpretation of these two texts; they do *not* claim to give access to Aristotle's own intentions and original meaning.

28. For this ordinary Greek view of virtue, see Plato, *Meno* 71e; and Ruby Blondell [as Mary Whitlock Blundell], *Helping Friends and Harming Enemies: A Study in Sophocles and Greek Ethics* (Cambridge: Cambridge University Press, 1989), 26–59.

29. If then, even. Discoveries about the "true" good intentions or revealed treachery of individuals sometimes continue long beyond the grave. Witness the cottage industry of revisionist biographical and historical studies.

30. Sachs, "Glossary," in Aristotle, *Poetics*, trans. Joe Sachs, 73.

31. See, for instance, Plato's *Republic* (387e–388d) and Lessing's defense of ancient male weeping against eighteenth-century critics in the *Laokoon* (1766). G. E. [Gotthold Ephraim] Lessing, *Werke und Briefe in zwölf Bänden* (Frankfurt am Main: Deutscher Klassiker Verlag, 1990), vol. 5, pt. 2, 20.

32. Though, as the previous chapter intimated, the "again" of recognition is figured in the king's familiarity with the epic cycle and the characters of the Trojan War. Alcinous connects the stranger to the heroic templates that Demodokos is enacting in his narrative imitation.

33. For an insightful study of the function of such similes that compare social opposites in the *Odyssey*, see Helen Foley, "'Reverse Similes' and Sex Roles in the *Odyssey*," in *Women in the Ancient World: The* Arethusa *Papers*, ed. John Peradotto and J. P. Sullivan (Albany: State University of New York Press, 1984), 59–78.

34. Others have remarked on how this simile connects Odysseus to the wives of Trojans he has slain. See R. B. Rutherford: "Now the victor and the victim are brought together in suffering grief" ("Philosophy of the *Odyssey*," *Journal of Hellenic Studies* 106 [1986]: 155).

35. For an ingenious and convincing explanation of Odysseus's motives and strategies in telling the tales at Alcinous's court, see Glenn Most, "The Structure and Function of Odysseus' *Apologoi*," *Transactions of the American Philological Association* 119 (1989): 15–30; for the challenges and strategies of rhetorical self-presentation in Greek narratives,

see also his "The Stranger's Strategem: Self-Disclosure and Self-Sufficiency in Greek Culture," *Journal of Hellenic Studies* 109 (1989): 114–133.

36. This translation has been modified for greater accuracy. Even the vigilantly literal Lattimore nods. He renders the final sentence, "He hid his tears *and deceived her*," which implies a narrator who confidently asserts that Penelope is taken in by the stranger's performance. The Homeric text is ambiguous in this point: "δόλῳ δ' ὅ γε δάκρυα κεῦθεν." The dative δόλῳ (as a ruse) shows that Odysseus *intends* deception by hiding his tears, but there is no signal at all about its success or failure with Penelope. The importance of this detail will become apparent in the next chapter, which interrogates the status of knowledge in recognition.

37. Richard Schechner and Victor Turner, *Between Theater and Anthropology* (Philadelphia: University of Pennsylvania Press, 1985), 36.

38. Schechner, *Performance Theory*, 35.

39. Schechner and Turner, *Between Theater*, 37, 41.

40. Schechner and Turner, 38–40 (figures 2.1–2.4).

41. Schechner and Turner, 113.

42. Schechner and Turner, 50.

43. Peggy Phelan, *Unmarked: The Politics of Performance* (London: Routledge, 1993), 146.

44. Rebecca Schneider, *Performing Remains: Art and War in Times of Theatrical Reenactment* (London: Routledge, 2011), 10.

45. Schneider, 2.

46. Rebecca Schneider, "Extending a Hand: Gesture, Duration and the (Non) Human Turn" (lecture, University of Washington, Seattle, Wash., April 24, 2015). For a fuller exposition on the temporality of performance, see her *Performing Remains*, 87–110.

47. At issue is Arthur Danto's refusal to recognize Cindy Sherman as a photographer and his projection of others' inability to recognize her as herself in self-portraits (Schneider, *Performing Remains*, 156; emphasis in the original).

48. Schneider, 6 (emphasis in the original).

49. J. D. Velleman, *How We Get Along* (Cambridge: Cambridge University Press, 2009), 11–33; Hilde Lindemann, *Holding and Letting Go: The Social Practice of Personal Identities* (Oxford: Oxford University Press, 2014), 97–102. Velleman's book even sports an engraving of commedia dell'arte actors on its cover.

50. Though Velleman's book appeared before Lindemann's *Holding and Letting Go*, her performative analysis is prefigured in her earlier work as well, which would have been available to him.

51. Lindemann, x.

52. Lindemann.

53. Lindemann, xiii.

54. Velleman, *How We Get Along*, 60.

55. "Reasoning such that being its (actual or possible) conclusion is what makes something an action" (Velleman, 30).

56. Velleman, 203–206.

57. Hilde Lindemann, *Damaged Identities, Narrative Repair* (Ithaca: Cornell University Press, 2001).

58. Velleman, *How We Get Along*, 11 (emphasis mine).

59. Lindemann, *Holding*, 204.
60. Lindemann, 22, 97–102.
61. Lindemann, 98.

Chapter Three

1. It is *poetological* and not simply *poetical* because it relies on the science or knowledge—the *logos*—of poetry. Penelope as weaver is the ultimate poet, but as an interpreter she is also the ultimate scholar of poetry.

2. This is evidenced by Seneca's epistle 88.8, which will receive greater attention later in this chapter. See Seneca, *Epistles 66–92*, trans. Richard M. Gummere, Loeb Classical Library 76 (Cambridge, Mass.: Harvard University Press, 1920).

3. Kostas Myrsiades, ed., "Special Issue: Early Recognition in Homer's *Odyssey*," *College Literature* 38, no. 2 (2011): i–xi, 1–185.

4. There is no space for an exhaustive summary of all scholars' positions on this question here. Lillian Eileen Doherty provides a helpful discussion of the scholarship in *Siren Songs: Gender, Audiences, and Narrators in the Odyssey* (Ann Arbor: University of Michigan Press, 1995), 31–63.

5. The case for early recognition has been convincingly made by Philip Whaley Harsh, "Penelope and Odysseus in *Odyssey* XIX," *American Journal of Philology* 71, no. 1 (1950): 1–21; Robert Fitzgerald's "Postscript" in his translation of Homer's *The Odyssey* (New York: Vintage Books, 1990), 499–506; Eva Brann, *Homeric Moments* (Philadelphia: Paul Dry, 2002), 274–284; and John Vlahos, "Homer's *Odyssey*: Penelope and the Case for Early Recognition," *College Literature* 38, no. 2 (2011): 1–75.

6. Anne Amory, "The Reunion of Odysseus and Penelope," in *Essays on the Odyssey: Selected Modern Criticism*, ed. Charles H. Taylor Jr. (Bloomington: Indiana University Press, 1963), 103.

7. Amory, 104–105. Other examples of this kind of interpretation include Norman Austin, *Archery at the Dark of the Moon: Poetic Problems in Homer's Odyssey* (Berkeley: University of California Press, 1975), 205–238; and Joseph Russo, "Interview and Aftermath: Dream, Fantasy, and Intuition in Odyssey 19 and 20," *American Journal of Philology* 103, no. 1 (1982): 4–18.

8. Russo, 10–11.

9. Sheila Murnaghan, "Penelope's *Agnoia*: Knowledge, Power, and Gender in the *Odyssey*," in *Homer's Odyssey*, ed. Lillian E. Doherty (Oxford: Oxford University Press, 2009), 245.

10. Murnaghan, 244.

11. Helene P. Foley, "Penelope as Moral Agent," in *The Distant Staff: Representing the Female in Homer's* Odyssey, ed. Beth Cohen (Oxford: Oxford University Press, 1995), 96.

12. Richard Heitman, *Taking Her Seriously: Penelope & the Plot of Homer's Odyssey* (Ann Arbor: University of Michigan Press, 2005), 10.

13. Erich Auerbach, *Mimesis: The Representation of Reality in Western Literature*, trans. Willard Trask (Garden City: Doubleday, 1953), 1–19. See criticisms of this claim below. To illustrate his point, curiously enough, Auerbach chooses the washing scene with the discovery and interjected story of Odysseus's distinctive scar—the very episode in which others contend that Homer subtly suggests Penelope's hidden recognition.

14. In an ingenious exegesis, Steve Reece combines a case for late recognition with an argument for the poem's narrative complexity. He posits other versions of the story that would have been familiar to archaic audiences in which Penelope explicitly recognizes Odysseus early and hypothesizes that the narrator of the *Odyssey* plays with these expectations to create suspense in the oral performance of the poem. He dubs this position "neoanalysis with an oral twist" ("Penelope's 'Early Recognition' of Odysseus from a Neoanalytic and Oral Perspective," *College Literature* 38, no. 2 [2011]: 110).

15. Marylin A. Katz, *Penelope's Renown: Meaning and Indeterminacy in the Odyssey* (Princeton: Princeton University Press, 1991), 194.

16. Katz, 3–19, 113, 192–195.

17. Doherty, *Siren Songs*, 191.

18. Doherty, 192, 145.

19. For earlier scholars of the analyst school, the same contradictions were proof of the multiple authorship of the *Odyssey*. See, for example, Wolfgang Schadewaldt, *Neue Kriterien zur Odyssee-Analyse: Die Wiedererkennung des Odysseus und der Penelope* (Heidelberg: Carl Winter Universitätsverlag, 1959).

20. See men from Agamemnon (*Od*, 24.192–198) to Heitman, *Taking Her Seriously*.

21. Georg Christoph Lichtenberg, *Sudelbüche*, E/213, in *Schriften Und Briefe*, ed. Franz Heinrich Mautner (Frankfurt am Main: Insel Verlag, 1983).

22. Most of the *Odyssey* is focalized through the implied rhapsodic narrator. Sometimes other characters receive embedded focalization. Sometimes Odysseus is the focalizer. Rarely is the narration focalized through Penelope, and never when the experience of her recognition is in question. See Irene de Jong, *Narratological Commentary on the Odyssey* (Cambridge: Cambridge University Press, 2001), 458–482.

23. In a dream or vision Odysseus has in the night after his interview with his wife, it seems that Penelope is standing by him "*having recognized him already*" (*gignōskousa*)—perhaps it is Odysseus, then, who "subconsciously" suspects that Penelope knows who he is (*Od*, 20.94; my emphasis).

24. Recall that Aristotle claims that anagnorisis can take place not only between persons but also in relation to objects and "whether or not someone has done something" (*P*, 11, 1452a, 36)—in this case, whether Penelope has recognized Odysseus.

25. "Ignorance evolving toward knowledge" is a good formula for the explication of anagnorisis offered here with the help of Aristotle and Homer. At best, the activity of recognition is asymptotic in approaching knowledge between people. By extension, all interpersonal recognition repeats this action in indeterminacy, though of course the stakes in daily life are rarely as dramatic or open to potential heroism as in the *Odyssey*.

26. See Barbara Clayton, *A Penelopean Poetics: Reweaving the Feminine in Homer's Odyssey* (Lanham: Lexington Books, 2003), 21–52; and Gregory Nagy, *Masterpieces of Metonymy: From Ancient Greek Times to Now* (Washington, D.C.: Center for Hellenic Studies, 2015), 4§127.

27. It is not surprising that strategies of reading should be intimately connected to practices of recognition: *anagnōsis*, a word related to *anagnōrisis*, means "recognition" as well as "reading." It comes from the verb *anagignōskein* ("*to know again, recognize: to acknowledge* . . . of written characters, *to know* them *again*, and so *to read*"; *LS*, 53, italics in original).

28. "The weaving, unweaving, and reweaving of the shroud parallel the poetic process of oral composition itself" (Clayton, *Penelopean Poetics*, 35).

29. Olga Levaniouk, *Eve of the Festival: Making Myth in Odyssey 19*, Hellenic Studies 46 (Cambridge, Mass.: Center for Hellenic Studies, Harvard University Press, 2011).

30. Aristotle, *The* Poetics *of Aristotle: Translation and Commentary*, trans. Stephen Halliwell (London: Duckworth, 1987), 144.

31. The first example Aristotle offers of this type of recognition is from Euripides's *Iphigenia among the Taurians*, in which Orestes blurts out his true identity to his sister after she has revealed herself through the artful and beautifully natural plot device of requesting Pylades take a letter to her brother. Aristotle goes so far as to name Orestes's action a fault (*hamartia*), since "he might have brought along some token or other" (*exēn gar an enia kai enegkein*; *P*, 16, 1454b, 35). It is tempting to read this as a rare instance of Aristotelian humor: surely he cannot seriously be suggesting that Euripides should have made Orestes pack several tokens to prove his identity during his travels on the off chance he should ever run into a long-lost loved one so that their reunion could be more artful. Imagine the situation: you have just realized that the woman before you is the sister you have long believed to be dead. The most likely—and Aristotle was a stickler for likelihood in fiction—reaction is joyfully to cry out "I am your brother!" In fact, any other reaction (such as fishing around for more artistic means of revelation) would be decidedly improbable and therefore no part of a good plot as Aristotle defines it.

32. On difference within tokens of identity, see Simon Goldhill, *The Poet's Voice: Essays on Poetics and Greek Literature* (Cambridge: Cambridge University Press, 1991), 19.

33. It would be anachronistic to project modern notions of verisimilitude on archaic epic, but for one reader in classical times, at least, naturalness and plausibility were requirements of good storytelling. For Aristotle, a plot only achieves the desired effect of striking wonder if the surprising reversal comes about through likely and believable events.

34. This is the active feature of Homeric ekphrasis praised by Lessing over Virgil's passive descriptions of objects (See *Laokoon*, chap. 18, in Gotthold Ephraim Lessing, *Werke und Briefe in zwölf Bänden*, vol. 5.2 [Frankfurt am Main: Deutscher Klassiker Verlag, 1990], 134–137).

35. See Sheila Murnaghan, *Disguise and Recognition in the Odyssey* (Princeton: Princeton University Press, 1987), 98–100.

36. See also Aristotle's *On Memory and Recollection*, where he contrasts the power of memory ("the active holding of an image as a likeness," 451a) with that of recollection (a deliberate search for something known or perceived before that involves reasoning, 453a). Even here, where Aristotle explicitly says that all thinking takes place through images, his language literally externalizes the image by insisting that one set it "before the eyes" (450a). Aristotle, *On the Soul and On Memory and Recollection*, trans. Joe Sachs (Santa Fe: Green Lion, 2004).

37. Lattimore's translation has been modified to be more literal and to better reflect Greek word order.

38. Homer, *Odyssey*, trans. Fitzgerald, 364.

39. See Lane Cooper, "The Fifth Form of 'Discovery' in the *Poetics* of Aristotle," *Classical Philology* 13, no. 3 (1918): 255; Aristotle, *Poetics*, trans. Sachs, 58n67; and Aristotle, Poetics *of Aristotle*, 60n2.

40. This scene serves as the prime example for Auerbach's famous claim that everything is present on the surface and in the foreground in Homer's poetry and that there are no hidden depths or ambiguities (*Mimesis*, chap. 1). See, however, corrections of this oversimplifying claim by Müller-Seidel, Köhnkern, Richardson, and Cave. Especially the latter two are interesting in terms of recognition, as they speculate on the role of *paralogismos* in anagnorisis. Helmut Müller-Seidel, *Versehen und Erkennen: Eine Studie über Heinrich von Kliest* (Köln: Böhlau, 1961), 9–14; Adolf Köhnkern, "Die Narbe des Odysseus," in *Darstellungsziele und Erzählstrategien in antiken Texten* (Berlin: De Gruyter, 2006), 49–63; Terence Cave, *Recognitions: A Study in Poetics* (Oxford: Clarendon, 1988), 22–24, 40–46; N. J. Richardson, "Recognition Scenes in the Odyssey and Ancient Literary Criticism," *Papers of the Liverpool Latin Seminar* 4 (1983): 230ff.

41. It is suggestive in this context to compare the central position of the caesura to Hölderlin's poetics with Paul North's investigation of diversion (*Zerstreuung*) in *The Problem of Distraction* (Stanford: Stanford University Press, 2012). The pregnant pause and the suspense-building diversion share an architecture of focus through interruption. In fact, both are echoed in Athena's divine distraction of Penelope as shown in the following.

42. Action in the face of uncertainty is grounds for Penelope's heroism according to Helene P. Foley, *Female Acts in Greek Tragedy* (Princeton: Princeton University Press, 2001), 127.

43. Cave, *Recognitions*, 43. Cave lays out scholars' claims for both Penelope and Eurycleia as paralogistic reasoners in the "washing scene," but he does not consider the position of the audience.

44. Levaniouk's *Eve of the Festival* demonstrates this in great detail.

45. Stephen Halliwell, *Aristotle's Poetics* (Chicago: University of Chicago Press, 1998), 164.

46. See epistle 88.8 in Seneca, *Epistles 66–92*, 353 (translation modified).

Chapter Four

1. Aristotle, *Aristotle's Poetics*, trans. Hippocrates Apostle, Elizabeth Dobbs, and Morris Parslow (Grinnell: Peripatetic, 1990), 12 (emphasis mine). Other examples of such addenda making friendship and enmity subordinate to knowledge: "bringing characters into" (Aristotle, *P*, 43); "leading toward" (Aristotle, *Poetics*, trans. Joe Sachs [Newburyport: Focus, 2005], 34); "bringing about" (Aristotle, *Aristotle's Poetics: A Translation and Commentary for Students of Literature*, trans. Leon Golden and O. B. Hardison Jr. [Englewood Cliffs: Prentice Hall, 1968], 19); "producing" (Aristotle, *Aristotle's Theory of Poetry and Fine Art, with a Critical Text and Translation of the Poetics*, trans. S. H. Butcher [London: Macmillan, 1895; 5th ed., New York: Dover, 1951], 41). Fuhrmann's authoritative German translation is most egregious in adding this causal language: "Die Widererkennung ist . . . ein Umschlag von Unkenntnis in Kenntnis, mit der Folge, dass Freundschaft oder Feindschaft eintritt" (Recognition is . . . a change from ignorance into knowledge with the consequence that friendship or enmity arises). Aristotle, *Poetik: Griechisch/Deutsch*, trans. and ed. Manfred Fuhrmann (Stuttgart: Reclam, 1982), 35.

2. For example, see translators Seth Benardete and Michael Davis: "Recognition . . . is a change from ignorance to knowledge, whether toward friendship or enmity" (Aristotle, *On Poetics* [South Bend: St. Augustine's Press, 2002], 30).

3. Plato, *Meno* 71e; Plato, *Complete Works*, ed. John M. Cooper (Indianapolis: Hackett, 1997).

4. Polemarchus in Plato's *Republic*, 332ab; Plato, *Complete Works*.

5. For an exhaustive catalog and insightful analysis, see Ruby Blondell, *Helping Friends and Harming Enemies: A Study in Sophocles and Greek Ethics* (Cambridge: Cambridge University Press, 1989), 26–59.

6. For a beautiful meditation on this problem, see Peter Fenves, "Politics of Friendship, Once Again," *Eighteenth-Century Studies* 32, no. 2 (1998): 133–155.

7. For a helpful comparison of Aristotelian versus modern friendship, see Alexander Nehamas, "Aristotelian *Philia*, Modern Friendship?," *Oxford Studies in Ancient Philosophy* 39 (2010): 213–247.

8. Alexander Nehamas, "The Good of Friendship," *Proceedings of the Aristotelian Society* 110, no. 3 (2010): 290.

9. Jacques Derrida, *Politics of Friendship*, trans. George Collins (New York: Verso, 1997), 290–291.

10. See, for example, Derrida, *Politics*, 65, 79, 106.

11. Fred Dallmayr points out this text's significant indebtedness to Levinas in his "Derrida and Friendship," *Critical Review of International Social and Political Philosophy* 2, no. 4 (1999):109.

12. Derrida, *Politics*, 75–106.

13. Derrida, 283.

14. Derrida, 282.

15. See chap. 3 of this book.

16. Some fictions do play with discoveries of hostility or friendship between characters and readers. Think of the revelations in Ian McEwan's *Atonement* (London: Jonathan Cape, 2001) that make many readers suddenly reevaluate their long investment of sympathy with the focalizing Briony, or think of the hated Professor Snape in J. K. Rowling's Harry Potter series, whom the sixth novel convicts of evil murder and betrayal before the seventh installment posthumously exonerates him by proving him to have been a disguised ally to Harry (*Harry Potter and the Half-Blood Prince* [London: Bloomsbury, 2005]; *Harry Potter and the Deathly Hallows* [New York: Arthur A. Levine Books, 2007]). Yet at no point is the reader threatened with anything direr than resentment at the narrator's duplicity or shame at his or her own gullibility.

17. Derrida, *Politics*, 250.

18. Derrida.

19. Three servants are named: Penelope upbraids Melantho for her rude treatment of the beggar (*Od*, 19.90–95), orders Eurynome to prepare him a cozy chair (*Od*, 19.96–99), and commands Eurycleia to wash his feet (*Od*, 19.357).

20. Derrida, *Politics*, 250 (emphasis in the original).

21. Derrida.

22. Derrida, 181. Although Derrida presents this model of friendship through readings of Nietzsche, Blanchot, and others, the articulation of it in *Politics of Friendship* is uniquely Levinasian and can be fairly attributed to Derrida.

23. Although Aristotle's demand for reciprocity in the highest forms of friendship is very clear, Derrida reads passages of the *Eudemian Ethics* that privilege loving over

being loved in order to cast the shadow of dissymmetry back into ancient friendship (Derrida, *Politics*, 9–11).

24. Derrida, 7–11.

25. Derrida, of course, would object to characterizing his interventions as a "conception" of friendship. He insists that the question "What is friendship?" must be replaced with "Who is the friend?" (*Politics*, 293–294). Yet the discursive nature of reading makes inevitable such reductive gestures as the one of which I am guilty here (and which I argue Derrida cannot avoid through his preference for modern friendship despite the mutual aporia he identifies between the two models).

26. Translation modified.

27. Translation modified.

28. Homer, *The Odyssey*, trans. Robert Fitzgerald (New York: Vintage Books, 1990), 354 (emphasis mine).

29. "In the contemplation of action, the friend seems to be nothing more than a mirror for the self; only in speaking together is it possible to discover the differences that individuate us." Ronna Burger, *Aristotle's Dialogue with Socrates: On the* Nicomachean Ethics (Chicago: Chicago University Press, 2008), 182. The principal virtue of *sight* in this respect for Aristotle is friendship's way of making it possible to behold conglomerations of various parts (such as the actions and episodes a person's life) as a whole. This problem becomes a focus of chapter 7 of this book. The virtue of *speech*, meanwhile, the "mirror for the self" provided by friends in the process of self-recognition, is explored in chapters 6 and 10.

30. Translation modified.

31. In order to display how dangerous inequality is for friendship, Aristotle points out the extreme case: no human could ever be friends with a god (*NE*, 1158b–1159a). This claim sheds instructive light on Odysseus's relation with Athena: no matter how darling and entertaining she finds her favorite mortal, no true relation of friendship can exist between them. Sophocles's Odysseus recognizes this well when he refuses to take up Athena's invitation to laugh and gloat over Ajax's demise (*Ajax*, lines 119–126, in *Sophocles I*, Loeb Classical Library 20 [Cambridge, Mass.: Harvard University Press, 1994]).

32. Penelope and Odysseus also need each other in order to become recognizable to the audience. See Helene P. Foley, "'Reverse Similes' and Sex Roles in the *Odyssey*," in *Women in the Ancient World: The* Arethusa *Papers*, ed. John Peradotto and J. P. Sullivan (Albany: State University of New York Press, 1984), 59–78.

33. Jacques Derrida, *Given Time: 1. Counterfeit Money* (Chicago: University of Chicago Press, 1992), 29–30.

34. Paul Ricoeur, *The Course of Recognition*, trans. David Pellauer (Cambridge, Mass.: Harvard University Press, 2005), 153–161; 232–246.

35. Ricoeur, 73.

36. For an opposite take on the consequences of positing Penelope's knowledge, see Sheila Murnaghan, *Disguise and Recognition in the Odyssey* (Princeton: Princeton University Press, 1987), 137ff.

37. Just think how often the disguised beggar Odysseus cites his own (fictional) past generosity to travelers as a reason for the suitors to be generous to him in turn (e.g., *Od*, 17.421).

38. Mutuality rules out such unrequited candidates of selfless gifting and friendship as Alcestis.

39. Derrida, *Politics*, 3–5.

40. For a cogent analysis of the Argos scene in the *Odyssey* and an enlightening comparison of its reception in antiquity and modernity, see Glenn Most, "Ansichten über einen Hund: Zu einigen Strukturen der Homerrezeption zwischen Antike und Neuzeit," *Antike und Abendland* 37 (1991): 144–168.

41. In this context, Socrates's claim in the *Republic* that dogs are philosophers because they love faces they know and hate faces they don't, regardless of how they are treated, could be interesting. In book 2, during his initial discussions with Glaucon about the character (*ēthos*) appropriate for the guardians of the city they have just begun constructing in words, Socrates claims that they ought to be like "pure-bred puppies," since they have to combine the seemingly contradictory dispositions of gentleness and high-spiritedness (375a). Recalling this image of the dog helps solve the apparent paradox because the puppies' "character (*tropos*) by nature [is] to be as gentle as possible with those they're accustomed to and know, but the opposite with those they don't know" (375e). This figure of canine virtue soon also becomes helpful for imagining the nature of philosophers (376a–b). Quoted from Plato, *Republic*, trans. Joe Sachs (Newburyport: Focus, 2007), 66–68.

42. Another way of expressing this difference would be to stress the fact that dogs do not *doubt*—for them, there is no difference between knowledge and opinion. Socrates's praise of them as philosophical is also rooted in their unshakeable devotion to what they *know* and their hostility to all they are ignorant of. But uncertainty is an unavoidable part of dealings between humans. Odysseus and Penelope share a strong dose of healthy skepticism about the performances of the people around them, which is why they are so good at the game of recognition, both as actors and as interpreting spectators.

43. I do not wish to make any kind of scientific claim about animal cognition here. Argos and dogs play a metaphorical role about the limits of human understanding in my argument; I do not pretend to know what an actual dog thinks, feels, or is capable of.

44. For thoughtful consideration of the Argos scene in terms of signs, see Simon Goldhill, *The Poet's Voice: Essays on Poetics and Greek Literature* (Cambridge: Cambridge University Press, 1991), 12–13; and Peter Gainsford, "Formal Analysis of Recognition Scenes in the *Odyssey*," *Journal of Hellenic Studies* 123 (2003): 57.

45. For a concise explanation of how this reading is due to pre-sixteenth-century editorial mistakes in the manuscript transmission of Diogenes's *Lives of the Philosophers*, see Giorgio Agamben, "The Friend," in *What Is an Apparatus? And Other Essays* (Stanford: Stanford University Press, 2009), 2–7.

46. Aristotle, *Rhetoric*, trans. Joe Sachs (Newburyport: Focus, 2009), bk. 2, chap. 13, 216 (1389b).

Chapter Five

1. Emphasis is mine to show the corresponding phrase in Greek. All full translations of the *Poetics* I have consulted follow this interpretation. The sole exception is Stephen Halliwell, who translates the clause: "concerning matters which bear on their prosperity or affliction" (Aristotle, *The* Poetics *of Aristotle: Translation and Commentary*, trans. Stephen Halliwell [London: Duckworth, 1987], 43). Halliwell's otherwise admirably clear and

insightful translation is puzzling here. His clause seems to modify two opposing antecedents and to be at once an objective and subjective genitive. On the one hand, recognition is a change from ignorance into knowledge "concerning matters which bear on . . ."; on the other hand, the added possessive pronoun "*their* prosperity or affliction" points back to the friends or enemies disjunction. Halliwell's final clause thus straddles the preceding elements of the definition and simultaneously refers to the *object* of recognition (what people come to know) and its *subject* (who is coming to know). This choice could be seen as an attempt to preserve the ambiguity present in Aristotle's Greek, but instead of allowing for *either* an objective *or* a subjective genitive, Halliwell's translation simultaneously forces *both*. This syntax unduly strains the logic of the action.

2. John MacFarlane, "Aristotle's Definition of Anagnorisis," *American Journal of Philology* 121, no. 3 (2000): 372 (emphasis in the original). The entire point of MacFarlane's article is to argue for this interpretation of the final clause.

3. Martha Craven Nussbaum, *The Fragility of Goodness: Luck and Ethics in Greek Tragedy and Philosophy* (Cambridge: Cambridge University Press, 1986), 3.

4. Nussbaum's reductive readings of Plato are less persuasive.

5. See Gerhard Neumann, "Erkennungs-Szene: Wahrnehmung zwischen den Geschlechtern im literarischen Text," in *Differenzen in der Geschlechterdifferenz—Differences within Gender Studies: Aktuelle Perspektiven der Geschlechterforschung*, ed. Kati Röttger and Heike Pau (Berlin: Erich Schmidt, 1999), 202–221; Neumann, "Die Entdeckung des Fremden: Goethe als Ethnograph," in *A Palavra e o Canto: Miscelânea de Homenagem a Rita Iriarte* (Lissabon: Edições Colibri, 2000), 85–94; and Neumann, "Erkennungsszene und Opferritual in Goethes Iphigenie und in Kleists Penthesilea," *Käthchen und seine Schwestern: Frauenfiguren im Drama um 1800*, ed. Günther Emig and Anton Philipp Knittel (Heilbronn: Stadtbücherei, 2000), 38–80.

6. See Gerhard Neumann, "Kleists ethnologisches Experiment: Zur Fetischisierung der Erkennungs-Szene in der Penthesilea," in *Kultur-Schreiben als romantisches Projekt: Romantische Ethnographie im Spannungsfeld zwischen Imagination und Wissenschaft*, ed. David Wellbery and Alexander von Bormann (Würzburg: Königshausen and Neumann, 2012), 155–156.

7. Presenting new conceptions as an interpretation of Aristotle is an age-old rhetorical device. Eighteenth-century critics such as Lessing and Goethe, for instance, invoke the authority of Aristotle for their clearly original ideas about literary theory. The attraction of contemporary scholars to this same strategy is more surprising but still popular. Like Neumann, Elinor Fuchs presents a highly original theory of dramatic recognition as an interpretation of the *Poetics* ("Waiting for Recognition: An Aristotle for 'Non-Aristotelian' Drama," *Modern Drama* 50, no. 4 [2007]: 533–534). A certain tradition of Aristotelian scholars may well level the same criticism at the present book.

8. See, for example, Carol Dougherty, *The Raft of Odysseus: The Ethnographic Imagination of Homer's* Odyssey (Oxford: Oxford University Press, 2001).

9. Many of the adventures in between can be read in this vein as well—just think how life among the Lotus-eaters stages the danger, ever-present to colonists far away from home, of forgetting the values of and ties to one's original culture.

10. See, for instance, *The Distaff Side: Representing the Female in Homer's Odyssey*, ed. Beth Cohen (New York: Oxford University Press, 1995); and Lillian Eileen Doherty, *Siren*

Songs: Gender, Audiences, and Narrators in the Odyssey (Ann Arbor: University of Michigan Press, 1995).

11. I do not mean to suggest that Circe's island represents any particular culture, but its initial dangerous hostility to the Ithacan travelers is evident.

12. J. L. Austin excludes performative utterances in fictional or theatrical contexts from consideration: they are "parasitic," "hollow," or "void" (*How to Do Things with Words* [Oxford: Clarendon, 1962], 22).

13. See Jacques Derrida, "Signature, Event, Context," in *Limited Inc.* (Evanston: Northwestern University Press, 1988), 1–21.

14. The Nausicaa episode is hence a good illustration of the nuanced emendations of Judith Butler's concept of gender as performance by Karen Bassi and Anne Duncan. Judith Butler's rejection of any biological (i.e., given by fate) ground to gender would make individuals unlimited agents of their own identities (*Gender Trouble: Feminism and the Subversion of Identity* [New York: Routledge, 1990], 128–141). Karen Bassi and Anne Duncan show how the theater and performed epic poetry invite a conscious negotiation of the fateful and free components of identity (Bassi, *Acting like Men: Gender, Drama, and Nostalgia in Ancient Greece* [Ann Arbor: University of Michigan Press, 1998], 5–8, 41; Duncan, *Performance and Identity in the Classical World* [Cambridge: Cambridge University Press, 2006], 10).

15. Later authors will not be able to resist converting this into a "love at first sight" scene as well (cf. Goethe's unfinished drama *Nausikaa*; HA, vol. 5).

16. This is precisely the function that Friedrich Schiller gives to the idyll in his enumeration of types of "sentimental" poetry ("Über naive und sentimentalische Dichtung," in *Theoretische Schriften*, ed. Rolf-Peter Janz [Frankfurt am Main: Deutscher Klassiker Verlag, 2008], 706–810). Homer is his preeminent example of a naive poet, and so the sentimentalizing potential of the Phaeacian books of the *Odyssey* (further emphasized in the self-referentiality of the scenes with the singer Demodokos as well as in Odysseus's own rhapsodizing self-narrations) challenges Schiller's theory in an interesting way. Peter Szondi, with very different examples, carries the implications of this challenge to their ultimate conclusion with his formula: "the naïve *is* the sentimental." See Peter Szondi, "Das Naive ist das Sentimentalische," in *Lektüren und Lektionen: Versuche über Literatur, Literaturtheorie und Litertatursoziologie* (Frankfurt am Main: Suhrkamp, 1973), 47–99; and Szondi, *Poetik und Geschichtsphilosophie I* (Frankfurt am Main: Suhrkamp, 1974), 149–183.

17. Homer, *The Odyssey*, trans. Robert Fitzgerald (New York: Vintage Books, 1990), 239.

18. *Euthyphro* 10a, in Plato, *Complete Works*, ed. John M. Cooper (Indianapolis: Hackett, 1997), 9.

19. Murnaghan, "The Plan of Athena," in *The Distaff Side: Representing the Female in Homer's* Odyssey, ed. Beth Cohen (New York: Oxford University Press, 1995), 61.

20. The poem simultaneously works to subvert the very power structures it ostensibly upholds, as the previous two chapters suggest.

21. Homer, *Odyssey*, trans. Fitzgerald, 186.

22. Recognition is not an issue at all for Elpenor: Odysseus sees him and laments, but the usual verbs of knowing and recognizing are absent from their entire encounter. Tiresias, on the other hand, although he could never have seen Odysseus before while alive,

immediately knows who he is: "*eme d' egnō kai proseeipen*" (he knew who I was and spoke to me; *Od*, 11.91). Tiresias's recognition of him is surprising enough at least for Odysseus to mention the fact of it with this verb of knowledge; the equally improbable circumstance that Odysseus also recognizes the previously unseen Tiresias goes entirely unremarked in his narration (though one might surmise that the "golden staff" Odysseus mentions might somehow have been a sign of the prophet's identity).

23. Curiously, although nearly all translators render this as "speak," the verb *enipein* means "to berate, chide, admonish." Can the dead not speak truly without recrimination?

24. Only Ajax refrains from approaching the pit and drinking—and this very refusal indicates that, unlike all the other spirits from Odysseus's past, he must be able to recognize the Ithacan from afar and without the libation. Does this mean that alone among human passions, envy and resentment survive death? Not even a mother's love allowed Anticlea to know her son unaided by the bloody potation; but Ajax's wounded pride over the allotment of Achilles's armor to Odysseus is strong enough to allow him to sense his perceived foe from beyond the grave.

Part II

1. See Stephen Greenblatt, *Renaissance Self-Fashioning: From More to Shakespeare* (Chicago: University of Chicago Press, 1980); and Harold Bloom, *Shakespeare: The Invention of the Human* (New York: Riverhead Books, 1998). For a less bombastic articulation of the essentialist position, see Terry G. Sherwood, *The Self in Early Modern Literature: For the Common Good* (Pittsburgh: Duquesne University Press, 2007).

2. For a helpful survey of Odysseus figures in literature up through the mid-twentieth century, see W. B. Stanford, *The Ulysses Theme: A Study in the Adaptability of a Traditional Hero* (1963; repr., Ann Arbor: University of Michigan Press, 1976).

3. See Hans Blumenberg, *Work on Myth*, trans. Robert M. Wallace (Cambridge, Mass.: MIT Press, 1985).

4. For variations of this narrative of the history of selfhood, see August Wilhelm von Schlegel, "Rezension zu Homers Werke von Voss," in *Dokumente zur Theorie der Übersetzung antiker Literatur in Deutschland seit 1800*, ed. J. Kitzbichler et al. (Berlin: De Gruyter, 2009), 7; Charles M. Taylor, *Sources of the Self: The Making of the Modern Identity* (Cambridge, Mass.: Harvard University Press, 1989); Raymond Martin and John Barresi, *Rise and Fall of the Soul and Self: An Intellectual History of Personal Identity* (New York: Columbia University Press, 2006); Rüdiger Campe and Julia Weber, eds., *Rethinking Emotion: Interiority and Exteriority in Pre-modern, Modern, and Contemporary Thought* (Berlin: De Gruyter, 2014), 1–18.

5. This enlightened view of the fractured self is true only for the elite cognoscenti who read James Joyce, Michel Foucault, or W. G. Sebald—not for the popular masses who are supposedly still ensconced in their Disney-induced illusions of real selves. Interestingly, this situation is the mirror image of the Renaissance Neoplatonists, who treasured their esoteric doctrine of the unity of the self in contrast to the fluid, volatile view of selfhood required for conducting practical affairs among the hoi polloi.

Chapter Six

1. Michel Foucault, *The Hermeneutics of the Subject: Lectures at the Collège De France, 1981–1982*, ed. Frédéric Gros et al. (New York: Palgrave Macmillan, 2005), 3–5.

2. Plato, *Plato's Sophist*, trans. Eva Brann et al. (Newburyport: Focus, 1996), 259D.

3. Hereafter this is referred to simply as *Alcibiades*.

4. This contention is one of the principle differences between my reading and that of Nancy Selleck, who sees Shakespeare's mirror imagery as rejecting Neoplatonic teachings about the soul and knowledge (*The Interpersonal Idiom in Shakespeare, Donne, and Early Modern Culture* [New York: Palgrave Macmillan, 2008], 94ff.). She is certainly right to point out this contrast in most cases, but as will become evident, *Alcibiades*—the text Neoplatonists considered the best introduction to their mystery—proves to be equally ambivalent about visual epistemology and the knowability of the self as Shakespeare's most unsettling scenes.

5. Foucault, *Hermeneutics of the Subject*, 65–71.

6. Foucault, 77–78.

7. Though, surprisingly, Foucault does not comment on the aporetic potential of the dialogue in revealing the problematic nature of its beautiful vision of self-knowledge.

8. See Ernst H. Kantorowicz's genealogy of the foundational Tudor political theory of the king's two bodies, which climaxes in a study of its echoes through Richard II: *The King's Two Bodies: A Study in Medieval Political Theology* (Princeton: Princeton University Press, 1957), 7–86.

9. Think of Queen Elizabeth's pregnant claim—realized with the visceral experience of watching the play rather than with the historical erudition of Kantorowicz's scholarship—"I am Richard II. Know ye not that?" (quoted in Charles Forker's introduction to Shakespeare, *Richard II*, ed. Charles Forker [London: Arden Shakespeare, 2004], 5).

10. See Ruby Blondell, *The Play of Character in Plato's Dialogues* (Cambridge: Cambridge University Press, 2002).

11. Interestingly, some readers have even equated Shakespeare with his Ulysses. E. M. W. Tillyard, for instance, quotes Ulysses's speech on degree as the unquestionable worldview not only of Shakespeare but of all his contemporaries (*The Elizabethan World Picture* [New York: Vintage Books, 1943], 9ff.). Yet the dramatic context of this speech forces one to question every irony-laden sentence. If read closely, it leads to a terrifying proto-Hobbesian vision of humanity (see Hugh Grady, *Shakespeare's Universal Wolf: Studies in Early Modern Reification* [Oxford: Clarendon, 1996], 58–94)—hardly the conformist Tudor worldview. George Bernard Shaw expresses the tendency well: "Ulysses, eminently 'respectable,' imposed by his gravity on the rest, as he imposed on his commentators, who had taken him to be 'Shakespeare drawn by Shakespeare himself'" (*Shakespeare, Troilus and Cressida: A Casebook*, ed. Priscilla Martin [London: Macmillan, 1976], 59). In one way, at least, Shakespeare's Ulysses is like his author: neither leaves any trace of personal intentions or convictions.

12. On the banishment of poetry from the Republic, see John White, "Afterword: Imitation," in Plato, *Republic*, trans. Joe Sachs (Newburyport: Focus, 2007), 323–346.

13. The *Phaedrus* itself showcases many ways in which written dialogues as well even as the unavoidable mediations of direct conversation still share in the dangers inherent in textuality.

14. For a persuasive account of Aristotelian catharsis as a form of aporetic wonder, see the introduction to Sachs's translation of Aristotle's *Poetics* (Newburyport: Focus, 2005), 10–17. See also chapter 8 of this book.

15. See David Bevington's note to 3.3.96ff., in *TC*, 365.

16. See Nicholas Denyer's introduction to Plato, *Alcibiades*, ed. Nicholas Denyer (Cambridge: Cambridge University Press, 2001), 14ff. All Greek citations are from this edition.

17. D. S. Hutchinson, "Introduction to *Alcibiades*," in *Al*, 558.

18. In fact, the Platonic authenticity of *Alcibiades* has had a few recent champions among classicists. For a thorough account of the authorship debate, see Denyer's introduction to Plato, *Alcibiades*, 14–25.

19. See Eric Mallin, "Emulous Factions and the Collapse of Chivalry: *Troilus and Cressida*," *Representations* 29 (Winter 1990):145–179. Mallin cleverly argues that both Achilles and Hector can be read as portraits of Essex, which alternately exhort and satirize the earl.

20. These parallels are further reinforced when one considers George Chapman's dedication of his *Iliads* to the Earl of Essex. The language of this dedication, in which Chapman expressly offers Achilles as both a natural comparison and future role model for his patron, Essex—with its revealingly self-contradictory insistence on the absolute division between body and soul, its curiously framed injunction to self-knowledge, and its professed fear of corruption through the desire to please the masses—reads like a convoluted mishmash of Socrates's advice to Alcibiades in Plato's dialog. This observation tempts one to read *Troilus and Cressida* as a ridiculous farce of Chapman's travesty of *Alcibiades* no less than as an intelligent commentary on the dialogue itself.

21. That is, Agamemnon, the Athenian assembly, and Elizabeth I, respectively.

22. In fact, after Odysseus returns unsuccessful from Achilles's tent at the end of book 9, Diomedes makes the precise suggestion that his buddy-in-trickery, Ulysses, will employ in *Troilus and Cressida*: "Would God, Atrides, thy request were yet to undertake, / And all thy gifts unoffered him! He's proud enough beside, / But this ambassage thou hast sent will make him burst with pride. / But let us suffer him to stay or go at his desire" (*Il*, 9.697–703, quoted here from Homer, *The Iliad*, trans. George Chapman [Princeton: Princeton University Press, 1956], 9.653–656). The line numbers of Chapman's translation diverge from the Greek. I quote Chapman's Homer in this chapter not out of any Keatsian sentimental attachment but because it is the version that Shakespeare would have had access to as he wrote *Troilus and Cressida*.

23. René Girard, *A Theater of Envy: William Shakespeare* (Oxford: Oxford University Press, 1991), chaps. 14–18.

24. One might call this is a strategy of reverse anagnorisis: Socrates first shows Alcibiades that he is a friend and then that he knows who Alcibiades really is. Insofar as Socrates attempts to implement a pedagogy of recognition, he is already involved in complications that make it suspect as a device of education or manipulation.

25. This is all the more so since Socrates says that only by knowing "the itself itself" can we come to know what a man is (or, in fact, anything itself), yet he proceeds to address the lesser and subsidiary question without tackling the more fundamental issue.

26. Foucault, *Hermeneutics of the Self*, 77.

27. For a beautiful and incisive meditation on the knowledge of self and others in Shakespeare, see Stanley Cavell, "The Avoidance of Love: A Reading of *King Lear*," in *Disowning Knowledge in Six Plays of Shakespeare* (Cambridge: Cambridge University Press, 1987), 39–124. Cavell reveals the polymorphous "avoidance of recognition" as the engine for the entire tragedy (46). Terrifyingly, true recognition of the other is predicated on acknowledgment of the other's honest recognition of the self (50, 72–73). No characters in *Troilus and Cressida* attain this kind of mutually vulnerable and redemptive recognition, and the play even calls the very possibility of "deep" interpersonal knowledge into question. Perhaps this radical superficiality contributes to the generic ambivalence of *Troilus and Cressida*: scholars and audiences are reluctant to grant this "problem play" the august designation of tragic depth.

28. Of course it is doubtful whether "personal versus political ends" would have had the same meaning for audiences of Homer and Shakespeare (or even for the earliest audiences of the Homeric poems and those in Classical Athens or later antiquity). The *oikos* versus *polis* [family/home versus city/state] distinction of Attic thinking is certainly very different from the vying claims of personal virtue and court politics in Early Modern England. But it is nevertheless significant that Shakespeare presents a Ulysses who, unlike Odysseus in the *Iliad*, is radically removed from any expression without rhetorical import.

29. Again, a historical caveat is needed: perhaps this is a kind of theatricality that is only possible in a Machiavellian world in which sovereignty is exercised from a small, central place: the court.

30. Alexander Leggatt, *Shakespeare's Tragedies: Violation and Identity* (Cambridge: Cambridge University Press, 2005), 2–7.

31. I do not mean to suggest that Plato's Socrates is ever as thoroughly soulless as Shakespeare's Ulysses. Despite his delightful impishness and hobgoblin's gift of hiding behind his winking pedagogical designs, it is hard to miss Socrates's demonstrable concern for many of his interlocutors. There are few more touching scenes in literature than his solicitous conversations with Phaedrus, for example, or with his followers before his death in the *Phaedo*. Ulysses is the epitome—and indictment—of several negating tendencies inherent in Plato's dialogues, but he by no means contains all of Socrates. For a fuller understanding of Socrates's complex paternal love for the disappointing and ultimately hateful Alcibiades, one would have to examine the relationship of Falstaff, whom Harold Bloom dubs "the Socrates of Eastcheap," with Hal (*Shakespeare: The Invention of the Human* [New York: Riverhead Books, 1998], 275).

32. Bloom, 330.

33. Of course there are important differences between the "self itself" that Socrates proposes but fails to investigate in *Alcibiades* and the notions of "self" that famously began to emerge in the Renaissance. But it is plausible to imagine that the consequences of neglecting the philosophical questions posed by Socrates will lead ultimately the same kind of moral bankruptcy for which the historical Alcibiades is notorious and which Shakespeare's Ulysses masterfully manipulates.

34. For a very suggestive reading of the "battle" between identity and subjectivity that is waged in the play, see Linda Charnes, "'So Unsecret to Ourselves': Notorious Identity and the Material Subject in Shakespeare's *Troilus and Cressida*," *Shakespeare Quarterly* 40 (Winter 1989): 413–440.

35. For explorations of the mirror imagery in Shakespeare's plays and poems with fascinating results, see two recent studies: Amy Cook extrapolates Hamlet's injunction that actors should "hold as 'twere the mirror up to nature" (*Hamlet*, 3.2.22) in terms of how cognitive science understands aesthetic operations (*Shakespearean Neuroplay: Reinvigorating the Study of Dramatic Texts and Performance through Cognitive Science* [New York: Palgrave Macmillan, 2010], 43–63). Selleck, meanwhile, cites the many instances of mirroring in Shakespeare's plays and sonnets in order to prove her general thesis that the Renaissance construction of self was radically interpersonal—that the genesis of identity only takes place in the active search for reflection of self in others (*Interpersonal Idiom*, 89–122). I agree with Selleck in her concern to show how Shakespeare's use of mirror imagery rejects the subjective, visually centered epistemology of Renaissance Neoplatonism and emphasizes instead the interpersonal creation of self(s). On the one hand, however, I hope to show that the Neoplatonists' favored "gateway text" to their mysteries, Plato's *Alcibiades*, already voices unease with the simplistic equations of Neoplatonism. On the other hand, I also argue that Plato's and Shakespeare's texts demonstrate the difficulties inherent in both notions of selfhood. Certainly self-knowledge is necessarily interpersonal—Plato's dialogues already show that with aplomb—but where does this material interpersonality leave the status of self-knowledge and knowledge of others? This is the question that drives this chapter. In regarding such mirroring scenes as instances of dramatic recognition, I am led to conclusions about their structure, inner workings, and roles within the larger play that go further to tie the textual mirrorings between characters (Selleck) to the aesthetic function of the plays as wholes (Cook, *Shakespearean Neuroplay*). In a way, then, my insistence on the anagnorisis formula builds a bridge between Selleck's understanding of identity and Cook's appreciation of cognitive blending in the apprehension of performances.

36. *Il*, trans. Chapman, 9.306–311.

37. Shakespeare, *Henry IV, Part 1* (5.1.127–140), ed. David Scott Kastan (London: Arden Shakespeare, 2002).

38. Interestingly, in Plutarch, Socrates's heroic actions in battle save Alcibiades's life, and it is precisely Socrates's insistence on giving Alcibiades the public honor of his own actions that later inspire the younger man to return the favor. This is perhaps the most productive kind of emulative mirroring that any account of the two men's relation offers. Plato's Socrates is clearly compromised at least partially by the narcissistic elements of his erotic desire to seduce Alcibiades into striving to imitate his own philosophical image.

39. Selleck points out many of the parallels to these arguments of Ulysses in Shakespeare's sonnets (*Interpersonal Idiom*, 99, 111–220).

40. "Time hath, my lord, a wallet at his back, / Wherein he puts alms for oblivion, / A great-sized monster of ingratitudes." The speech goes on to list the many personal attributes and virtues that are "subjects all / To envious and calumniating Time": "beauty, wit, / High birth, vigour of bone, desert in service, / Love, friendship, charity" (*TC*, 3.3.146–189).

41. Girard, *Theater of Envy*, 157.

42. Girard, 147.

43. See glossary entry on *hexis* in Aristotle, *Nicomachean Ethics*, trans. Joe Sachs (Newburyport: Focus, 2002), 201.

Chapter Seven

1. “Goethe’s structuring persona is Ulysses. . . . The journey is Goethe’s *Urmythos*.” Jane K. Brown, “Goethe: From my Life: Poetry and Truth,” from *Handbuch der Autobiographie und Selbstfiktion*, ed. Martina Wagner-Egelhaaf (Amsterdam: De Gruyter, forthcoming).

2. “Mediterranean wanderings” is a bit of hyperbole: Goethe only made one sea voyage (to Sicily and back) during his Italian sojourn. Yet Goethe often imagines himself in the role of Odysseus, seeing the same sights as the Ithacan hero (cf., *Italienische Reise*, in HA, 11, 241, 266, 298–300, 323).

3. At the microlevel, Goethe’s morphology plays a pivotal role in the development from Kant to Hegel, according to Eckart Förster; see Eckart Förster, *The Twenty-Five Years of Philosophy: A Systematic Reconstruction* (Cambridge, Mass.: Harvard University Press, 2012). At the macrolevel, Goethe’s concept of form opens up a long and dangerous history of Gestalt thinking according to Annette Simonis; see her *Gestalttheorie von Goethe bis Benjamin: Diskursgeschichte einer deutschen Denkfigur* (Köln: Böhlau, 2001). For insightful studies of the consequences and implications of Goethe’s morphological thinking, see Kirk Wetters, *Demonic History from Goethe to the Present* (Evanston: Northwestern University Press, 2014), 39–57; Eva Geulen, *Aus dem Leben der Form: Goethes Morphologie und die Nager* (Berlin: August Verlag, 2016); and David Wellbery, “Form und Idee: Skizze eines Begriffsfeldes um 1800,” in *Morphologie und Moderne: Goethes ‘Anschauliches Denken’ in den Geistes- und Kulturwissenschaften seit 1800*, ed. Jonas Maatsch (Berlin: De Gruyter, 2014), 17–43.

4. For the historical details, see Nicholas Boyle, *Goethe: The Poet and the Age, Revolution and Renunciation* (Oxford: Clarendon, 2000), 2:218–237 and the footnotes 837–838; and Goethe, *Begegnungen und Gespräche*, ed. Ernst Grumach and Renate Grumach (Berlin: De Gruyter, 1980), 4:97–99.

5. “gelähmt.” “Bund, der ununterbrochen gedauert, und für uns und andere manches Gute gewirkt hat” (HA, 10, 541).

6. “Nach meiner Rückkunft aus Italien . . . fand ich neuere und ältere Dichterwerke in großem Ansehen, von ausgebreiteter Wirkung, leider solche, die mich äußerst anwiderten, ich nenne nur Heinses ‘Ardinghello’ und Schillers ‘Räuber.’ Jener war mir verhaßt, weil . . . , dieser, weil ein kraftvolles, aber unreifes Talent gerade die ethischen und theatralischen Paradoxen, von denen ich mich zu reinigen gestrebt, recht im vollen hinreißenden Strome über das Vaterland ausgegossen hatte” (HA, 10, 538). This passage is especially interesting in the context of recognition (*anagnorisis*) since it shows that Goethe also recognized *himself* (at an earlier *Bildungstufe* [stage of development]) in Schiller. The manner in which Schiller presented Goethe with a mirror image of his earlier self (which he now could recognize as unflattering, immature, and undesirable) is an uncanny encounter that accounts for much of the virulence of Goethe’s reaction.

7. “An keine Vereinigung war zu denken” (HA, 10, 540).

8. “einstmals fand ich Schillern daselbst, wir gingen *zufällig* beide zugleich hinaus, ein Gespräch knüpfte sich an” (HA, 10, 540; emphasis mine). It is only fair to remark, however, that the extent of Goethe’s awareness of the staged nature of this encounter is unclear. It seems that mutual friends who knew that Goethe would be at the lecture encouraged the sedentary homebody Schiller (“whose interest in botany was limited”; Boyle, *Goethe*, 222) to attend in order to facilitate a meeting between the two in congenial circumstances.

9. "Das kann mir sehr lieb sein, daß ich Ideen habe ohne es zu wissen, und sie sogar mit Augen sehe!" (HA, 10, 541).

10. "durch den größten, vielleicht nie ganz zu schlichtenden Wettkampf zwischen Objekt und Subjekt" (HA, 10, 541).

11. In this chapter only, quotations from Aristotle's *Poetics* are from Joe Sachs's translation of *Poetics* (Newburyport: Focus, 2005).

12. "der Punkt, der uns trennte, war dadurch aufs strengste bezeichnet" (HA, 10, 541).

13. See Schiller's famous *Geburtstagsbrief* [birthday letter] with its distillation of each poet's peculiar genius (August 23, 1794) and Goethe's responsive reply (August 27, 1794), in Friedrich Schiller and Johann Wolfgang von Goethe, *Der Briefwechsel zwischen Goethe und Schiller*, ed. Siegfried Seidel (Munich: Beck, 1984), 1:9–12. These first tableaux are still implicit in the elaborate typology of poetry in Schiller's treatise on *Naive und sentimentalische Dichtung* and explicit in Goethe's many later accounts of himself and Schiller as realist versus idealist. I'm not interested in assessing the accuracy of the content of these various models at the moment but rather their structural commonality.

14. Goethe claims that he comes to understand himself in this encounter. For more on the trope of recognizing self in the reflection of a friend, see chapter 6 of this book.

15. "Eine solche muß es doch geben! Woran würde ich sonst erkennen, daß dieses oder jenes Gebilde eine Pflanze sei, wenn sie nicht alle nach einem Muster gebildet wären-?" (HA, 11, 266).

16. "Gestört war mein guter poetischer Vorsatz, der Garten des Alcinous war verschwunden, ein Weltgarten hatte sich aufgetan" (HA, 11, 267).

17. This level of recognition of course will work a bit differently in a read narrative than in a watched play. For the latter, one can (usually) dispense with the very superficial "aha!" moment of guessing which actor is portraying which well-known character ("The one in black must be Hamlet!"). But both are also typified by a spectator's or reader's sense of the trueness of the portrayal, whether in a narrated character sketch or in an acted gesture. Whether one sees Wilhelm Meister acting on stage or reads his character analysis on the page, for instance, one will respond with a "Yes, that's just like Hamlet!" or "No, that's not Hamlet at all!"

18. As a side note, it would be interesting to compare Goethe's *Natürliche Tochter* with his *Iphigenie* in light of this operation. It too is a play on recognition in the sense of acknowledgment as its central action, and all of its characters with the exception of Eugenie [well-born], the daughter to be recognized, are never given names but rather only have general social titles throughout the play.

19. For more on how Aristotle's disdain for spectacle (*opsis*) "seems" more than it "is," see chapters 2 and 8 in this book.

20. But then, this is supposedly precisely what Goethe did when he conceived of his aborted tragedy, *Nausikaa* (HA, 5). Immersing oneself in the immediacy of an episode from an epic runs the risk of conceiving the central story of a tragedy.

21. Golden nicely renders *kathalou* as "in universal form." See *Aristotle's Poetics: A Translation and Commentary for Students of Literature,* trans. and ed. Leon Golden and O. B. Hardison Jr. (Englewood Cliffs: Prentice Hall, 1968), 30.

22. Compare, for instance, Boyle, *Goethe*, 223ff., who takes great pains to point out the historical inaccuracies of the account in "Glückliches Ereignis" only in order to further

challenge the simplified, canonic views Goethe and Schiller present of themselves as "realist" versus "idealist." Compare Boyle's revisionist account with Gisela Horn and Detlef Ignasiak, *"Glückliches Ereignis": Der Arbeitsbund zwischen Goethe und Schiller* (Rudolstadt: Hain Verlag, 1994); and Klaus F. Gille, "'Glückliches Ereignis': Zum Freundschaftsbund zwischen Schiller und Goethe," *Weimarer Beiträge* 48, no. 4 (2004): 520–530. Both of these German monographs accept Goethe's story at face value. The former is a sentimentalizing collection of quotations and pictures from Goethe's and Schiller's independent and mutual engagement with the city of Jena; the latter, despite its title (friendship bond), is much more an analysis of the *Arbeitsbund* (working bond) between the two men, taking off with Goethe's account in "Glückliches Ereignis" and focusing on the exchange of letters about *Wilhelm Meister.* Eckart Förster uses the text instead to illustrate his understanding of Goethe's epistemology ("Goethe and the 'Auge des Geistes,'" *Deutsche Vierteljahrsschrift für Literaturwissenschaft und Geistesgeschichte* 75, no. 1 [2001]: 87–101). Simonis reads it as a confirmation of the totalizing and ideological tendency of Gestalt thinking (*Gestalttheorie*, 57–70).

23. For example, see Horn und Ignasiak, *"Glückliches Ereignis."*

24. This structure of the fourteen paragraphs is reminiscent of a traditional fourteen-line Petrarchan sonnet: roughly, an octet descriptively sets up the problem (1–7), and a sestet then presents the resolution (8–14). Here, the sestet is divided into two tercets: one for the "fortunate event" (8–11) and then one of suggestive reflection (12–14).

25. Remember that for Aristotle, it is the serious subject matter of a story, and not its unhappy outcome, that makes a tragedy. *Iphigenie in Tauris*, where the recognition between Orestes and his sister provide for the reversal from bad to good fortune, is just as "tragic" for Aristotle as *Oedipus* with its change from good to bad. "Glückliches Ereignis" is an example of the former type of tragedy, which Aristotle even describes as the "most powerful" (*P*, 14, 1454a, 5).

26. In fact, one English translator gives up on rendering the conditional structure of this sentence at all, opting instead for a series of indicative declarations: "The happiest moments of my life were experienced during my study of the metamorphosis of plants, as the sequence of their growth gradually became clear to me. This method of regarding the plant world inspired me during my stay at Naples and Sicily; it became more and more precious to me; everywhere I gave myself practice in its application. And these pleasant pursuits were to achieve priceless value by providing the occasion for one of the noblest relationships granted me in my later years." Goethe, *Goethe's Botanical Writings*, trans. Bertha Mueller (Woodbridge: Ox Bow, 1952), 215. This misses the spiraling force of conditionality that winds up the opening sentence like an overloaded spring that will propel the narrative forward.

27. See chapter 1 of this book.

28. "jenen wunderlichen Ausgeburten . . . erschreckte mich, denn ich glaubte all mein Bemühen völlig verloren zu sehen" (HA, 11, 538–539).

29. "Daher denn so viel Treffliches und Albernes sich über die Welt verbreitet, und Verwirrung aus Verwirrung sich entwickelt" (HA, 11, 538).

30. "Gewisse harte Stellen sogar konnte ich direkt auf mich deuten" (HA, 11, 539). These were some rather snide allusions to Goethe's corpulence.

31. "sie zeigten mein Glaubensbekenntnis in einem falschen Lichte" (HA, 11, 539).

32. "Anstatt sie [die große Mutter, die Natur] selbständig, lebendig vom Tiefsten bis zum Höchsten gesetzlich hervorbringend zu betrachten, nahm er sie von der Seite einiger empirischen menschlichen Natürlichkeiten" (HA, 11, 539).

33. Simonis points out the perceptual fallacy of assuming that the appearance of forms, shapes, and continuities implies their underlying presence. Her book diagnoses Gestalt-based thinking (attending to the whole) as leading to specific ideological formations and deformations (see *Gestalttheorie*, 60–64). I fully concur with her apprehensions about the attendant dangers of thinking from wholes to parts, but instead of believing "Glückliches Ereignis" to be an attempt to plaster over and hide these shortcomings and pitfalls, in my reading, the text exposes these difficulties with helpfully warning precision. The text, in other words, is open-eyed about the blindness to which its own methodology is liable.

34. The near kinship of the anagnorisis scenario elaborated in "Glückliches Ereignis" with the mode of scientific knowledge advocated by Goethe is further evidenced by the very place in which he chose to publish the small text. One might have expected such a moving monument to Goethe's debt to Schiller to appear as an introductory piece to an edition of the deceased poet's works that Goethe helped see through the press in the decades following Schiller's death. Better yet, Goethe may well have saved it for the publication of his correspondence with Schiller, which he brought out with great love and care in 1828. Instead, the anecdote reaches the public at the tail end of the first issue of his *Morphologische Hefte* in 1817 (*Zur Morphologie* I, 1; see HA, 11, 758). Together with "Geschichte meines botanischen Studiums," which is the first piece in the edition, the two texts frame a slightly reworked version of Goethe's *Morphologie der Pflanzen*, which had originally appeared—and been largely ignored—in 1790, shortly after his return from Italy. The entire issue can be seen as a way of working through the initial trauma of Goethe's homecoming. One could even read the three pieces that make up the edition together with "recognition" as a key central action, just as the *Blatt* had been Goethe's *Schlüssel* [key] to reading the *Geheimnisse der Pflanzenwelt* [mysteries of the plant world]. Geulen has a very provocative reading of the *Morphologische Hefte* and the question of form (see her *Aus dem Leben der Form*).

35. Immanuel Kant, *Kritik der Urteilskraft*, §§76, 77, in *Werke: Akademie Textausgabe* (Berlin: De Gruyter, 1968), 5:405–415.

36. "Das kann mir sehr lieb sein, daß ich Ideen habe ohne es zu wissen, und sie sogar mit Augen sehe!" (HA, 11, 541). Förster has written convincingly on what must be involved in the "Auge des Geistes." Compare, for example, *Die Farbenlehre*, §242, HA, 13, 382.

37. Förster, "Auge," 90.

38. "(Aus seinem [Goethes] Munde [27.3.1813] abgeschrieben) von Johannes Daniel Falk, 'Schillers erste Bekanntschaft mit Göthen'" (**Magdeburgische Ztg.*, Montagsbl. 16.1.1933, Goethe-Museum Düsseldorf, Falk IV 7), quoted in Goethe, *Begegnungen und Gespräche*, ed. Grumach, 4:85 (emphasis mine).

39. Förster, "Auge," 92 (emphasis mine).

40. Aristotle, *On Poetics*, trans. Seth Benardete and Michael Davis (South Bend: St. Augustine's Press, 2002), 43.

41. "Und eine Naturwirkung, die wir der Idee gemäß als simultan und sukzessiv zugleich denken sollen, scheint uns in eine Art Wahnsinn zu versetzen. Der Verstand kann

nicht vereinigt denken, was die Sinnlichkeit ihm gesondert überlieferte" ("Bedenken und Ergebung," in HA, 13, 31–32).

42. Förster, "Auge," 92.

43. Falk, quoted in Goethe, *Begegnungen und Gespräche*, ed. Grumach, 4:85.

44. The key to understanding *Hamlet* the play, according to Wilhelm, is recognition of Hamlet's character: "eine große Tat auf eine Seele gelegt, die der Tat nicht gewachsen ist" (HA, 7, 245–246).

45. It would be hard to demonstrate these difficulties more assiduously than Peter Szondi manages in his analysis of Schiller's *Über naive und sentimentalische Dichtung*, which itself developed out of the vision he and Goethe had of each other in the encounter described in "Glückliches Ereignis." Szondi's relentless comparison of the two archetypal modes of poeticizing intentionally confuses the distinctions (or rather reveals the contradictions contained in Schiller's treatment of his own concepts) only in order to clarify their inherent dialectical relation. Szondi leads us down the never-ending spirals of confusion so as to reach a conclusion that climaxes with (but can by no means be contained by) the paradoxical title of his essay, "Das Naive *ist* das Sentimentalische." See Szondi, *Lektüren und Lektionen: Versuche über Literatur, Literaturtheorie und Litertatursoziologie* (Frankfurt am Main: Suhrkamp, 1973), 47–102; and Szondi, *Poetik und Geschichtsphilosophie* (Frankfurt am Main: Suhrkamp, 1974), 1:149–182.

46. "daß ein fast Unmögliches unternommen werde, wenn man *die Übergänge* in einen geläuterten, freieren, selbstbewußten Zustand, deren es tausend und aber tausend geben muß, zu schildern unternimmt" (HA, 11, 542).

47. "Von Bildungsstufen kann die Rede nicht sein, wohl aber von Irr-, Schleif- und Schleichwegen" (HA, 11, 542).

48. "*der Punkt*, der uns trennte, war dadurch aufs strengste bezeichnet" (HA, 11, 541).

49. Falk, quoted in Goethe, *Begegnungen und Gespräche*, ed. Grumach, 4:85 (emphasis mine).

50. For Lessing's articulation of the "pregnant moment," see *Laokoon*, chap. 16, in *Werke und Briefe in zwölf Bänden*, vol. 5.2 (Frankfurt am Main: Deutscher Klassiker Verlag, 1990).

51. See Scott Goddard, "Beethoven and Goethe," *Music & Letters* 8, no. 2 (1927): 165–171.

52. Compare Goethe's letter to Herder (in which he claimed that "Die Urpflanze wird das wunderlichste Geschöpf von der Welt, um welches mich die Natur selbst beneiden soll. Mit diesem Modell und dem Schlüssel dazu kann man alsdann noch Pflanzen ins Unendliche erfinden, die konsequent sein müssen, das heißt, die, wenn sie auch nicht existieren, doch existieren könnten und nicht etwa malerische oder dichterische Schatten und Scheine sind, sondern eine innerliche Wahrheit und Notwendigkeit haben" [HA, 11, 324]), with Aristotle's declaration in chap. 9 ("the work of the poet is to speak not of things that have happened but of the sort of things that might happen and possibilities that come from what is likely or necessary. . . . For this reason too, poetry is a more philosophical and serious thing than history, since poetry speaks more of things that are universal, and history of things that are particular" [*P*, 9, 1451a, 37–1451b, 7]). This is why Goethe is a more philosophical scientist than, say, Linneas, for the latter describes and classifies particular plants

that actually exist, whereas the former writes of plants that are more universal. Hence the poet is the true knower of human nature—because she can create individuals who are instances of universal humanity.

53. See Aristotle's discussion of magnitude and unity (*P*, 7, 1450b, 37–1451a, 15).

Chapter Eight

1. Detlev W. Schumann, "Die Bekenntnisszenen in Goethes *Iphigenie*: Symmetrie und Steigerung," *Jahrbuch der deutschen Schillergesellschaft* 4 (1960): 229–246. Michael Mandelartz expands on this reading by including parallels from Goethe's other works to the levels of personal and social development in the play. Mandelartz limits the botanical metaphors to the first stage of his analysis, after which he turns to cosmogonic and biographical readings. See Mandelartz, "Die 'reine Seele' und die Politik: Partikularität und Universalität in Goethes *Iphigenie*," *Goethe Yearbook* 16 (2009): 51–66.

2. See "Spiraltendenz der Vegetation" (HA, 13, 130–148).

3. "edle Einfalt, stille Große" (J. J. Winckelmann, *Gedanken über die Nachahmung der griechischen Werke in der Malerey und Bildhauerkunst* [Dresden: Waltherische Handlung, 1756], 21).

4. "ein Mensch wie Du und ich"; "In Goethes klassischen Stücken treten nur noch Weimaraner auf" (Martin Walser, *Erfahrungenund Leseerfahrungen* [Frankfurt am Main: Suhrkamp Verlag, 1965], 69, 77). Walser's essay decries the universalizing tendency of schoolroom readings of classical texts like *Iphigenie*. The first quote is his representation of others' readings of Iphigenie's character; the second, his own.

5. For an overview of the critical tradition around *Iphigenie* and its historical and cultural implications, see Irmgard Wagner, *Critical Approaches to Goethe's Classical Dramas:* Iphigenie, Torquato Tasso, *and* Die natürliche Tochter (Columbia: Camden House, 1995), 5–90.

6. I do not mean anything as complex as Adorno's "mythic moment"—myth as "Schuldzusammenhang des Lebendigen" or "gegenwärtige Vorwelt"—to the recognition of which Adorno ascribes the dignity of Goethe's work in his august essay on *Iphigenie* but rather quite simply myth as shared story. Theodor Adorno, "Zum Klassizismus von Goethes *Iphigenie*," in *Noten zur Literatur* (Frankfurt am Main: Suhrkamp, 1974), 495.

7. Unless otherwise noted, English translations are from David Luke's version, which includes the equivalent line numbers: *Iphigenia in Tauris*, trans. David Luke, in Johann Wolfgang von Goethe, *Collected Works*, vol. 8, *Verse Plays and Epic*, ed. Cyrus Hamlin and Frank Ryder (Princeton: Princeton University Press, 1987), 1–53. Althouth Luke renders the title character's name as "Iphigenia," I use "Iphigenie" to refer to Goethe's character and "Iphigenia" to refer to Euripides's character throughout.

8. George Steiner, *Antigones* (New Haven: Yale University Press, 1984), 43–51.

9. Martin Mueller, *Children of Oedipus and Other Essays on the Imitation of Greek Tragedy 1550–1800* (Toronto: University of Toronto Press, 1980), 79–91. Pylades's identification with Odysseus goes much deeper than the broad parallels Mueller points out, as shown below.

10. Helga Gallas, *Kleist: Gesetz, Begehren und Sexualität* (Frankfurt am Main: Stroemfeld, 2005), 209–216.

11. The translation has been modified.

12. To Athena (*Od*, 13), the swineherd (*Od*, 14), and Penelope (*Od*, 19).

13. She cannot know that Athena will intervene to save them in the final deus ex machina.

14. The translation has been modified: *deinai gar hai gunaikes heuriskein tekhnas*.

15. Gerhard Neumann makes a similar point about female protagonists of ancient tragedies and eighteenth-century heroines in general ("Erkennungs-Szene: Wahrnehmung zwischen den Geschlechtern im literarischen Text," in *Differenzen in der Geschlechterdifferenz—Differences within Gender Studies: Aktuelle Perspektiven der Geschlechterforschung*, ed. Kati Röttger and Heike Pau [Berlin: Erich Schmidt, 1999], 202–221). Neumann's general thesis is that anagnorisis between sexes as a ritual of perception (*Wahrnehmungsritual*) takes on the same role in literary texts as the first contact situation between cultures in the exploration of the world (*Erkundung der Welt*). He further shows how these scenes question the very possibility of making intelligible signs for and about such acts of recognition (Neumann, 214). See also Ritta Jo Horsley, "Dies Frauenschicksal: A Critical Appraisal of Goethe's *Iphigenie*," in *Beyond the Eternal Feminine: Critical Essays on Women and German Literature*, ed. Susan Cocalis and Kay Goodman (Stuttgart: Akademischer Verlag Hans-Peter Heinz, 1982), 47–74.

16. The translation has been modified.

17. Fritz Breithaupt, "How I Feel Your Pain: Lessing's Mitleid, Goethe's Anagnorisis, and Fontane's Quiet Sadism," *Deutsche Vierteljahrsschrift für Literaturwissenschaft und Geistesgeschichte* 82, no. 3 (2008): 400–423.

18. Johann Gottlieb Fichte, *Grundlage des Naturrechts nach Principien der Wissenschaftslehre*, in *Gesamtausgabe der Bayerischen Akademie der Wissenschaften*, vol. 1.3 (Stuttgart: Fromman-Holzboog, 1966), 342.

19. Jane K. Brown, *Goethe's Allegories of Identity* (Philadelphia: University of Pennsylvania Press, 2014), 73.

20. Thus long before the modernist and postmodernist templates that Julia Kristeva likes to cite, the unified and stable identity of any subject is already problematized as a *mise en procès*, a site of intertextual interplay. See her *Desire in Language: A Semiotic Approach to Literature and Art* (New York: Columbia University Press, 1980), 124–147.

21. Brown, *Goethe's Allegories*, 60 (emphasis mine).

22. Brown, 9, 38.

23. Cyrus Hamlin, "'Myth and Psychology': The Curing of Orest in Goethe's *Iphigenie auf Tauris*," *Goethe Yearbook* 12 (2004): 59–80; and Brown, *Goethe's Allegories*, 65–66.

24. See, for example, Terence Cave, *Recognitions: A Study in Poetics* (Oxford: Clarendon, 1988), 371: "[*Iphigenie*] can be read even at a literal level as the triumph of character over plot."

25. Terence Cave cleverly notes that the whole arsenal of proofs and tests for identity that usually attend recognition scenes (the production of signs and tokens) have been dispensed with in the scene between brother and sister but show up again at this late stage. Iphigenie produces a traditional series of proofs of Orestes's identity for Thoas's benefit (Cave, *Recognitions*, 385). What he reads as a surreptitious return of the scandalous nature of anagnorisis in literature can also be viewed as a transfer of the *scene* of recognition: from the private (in the world of the play) to the public performance for the political leader, as will be argued in the next chapter.

26. Considering that Iphigenie's father was willing to sacrifice her for the sake of sailing winds for an army, one may question just how "wert" and "teuer" he should be to her, but she displays herself as remarkably loyal to his memory throughout the play, twice even fondly imagining a recognition scene that could occur between herself and Agamemnon (cf., HA, 5, 45ff.; and 440ff.).

27. This aporia will necessarily disappear in most staged versions of the play, because actors and directors are forced to make an interpretive decision for Thoas's behavior in their production. Yet the spectacular nature of the impasse is integral to the experience of reading the text: the reader must puzzle over how to imagine Thoas's reactions. Actual stage performance closes off the performative ambiguities inherent in reading.

28. There is a similar textual ambiguity that performance cannot help but make clear in the silence of Isabel after the duke's revelation and marriage proposal in the final scene of Shakespeare's *Measure for Measure*.

29. For a persuasive account of this interpretation of catharsis, see *P*, trans. Sachs, 10–17.

30. See, for example, Hamlin, "Myth and Psychology," 63; Brown, *Goethe's Allegories*, 65.

31. Jacob Bernays, *Grundzüge der verlorenen Abhandlung des Aristoteles über die Wirkung der Tragödie* (Hildesheim: Georg Olms Verlag, 1970); and Bernays, "On Catharsis: From *Fundamentals of Aristotle's Lost Essay on the 'Effect of the Tragic' (1857)*," trans. Peter Rudnytsky, *American Imago* 61, no. 5 (2004): 329.

32. Orest's issues are not limited to his own crime against his mother but also include the psychic damage inflicted by his father's early abandonment, blame for which he transferred to his mother.

33. Bernays, *Grundzüge*, 36; Bernays, "Catharsis," 339.

34. See chapter 9 of this book.

35. The translation has been altered.

36. See Leon Golden, "Catharsis," *Transactions and Proceedings of the American Philological Association* 93 (1962): 58; Stephen Halliwell, *Aristotle's Poetics* (Chicago: University of Chicago Press, 1998), 200–201; Martha Craven Nussbaum, "Tragedy and Self-Sufficiency: Plato and Aristotle on Fear and Pity," in *Essays on Aristotle's* Poetics, ed. Amélie Oksenberg Rorty (Princeton: Princeton University Press, 1992), 280–283.

37. G. E. Lessing, in contrast, for whom catharsis is the object and purpose of tragedy's *Bewirken*, would not stint the appellation "tragedy" from a play that fails to effect a purification; he would just call it a *bad* tragedy. See *Hamburgische Dramaturgie*, 77. Stück, in Gotthold Ephraim Lessing, *Werke und Briefe in zwölf Bänden*, vol. 6 (Frankfurt am Main: Deutscher Klassiker Verlag, 1985).

38. "[Aristotle] versteht unter Katharsis diese aussöhnende Abrundung, welche eigentlich von allem Drama, ja sogar von allen poetischen Werken gefordert wird" (HA, 12, 343).

39. Gerald Else, *Aristotle's Poetics: The Argument* (Cambridge, Mass.: Harvard University Press, 1957), 439.

40. This was attested by Todd London, executive director at the University of Washington School of Drama, during Q&A, "Performing Arts Lectures: Revisiting the Newness of New Drama," February 16, 2016.

41. Goethe's translation of Aristotle's definition garnered the ridicule of nineteenth-century classicists and has been largely ignored by modern scholars. See Butcher's scathing review in his authoritative nineteenth-century commentary (Aristotle, *Aristotle's Theory of Poetry and Fine Art, with a Critical Text and Translation of the Poetics*, trans. S. H. Butcher [London: Macmillan, 1895; 5th ed., New York: Dover, 1951], 244). Else does not attribute Goethe in his own "Goethean" reading of catharsis.

42. *P*, trans. Sachs, 16.

43. *P*, trans. Sachs, 15.

44. "Alle Poesie soll belehrend seyn, aber unmerklich; sie soll den Menschen aufmerksam machen, wovon sich zu belehren werth wäre; er muß die Lehre selbst daraus ziehen wie aus dem Leben" (Goethe, "Über das Lehrgedicht," in *Goethes Werke: Herausgegeben im Auftrage der Großherzogin Sophie von Sacshen* [Munich: DTV, 1987], section 1, vol. 41, pt. 2, 226).

45. Rainer Maria Rilke, "Archaïscher Torso Apollos," in *Sämtliche Werke* (Wiesbaden: Insel-Verlag, 1955), 1:557.

Chapter Nine

1. Charles M. Taylor, *Multiculturalism: Examining the Politics of Recognition* (Princeton: Princeton University Press, 1994), 25–73; Axel Honneth, *Der Kampf um Anerkennung: zur moralischen Grammatik sozialer Konflikte* (Frankfurt am Main: Suhrkamp Verlag, 1992). See also Ludwig Siep, *Anerkennung Als Prinzip Der Praktischen Philosophie: Untersuchungen zu Hegels Jenaer Philosophie des Geistes* (München: Alber, 1979); and Robert R. Williams, *Recognition: Fichte and Hegel on the Other* (Albany: State University of New York Press, 1992).

2. For a thorough and helpful taxonomy of literary scholars' "appropriations" of recognition theories, see Andrea Albrecht, "Theorien der Anerkennung: Literaturwissenschaftliche Appropriationen," *Internationales Archiv für Sozialgeschichte der deutschen Literatur* (*IASL*) 37, no. 2 (2012): 323–343

3. Walter Erhart, "Drama der Anerkennung: Neue gesellschaftstheoretische Überlegungen zu Goethes *Iphigenie auf Tauris*," *Jahrbuch der Deutschen Schiller-Gesellschaft* 51 (2007): 149.

4. Erhart, 160.

5. "spielt sämtliche Formen moderner Anerkennungsverhältnisse durch" (Erhart, 164; translations mine).

6. "es verweist zugleich auf eine neue Funktion moderner Literatur, nämlich soziale Anerkennungsverhältnisse und Anerkennungspathologien zu simulieren. Die Literaturwissenschaft jedenfalls . . . gewönne durch eine solche Perspektive ein gesellschaftstheoretische Potential zurück" (Erhart, 165).

7. See Irmgard Wagner, *Critical Approaches to Goethe's Classical Dramas*: Iphigenie, Torquato Tasso, *and* Die natürliche Tochter (Columbia: Camden House, 1995), 5–30.

8. Hans Blumenberg, *Work on Myth*, trans. Robert M. Wallace (Cambridge, Mass.: MIT Press, 1985), 3–32.

9. Wolfdietrich Rasch, *Goethes* Iphigenie auf Tauris *als Drama der Autonomie* (München: Beck, 1979).

10. Erhart, "Drama der Anerkennung," 155.

11. Patchen Markell, *Bound by Recognition* (Princeton: Princeton University Press, 2003). He sketches the argument in the introduction (4–7), and then proceeds to repeat its logic in his readings of Taylor and Herder (39–61), Sophocles and Aristotle (62–89), and Hegel (90–121).

12. Markell, *Bound*, 7 and passim. Markell's technical appropriation of "acknowledgment" should not be confused with its common usage as "public recognition" nor with the more accurate translation of Hegel's *Anerkennung* than the common "recognition." In fact, Markell opposes his "acknowledgment" to both these concepts.

13. For the sake of clarity in the ensuing discussion, I will refer to Markell's political recognition as *Anerkennung*. Unless otherwise modified, *recognition* will refer to the broader nexus of activities involved in the relational process of identity (re)construction and (re)enactment as developed over the preceding chapters of this book.

14. Markell, *Bound*, 62.

15. Markell, 86.

16. Markell, 190–193.

17. Markell, 112.

18. Carl Schmitt, *Der Begriff des Politischen: Text von 1932 mit eimen Vorwort und drei Corollarien* (Berlin: Duncker and Humblot, 1991), 26; Schmitt, *The Concept of the Political*, trans. George Schwab (Chicago: University of Chicago Press, 1996), 26.

19. Schmitt, *Begriff*, 29; *Concept*, 28.

20. See Ruby Blondell, *Helping Friends and Harming Enemies: A Study in Sophocles and Greek Ethics* (Cambridge: Cambridge University Press, 1989), 26–59.

21. For the lexical information in this paragraph, see *LS*, 340, 653. See also Blondell, *Helping Friends*, 39.

22. Schmitt, *Begriff*, 38; *Concept*, 38.

23. Schmitt, *Begriff*, 33; *Concept*, 33.

24. Schmitt, *Begriff*, 38; *Concept*, 38.

25. White House, "Remarks by President Obama at Leaders Summit on Refugees," released September 20, 2016, https://www.whitehouse.gov; Oscar Brown Jr., "The Snake," sung by Al Wilson, released by Bell Records, 1968.

26. See Cicero's *On Friendship*, Ovid's *Tristia*, and Gluck's, *Iphigénie en Tauride*. For an engaging account of the reception of this story, see Edith Hall, *Adventures with Iphigenia in Tauris: A Cultural History of Euripides' Black Sea Tragedy* (Oxford: Oxford University Press, 2013), 92–110. This marginalization of Iphigenia showcases Jacques Derrida's claim about the exclusion of women from models of friendship based on fraternity (see Derrida, *Politics of Friendship*, trans. George Collins [New York: Verso, 1997], 290). In these versions of the myth, even the consanguine sister is discounted for the sake of the elective brother.

27. Of course, an ancient Greek audience would not have conceived of it in these terms. For them, the Taurians represent the extreme case of the violation of the sacred laws of *xenia*, the guest/host relation.

28. Carl Schmitt, *Politische Theologie: Vier Kapitel zur Lehre von der Souveränität*, 6th ed. (Berlin: Duncker and Humblot, 1993), 13.

29. The modern roots of the state of exception originate during the French Revolution (just five years after the publication of the verse version of *Iphigenie*), but Giorgio

Agamben traces its conceptual history back to the Roman *justitium* and *auctoritas*. Agamben, *State of Exception* (Chicago: University of Chicago Press, 2005).

30. Unless otherwise noted, English translations are from David Luke's version, which includes the equivalent line numbers: *Iphigenie in Tauris*, trans. David Luke, in Johann Wolfgang von Goethe, *Collected Works: Vol. 8: Verse Plays and Epic*, ed. Cyrus Hamlin and Frank Ryder (Princeton: Princeton University Press, 1987), 1–53. Here, the translation has been modified for greater literal accuracy.

31. Iphigenie neatly turns the tables on Thoas here, who had earlier accused her of similarly choosing the divine laws that most accord with her desires: "Es spricht kein Gott, es spricht dein eignes Herz" (HA, 5, 493).

32. The translation has been modified to reflect German syntax and word choice more accurately.

33. Thomas Hobbes, *Leviathan*, ed. Richard E. Flathman and David Johnston (New York: W. W. Norton, 1997), chap. 14, p. 77.

34. See, for instance, Dieter Borchmeyer, *Weimarer Klassik: Portrait einer Epoche* (Weinheim: Beltz Athenäum, 1994), 153. Immanuel Kant, *Werke: Akademie Textausgabe* (Berlin: De Gruyter, 1968), 8:425–430.

35. This maxim clearly motivated Euripides's Iphigenia, who had no qualms about deceiving the Taurian king who had so long held her captive and forced her to prepare victims for sacrifice.

36. Derrida, *Politics*, 112–137. See also chapter 4 of this book.

37. Derrida, 282.

38. See, for instance, Immanuel Kant, *Zum ewigen Frieden*, in *Werke*, 8:341–386.

39. Derrida, *Politics*, 218–219.

40. Hannah Arendt, *The Human Condition* (Chicago: Chicago University Press, 1958), 181.

41. Arendt, 244.

42. Arendt, 245.

43. Theodor Adorno, "Zum Klassizismus von Goethes *Iphigenie*," in *Noten zur Literatur* (Frankfurt am Main: Suhrkamp, 1974), 509.

44. The echo holds true for Luther's translation as well: "Was ihr nicht getan habt einem unter diesen Geringsten, das habt ihr mir auch nicht getan," Matthäus 25:45; Martin Luther, *Die Bibel, oder die ganze heilige Schrift des alten und neuen Testaments* (New York: Amerikanische Bibel-Gesellschaft, 1898), 32.

45. Arendt, *Human Condition*, 238.

46. Martin Mueller picks up on other clues to see Iphigenie as a Christ figure: *Children of Oedipus and Other Essays on the Imitation of Greek Tragedy 1550–1800* (Toronto: University of Toronto Press, 1980), 91.

47. Schmitt, *Begriff*, 29; *Concept*, 29.

48. Arendt, *Human Condition*, 243.

49. Carl Schmitt, *Verfassungslehre* (Berlin: Duncker and Humblot, 1965), 90.

50. Arendt, *Human Condition*, 184–186.

51. Arendt, 186 (emphasis in the original).

52. Arendt, 188.

53. The translation has been modified.

54. This was in a letter to Schiller dated January 19, 1802 (HA, 8, 405).

55. See, for instance, Rainer Forst and Jeffrey Flynn, *The Right to Justification: Elements of a Constructivist Theory of Justice* (New York: Columbia University Press, 2012), 139; and Rainer Forst, *Toleration in Conflict: Past and Present* (New York: Cambridge University Press, 2013), 3, 15, 28, 61, 136, 146, 328–329, 568.

56. Goethe, *Maximen und Reflexionen*, Nr. 136–150, "eine Idee darf nicht liberal sein! . . . Noch weniger darf der Begriff liberal sein" (HA, 12, 384).

57. Goethe, Nr. 147–148, "Wo man die Liberalität suchen muß, das ist in den Gesinnungen . . . Gesinnungen aber sind selten liberal, weil die Gesinnung unmittelbar aus der Person, ihren nächsten Beziehungen und Bedürfnissen hervorgeht" (HA, 12, 384).

Chapter Ten

1. "Always a different stage." Sigmund Freud's famous allegorical staging of the subconscious is apt here for the displaced scene of recognition, which by its very definition would seem to consist in becoming *conscious* of a person, place, or thing. See his *Traumdeutung*, in *Gesammelte Werke*, ed. Anna Freud et al., vols. 2–3 (Frankfurt am Main: Fischer, 1999), 51.

2. Gerhard Neumann, "Kleists ethnologisches Experiment: Zur Fetischisierung der Erkennungs-Szene in der Penthesilea," in *Kultur-Schreiben als romantisches Projekt: Romantische Ethnographie im Spannungsfeld zwischen Imagination und Wissenschaft*, ed. David Wellbery and Alexander von Bormann (Würzburg: Königshausen and Neumann, 2012), 155–178.

3. See Carol Jacobs, *Uncontainable Romanticism* (Baltimore: Johns Hopkins University Press, 1989), 85–114; Katrin Pahl, "Forging Feeling: Kleist's Theatrical Theory of Re-layed Emotionality," *MLN* 124, no. 3 (2009): 680; Michel Chaouli, "Devouring Metaphor: Disgust and Taste in Kleist's Penthesilea," *German Quarterly* 69, no. 2 (1996): 126.

4. See more on Lacanian readings of the play below, but for incisive political readings, see (on Foucault) Rüdiger Campe, "Zweierlei Gesetz in Kleists *Penthesilea*: Naturrecht und Biopolitik," in *Penthesileas Versprechen*: *Exemplarische Studien über die literarische Referenz* (Freiburg: Rombach Verlag, 2008), 313–342; and (on Legendre) Girard Raulet, "Der opake Punkt des Politischen," in *Penthesileas Versprechen*, ed. Campe, 343–374.

5. See Bianca Theisen, *Bogenschluss: Kleists Formalisierung des Lesens* (Freiburg: Rombach, 1996), 155; Bettina Menke, "Penthesilea: das Bild des Körpers und seine Zerfällung," in *Erotik und Sexualität im Werk Heinrich von Kleists: Internationales Kolloquium des Kleist-Archivs Sembdner* (Heilbronn: Stadtbücherei, 2000), 127.

6. Jacobs, *Uncontainable*, 126.

7. Much of interest has been teased out from *Penthesilea* in the context of recognition yet not in the Aristotelian vein pursued here. Walter Müller-Seidel explores the recurrent theme of *Versehen*—which he combines with a host of revealing imagery about the interdependence of sight and knowledge—in Kleist's work, *Versehen und Erkennen: Eine Studie über Heinrich von Kliest* (Köln: Böhlau, 1961). Helmut J. Schneider carries further this analysis of visuality into the realm of theatricality by showing how *Penthesilea*'s staging of recognition is in direct dialogue with earlier German plays of the Enlightenment and Classicism; see Schneider's "Entzug der Sichtbarkeit: Kleist's *Penthesilea* und die klassische Humanitätsdramaturgie," in *Penthesileas Versprechen*, ed. Campe, 127–152.

8. Alva Noë, *Action in Perception* (Cambridge, Mass.: MIT Press, 2004), 39–48.

9. Rüdiger Campe, "Presenting the Affect: The Scene of *Pathos* in Aristotle's *Rhetoric* and its Revision in Descartes' *Passions of the Soul*," in *Rethinking Emotion: Interiority in Premodern, Modern, and Contemporary Thought*, ed. Rüdiger Campe and Julia Weber (Berlin: De Gruyter, 2014), 49–54.

10. See, for instance, Catherine Newmark, *Passion—Affekt—Gefühl: Philosophische Theorien der Emotionen zwischen Aristoteles und Kant* (Hamburg: Meiner, 2008).

11. Michel Foucault, *The Hermeneutics of the Subject: Lectures at the Collège De France, 1981–1982*, ed. Frédéric Gros et al. (New York: Palgrave Macmillan, 2005), 14–19.

12. Pahl persuasively shows how Kleist's play offers a model for conceiving of feeling beyond "the antagonism of (body-bound) emotionality and (language-bound) rationality" ("Forging Feeling," 668). By arguing that Penthesilea figures as an emblem of Cartesian interiority, this chapter may seem at odds with her conclusions. In fact, my reading complements her claims. Penthesilea's inability to engage in classical practices of intersubjectivity is the tragedy of the modern subject at its extreme of inaccessible interiority. Other figures and passages in the drama open up alternative ways of understanding consciousness.

13. "Was in ihr walten mag, das weiß nur sie, / Und jeder Busen ist, der fühlt, ein Rätsel." I often modify Agee's metrical translation for greater accuracy—to the unfortunate detriment of his elegant iambs—and indicate this with "mod." after the page number. Here, *Penth*, 9, 1285–1286; 59, mod.

14. See Christa Wolf, "Kleists *Penthesilea*," in *Die Dimension des Autors: Essays und Aufsätze, Reden und Gespräche 1959–1985* (Neuwied: Luchterhand, 1987), 660–676; Neumann, "Kleists ethnologisches Experiment."

15. James Phillips offers a suggestive reading of *Penthesilea* through the lens of Kleist's engagement with Kant's critical philosophy. My reading of the play takes up Phillips's early but unpursued suggestion that Kleist's *Kantkrise* "is not so much Kantian as Cartesian." See his *Equivocation of Reason: Kleist Reading Kant* (Stanford: Stanford University Press, 2007), 3.

16. See chapter 6 of this book.

17. See Helga Gallas, *Kleist: Gesetz, Begehren und Sexualität* (Frankfurt am Main: Stroemfeld, 2005), 181–183; Evelyn Moore, "The Deadly Gaze: Penthesilea and Achilles in Love," *(Re-)turn: A Journal of Lacanian Studies* 3–4 (Spring 2008): 41; and Anthony Stephens, "Verzerrungen im Spiegel: Das Narziß-Motiv bei Heinrich von Kleist," in *Heinrich von Kleist: Kriegsfall—Rechtsfall—Sündenfall*, ed. Gerhard Neumann (Freiburg im Briesgau: Rombach, 1994), 292. All three scholars mention one or two of the mirroring scenes as incidental support for their readings. Chris Cullens and Dorothea von Mücke, in contrast, make all four mirror scenes central to their Lacanian analysis of desire ("Love in Kleist's *Penthesilea* and *Kätchen von Heilbronn*," *DVJS* 63, no. 3 [1989]: 461–493).

18. Interestingly, the first scholar to question the authenticity and to lament the pervasive high opinion of *Alcibiades* was Kleist's Berlin contemporary, Friedrich Schleiermacher.

19. Foucault, *Hermeneutics*, 36–38; 74–76.

20. "So viel ich weiß, gibt es in der Natur / Kraft bloß und ihren Widerstand, nichts Drittes" (*Penth*, 1, 125; 8).

21. For Aristotle too, recognition leads either to friendship or hostility: there is no third relational term.

22. Neumann, "Kleists ethnologisches Experiment." Carol Jacobs agrees that "[Penthesilea] is the third term, the 'Drittes,' which violates the natural law declaring power and its resistance as the only conceivable forces." But she also sees that Odysseus's speech manages to include and assimilate the inexplicable phenomenon into his worldview: "Indeed all this is spoken by a tongue that knows whereof it speaks ('This much I know'), that knows not only what it knows but also both what it desires and is its opposite. . . . Odysseus intends to speak about a crisis in self-identity, but to speak about it from the distance of his own sure knowledge" (Jacobs, *Uncontainable*, 93). She elegantly shows how Odysseus's confident avowal of what he understands about force and counterforce is already implicated in inherent contradictions.

23. "als schlüge rings um ihr / Die Welt in helle Flammenlohe auf" (*Penth*, 1, 70–71; 7).

24. The red face for Odysseus, like the white flag for Foster's adventurers, at the very least announces the possibility of relation, even if the precise catalog of correspondences is yet to be deciphered.

25. Foucault, *Hermeneutics*, 76.

26. Foucault, 58.

27. Although etymologists derive *Gleisner* from older versions of *gleich* (same), they admit that it "im heutigen Sprachgefühl auf 'gleißen' bezogen wird" (Paul Grebe, ed., *Der Große Duden, Band 7—Etymologie: Herkunftswörterbuch der deutschen Sprache* [Mannheim: Dudenverlag, 1963], 225). *Gleißen* means to glisten, glitter, or gleam.

28. Foucault, *Hermeneutics*, 75.

29. See *Laokoon*, chaps. 16–18, in Gotthold Ephraim Lessing, *Werke und Briefe in zwölf Bänden*, vol. 5.2 (Frankfurt am Main: Deutscher Klassiker Verlag, 1990), 116–137.

30. Stephens points to this scene to illustrate Lacanian narcissism and trauma ("Verzerrungen," 249–251). For another treatment of mirrors in Kleist, see Ilse Graham, who borrows the image of a mirror that is "schief und schmutzig" from one of the early letters during his "Kantkrise" to tease out an elegant reading of Penthesilea, whose "warped and sullied mirror of a soul conditioned to unrelatedness" makes the play's tragic outcome inevitable (*Word into Flesh: A Poet's Quest for the Symbol* [Berlin: De Gruyter, 1977], 124ff.). She does not, however, mention the several instances of mirrors within the language of the first half of the play explored here.

31. Foucault, *Hermeneutics*, 68.

32. Chapter 6 of this book established the relation of Plato to Shakespeare thusly:

Socrates : Alcibiades :: Ulysses : Achilles

With Kleist, the present chapter adds the further analogy for both predecessors:

:: Ulysses/Achilles : Penthesilea

Both terms from the middle ratio become the first term of the third. Despite the many differences of cultural context, unspoken assumptions, and historical realities between Attic Greece, Early Modern England, and Romantic Germany, one constant of flux becomes clear within these three ratios. In all three cases of interpersonal mirrorings, an unsustainable reflector gives an image of an unknowable reflection.

33. Neumann, "Kleists ethnologisches Experiment."

34. Gerhard Neumann, "Erkennungsszene und Opferritual in Goethes Iphigenie und in Kleists Penthesilea," in *Käthchen und seine Schwestern: Frauenfiguren im Drama um 1800: Internationales Kolloquium des Kleist-Archivs Sembdner*, ed. Günther Emig and Anton Philipp (Knittel. Heilbronn: Stadtbücherei, 2000), 38–80.

35. "Was hier artikuliert, was hier beobachtet wird, ist nichts Geringeres als der Kollaps jener Denk-, Schicksals- und kulturellen Ordnungsmuster, die am Anfang jeden menschlichen Handelns stehen" (Neumann, "Kleists ethnologisches Experiment," 11).

36. "Fürwahr! Man mögte, wenn er so erscheint, fast zweifeln, / Daß er es sei" (*Penth*, 15, 1792; 88).

37. Gallas, *Kleist*, 209–216.

38. "Wo bin ich?" "Kennst du die Stimme deiner Schwester nicht?" (*Penth*, 14, 1549; 77, mod.).

39. Terence Cave, *Recognitions: A Study in Poetics* (Oxford: Clarendon, 1988), 242–255.

40. Though Hegel's *Phenomenology of Spirit* was published one year earlier than *Penthesilea*, it is highly unlikely that Kleist would have read it. Nonetheless, the *Anerkennung* narrative of the master/slave dialectic is strikingly apt here. The struggle for recognition between subjects as a question of lordship and bondage (as an inevitable objectification of the other subject) is dramatized in many of Kleist's works. Though Campe convincingly shows how Penthesilea later proves herself to be an anti-Hegelian constructivist in contrast to Achilles's essentialist political assumptions (*Penth*, 15, 1902–1911; Campe, "Zweierlei," 321–324), in this recognition scene, Penthesilea is committed to the first steps of Hegel's dialectic, without, however, ever achieving any *Aufhebung* of the subject/object divide.

41. René Descartes, *Discourse on Method and Meditations on First Philosophy*, trans. Donald Cress (Indianapolis: Hackett, 1993), 66.

42. Descartes, 68.

43. Michel Foucault, *The Order of Things: An Archaeology of the Human Sciences* (New York: Vintage, 1994), 58–70.

44. Though for the sake of literalness I have rendered *nur zum Schein* as "just for show," Agee translated it as "playfully," which captures the spirit of my reading perfectly.

45. "wer recht von Herzen liebt, / Kann schon das eine für das andre greifen" (*Penth*, 24, 2982–2983; 145, mod.).

46. Judith Butler, "Performative Acts and Gender Constitution: An Essay in Phenomenology and Feminist Theory," *Theatre Journal* 49, no. 1 (1988): 524–528.

47. Penthesilea might thus be seen to embody the Kantian duty not to lie, though in her case truth-telling is not a free choice but an ineluctable feature of her character.

48. Nor am I trying in any way to downplay the very real difficulties and often insurmountable obstacles of communication between cultures, genders, or individuals.

49. Descartes, *Meditations*, 62.

50. See Jacobs, *Uncontainable*, ix–xiv, 85–114.

51. "Der Mensch kennt nur sich selbst, insofern er die Welt kennt, die er nur in sich und sich nur in ihr gewahr wird. Jeder neue Gegenstand, wohl beschaut, schließt ein neues Organ in uns auf" (HA, 13, 38).

Concluding Reflections

1. Margaret Atwood makes the twelve handmaidens, who are hanged for colluding with the suitors in the *Odyssey*, innocent of treachery. This move actually deprives the plot of its potential for social commentary. The discomfort readers feel in the *Odyssey* at the hanging of the handmaidens, who are only guilty of navigating the social realities of serving women in archaic Greek culture, is a much more subversive denunciation of patriarchal norms. Even a Greek audience would wholeheartedly agree that the handmaidens who remained loyal to Penelope should not be punished. Atwood's unproblematic version thus fails to challenge the common moral sensibilities of both Homeric culture and our own. A Penelope who interceded on behalf of handmaidens who *had been* conniving with the suitors and trading sexual favors for social advantages, on the other hand, would be a much more provocative figure and could orchestrate a very powerful recognition scenario.

2. Such work would also rely on much that has already been accomplished. Jane K. Brown's *Goethe's Faust: The German Tragedy* (Ithaca: Cornell University Press, 1986), for instance, would be a necessary playbook for any game of tracing the course of recognition through *Faust*.

3. With good reason, Wallace translates this term as "significance," but a more literal rendering of its connotative import into English would be something like "meaningfulness." Hans Blumenberg's *Arbeit am Mythos* (Frankfurt: Suhrkamp, 2004), 77; and its translation *Work on Myth*, trans. Robert M. Wallace (Cambridge, Mass.: MIT Press, 1985), 67.

4. Blumenberg, *Arbeit*, 80; Blumenberg, *Work*, 70.

5. Blumenberg, *Arbeit*, 80; Blumenberg, *Work*, 70.

6. Though Blumenberg denies mythological power of consciously authored fictions, authors still avail themselves of mythic patterns to shape and craft their stories. It is no coincidence that the techniques of plot construction recommended by Aristotle should match the "operations" for generating "significance" at work in myth.

7. Blumenberg, *Arbeit*, 80–86; Blumenberg, *Work*, 70–75.

8. Blumenberg, *Arbeit*, 85; Blumenberg, *Work*, 75.

9. Blumenberg, *Arbeit*, 85; Blumenberg, *Work*, 75.

10. Blumenberg, *Arbeit*, 86–87; Blumenberg, *Work*, 75–76.

11. Blumenberg, *Arbeit*, 89; Blumenberg, *Work*, 78.

12. Blumenberg, *Arbeit*, 90; Blumenberg, *Work*, 79.

13. Blumenberg, *Arbeit*, 87; Blumenberg, *Work*, 76.

14. Blumenberg, *Arbeit*, 77; Blumenberg, *Work*, 84.

15. Blumenberg, *Arbeit*, 92; Blumenberg, *Work*, 81.

16. Blumenberg, *Arbeit*, 95; Blumenberg, *Work*, 84.

17. "Es ist zwar nicht geschehen, aber vielleicht denkbar, daß sich jemand vor ihrem Gesang gerettet hätte, vor ihrem Schweigen gewiß nicht" (Franz Kafka, *Die Erzählungen* [Frankfurt am Main: Fischer, 1961], 301; translations from Kafka are mine).

18. Max Horkheimer and Theodor Adorno, *Dialectic of Enlightenment: Philosophical Fragments* (Stanford: Stanford University Press, 2002), 25–26; and Horkheimer and Adorno, *Dialektik der Aufklärung: Philosophische Fragmente* (Frankfurt: Fischer Verlag, 1988), 39.

19. "Odysseus, sagt man, war so listenreich, war ein solcher Fuchs, daß selbst die Schicksalsgöttin nicht in sein Innerstes dringen konnte" (Kafka, *Erzählungen*, 301).

20. "die Wendungen ihrer Hälse, das tiefe Atmen, die tränenvollen Augen, den halb geöffneten Mund" (Kafka, 300).

21. Horkheimer and Adorno, *Dialectic of Enlightenment*, 39, *Dialektik der Aufklärung*, 55 (translation modified).

22. See chapter 1 of this book.

23. She does this twice: the logic of time in the drama makes it very doubtful that there was any chance for the exhaustive exchange of signs with Orest that Iphigenie reports to Thoas (HA, 5, 2079–2094). More damning, though, is her admonition to the struggling Thoas that "Um Guts zu tun braucht's keiner Überlegung" (HA, 5, 1989). In the previous act, she had pleaded with Pylades, "O laß mich zaudern!" (HA, 5, 1669). She *does* need "Überlegung" to do good, though she denies it to Thoas.

BIBLIOGRAPHY

Abrams, J. J., Jeffrey Lieber, and Damon Lindelof. *Lost. The Complete Sixth Season: The Final Season*. Los Angeles: ABC Studios, Touchstone Home Video, 2010. DVD.

Adorno, Theodor. *Noten zur Literatur*. Frankfurt am Main: Suhrkamp, 1974.

Agamben, Giorgio. "The Friend." In *What Is an Apparatus? And Other Essays*, translated by David Kishik and Stefan Pedatella, 25–38. Stanford: Stanford University Press, 2009.

———. *State of Exception*. Chicago: University of Chicago Press, 2005.

Albrecht, Andrea. "Theorien der Anerkennung: Literaturwissenschaftliche Appropriationen." *Internationales Archiv für Sozialgeschichte der deutschen Literatur* (*IASL*) 37, no. 2 (2012): 323–343.

Amory, Anne. "The Reunion of Odysseus and Penelope." In *Essays on the Odyssey: Selected Modern Criticism*, edited by Charles H. Taylor Jr., 100–121. Bloomington: Indiana University Press, 1963.

Arendt, Hannah. *The Human Condition*. Chicago: Chicago University Press, 1958.

Aristotle. *Aristotle's Physics: A Guided Study. Translated and edited with commentary by Joe Sachs*. New Brunswick: Rutgers University Press, 1995.

———. *Aristotle's Poetics*. Translated by Hippocrates Apostle, Elizabeth Dobbs, and Morris Parslow. Grinnell: Peripatetic, 1990.

———. *Aristotle's Poetics: A Translation and Commentary for Students of Literature*. Translated by Leon Golden and O. B. Hardison Jr. Englewood Cliffs: Prentice Hall, 1968.

———. *Aristotle's Theory of Poetry and Fine Art, with a Critical Text and Translation of the Poetics*. Translated by S. H. Butcher. 5th ed. New York: Dover, 1951. First published 1895.

———. *The Basic Works of Aristotle*. Edited by Richard McKeon. Lifetime Library. New York: Random House, 1941.

———. *Nicomachean Ethics*. Translated by Joe Sachs. Newburyport: Focus, 2002.

———. *The Nicomachean Ethics*. Translated and edited by H. Rackham. Loeb Classical Library 73. 2nd ed. Cambridge, Mass.: Harvard University Press, 1934.

———. *On Memory and Recollection*. In *On the Soul and On Memory and Recollection*. Translated by Joe Sachs, 165–181. Santa Fe: Green Lion, 2004.

———. *On Poetics*. Translated by Seth Benardete and Michael Davis. South Bend: St. Augustine's Press, 2002.

———. *On the Soul*. In *On the Soul and On Memory and Recollection*. Translated by Joe Sachs, 45–164. Santa Fe: Green Lion, 2004.

———. *Physica*. 1950. Edited by W. D. Ross. Oxford: Oxford University Press, 1988.

———. *Poetics*. Edited and translated by Stephen Halliwell et al. Loeb Classical Library 199. Cambridge, Mass.: Harvard University Press, 1995.

———. *Poetics*. Translated by Joe Sachs. Newburyport: Focus, 2005.

———. *The* Poetics *of Aristotle: Translation and Commentary*. Translated by Stephen Halliwell. London: Duckworth, 1987.

———. *Poetik: Griechisch/Deutsch*. Translated and edited by Manfred Fuhrmann. Stuttgart: Reclam, 1982.

———. *Rhetoric*. Translated by Joe Sachs. Newburyport: Focus, 2009.

Aristotle, Horace, and Longinus. *Classical Literary Criticism*. Translated by T. S. Dorsch. London: Penguin Books, 1965.

Atwood, Margaret. *The Penelopiad: The Play*. London: Faber and Faber, 2007.

Auerbach, Erich. *Mimesis: The Representation of Reality in Western Literature*. Translated by Willard Trask. Garden City: Doubleday, 1953.

Austin, J. L. *How to Do Things with Words*. Oxford: Clarendon Press, 1962.

Austin, Norman. *Archery at the Dark of the Moon: Poetic Problems in Homer's Odyssey*. Berkeley: University of California Press, 1975.

———. "Homeric Nostalgia." *Yale Review* 98, no. 2 (2010): 37–64.

———. "Name Magic in the *Odyssey*." *California Studies in Classical Antiquity* 5 (1972): 1–19.

Autenrieth, Georg, and Robert P. Keep. *A Homeric Dictionary for Schools and Colleges*. Norman: University of Oklahoma Press, 1958.

Bassi, Karen. *Acting like Men: Gender, Drama, and Nostalgia in Ancient Greece*. Ann Arbor: University of Michigan Press, 1998.

Bernays, Jacob. *Grundzüge der verlorenen Abhandlung des Aristoteles über die Wirkung der Tragödie*. Hildesheim: Georg Olms Verlag, 1970.

———. "On Catharsis: From *Fundamentals of Aristotle's Lost Essay on the 'Effect of the Tragic'* (1857)." Translated by Peter Rudnytsky. *American Imago* 61, no. 5 (2004): 319–341.

Bial, Henry, and Sara Brady, eds. *The Performance Studies Reader*. 3rd ed. London: Routledge, 2015.

Blondell, Ruby. *Helen of Troy: Beauty, Myth, Devastation*. Oxford: Oxford University Press, 2013.

——— [Mary Whitlock Blundell]. *Helping Friends and Harming Enemies: A Study in Sophocles and Greek Ethics*. Cambridge: Cambridge University Press, 1989.

———. *The Play of Character in Plato's Dialogues*. Cambridge: Cambridge University Press, 2002.

Bloom, Harold. *Shakespeare: The Invention of the Human*. New York: Riverhead Books, 1998.

Blumenberg, Hans. *Arbeit am Mythos*. Frankfurt am Main: Suhrkamp, 2004. First published 1979.

———. *Work on Myth*. Translated by Robert M. Wallace. Cambridge, Mass.: MIT Press, 1985.

Borchmeyer, Dieter. *Weimarer Klassik: Portrait Einer Epoche*. Weinheim: Beltz Athenäum, 1994.

Boyle, Nicholas. *Goethe: The Poet and the Age*. Vol. 2, *Revolution and Renunciation*. Oxford: Clarendon, 2000.

Boym, Svetlana. *The Future of Nostalgia*. New York: Basic Books, 2001.

Brann, Eva. *Homeric Moments*. Philadelphia: Paul Dry, 2002.

Breithaupt, Fritz. "How I Feel Your Pain: Lessing's Mitleid, Goethe's Anagnorisis, and Fontane's Quiet Sadism." *Deutsche Vierteljahrsschrift für Literaturwissenschaft und Geistesgeschichte* 82, no. 3 (2008): 400–423.

Brown, Jane K. "Goethe: From My Life: Poetry and Truth." In *Handbuch der Autobiographie und Selbstfiktion*, edited by Martina Wagner-Egelhaaf. Amsterdam: De Gruyter. Draft shared before publication. Forthcoming.

———. *Goethe's Allegories of Identity*. Philadelphia: University of Pennsylvania Press, 2014.

———. *Goethe's Faust: The German Tragedy*. Ithaca: Cornell University Press, 1986.

Burger, Ronna. *Aristotle's Dialogue with Socrates: On the "Nicomachean Ethics."* Chicago: Chicago University Press, 2008.

Butler, Judith. *Gender Trouble: Feminism and the Subversion of Identity*. New York: Routledge, 1990.

———. "Performative Acts and Gender Constitution: An Essay in Phenomenology and Feminist Theory." *Theatre Journal* 49, no. 1 (1988): 519–548.

Campe, Rüdiger, ed. *Penthesileas Versprechen: Exemplarische Studien über die literarische Referenz*. Freiburg: Rombach Verlag, 2008.

———. "Presenting the Affect: The Scene of *Pathos* in Aristotle's *Rhetoric* and Its Revision in Descartes' *Passions of the Soul*." In *Rethinking Emotion: Interiority in Premodern, Modern, and Contemporary Thought*, edited by Rüdiger Campe and Julia Weber, 36–57. Berlin: De Gruyter, 2014.

———. "Zweierlei Gesetz in Kleists *Penthesilea*: Naturrecht und Biopolitik." In *Penthesileas Versprechen: Exemplarische Studien über die literarische Referenz*, edited by Rüdiger Campe, 313–342. Freiburg: Rombach Verlag, 2008.

Campe, Rüdiger, and Julia Weber, eds. *Rethinking Emotion: Interiority and Exteriority in Pre-modern, Modern, and Contemporary Thought*. Berlin: De Gruyter, 2014.

Cave, Terence. *Recognitions: A Study in Poetics*. Oxford: Clarendon, 1988.

Cavell, Stanley. *Disowning Knowledge in Six Plays of Shakespeare*. Cambridge: Cambridge University Press, 1987.

Chaouli, Michel. "Devouring Metaphor: Disgust and Taste in Kleist's Penthesilea." *German Quarterly* 69, no. 2 (1996): 125–143.

Charnes, Linda. "'So Unsecret to Ourselves': Notorious Identity and the Material Subject in Shakespeare's *Troilus and Cressida*." *Shakespeare Quarterly* 40 (Winter 1989): 413–440.

Clayton, Barbara. *A Penelopean Poetics: Reweaving the Feminine in Homer's Odyssey*. Lanham: Lexington Books, 2003.

Cocalis, Susan, and Kay Goodman, eds. *Beyond the Eternal Feminine: Critical Essays on Women and German Literature*. Stuttgart: Akademischer Verlag Hans-Peter Heinz, 1982.

Cohen, Beth, ed. *The Distaff Side: Representing the Female in Homer's Odyssey*. New York: Oxford University Press, 1995.

Cook, Amy. *Shakespearean Neuroplay: Reinvigorating the Study of Dramatic Texts and Performance through Cognitive Science*. New York: Palgrave Macmillan, 2010.

Cooper, Lane. "The Fifth Form of 'Discovery' in the *Poetics* of Aristotle." *Classical Philology* 13, no. 3 (1918): 251–261.

Culbertson, Diana. *The Poetics of Revelation: Recognition and the Narrative Tradition.* Macon: Mercer University Press, 1989.

Cullens, Chris, and Dorothea von Mücke. "Love in Kleist's *Penthesilea* and *Kätchen von Heilbronn*." *DVJS* 63, no. 3 (1989): 461–493.

Dallmayr, Fred. "Derrida and Friendship." *Critical Review of International Social and Political Philosophy* 2, no. 4 (1999): 105–130.

Davis, Michael. Introduction to *On Poetics*, by Aristotle, ix–xxx. Translated by Seth Benardete and Michael Davis. South Bend: St. Augustine's Press, 2002.

Deleuze, Gilles. *Difference and Repetition.* Translated by Paul Patton. New York: Columbia University Press, 1994.

———. *The Fold: Leibniz and the Baroque.* Translated by Tom Conley. Minneapolis: University of Minnesota Press, 1993.

Derrida, Jacques. *Given Time: 1. Counterfeit Money.* Chicago: University of Chicago Press, 1992.

———. *Limited Inc.* Evanston: Northwestern University Press, 1988.

———. *Margins of Philosophy.* Chicago: University of Chicago Press, 1982.

———. *Politics of Friendship.* Translated by George Collins. New York: Verso, 1997.

Descartes, René. *Discourse on Method and Meditations on First Philosophy.* Translated by Donald Cress. Indianapolis: Hackett, 1993.

Detienne, Marcel, and Jean-Pierre Vernant. *Cunning Intelligence in Greek Culture and Society.* Translated by Janet Lloyd. Hassocks, U.K.: Harvester, 1978.

Doherty, Lillian Eileen, ed. *Homer's Odyssey.* Oxford: Oxford University Press, 2009.

———. *Siren Songs: Gender, Audiences, and Narrators in the Odyssey.* Ann Arbor: University of Michigan Press, 1995.

Dougherty, Carol. *The Raft of Odysseus: The Ethnographic Imagination of Homer's* Odyssey. Oxford: Oxford University Press, 2001.

Duncan, Anne. *Performance and Identity in the Classical World.* Cambridge: Cambridge University Press, 2006.

Edwards, Mark W. *Sound, Sense, and Rhythm: Listening to Greek and Latin Poetry.* Princeton: Princeton University Press, 2009.

Else, Gerald. *Aristotle's Poetics: The Argument.* Cambridge, Mass.: Harvard University Press, 1957.

Erhart, Walter. "Drama der Anerkennung: Neue gesellschaftstheoretische Überlegungen zu Goethes *Iphigenie auf Tauris*." *Jahrbuch der Deutschen Schiller-Gesellschaft* 51 (2007): 140–165.

Euripides. *Euripides.* Edited and translated by David Kovacs. Loeb Classical Library, 9–12, 485, 496. 6 vols. Cambridge, Mass.: Harvard University Press, 1994–1999.

Fenves, Peter. "Politics of Friendship, Once Again." *Eighteenth-Century Studies* 32, no. 2 (1998): 133–155.

Fichte, Johann Gottlieb. *Grundlage des Naturrechts nach Principien der Wissenschaftslehre.* In *Gesamtausgabe der Bayerischen Akademie der Wissenschaften*, vol. 1.3. Stuttgart: Fromman-Holzboog, 1966.

Fischer-Lichte, Erika. *The Routledge Introduction to Theatre and Performance Studies.* Translated by Minou Arjomand. London: Routledge, 2013.

———. *The Semiotics of Theater.* Bloomington: Indiana University Press, 1992.

Fleming, Paul. "Belatedness: A Theory of the Epic." *MLN* 129, no. 3 (2014): 525–534.

Foley, Helene P. *Female Acts in Greek Tragedy*. Princeton: Princeton University Press, 2001.

———. "Penelope as Moral Agent." In *The Distant Staff: Representing the Female in Homer's* Odyssey, edited by Beth Cohen, 93–115. Oxford: Oxford University Press, 1995.

———. "'Reverse Similes' and Sex Roles in the *Odyssey*." In *Women in the Ancient World: The* Arethusa *Papers*, edited by John Peradotto and J. P. Sullivan, 59–78. Albany: State University of New York Press, 1984.

Ford, Andrew. "Epic as Genre." In *A New Companion to Homer*, edited by Ian Morris and Barry Powell, 103–120. Leiden: Brill, 1997.

Forst, Rainer. *Toleration in Conflict: Past and Present*. Cambridge: Cambridge University Press, 2013.

Forst, Rainer, and Jeffrey Flynn. *The Right to Justification: Elements of a Constructivist Theory of Justice*. New York: Columbia University Press, 2012.

Förster, Eckart. "Goethe and the 'Auge des Geistes.'" *Deutsche Vierteljahrsschrift für Literaturwissenschaft und Geistesgeschichte* 75, no. 1 (2001): 87–101.

———. *The Twenty-Five Years of Philosophy: A Systematic Reconstruction*. Cambridge, Mass.: Harvard University Press, 2012.

Foucault, Michel. *The Hermeneutics of the Subject: Lectures at the Collège De France, 1981–1982*, edited by Frédéric Gros, François Ewald, and Alessandro Fontana. New York: Palgrave Macmillan, 2005.

———. *The Order of Things: An Archaeology of the Human Sciences*. New York: Vintage, 1994.

Frame, Douglas. *The Myth of Return in Early Greek Epic*. New Haven: Yale University Press, 1978.

Fraser, Nancy, and Axel Honneth. *Redistribution or Recognition? A Political-Philosophical Exchange*. London: Verso, 2003.

Freeman, Lauren. "Recognition Reconsidered: A Re-reading of Heidegger's Being and Time §26." *Philosophy Today* 53, no. 1 (2009): 85–99.

Freud, Sigmund. *Gesammelte Werke*. Edited by Anna Freud et al. 18 vols. Frankfurt am Main: Fischer, 1999.

Fuchs, Elinor. "Waiting for Recognition: An Aristotle for 'Non-Aristotelian' Drama." *Modern Drama* 50, no. 4 (2007): 532–544.

Gainsford, Peter. "Formal Analysis of Recognition Scenes in the *Odyssey*." *Journal of Hellenic Studies* 123 (2003): 41–59.

Gallas, Helga. *Kleist: Gesetz, Begehren und Sexualität*. Frankfurt am Main: Stroemfeld, 2005.

Genette, Gérard. *Narrative Discourse: An Essay in Method*. Translated by Jane E. Levin. Ithaca: Cornell University Press, 1980.

Geulen, Eva. *Aus Dem Leben Der Form: Goethes Morphologie und die Nager*. Berlin: Im Verlag der Buchhandlung Walther König, Köln, an imprint of August Verlag, 2016.

Gille, Klaus F. "'Glückliches Ereignis': Zum Freundschaftsbund zwischen Schiller und Goethe." *Weimarer Beiträge* 48, no. 4 (2004): 520–530.

Girard, René. *A Theater of Envy: William Shakespeare*. Oxford: Oxford University Press, 1991.

Goddard, Scott. "Beethoven and Goethe." *Music & Letters* 8, no. 2 (1927): 165–171.

Goethe, Johann Wolfgang von. *Begegnungen und Gespräche*. Edited by Ernst Grumach and Renate Grumach. Berlin: De Gruyter, 1980.

———. *Collected Works*. Vol. 8, *Verse Plays and Epic*. Edited by Cyrus Hamlin and Frank Ryder. Princeton: Princeton University Press, 1987.

———. *Goethe's Botanical Writings*. Translated by Bertha Mueller. Woodbridge: Ox Bow, 1952.

———. *Goethes Werke: Herausgegeben im Auftrage der Großherzogin Sophie von Sacshen*. Weimar: Böhlau, 1887–1919. Sections 1–4, 133 vols. in 143 parts, plus 3 supplementary vols. Reprint, Munich: Deutscher Taschenbuch Verlag, 1987.

———. *Werke*. Hamburger Ausgabe, edited by Erich Trunz, 14 vols. Munich: Deutscher Taschenbuch Verlag, 1986.

Goffman, Erwin. *The Presentation of Self in Everyday Life*. New York: Anchor Books, Doubleday, 1959.

Golden, Leon. "Catharsis." *Transactions and Proceedings of the American Philological Association* 93 (1962): 51–60.

Goldhill, Simon. *The Poet's Voice: Essays on Poetics and Greek Literature*. Cambridge: Cambridge University Press, 1991.

Grady, Hugh. *Shakespeare's Universal Wolf: Studies in Early Modern Reification*. Oxford: Clarendon, 1996.

Graham, Ilse. *Word into Flesh: A Poet's Quest for the Symbol*. Berlin: De Gruyter, 1977.

Grebe, Paul, ed. *Der Große Duden, Band 7—Etymologie: Herkunftswörterbuch der deutschen Sprache*. Mannheim: Dudenverlag, 1963.

Greenblatt, Stephen. *Renaissance Self-Fashioning: From More to Shakespeare*. Chicago: University of Chicago Press, 1980.

Hall, Edith. *Adventures with Iphigenia in Tauris: A Cultural History of Euripides' Black Sea Tragedy*. Oxford: Oxford University Press, 2013.

Halliwell, Stephen. *Aristotle's Poetics*. Chicago: University of Chicago Press, 1998.

Hamilton, John T. *Security: Politics, Humanity, and the Philology of Care*. Princeton: Princeton University Press, 2013.

Hamlin, Cyrus. "'Myth and Psychology': The Curing of Orest in Goethe's *Iphigenie auf Tauris*." *Goethe Yearbook* 12 (2004): 59–80.

Harsh, Philip Whaley. "Penelope and Odysseus in *Odyssey* XIX." *American Journal of Philology* 71, no. 1 (1950): 1–21.

Hartog, François. *Memories of Odysseus: Frontier Tales from Ancient Greece*. Chicago: University of Chicago Press, 2001.

Hegel, Georg Wilhelm Friedrich. *Phänomenologie des Geistes*. Hamburg: Felix Meiner Verlag, 1988.

Heidegger, Martin. *Sein und Zeit*. Tübingen: Max Niemeyer Verlag, 1993.

Heitman, Richard. *Taking Her Seriously: Penelope and the Plot of Homer's Odyssey*. Ann Arbor: University of Michigan Press, 2005.

Hobbes, Thomas. *Leviathan*. Edited by Richard E. Flathman and David Johnston. New York: W. W. Norton, 1997.

Hölderlin, Friedrich. *Sämtliche Werke*. Edited by Friedrich Beissner. Frankfurt am Main: Insel-Verlag, 1961.

Homer. *Iliad*. Translated and edited by A. T. Murray and William F. Wyatt. Loeb Classical Library 170–171. Vols. 1–2. 2nd ed. Cambridge, Mass.: Harvard University Press, 1999.

———. *The Iliad.* Translated by George Chapman. Princeton: Princeton University Press, 1956. First published as *Seaven Bookes of the Iliades of Homere, Prince of Poets* in 1598 by John Windet (London).

———. *The Iliad.* Translated by Richmond Lattimore. 1951. Reprint, Chicago: University of Chicago Press, 1961.

———. *Odyssey.* Translated and edited by A. T. Murray and George E. Dimock. Loeb Classical Library 104–105. Vols. 1–2. Cambridge, Mass.: Harvard University Press, 1998.

———. *The Odyssey.* Translated by Robert Fitzgerald. 1961. Reprint, New York: Vintage Books, 1990.

———. *The Odyssey.* Translated by Richmond Lattimore. 1965. Reprint, New York: Harper Perennial, 1991.

Honneth, Axel. *Der Kampf um Anerkennung: zur moralischen Grammatik sozialer Konflikte.* Frankfurt am Main: Suhrkamp Verlag, 1992.

———. *The I in We: Studies in the Theory of Recognition.* Cambridge: Polity, 2012.

———. *The Struggle for Recognition: The Moral Grammar of Social Conflicts.* Cambridge: Polity, 1995. Reprint, Hoboken: Blackwell, 1995.

Honneth, Axel, Judith Butler, Raymond Geuss, Jonathan Lear, and Martin Jay. *Reification: A New Look at an Old Idea.* Berkeley Tanner Lectures. Oxford: Oxford University Press, 2008.

Honneth, Axel, Jacques Rancière, and Katia Genel. *Recognition or Disagreement: A Critical Encounter on the Politics of Freedom, Equality, and Identity.* New York: Columbia University Press, 2016.

Horkheimer, Max, and Theodor Adorno. *Dialectic of Enlightenment: Philosophical Fragments.* Translated by Edmund Jephcott. Stanford: Stanford University Press, 2002.

———. *Dialektik der Aufklärung: Philosophische Fragmente.* 1947. Reprint, Frankfurt am Main: Fischer Verlag, 1988.

Horn, Gisela, and Detlef Ignasiak. *"Glückliches Ereignis": Der Arbeitsbund zwischen Goethe und Schiller.* Rudolstadt: Hain Verlag, 1994.

Horsley, Ritta Jo. "'Dies Frauenschicksal': A Critical Appraisal of Goethe's *Iphigenie.*" In *Beyond the Eternal Feminine: Critical Essays on Women and German Literature*, edited by Susan Cocalis and Kay Goodman, 47–74. Stuttgart: Akademischer Verlag Hans-Peter Heinz, 1982.

Huntington, Patricia J. *Ecstatic Subjects, Utopia, and Recognition: Kristeva, Heidegger, Irigaray.* Albany: State University of New York Press, 1998.

Hurley, Susan. *Consciousness in Action.* Cambridge, Mass.: Harvard University Press, 1998.

Hutchinson, D. S. "Introduction to *Alcibiades.*" In Plato, *Complete Works*, edited by John M. Cooper, 557–558. Indianapolis: Hackett, 1997.

Jacobs, Carol. *Uncontainable Romanticism.* Baltimore: Johns Hopkins University Press, 1989.

Jong, Irene de. *A Narratological Commentary on the Odyssey.* Cambridge: Cambridge University Press, 2001.

Joyce, James. *Ulysses.* New York: Random House, 1946.

Kafka, Franz. *Die Erzählungen.* Frankfurt am Main: Fischer, 1961.

Kant, Immanuel. *Kants Werke: Akademie Textausgabe.* 9 vols. Berlin: De Gruyter, 1968.

Kantorowicz, Ernst H. *The King's Two Bodies: A Study in Medieval Political Theology*. Princeton: Princeton University Press, 1957.

Katz, Marylin A. *Penelope's Renown: Meaning and Indeterminacy in the Odyssey*. Princeton: Princeton University Press, 1991.

Kirschenblatt-Gimblett, Barbara. "Performance Studies." In *The Performance Studies Reader*, edited by Henry Bial and Sara Brady, 25–36. 3rd ed. London: Routledge, 2015.

Kleist, Heinrich von. *Penthesilea*. Translated by Joel Agee. Illustrated by Maurice Sendak. New York: Harper Perennial, 1998.

———. *Sämtliche Werke und Briefe*. Carl Hanser Verlag: Munich, 1993.

Köhnkern, Adolf. *Darstellungsziele und Erzählstrategien in antiken Texten*. Berlin: De Gruyter, 2006.

Kristeva, Julia. *Desire in Language: A Semiotic Approach to Literature and Art*. Translated by Thomas Gora, Alice Jardine, and Leon S. Roudiez. New York: Columbia University Press, 1980.

Lattimore, Richmond. *Story Patterns in Greek Tragedy*. Ann Arbor: University of Michigan Press, 1964.

Laubscher, Leswin. "Of Odysseus and Abraham: Nostalgia, Heimweë, and the Ways (of) Home." *Peace and Conflict: Journal of Peace Psychology* 18, no. 3 (2012): 214–224.

Leggatt, Alexander. *Shakespeare's Tragedies: Violation and Identity*. Cambridge: Cambridge University Press, 2005.

Lessing, Gotthold Ephraim. *Werke und Briefe in zwölf Bänden*. Frankfurt am Main: Deutscher Klassiker Verlag, 1985–2003.

Levaniouk, Olga. *Eve of the Festival: Making Myth in Odyssey 19*. Hellenic Studies 46. Cambridge, Mass.: Center for Hellenic Studies, Harvard University Press, 2011.

Lichtenberg, Georg Christoph. *Schriften Und Briefe*. Edited by Franz Heinrich Mautner. Frankfurt am Main: Insel Verlag, 1983.

Liddell, H. G., and Robert Scott. *An Intermediate Greek-English Lexicon*. Oxford: Oxford University Press, 1945.

Liddell, H. G., Robert Scott, and Henry Jones. *A Greek-English Lexicon*. Oxford: Oxford University Press, 1996.

Lindemann, Hilde. *Damaged Identities, Narrative Repair*. Ithaca: Cornell University Press, 2001.

———. *Holding and Letting Go: The Social Practice of Personal Identities*. Oxford: Oxford University Press, 2014.

Lord, Albert. *Singer of Tales*. 2nd ed. Cambridge, Mass.: Harvard University Press, 2000. First published 1960.

Lucas, George, with Leigh Brackett and Lawrence Kasdan. *The Empire Strikes Back*. Directed by Irvin Kershner. Los Angeles: Twentieth Century Fox, 1980. DVD.

Lukács, Georg. *The Theory of the Novel*. Translated by Anna Bostock. Cambridge, Mass.: MIT Press, 1971.

Luther, Martin. *Die Bibel, oder die ganze heilige Schrift des alten und neuen Testaments*. Translated by American Bible Society. New York: Amerikanische Bibel-Gesellschaft, 1898.

———. *Die Bibel, oder, die ganze heilige Schrift des alten und neuen Testaments. Nach der Übersetzung Martin Luthers*. Stuttgart: Württembergische Bibelanstalt, 1972.

Maatsch, Jonas, ed. *Morphologie und Moderne: Goethes 'Anschauliches Denken' in den Geistes- und Kulturwissenschaften seit 1800*. Berlin: De Gruyter, 2014.

MacFarlane, John. "Aristotle's Definition of Anagnorisis." *American Journal of Philology* 121, no. 3 (2000): 367–384.

Mallin, Eric. "Emulous Factions and the Collapse of Chivalry: *Troilus and Cressida*." *Representations* 29 (Winter 1990):145–179.

Mandelartz, Michael. "Die 'reine Seele' und die Politik: Partikularität und Universalität in Goethes *Iphigenie*." *Goethe Yearbook* 16 (2009): 47–68.

Manson, Graeme, and John Fawcett. *Orphan Black* (TV series). Toronto: Temple Street Productions, BBC America, 2013–2018.

Markell, Patchen. *Bound by Recognition*. Princeton: Princeton University Press, 2003.

Martin, Priscilla, ed. *Shakespeare, Troilus and Cressida: A Casebook*. London: Macmillan, 1976.

Martin, Raymond, and John Barresi. *The Rise and Fall of Soul and Self: An Intellectual History of Personal Identity*. New York: Columbia University Press, 2006.

McEwan, Ian. *Atonement*. London: Jonathan Cape, 2001.

Menke, Bettina. "Penthesilea: das Bild des Körpers und seine Zerfällung." In *Erotik und Sexualität im Werk Heinrich von Kleists: Internationales Kolloquium des Kleist-Archivs Sembdner*, 117–136. Heilbronn: Stadtbücherei, 2000.

Moore, Evelyn. "The Deadly Gaze: Penthesilea and Achilles in Love." *(Re-)turn: A Journal of Lacanian Studies* 3–4 (Spring 2008): 33–47.

Morris, Ian, and Barry Powell, eds. *A New Companion to Homer*. Leiden: Brill, 1997.

Most, Glenn. "Ansichten über einen Hund: Zu einigen Strukturen der Homerrezeption zwischen Antike und Neuzeit." *Antike und Abendland* 37 (1991): 144–168.

———. "The Stranger's Strategem: Self-Disclosure and Self-Sufficiency in Greek Culture." *Journal of Hellenic Studies* 109 (1989): 114–133.

———. "The Structure and Function of Odysseus' *Apologoi*." *Transactions of the American Philological Association* 119 (1989): 15–30.

Mueller, Martin. *Children of Oedipus and Other Essays on the Imitation of Greek Tragedy 1550–1800*. Toronto: University of Toronto Press, 1980.

Müller-Seidel, Helmut. *Versehen und Erkennen: Eine Studie über Heinrich von Kliest*. Köln: Böhlau, 1961.

Murnaghan, Sheila. *Disguise and Recognition in the Odyssey*. Princeton: Princeton University Press, 1987.

———. "Penelope's *Agnoia*: Knowledge, Power, and Gender in the *Odyssey*." In *Homer's Odyssey*, edited by Lillian E. Doherty, 231–246. Oxford: Oxford University Press, 2009.

———. "The Plan of Athena." In *The Distaff Side: Representing the Female in Homer's* Odyssey, edited by Beth Cohen, 61–80. New York: Oxford University Press, 1995.

Myrsiades, Kostas, ed. "Special Issue: Early Recognition in Homer's *Odyssey*." *College Literature* 38, no. 2 (2011): i–xi, 1–185.

Nagy, Gregory. *Homer the Preclassic*. Berkeley: University of California Press, 2010.

———. *Masterpieces of Metonymy: From Ancient Greek Times to Now*. Hellenic Studies 72. Washington, D.C.: Center for Hellenic Studies, 2015.

———. *Poetry as Performance: Homer and Beyond*. Cambridge: Cambridge University Press, 1996.

Nehamas, Alexander. "Aristotelian *Philia*, Modern Friendship?" *Oxford Studies in Ancient Philosophy* 39 (2010): 213–247.

———. "The Good of Friendship." *Proceedings of the Aristotelian Society* 110, no. 3 (2010): 267–294.

Neumann, Gerhard. "Die Entdeckung des Fremden: Goethe als Ethnograph." In *A Palavra e o Canto: Miscelânea de Homenagem a Rita Iriarte*, edited by the Department of German Studies at the University of Lisbon, 85–94. Lissabon: Edições Colibri, 2000.

———. "Erkennungsszene und Opferritual in Goethes Iphigenie und in Kleists Penthesilea." In *Käthchen und seine Schwestern: Frauenfiguren im Drama um 1800: Internationales Kolloquium des Kleist-Archivs Sembdner*, edited by Günther Emig and Anton Philipp Knittel, 38–80. Heilbronn: Stadtbücherei, 2000.

———. "Erkennungs-Szene: Wahrnehmung zwischen den Geschlechtern im literarischen Text." In *Differenzen in der Geschlechterdifferenz—Differences within Gender Studies: Aktuelle Perspektiven der Geschlechterforschung*, edited by Kati Röttger and Heike Pau, 202–221. Berlin: Erich Schmidt, 1999.

———, ed. *Heinrich von Kleist: Kriegsfall—Rechtsfall—Sündenfall.* Freiburg im Briesgau: Rombach, 1994.

———. "Kleists Ethnologisches Experiment: Zur Fetischisierung der Erkennungs-Szene in der Penthesilea." In *Kultur-Schreiben als romantisches Projekt: Romantische Ethnographie im Spannungsfeld zwischen Imagination und Wissenschaft*, edited by David Wellbery and Alexander von Bormann, 155–178. Würzburg: Königshausen and Neumann, 2012.

Newmark, Catherine. *Passion—Affekt—Gefühl: Philosophische Theorien der Emotionen zwischen Aristoteles und Kant.* Hamburg: Meiner, 2008.

Noë, Alva. *Action in Perception.* Cambridge, Mass.: MIT Press, 2004.

———. *Out of Our Heads: Why You Are Not Your Brain, and Other Lessons from the Biology of Consciousness.* New York: Hill and Wang, 2009.

North, Paul. *The Problem of Distraction.* Stanford: Stanford University Press, 2012.

Novalis. *Schriften.* Vol. 3. Edited by Richard Samuel. Stuttgart: W. Kohlhammer Verlag, 1960.

Nussbaum, Martha Craven. *The Fragility of Goodness: Luck and Ethics in Greek Tragedy and Philosophy.* Cambridge: Cambridge University Press, 1986.

———. "Tragedy and Self-Sufficiency: Plato and Aristotle on Fear and Pity." In *Essays on Aristotle's* Poetics, edited by Amélie Oksenberg Rorty, 261–290. Princeton: Princeton University Press, 1992.

Pahl, Katrin. "Forging Feeling: Kleist's Theatrical Theory of Re-layed Emotionality." *MLN* 124, no. 3 (2009): 666–682.

Peradotto, John, and J. P. Sullivan, eds. *Women in the Ancient World: The* Arethusa *Papers.* Albany: State University of New York Press, 1984.

Phelan, Peggy. *Unmarked: The Politics of Performance.* London: Routledge, 1993.

Phillips, James. *The Equivocation of Reason: Kleist Reading Kant.* Stanford: Stanford University Press, 2007.

Plato. *Alcibiades.* Edited by Nicholas Denyer. Cambridge: Cambridge University Press, 2001.

———. *Complete Works.* Edited by John M. Cooper. Indianapolis: Hackett, 1997.

———. *Plato's Sophist*. Translated by Eva Brann, Peter Kalkavage, and Eric Salem. Newburyport: Focus, 1996.

———. *Republic*. Translated by Joe Sachs. Newburyport: Focus, 2007.

Poincaré, Henri. *The Measure of Time*. In *The Foundations of Science (The Value of Science)*, translated by George Bruce Halsted, 222–234. New York: Science Press, 1913. Available online at https://en.wikisource.org.

Rasch, Wolfdietrich. *Goethes* Iphigenie auf Tauris *als Drama der Autonomie*. München: Beck, 1979.

Raulet, Gerard. "Der opake Punkt des Politischen." In *Penthesileas Versprechen: Exemplarische Studien über die literarische Referenz*, edited by Rüdiger Campe, 343–374. Freiburg: Rombach Verlag, 2008.

Reece, Steve. "Penelope's 'Early Recognition' of Odysseus from a Neoanalytic and Oral Perspective." *College Literature* 38, no. 2 (2011): 101–117.

Richardson, N. J. "Recognition Scenes in the Odyssey and Ancient Literary Criticism." *Papers of the Liverpool Latin Seminar* 4 (1983): 219–235.

Richardson, Scott Douglas. *The Homeric Narrator*. Nashville: Vanderbilt University Press, 1990.

Richter, Gerhard. *Afterness: Figures of Following in Modern Thought and Aesthetics*. New York: Columbia University Press, 2011.

Ricoeur, Paul. *The Course of Recognition*. Translated by David Pellauer. Cambridge, Mass.: Harvard University Press, 2005.

———. *The Rule of Metaphor: Multi-disciplinary Studies of the Creation of Meaning in Language*. Toronto: University of Toronto Press, 1977.

Rilke, Rainer Maria, and Ruth Sieber-Rilke. *Sämtliche Werke*. 7 vols. Wiesbaden: Insel-Verlag, 1955.

Rorty, Amélie Oksenberg, ed. *Essays on Aristotle's* Poetics. Princeton: Princeton University Press, 1992.

Röttger, Kati, and Heike Pau, eds. *Differenzen in der Geschlechterdifferenz—Differences within Gender Studies: Aktuelle Perspektiven der Geschlechterforschung*. Berlin: Erich Schmidt, 1999.

Rowling, J. K. *Harry Potter and the Deathly Hallows*. New York: Arthur A. Levine Books, 2007.

———. *Harry Potter and the Half-Blood Prince*. London: Bloomsbury, 2005.

Russo, Joseph. "Interview and Aftermath: Dream, Fantasy, and Intuition in Odyssey 19 and 20." *American Journal of Philology* 103, no. 1 (1982): 4–18.

Rutherford, R. B. "The Philosophy of the Odyssey." *Journal of Hellenic Studies* 106 (1986): 145–162.

Schadewaldt, Wolfgang. *Neue Kriterien zur Odyssee-Analyse: Die Wiedererkennung des Odysseus und der Penelope*. Heidelberg: Carl Winter Universitätsverlag, 1959.

Schechner, Richard. *Performance Theory*. London: Routledge, 1988.

Schechner, Richard, and Victor W. Turner. *Between Theater and Anthropology*. Philadelphia: University of Pennsylvania Press, 1985.

Schiller, Friedrich. *Theoretische Schriften*. Edited by Rolf-Peter Janz. Frankfurt am Main: Deutscher Klassiker Verlag, 2008.

Schiller, Friedrich, and Johann Wolfgang von Goethe. *Der Briefwechsel Zwischen Schiller und Goethe*. Edited by Siegfried Seidel. München: Beck, 1984.

Schlegel, August Wilhelm von. "Rezension zur Homers Werke von Voss." In *Dokumente zur Theorie der Übersetzung antiker Literatur in Deutschland seit 1800*, edited by J. Kitzbichler, Katja Lubitz, and Nina Mindt, 3–38. Berlin: De Gruyter, 2009.

Schmitt, Carl. *Der Begriff des Politischen: Text von 1932 mit eimen Vorwort und drei Corollarien*. Berlin: Duncker and Humblot, 1991.

———. *The Concept of the Political*. Translated by George Schwab. Chicago: University of Chicago Press, 1996.

———. *Politische Theologie: Vier Kapitel zur Lehre von der Souveränität*. 6th ed. Berlin: Duncker and Humblot, 1993. First published 1934.

———. *Verfassungslehre*. Berlin: Duncker and Humblot, 1965. First published 1928.

Schneider, Helmut J. "Entzug der Sichtbarkeit: Kleist's *Penthesilea* und die klassische Humanitätsdramaturgie." In *Penthesileas Versprechen: Exemplarische Studien über die literarische Referenz*, edited by Rüdiger Campe, 127–152. Freiburg: Rombach Verlag, 2008.

Schneider, Rebecca. "Extending a Hand: Gesture, Duration and the (Non)Human Turn." Lecture at the Performance Studies Research Group, University of Washington, Seattle, April 24, 2015.

———. *Performing Remains: Art and War in Times of Theatrical Reenactment*. London: Routledge, 2011.

Schumann, Detlev W. "Die Bekenntnisszenen in Goethes *Iphigenie*: Symmetrie und Steigerung." *Jahrbuch der deutschen Schillergesellschaft* 4 (1960): 229–246.

Selleck, Nancy. *The Interpersonal Idiom in Shakespeare, Donne, and Early Modern Culture*. New York: Palgrave Macmillan, 2008.

Seneca. *Epistles 66–92*. Translated by Richard M. Gummere. Loeb Classical Library 76. Cambridge, Mass.: Harvard University Press, 1920.

Shakespeare, William. *Henry IV Part 1*. Edited by David Scott Kastan. London: Arden Shakespeare, 2002.

———. *Richard II*. Edited by Charles Forker. London: Arden Shakespeare, 2004.

———. *Troilus and Cressida*. Edited by David Bevington. London: Arden Shakespeare; Thomson Learning, 1998. First published 1609.

Shaw, George Bernard. "Transactions of the New Shakespere Society, 29 Feb. 1884." In *Shakespeare, Troilus and Cressida: A Casebook*, edited by Priscilla Martin, 57–59. London: Macmillan, 1976.

Sherwood, Robert E. *The Best Years of Our Lives*. Directed by William Wyler. Los Angeles: Samuel Golden, 1946.

Sherwood, Terry G. *The Self in Early Modern Literature: For the Common Good*. Pittsburgh: Duquesne University Press, 2007.

Siep, Ludwig. *Anerkennung als Prinzip der praktischen Philosophie: Untersuchungen zu Hegels Jenaer Philosophie des Geistes*. München: Alber, 1979.

Simonis, Annette. *Gestalttheorie von Goethe bis Benjamin: Diskursgeschichte einer deutschen Denkfigur*. Köln: Böhlau, 2001.

Sophocles. *Sophocles*. Translated and edited by Hugh Lloyd-Jones. Loeb Classical Library 1–2. Cambridge, Mass.: Harvard University Press, 1994.

———. *The Theban Plays: Antigone, King Oidipous, Oidipous at Colonus*. Translated by Ruby Blondell. Newburyport: Focus, 2002.

Smith, Adam. *The Theory of Moral Sentiments*. London: Penguin Classics, 2010. First published 1759.

Snell, Bruno. *The Discovery of the Mind: The Greek Origins of European Thought*. Translated by T. G. Rosenmeyer. New York: Harper, 1960.

Stanford, W. B. "The Homeric Etymology of the Name Odysseus." *Classical Philology* 47, no. 4 (1952): 209–213.

———. *The Ulysses Theme: A Study in the Adaptability of a Traditional Hero*. 1963. Reprint, Ann Arbor: University of Michigan Press, 1976.

Steiner, George. *Antigones*. New Haven: Yale University Press, 1984.

Stephens, Anthony. "Verzerrungen im Spiegel: Das Narziß-Motiv bei Heinrich von Kleist." In *Heinrich von Kleist: Kriegsfall—Rechtsfall—Sündenfall*, edited by Gerhard Neumann, 249–251. Freiburg im Briesgau: Rombach, 1994.

Szondi, Peter. *Lektüren und Lektionen: Versuche über Literatur, Literaturtheorie und Litertatursoziologie*. Frankfurt am Main: Suhrkamp, 1973.

———. *Poetik und Geschichtsphilosophie*. Frankfurt am Main: Suhrkamp, 1974.

Taylor, Charles H., Jr., ed. *Essays on the Odyssey: Selected Modern Criticism*. Bloomington: Indiana University Press, 1963.

Taylor, Charles M. *Multiculturalism: Examining the Politics of Recognition*. Princeton: Princeton University Press, 1994.

———. *Sources of the Self: The Making of the Modern Identity*. Cambridge, Mass.: Harvard University Press, 1989.

Theisen, Bianca. *Bogenschluss: Kleists Formalisierung des Lesens*. Freiburg: Rombach, 1996.

Tillyard, E. M. W. *The Elizabethan World Picture*. New York: Vintage Books, 1943.

Tilman, Nancy. *I'd Know You Anywhere, My Love*. New York: Feiwel and Friends, 2013.

Velleman, J. David. *How We Get Along*. Cambridge: Cambridge University Press, 2009.

Virgil. *The Aeneid*. Translated by Robert Fitzgerald. 1981. Reprint, New York: Vintage Classics, 1990.

Vlahos, John B. "Homer's *Odyssey*: Penelope and the Case for Early Recognition." *College Literature* 38, no. 2 (2011): 1–75.

Wagner, Irmgard. *Critical Approaches to Goethe's Classical Dramas:* Iphigenie, Torquato Tasso, *and* Die natürliche Tochter. Columbia: Camden House, 1995.

Walcott, Derek. *The Odyssey: A Play*. New York: Farrar Straus Giroux, 1993.

Walser, Martin. *Erfahrungen und Leseerfahrungen*. Frankfurt am Main: Suhrkamp Verlag, 1965.

Wellbery, David. "Form und Idee: Skizze eines Begriffsfeldes um 1800." In *Morphologie und Moderne: Goethes 'Anschauliches Denken' in den Geistes- und Kulturwissenschaften seit 1800*, edited by Jonas Maatsch, 17–43. Berlin: De Gruyter, 2014.

Wellbery, David, and Alexander von Bormann, eds. *Kultur-Schreiben als romantisches Projekt: Romantische Ethnographie im Spannungsfeld zwischen Imagination und Wissenschaft*. Würzburg: Königshausen and Neumann, 2012.

Wetters, Kirk. *Demonic History from Goethe to the Present*. Evanston: Northwestern University Press, 2014.

White, John. "Afterword: Imitation." In Plato, *Republic*, 323–346. Translated by Joe Sachs. Newburyport: Focus, 2007.

White House. "Remarks by President Obama at Leaders Summit on Refugees." Released September 20, 2016. https://www.whitehouse.gov.

Williams, Robert R. *Recognition: Fichte and Hegel on the Other*. Albany: State University of New York Press, 1992.

Winckelmann, Johann Joachim. *Gedanken über die Nachahmung der griechischen Werke in der Malerey und Bildhauerkunst*. 2nd ed. Dresden: Waltherische Handlung, 1756.

Wolf, Christa. *Die Dimension des Autors: Essays und Aufsätze, Reden und Gespräche 1959–1985*. Neuwied: Luchterhand, 1987.

INDEX

ABOUT THE AUTHOR

ELLWOOD WIGGINS is an assistant professor of German at the University of Washington in Seattle.